Main
Problems in
American
History

THE DORSEY SERIES IN AMERICAN HISTORY

EDITOR   IRVIN G. WYLLIE   *UNIVERSITY OF WISCONSIN*

SALE & KARN   *American Expansion: A Book of Maps*

GLAAB   *The American City: A Documentary History*

QUINT, ALBERTSON, & CANTOR   *Main Problems in American History*

Main
Problems in
American
History

VOLUME TWO

Edited by

HOWARD H. QUINT

Professor of History
University of Massachusetts

DEAN ALBERTSON

Professor of History
University of Massachusetts

MILTON CANTOR

Assistant Professor of History
University of Massachusetts

1964　　**THE DORSEY PRESS**

HOMEWOOD, ILLINOIS

First Printing, September, 1964
Second Printing, June, 1965

Library of Congress Catalog Card No. 64–24701

PRINTED IN THE UNITED STATES OF AMERICA

To the memory of our friend and colleague

The late NORMAN FURNISS

Preface

WE HAVE designed this two-volume work, the collaborative effort of thirty-one scholars, primarily for use in college survey courses in American history. It does not replace textbooks customarily used to impart basic information to the student. Nor does it serve as a substitute for the reading of historical literature. Its function rather is to acquaint students with historical problems that are directly related to the general context of a survey course yet highly significant in themselves.

These problems, we believe, are particularly well adapted for use in small discussion sections of large lecture courses, inasmuch as they offer both a focus and a direction to such class meetings. As instructors and students well know, such sessions are frequently a chore for the former and a bore to the latter. And the reasons are not hard to discover: either the law of diminishing returns is defied by a review of the week's work, or a brave but futile effort is made to discuss documentary readings, assigned with little or no relationship to an understood frame of reference. In recent years, efforts have been made to have students read articles giving conflicting interpretations of historical events in the hope that they will see the exciting clashes of issues which make history the fascinating discipline that it is. But often such articles, appearing in scholarly journals, and written for specialists, have a strong historiographical emphasis. They may confuse more than enlighten freshmen and sophomores.

We have attempted to write, each in his own way, an interpretive essay which will serve as a point of departure for a challenging class discussion. We do not claim to have said the final word on any subject; we have sought only to open up problems for further probing. Doubtless many instructors and students will take issue with our analyses or interpretations; their independent reactions should generate the intellectual interplay that must be at the very heart of any really satisfactory class discussion. We have made no effort to shape the essays to any particular pattern or to prevent the various writers from stepping on each other's scholarly toes, or at times from traversing the same historical ground.

Appended to each essay is a small number of documents which have a direct relationship to points raised in the essays. In this way, documents which by themselves might be dull and insignificant, become alive and meaningful. This method of presentation helps the students understand how the historian makes use of primary source materials in arriving at conclusions and in writing history. Whenever possible, the contributors have selected documents which have not been overworked in source books and consequently will be reasonably fresh for students and instructors alike.

July, 1964

HOWARD H. QUINT
DEAN ALBERTSON
MILTON CANTOR

Table of Contents

FRANCIS BUTLER SIMKINS
Longwood College

Reconstruction in the South

PRE-EMINENT among the issues that engaged the attention of the American people after the Civil War was the reordering of southern society. The focal issue was whether the Negro should be given the rights of white Americans. The more articulate element of northern opinion believed the Union's victory should be followed by applying to the four million ex-slaves the principles of the Declaration of Independence. The white South, on the other hand, was determined to hold the Negro within the bonds of an accustomed caste system. With scarcely more than a whimpering regret, the South acceded to what force of arms had imposed: the freeing of the Negroes and the restoration of the Union. But these concessions were essentially all that the region was willing to make. That there should be a fundamental alteration of the low-caste status of the ex-slaves was not contemplated.

To maintain its position, the white South had formidable resources. The waging of "total" war, with its physical destruction and impoverishment, was not followed by the imposition of "total" peace. Only one man was put to death for participation in the "Great Rebellion." General amnesty was extended to former rebels, and the only property confiscated was for nonpayment of federal taxes. No one was forced to migrate or denied the privilege of living anywhere in the United States. Generals of the defunct Confederacy came out of defeat with almost as much prestige as they would have had had they been victorious. Unrepentant, the defeated leaders, if shorn of their "fire-eating" qualities, were surrounded by a tragic aura. Behind their leadership was the great mass of southern white men, assertive country folk who still controlled lands of their own and who had a profound contempt for northerners and for Negroes except as servants. These hard-bitten rural people had proved their stamina through service in the Confederate army. They were prepared to terrorize Yankees and Negroes alike if either group tried to upset the traditional social order.

1

If the victorious North was not motivated by vengeance for vengeance's sake, it was moved by what white southerners considered worse: the desire to make over the defeated section in the Abolitionist image. Northerners represented "the bitter zeal of righteous men," not desirous of putting ex-rebels to death but of making Mississippi and South Carolina like Massachusetts and Connecticut. The North, it was inferred, planned to make the Negro in many respects equal to the white man. Therein lay the threat to a doctrine patiently nourished by most southerners for more than two hundred years—white supremacy. Conflicts of bitter emotions were inevitable. To uproot this most unique and distinct feature of southern life was considered a greater disaster than the bloodshed of a long war.

Even today, many southern white people accept this judgment as axiomatic. They may argue over the merits of the Confederacy, but only a few academic scholars question the alleged "horrors" of Negro rule. The wickedness of this period and the righteousness of the manner in which it was destroyed are fundamentals of the civic code.

Most chroniclers of Reconstruction still blunder in that they treat the period like Thomas Carlyle's portrayal of the French Revolution— a melodrama involving wild-eyed conspirators operating within a society frenzied by misery. At its best, this is the pageantry of the dramatist; at its worst, it is the sensationalism of the journalist or scenario writer. Of course, the South during Reconstruction had prophets of despair and unprincipled knaves. Fortunately, the record of their behavior constitutes only a partial rendering of the political aspects of Reconstruction.

Aberrations of Reconstruction politicians were not accurate barometers of the actual behavior of the southern people. Reconstruction governments were not natural developments from conditions inherent in southern life; in a sense, they were artificial impositions from without. They did not fit, as Montesquieu would have said, "the humor and disposition" of the people in whose interests they were established. Frenzied politics did not necessarily reflect a frenzied society. Despite strange doings in statehouses, southerners usually lived as quietly and as normally during Reconstruction as in any other period of the South's history. Defiance of inherited caste divisions, as reflected in an occasional official reception or in acts of legislatures, was not reflected in common social relations. Little attempt was made to destroy white supremacy in social and economic intercourse. In general, the political aggressiveness of the Negroes characteristic of the period did not extend to social relations. Although racially desegregated schools were made lawful in some states, such a violation of the inherited caste system was not widely practiced.

The Reconstruction period as a whole was characterized by cordiality between the races except in politics. Most Negroes accorded their former masters the same servile respect that they had previously shown them. Tipping of hats and curtseying to passing whites were in evidence, and the words "master" and "mistress" were in general use. As postbellum life became more settled, social relations between the races often became cordial. The conduct of Robert Smalls, the Negro who rose highest in South Carolina politics, was not exceptional. When Smalls entered the home of his former mistress, he ate at a separate table. Mrs. Robert B. Elliott, the wife of the Negro speaker of the South Carolina House of Representatives, lived ostentatiously in the political circles of the state capital; but when she visited her former mistress, she acted as though she were still a servant.

Reconstruction was a precise step forward toward the Americanization of the Negroes. As historian William A. Dunning has written, the newly liberated freedmen were "fascinated with the pursuit of the white man's culture." This passion was a dominant feature. The zeal with which the ex-slaves sought the benefits of literary culture was perhaps unparalleled in history. Although Negro society during the first years of freedom tended to grow independently of white society, it continued to imitate the culture of the superior caste. Among cultivated Negroes, the more independent of the whites their society was, the stronger was the resemblance. Radical changes in Negro religion which grew out of freedom were decidedly in the direction of white church practices. The bad manners of the Negro were those of American rustics, and their political vices were not unlike those of contemporary urban politicians everywhere. White southerners ridiculed Negro politicians who attempted to imitate Henry Clay or Charles Sumner. Undue emphasis was placed upon the impracticability of loading the curricula of Negro schools with items taken from the classical schools of the eastern states. Yet, measured according to the ubiquitous standards of American civilization, were these aspirations in the wrong direction? Were they not in the direction all Americans sought to move, particularly those relegated to the lowest caste? The major problem of the former slave has been to attain the standards of American civilization. This was the decree of circumstances which the American Negro has accepted without complaint. Reconstructionists who held up Boston and Massachusetts as ideals for the Negroes were not giving the wrong advice. That this advice moved

Negroes profoundly is a tribute to the sound instincts of the ex-slaves.

It is an accepted convention of scholarship that the Reconstruction experiment was excessively radical. We are told how 4,000,000 Negroes were suddenly hurled from slavery into freedom; how freedmen were forcéd into the roles of New England gentlemen; how 700,000 illiterate ex-slaves were given the privileges of voting and officeholding. But were these measures genuine radicalism, followed by fundamental changes in southern society? The answer was that they were superimposed innovations that in no thorough sense struck at the foundations of southern life. A truly radical program would have called for the confiscation of land for the freedmen. Land, the wartorn South's principal form of wealth, was the former slave's only possible weapon in his battle for economic and social rights. Efforts of the Freedmen's Bureau in behalf of land endowments were fitful or abortive. Conservative constitutional theory opposed any such meaningful sequestration.

The dominant Radicals of the day naïvely assumed that Negro advancement could be obtained through the ballot box and the spelling book. The freedmen obtained these, though they were allowed to continue in physical want. But as colored people became sufficiently encouraged to demand the confirmation of their freedom and implementation of their voting privilege, the whites showed an aggressiveness that went beyond maintenance of their traditional position. They tightened the bonds of caste, they deprived the subordinate caste of many of the industrial callings the Negro had practiced under slavery, and they welcomed abandonment of the land by colored farmers. The growth of white democracy and disappearance of aristocratic prejudices against many forms of honest labor created the impression that southern society could function without the despised African. At the end of Reconstruction, victory was largely in white hands—the actuality as well as the sentiment and the tradition.

There *was* corruption and ignorance in the Radical state governments—expensive spittoons, thousand-dollar bribes, fraudulent bond issues. For several years following 1868, buffoonery and corruption ran riot in state capitols. Votes were for sale at fixed prices. A carpetbagger governor asserted, probably with exaggeration, that two hundred illiterate magistrates conducted courts in his state. Governors confessed receiving bribes, and some retired from office with considerable fortunes. James S. Pike, anti-Radical Republican from Maine, described the South Carolina legislature as composed of former slaves "rioting in the halls of their master." "Seven years ago," remarked Pike in the late 1860's, "these men were raising corn and cotton under the whip of the overseer. Today they are raising points of order. . . . It is easier and better paid. . . . This is their day of jubilee." Expenditures for state governments increased as much as 1,400 per cent.

Little was unique in the financial behavior of the southern Reconstructionists. The rebuilding of railroads and other public utilities disrupted by war required heavy expenditures, as did the extension of schools and other services made necessary by the entrance of the Negroes into freedom. But corruption was hardly confined to the South. Scandals of the Grant administration and of the Tweed Ring in New York City were in a sense far less excusable than happenings in southern capitals. Nor were the white-dominated regimes that preceded and followed the Radical regimes spotless. Public misconduct, including that of Reconstruction, formed an integral part of a national era of expansion which prompted unwise expenditures of public funds.

The period of southern history that came after the Civil War has often been called "Black Reconstruction," implying that Negroes were the principal actors in the drama—especially in the scandals. This was true only in a limited sense. Greatest extravagances of the period actually came from state endorsement of railroad securities. When railroad companies defaulted, as many did, the state governments were left "holding the bag." White lobbyists and white politicians made off with the lion's share of the profits from these transactions. Officeholders of the scandalous period, it should be mentioned, were mostly whites. Only South Carolina had a legislature with a Negro majority. One Negro served briefly as governor of a state; only two held office as United States senators; fifteen became members of the national House of Representatives; three became lieutenant governors; only one sat on a state supreme court.

Several generations of historians have maintained that the profligacy of Reconstruction governments checked economic recovery. But the actual financial burdens of governments that tolerated waste and extravagance have been exaggerated. Increases in tax rates and debts characteristic of the Radical governments were small when compared with those of northern states during the same period. It has been pointed out that Illinois in 1870 had a tax rate of 55 mills as compared with 15 mills in the eleven states of the former Confederacy; and that in the same year, these same southern states received only $32 million in state, county, and municipal taxes, while the state of New York alone collected $48 million. The extravagant bond issues of the Reconstruction governments were no immediate burden upon contemporaries and afflicted subsequent generations only to the extent to which the bonds were not repudiated. Reconstruction governments failed not because their expenditures were burdensome, but because they did not enjoy enough respect to force prospective taxpayers to yield funds sufficient to meet the obligations of effective government. There was a taxpayers' strike rather than a tax collectors' orgy. Some Reconstruction governments could not pay the gas bills of legislative halls.

Corruption in the legislatures did not prevent social and economic progress. Social activities of both races remained relatively stable; absent were the misery, hatred, and repressions frequently ascribed to the period. There were camp meetings, balls, ring tournaments, picnics, banquets, and indulgence in the vanities of personal adornment. There was, of course, the shadow of the Lost Cause and an apprehension concerning political happenings. But there were also memories of recent heroic events of war and surviving war heroes to give them reality. Gayety was disciplined by recent tragedy but not dampened by the utilitarianism of a more progressive age.

Commercial and industrial expansion, so pronounced in later times, was inaugurated during Reconstruction. Numerous towns and commercial establishments came into existence. New railroads and cotton mills were built, and the mining of phosphates was begun. The small town and the crossroads storekeeper took the place of the antebellum cotton planter as the dominant personality of the community.

The groundwork was laid for a new system of farming. While official agencies, through "black codes" and the Freedmen's Bureau, were making unsuccessful attempts to redefine a shattered rural economy, ex-slaves bargained themselves into an ordered agricultural situation unlike that of slavery and, from their viewpoint, advantageous. They worked outside official purview. Though unable to gain title to the land, they forced white competitors for their labor to allow them separate houses in the expanding cotton fields. Abandonment of the communal life of the slave plantation bestowed upon the Negro the American farmer's ideal of a separate existence. Here was a revolutionary change far more important in the life of the freedmen than sensational political reforms. Then followed negotiation of share-crop arrangements and other types of labor contracts between freedmen and landlords. These agreements were a *modus vivendi* which allowed Negroes and their one-time owners to work together for many decades.

Reconstructionists helped point the way for southern communities to change from slave states to modern commonwealths. State constitutions evolved that were so in tune with progressive political principles that they substantially have survived to the present day. These constitutions achieved reforms in the organization of courts, in county government, in school administration, and in the conduct of elections. Also projected were state school systems. A sense of identity with the United States was so thoroughly acquired that the time when the South wished a separate existence was completely forgotten. White southerners were to join Negroes, carpetbaggers, and scalawags in embracing the idea of a consolidated United States. Perhaps southerners of both races became more chauvinistic than other Americans. The southern Negro for the first time discovered independence in church life, and a beginning was made in the rebuilding of southern industry and commerce.

But the white South was determined that the Reconstruction experiment must be done away with, at least to the extent of eliminating Negroes from all political activities. Although Negroes were not in any real sense in control of state governments, they held some offices of honor and trust, and enjoyed freedom to elect political opportunists from both North and South—scalawags and carpetbaggers. Negroes and their sympathizers in high office were to white men a humiliation almost as great as that of black men marrying white women. The hated word "Radical" entered the local vocabulary. It was thought that the aim of the victors in the Civil War was to convince the southern white man that he must not regard himself as superior to the Negroes. "White supremacy" became the new watchword and war cry. That tens of thousands of white southerners had died on battlefields had not changed this view. White fathers killed in war were replaced by more numerous sons, who called the dead blessed and dedicated themselves fervently to the belief that the Negro was inferior to the white man and should not take an equal place in the white man's world.

To destroy manifestations of Negro equality, southern whites employed all the weapons at their command, including force when it did not invite federal intervention. Corruption and extravagance justified the intolerance shown to the Radical regimes. Indeed, had these regimes manifested the exemplary statesmanship of a Bismarck or a Gladstone, they still would not have been acceptable.

The first step in eliminating the Negro and his Radical allies from politics was to unite all men of the supposedly superior race in a *Conservative* political party. This designation was to quiet the antagonism of former Whigs, who could not abide the word *Democratic*. By mere fact of numerical superiority of whites over Negroes, those who had ruled in the antebellum South quickly won control in Virginia, North Carolina, Tennessee, and Georgia.

In states where Negroes possessed a majority or a near majority, the problem of eliminating them from politics was more difficult. It was solved by the growing tendency of whites to match Negro intransigence with violence. Every prominent Negro or white Radical feared assassination when he ventured into rural areas; and as a consequence, the more prudent remained in the towns behind the protection of federal garrisons. Despite experience in use of firearms, the Negro militia, organized to protect the Radical governments against violence, was psychologically unable to resist a show of force by the whites. When race riots took place, almost invariably more Negroes than whites were killed.

Although whites, by direct action, might easily free themselves of Negro participation in politics, such conduct tended to provoke the intervention of federal troops. More subtle tactics were used by societies loosely called the Ku-Klux Klan, organizations which aimed at the destruction of Radical power through intimidation and outright terrorism. When the officially designated Ku-Klux Klan was suppressed by federal troops, other less ostentatious but more effective agencies of violence were devised. Instead of wearing ghostly disguises, the white terrorists went about in plain clothes with unconcealed weapons in their hands. Such naked threats as these carried elections in Alabama, Arkansas, and Texas. By the early 1870's, only Mississippi, Louisiana, Florida, and South Carolina remained in control of the Negroes and their allies.

Conditions developed in these four states that made recovery of white supremacy easy. Mississippi settled into what a historian calls "a peculiar quiet" after bloody onslaughts against Negroes. A victory for the whites at the polls was so overwhelming that advocates of further federal intervention became too discouraged to continue the struggle.

In the three other states the members of the former ruling class set out to attain their return to power by any and all methods short of open conflict with the army of occupation. White leagues, rifle clubs, and other agencies of potential violence neutralized the weight of Negro majorities. Dual governments, one Radical and one Conservative, came into existence in each of the three states. They sent dual election returns to Washington in the contested presidential election of 1876. So close was the electoral count that the votes of the three southern states in question could determine whether a Democrat or a Republican would be president of the United States. Compromise was effected. The electoral votes of the three contested states, with Democratic consent, were given to the Republicans, thereby assuring the choice of a Republican president. In return for this concession, Rutherford B. Hayes, the Republican victor, agreed to withdraw federal troops from the three states under Radical control. When this occurred early in 1877, the last of the Radical state governments collapsed. White supremacy was completely re-established. Justified by a wave of industrial development, within a generation "Jim Crow" laws had separated the Negro socially, and southern constitutional amendments had taken his last vestiges of political rights. The colored American citizen, set free in law and fact by the Thirteenth Amendment, asserted equal in law if not in fact by the Fourteenth and Fifteenth amendments, would remain for the greatest part of the succeeding century a monument to the failure of the postwar Reconstructionists to place him permanently within the main stream of American political life.

SUGGESTED READINGS

Buck, Paul. *Road To Reunion.* Boston: Little, Brown & Co., 1937.

Coulter, E. Merton. *The South during Reconstruction, 1865–1877.* Baton Rouge: Louisiana State University Press, 1947.

Du Bois, W. E. Burghardt. *Black Reconstruction.* New York: Russell & Russell, Inc., 1935.

Dunning, William A. *Reconstruction: Political and Economic.* New York: Harper & Bros., 1907.

Fleming, Walter L. *Civil War and Reconstruction in Alabama.* Gloucester, Mass.: Peter Smith, 1949.

Fleming, Walter L. (ed.). *Documentary History of Reconstruction: 1865 to the Present Time.* 2 vols. Cleveland: Arthur H. Clark Co., 1906–7.

Fleming, Walter L. *The Sequel of Appomattox.* New Haven: Yale University Press, 1919.

Franklin, John Hope. *Reconstruction.* Chicago: University of Chicago Press, 1962.

Garner, James W. *Reconstruction in Mississippi.* New York: Macmillan Co., 1901.

McKitrick, Eric. *Andrew Johnson and Reconstruction.* Chicago: University of Chicago Press, 1960.

Simkins, Francis B., and Woody, Robert H. *South Carolina during Reconstruction.* Chapel Hill: University of North Carolina Press, 1932.

Wharton, Vernon L. *The Negro in Mississippi, 1865–1890.* Chapel Hill: University of North Carolina Press, 1947.

Woodward, C. Vann. *Reunion and Reaction.* Boston: Little, Brown & Co., 1951.

Document 16.1

THE ARGUMENT FOR CONGRESSIONAL RECONSTRUCTION

Vermont-born Thaddeus Stevens knew poverty in his early years—a factor of some importance, since it helped shape his later antagonism toward aristocracy and his firm belief in economic and political democracy. After a legal and business career in Pennsylvania, he entered Congress in 1848 and became the authoritative voice of Radical Republicanism. During the period of Reconstruction, he was a leading spokesman in favor of Congressional control over the ex-Confederates, military occupation of the South, and the imposition of a harsh peace. In the following selection, Stevens enunciates the "conquered province" theory, which became the legal basis for his attitude toward the South.

(From Thaddeus Stevens, "Reconstruction: Speech of the Hon. Thaddeus Stevens, Delivered in the City of Lancaster," *Lancaster [Pa.] Examiner and Herald*, September 7, 1865)

In compliance with your request I have come to give my views of the present condition of the rebel States; of the proper mode of reorganizing the Government, and the future prospects of the Republic. During the whole progress of the war I never for a moment felt doubt or despondency. I knew that the loyal North would conquer the rebel despots who sought to destroy freedom. But since that traitorous confederation has been subdued, and we have entered upon the work of "reconstruction" or "restoration," I cannot deny that my heart has become sad at the gloomy prospects before us.

Four years of bloody and expensive war waged against the United States by eleven States, under a government called the "Confederate States of America" to which they acknowledged allegiance, have overthrown all governments within those States, which could be acknowledged as legitimate by the Union. The armies of the Confederate States having been conquered and subdued, and their territories possessed by the United States, it becomes necessary to establish governments therein, which shall be republican in "form and principles, and form a more perfect union" with the parent government. It is desirable that such a course should be pursued as to exclude from those governments every vestige of human bondage and render the same forever impossible in this nation, and to take care that no principles of self-destruction shall be incorporated there in. In effecting this, it is to be hoped that no provision of the Constitution will be infringed, and no principle of the law of nations disregarded. Especially must we take care that in rebuking this unjust and treasonable war, the authorities of the Union shall indulge in no acts of usurpation which may tend to impair the stability and permanency of the nation within these limitations. We hold it to be the duty of the Government to inflict condign punishment on the rebel belligerents, and so weaken their hands that they can never again endanger the Union; and so reform their municipal institutions as to make them republican in spirit as well as in name.

We especially insist that the property of the chief rebels should be seized and appropriated to the payment of the National debt, caused by the unjust and wicked war which they instigated.

How can such punishments be inflicted and such forfeitures produced without doing violence to established principles?

Two positions have been suggested.

1st—To treat those States as never having been out of the Union, because the Constitution forbids secession, and, therefore, a fact forbidden by law could not exist.

2nd—To accept the position in which they placed themselves as severed from the union; an independent government *de facto*, and an alien enemy to be dealt with according to the laws of war.

It seems to me that while we do not aver that the United States are bound to treat them as an alien enemy, yet they have a right to elect so to do if it be for the interest of the nation; and that the "Confederate States" are estopped from denying that position. . . .

The Confederate States were for four years what they claimed to be, an alien enemy in all their rights and liabilities. To say that they were states under the protection of that constitution which they were assaulting with bloody defeats, simply because they became belligerents through crime, is making theory over-rule fact to an absurd degree. It will I suppose at least be conceded that the United States if not obliged so to do, have a right to treat them as an alien enemy now conquered, and subject to all the liabilities of a vanquished foe. . . .

All writers agree that the victor may inflict punishment upon the vanquished enemy even to the taking of his life, liberty, or the confiscation of his property; but that this extreme right is never exercised, except upon a cruel, barbarous, obstinate, or dangerous foe who has waged an unjust war.

Upon the character of the belligerent, and the justice of the war, and the manner of conducting it, depends our right to take the lives, liberty, and property of the belligerent. This war had its origin in treason without one spark of justice. It was prosecuted before notice of it, by robbing our forts and armories, and our navy-yards; by stealing our money from the mints and depositories, and by surrendering our forts and navies by perjurers who had sworn to support the Constitution. In its progress our prisoners, by the authority of their government were slaughtered in cold blood. Ask Fort Pillow and Fort Wagner. Sixty thousand of our prisoners have been deliberately starved to death because they would not enlist in the rebel armies. The graves at Andersonville have each an accusing tongue. The purpose and avowed object of the enemy "to found an empire whose corner-stone should be slavery," render its perpetuity or revival dangerous to human liberty.

Surely, these things are sufficient to justify the exercise of the extreme rights of war—"to execute, to imprison, to confiscate." How many captive enemies it would be proper to execute, as an example to nations, I leave others to judge. I am not fond of sanguinary punishments, but surely some victims must propitiate the *manes* [shades of the departed] of our starved, murdered, slaughtered martyrs. A court martial could do justice according to law.

But we propose to confiscate all the estate of every rebel belligerent whose estate was worth $10,000, or whose land exceeded two hundred acres in quantity. Policy if not justice would require that the poor, the ignorant, and the coerced should be forgiven. They followed the example and teachings of their wealthy and intelligent neighbors. The rebellion would never have originated with them. Fortunately those who would thus escape form a large majority of the people though possessing but a small portion of the wealth. The proportion of those exempt compared with the punished would be I believe about nine tenths."

There are about six millions of freemen in the South. The number of acres of land is 465,000,000. Of this those who own above two hundred acres each, number about 70,000 persons, holding in the aggregate (together with the States) about 394,000,000 acres, leaving for all the others below 200 each about 71,000,000 of acres. By thus forfeiting the estates of the leading rebels, the Government would have 394,000,000 of acres beside their town property, and yet nine tenths of the people would remain untouched. Divide this land into convenient farms. Give if you please forty acres to each adult male freedman. . . .

Look again, and see loyal men reduced to poverty by the confiscations by the Confederate States, and by the rebel States—see Union men robbed of their property, and their dwellings laid in ashes by rebel raiders, and say if too much is asked for them. But above all, let us inquire whether imperative duty to the present generation and to posterity does not command us to compel the wicked enemy to pay the expense of this unjust war. In ordinary transactions he whose raises a false clamor and prosecutes an unfounded suit, is adjudged to pay the costs in his defeat. We have seen that, by the law of nations, the vanquished in an unjust war must pay the expense.

Our war debt is estimated at from three to four billions of dollars. . . . Four hundred and seventy millions to be raised by taxation—our present heavy taxes will not in ordinary years, produce but little more than half that sum. Can our people bear double their present taxation? He who unnecessarily causes it will be accursed from generation to generation. It is fashionable to belittle our public debt, lest the people should become alarmed, and political parties should suffer. I have never found it wise to deceive the people. They can always be trusted with the truth. Capitalists will not be affected for they can not be deceived. Confide in the people, and you will avoid repudiation. Deceive them, and lead them into false measures, and you may produce it. . . .

The plan we have proposed would pay at least three fourths of our debt. The balance could be managed with our present taxation. . . .

While I hear it said everywhere that slavery is dead, I cannot learn who killed it. No thoughtful man has pretended that Lincoln's proclamation, so noble in sentiment, liberated a single slave. It expressly excluded from its operation all those within our lines. No slave within any part of the rebel States in our possession or in Tennessee, but only those beyond our limit and beyond our power were declared free. . . .

But, it is said, by those who have more sympathy with rebel wives and children than for the widows and orphans of loyal men, that this stripping the rebels of their estates and driving them to exile or to honest labor would be harsh and severe upon innocent women and children. It may be so; but that is the result of the necessary laws of war. But it is revolutionary, they say. This plan would, no doubt, work a radical reorganization in southern institutions, habits and manners. It is intended to revolutionize their principles and feelings. This may startle feeble minds and shake weak nerves. So do all great improvements in the political and moral world. It requires a heavy impetus to drive forward a sluggish people. When it was first proposed to free the slaves, and arm the blacks, did not half the nation tremble? The prim conservatives, the snobs, and the male waiting maids in Congress, were in hysterics.

The whole fabric of southern society *must* be changed and never can it be done if this opportunity is lost. Without this, this Government can never be, as it never has been, a true republic. Heretofore, it had more the features of aristocracy than of democracy.—The Southern States have been despotisms, not goverments of the people. It is impossible that any practical equality of rights can exist where a few thousand men monopolize the whole landed property. The larger the number of small proprietors the more safe and stable the government. As the landed interest must govern, the more it is subdivided and held by independent owners, the better. . . . —If the south is ever to be made a safe republic let her lands be cultivated by the toil of the owners or the free labor of intelligent citizens. This must be done even though it drive her nobility into exile. If they go, all the better.

It will be hard to persuade the owner of ten thousand acres of land, who drives a coach and four, that he is not degraded by sitting at the same table, or in the same pew, with the embrowned and hard-handed farmer who has himself cultivated his own thriving homestead of 150 acres. This subdivision of the lands will yield ten bales of cotton to one that is made now, and he who produced it will own it and *feel himself a man.*

It is far easier and more beneficial to exile 70,000 proud, bloated, and defiant rebels, than to expatriate four millions of labourers, native to the soil and loyal to the Government. . . .

This remodeling the institutions, and reforming the rooted habits of a proud aristocracy, is undoubtedly a formidable task; requiring the broad mind of enlarged statesmanship, and the firm nerve of the hero. But will not this mighty occasion produce—will not the God of Liberty and order give us such men? Will not a Romulus, a Lycurgus, a Charlemagne, a Washington arise, whose expansive views will found a free empire, to endure till time shall be no more?

This doctrine of restoration shocks me.—We have a duty to perform which our fathers were incapable of, which will be required at our hands by God and our Country. When our ancestors found a "more perfect Union" necessary, they found it impossible to agree upon a Constitution without tolerating, nay guaranteeing Slavery. They were obliged to acquiesce, trusting to time to work a speedy cure, in which they were disappointed. *They* had some excuse, some justification. But we can have none if we do not thoroughly eradicate Slavery and render it forever impossible in this republic. The Slave power made war upon the nation. They declared the "more perfect Union" dissolved. Solemnly declared themselves a foreign nation, alien to this republic; for four years were in fact what they claimed to be. We accepted the war which they tendered and treated them as a government capable of making war. We have conquered them, and as a conquered enemy we can give them laws; can abolish all their municipal institutions and form new ones. If we do not make those institutions fit to last through generations of free men, a heavy curse will be on us. Our glorious, but tainted republic, has been born to new life through bloody, agonizing pains. But this frightful "Restoration" has thrown it into "cold obstruction, and to death." If the rebel states have never been out of the Union, any attempt to reform their State institutions either by Congress or the President, is rank usurpation.

Is then all lost? Is this great conquest to be in vain? That will depend upon the virtue and intelligence of the next Congress. To Congress alone belongs the power of the Re-construction—of giving law to the vanquished. . . . If a majority of Congress can be found wise and firm enough to declare the Confederate States a conquered enemy. Re-construction will be easy and legitimate; and the friends of freedom will long rule in the Councils of the Nation. If Restoration prevails the prospect is gloomy, and new "Lords will make new laws." The Union party will be overwhelmed. The Copperhead party has become extinct with Secession. But with Secession it will revive. Under "restoration" every rebel State will send rebels to Congress; and these, with their allies in the North, will control Congress, and occupy the White House. Then Restoration of Laws and ancient Constitutions will be sure to follow; our public debt will be repudiated or the rebel National debt will be added to ours, and the people be crushed beneath heavy burdens.

Let us forget all parties, and build on the broad platform of "reconstructing the Government out of the conquered territory, converted into new and free States, and admitted into the Union by the sovereign power of Congress, with another plank,"—THE PROPERTY OF THE REBELS SHALL PAY OUR NATIONAL DEBT, *and indemnify freed-men and loyal sufferers,*—and that under no circumstances will we suffer the National debt to be repudiated, or the interest scaled below the contract rates; nor permit any part of the rebel debt to be assumed by the nation.

Let all who approve of these principles tarry with us. Let all others go with Copperheads and rebels. Those will be the opposing parties. Young men, this duty devolves on you. Would to God, if only for that, I were still in the prime of life, that I might aid you to fight through this last and greatest battle of Freedom.

Document 16.2

A SOUTHERN VIEW OF THE FREEDMEN

The problems of social, economic, and psychological adjustment between southern whites and the new freedmen in the immediate postwar period are revealed in this excerpt from a letter written by a white Alabaman in 1866

(From *Transactions of the Alabama Historical Society*, Vol. IV, "Letters of William F. Samford," reproduced in Walter L. Fleming [ed.], *Documentary History of Reconstruction: 1865 to the Present Time*, Vol. I [Cleveland: Arthur H. Clark Co., 1906], pp. 92–93)

Here, in a mile of me, is a negro woman dying, who says an old African hag put a snake in her four years ago, and the Obi doctor has gone to deliver her. "Civilization" is "marching two steps backwards" like the truant boy went to school, "to one forward" in our "Africa" down here. The negroes here spend their time going to "funerals," religious howlings, promiscuous sexual intercourse, thieving and "conjuring." At their "funerals" they bellow like cattle when one of their number is slaughtered. . . .

Emancipation is a fact. I have sworn to support it, and I shall keep my oath. Sambo is a freeman by force of presidential proclamation. But it is not unlawful to see certain evils of emancipation which call for the active interposition of the philanthropists. Sambo will flog his child unmercifully, and Sally will neglect it in sickness, and so between paternal action and maternal non-action little Cuffy has a "hard road to travel" for twenty-one years of his infancy—a terrible preparatory training for the bliss of being "free to starve."

The stupendous wrong and folly consists in taking a poor, ignorant, childlike race from under the fostering care of a patriarchal government and withdrawing from it the protection of interest. . . .

The Christmas holidays here are cold, rainy, cheerless. The heart of the South is beginning to sink in despair. The streets are full of negroes, who refuse to make contracts to labor the next year. The short crop of 1866 causes much dissatisfaction. They will not engage to work for anything but wages, and few are able to pay wages. They are penniless but resolute in their demands. They expect to see all the land divided out equally beween them and their old masters, in time to make the next crop. One of the most intelligent black men I know told me that in a neighboring village where several hundred negroes were congregated, he does not think that as many as three made contracts, although the planters are urgent in their solicitations, and offering the highest prices for labor they can possibly afford to pay. The same man informed me that the impression widely prevails that Congress is about to divide out the lands, and that this impression is given out by Federal soldiers at the nearest military station. It cannot be disguised that in spite of the most earnest efforts of their old master to conciliate and satisfy them, the estrangement between the races increases in its extent and bitterness. Nearly all the negro men are armed with repeaters and many of them carry them openly, day and night. The status is most unsatisfactory, and really full of just apprehensions of the direst results. The negro children are growing up in ignorance and vice. The older ones, men and women, abandon themselves to dissipation of the lowest sort. Their schools, "so-called," are simply a farce.

Document 16.3

THE SOUTHERN FEAR OF NEGRO DOMINATION

The white South's determination to deny political rights to the Negro and thereby to maintain "Anglo-Saxon" dominance in all aspects of southern life may be seen in this protest of South Carolina whites, dated September 21, 1867, against Congressional efforts to insure equality for the new freedmen by the Reconstruction acts.

(From J. S. Reynolds, "Reconstruction in South Carolina," reproduced in Walter L. Fleming [ed.], *Documentary History of Reconstruction: 1865 to the Present Time*, Vol. I [Cleveland: Arthur H. Clark Co., 1906], pp. 424–26)

We desire peace for its own sake, for its holy Christian influence, and for the civilization and refinement which spring up in its path. Do the Reconstruction acts of Congress propose to give us this peace? No—they give us war and anarchy, rather. They sow the seeds of discord in our midst and place the best interests of society in the hands of an ignorant mob. They disfranchise the white citizen and enfranchise the newly emancipated slave. The slave of yesterday, who knew no law but the will of the master, is today about to be invested with the control of the government. In all popular governments the two great sources of power may be traced, (1) to the exercise of the ballot, (2) to the franchise of the jury box. Invest any people with these two great powers, and they have at once the government of the country in their hands. By the Reconstruction acts of Congress these powers are conferred upon the negro—he can make and unmake the Constitution and the laws which he will administer according to the dictates of another or his own caprice.

We are not unfriendly to the negro. . . . In his property, in his life and in his person we are willing that the black man and the white man shall stand together upon the same platform and be shielded by the same equal laws. We venture the opinion that the people of South Carolina are prepared to adopt as their own the Constitution of any New England or other Northern State, wherein it is supposed that the civil rights of the negro are more fully and amply secured. But upon a question involving such great and momentous issues we should be untrue to ourselves and unfair to our opponents were we to withhold the frank and full expression of our opinions. We, therefore, feeling the responsibility of the subject and the occasion, enter our most solemn protest against the policy of investing the negro with political rights. The black man is what God and nature and circumstances have made him. That he is not fit to be invested with these important rights may be no fault of his. But the fact is patent to all that the negro is utterly unfitted to exercise the highes function of the citizen. The government of the country should not be permitted to pass from the hands of the white man into the hands of the negro. The enforcement of the Reconstruction acts by military power under the guise of negro voters and negro conventions cannot lawfully reëstablish civil government in South Carolina. It may for a time hold us in subjection to a quasi-civil government backed by military force, but it can do no more. As citizens of the United States we should not consent to live under negro supremacy, nor should we acquiesce in negro equality. Not for ourselves only, but on behalf of the Anglo-Saxon race and blood in this country, do we protest against this subversion of the great social law, whereby an ignorant and depraved race is placed in power and influence above the virtuous, the educated and the refined. By these acts of Congress intelligence and virtue are put under foot, while ignorance and vice are lifted into power.

Document 16.4
THE KLAN VISITS A NEGRO

The Ku-Klux Klan, organized originally as a secret fraternal order, became the most sensational means of southern white resistance to the carpetbagger-scalawag-Negro-dominated southern state governments during the years 1868–71. The following selection tells how Klan night riders intimidated a Negro voter.

(From "Ku Klux Report, South Carolina Testimony . . . 1871," reproduced in Walter L. Fleming [ed.], *Documentary History of Reconstruction: 1865 to the Present Time*, Vol. II [Cleveland: Arthur H. Clark Co., 1907], pp. 371–73)

They came to my door and they said "Hey!" I was asleep. They called "Hey, hey!" My wife says, "Lewis listen." . . . "What are you doing there?" I says; and they said, "By Christ, come out; I will show you what I am doing." . . . and I got up and sat on the bed, with my legs hanging out, and peeped out. . . . They says, "Lewis, by Christ, arn't you going to get up and open the door?" . . . I spoke and said, "What do you want; do you want to whip me?" I have done nothing to be whipped; . . . He says, "By Christ, open the door; I will tell you by Christ, what I am to whip you for." I hung down my head and studied, and said, "I have done nothing to be whipped for; and I don't think I can open the door." My wife jumped up to open the door; they said, "Open the door, Adeline"; . . . They said, "Lewis, you get up and come out." . . . After so long a time I went to the door. . . . Then one come running right up to me, a great big fellow . . . he says, "Come down on the ground, by Christ, among your friends!" I says, "I can do that and let the trouble be over with; short or long, let it be over with," and out on the ground I went. Says he, "How did you vote?" I says, "I voted the radical ticket." "You has, sir?" he says. I says, "Yes, sir." "Well, by Christ," says he, "Ain't you had no instruction?" I says, "I can't read, and I can't write, and I can't much more than spell." . . . I says, "How can a black man get along without there is some white gentleman or other with them? We go by instructions. We don't know nothing much." "O, by Christ," says he, "you radicals go side by side with one another, and by Christ us democrats go side and side with one another." I says, "I can't help that." He says, "You can't by Christ." I says, "No sir; I can't." He says, "Well, sir, are you going up in the morning to see to your crop, and go to work?" I says, "Just as quick as I get my breakfast I am going." He says, "Is you tending to your crop?" I says, "Yes, I am." He says, "Is there any grass in your crop?" I says, "Yes, a little; according to the chances, I had a little grass there." He says, "By Christ, you have got to tend to the crop." I says, "I am tending to it." I says, "When I get out of corn and out of meat both, and anybody has got corn and meat, I jump out and work for a bushel of corn and a piece of meat, and work until I get it." . . . I says, "What do you want to whip me for? I have done nothing." "Come out in the road," he says. I stopped and studied and hung down my head. "I can't study up nothing," I said, "for what you ought to whip me." They said, "You didn't think about this when you voted the radical ticket." One of them threw a pistol right up here under my chin, and one grabbed me by the sleeve, and he says, "You must come." I says, "I can come without holding, I reckon, but it is mighty hard to take a whipping for nothing; the gentleman on the plantation . . . says I am a good hand; . . . and anybody that wants to know whether I am a good hand or not needs no more than to go and look at my crop." He says . . . "Get in the road and march," and in the road I went. They took me up the road pretty near to the edge of the woods; . . . Says he, "Off with your shirt." I says, "What do you all want to whip me for; what have I done?" "By Christ," he says, "Off with your shirt; if you don't you shall go dead. We come from Manassas grave-yard; and by Christ we want to get back to our grave-yard and cover up before day, by Christ." . . . I threw my shirt off. The one talking to me says, "You must hit him forty;" the other says, "thirty will do him." He says, "Now Lewis, by Christ, you get down on your knees." I says, "It is hard to get down on my knees and take a whipping for nothing." Then I dropped down. He says, "By Christ, don't you get up until we get done with you." They set to work on me and hit me ten or fifteen licks pretty keen, and I raised up. "Get down," he says; "if you ever raise up again you'll go dead before we quit you." Down I went again, and I staid down until they got done whipping me. Says he, "Now, by Christ, you must promise you will vote the democratic ticket?" I says, "I don't know how I will vote; it looks hard when a body thinks this way and that way to take a beating." . . . "You must promise to vote the democratic ticket, or you go dead before we leave you," he says. Then I studied and studied. They gathered right close up around me. "Come out with it —come, out with it, by Christ." Then I says, "Yes, sir, I reckon so." . . . Well, after I told them that, they said, "By Christ, now get up and put on your shirt." . . . I stopped and studied, and had to put on my shirt. "Now," he says, "by Christ, you go; we are done with you; . . . if you let it get out you must go dead for it all; I will come back." I says, "Yes," and back I went to my house, and off they went.

17

GRADY McWHINEY
Northwestern University

The Negro in the "New South"

No PERIOD of American history was more promising or more disillusioning to the Negro than the last forty years of the nineteenth century. In 1860, nearly 90 per cent of America's four and a half million Negroes were slaves. Of those who were free the vast majority were second-class citizens, even in the North. Usually, only the most menial jobs were open to them. They were segregated; they were forbidden to migrate from state to state. Hardly any of them could vote. They were barred from jury duty and from the witness stand. The federal government seemed oblivious to their condition. As a free Negro remarked: "Under the Constitution and Government of the United States, the colored people are nothing and can be nothing but an alien, disfranchised and degraded class." In 1854, Abraham Lincoln admitted that he objected to social and political equality for Negroes." My own feelings will not admit of this," he said, "and if mine would, we well know that those of the great mass of white people will not."

During the Civil War period, this prejudice against Negroes appeared to change. By 1870, every Negro had been emancipated and given full citizenship. Not only could he travel freely about the country; he could vote and hold public office. No state or local government post in the South was beyond his grasp. For forty-three days, Louisiana had a black governor; in other states, Negroes served as lieutenant governors, supreme court justices, secretaries of state, superintendents of public education, legislators, treasurers, sheriffs, and city councilmen. Between 1869 and 1877, sixteen Negroes sat in the Congress of the United States. Such a change in the Negro's status suggests that white Americans were adopting the view expressed by Senator Charles Sumner in 1866—that a "man, of whatever country or race, whether browned by equatorial sun or blanched by northern cold, is with you a child of the Heavenly Father, and equal with you in all the rights of Human Nature."

But Sumner's hopes were premature. By the beginning of the twentieth century, color-blind democracy was a mockery in America. The Negro was one of the most discriminated-against men in all Christendom. Systematically, he had been stripped of nearly all his rights; even his freedom had been circumscribed. He had been relegated to a subservient position in society, disfranchised throughout most of the South, and deserted by both the federal government and the United States Supreme Court. He was being lynched, vilified, and exploited; he was "Jim Crowed" nearly everywhere.

What happened to the Negro between 1860 and 1900 is clear; why it happened is often misunderstood. It seems paradoxical that a nation so apparently committed to liberty and democracy would give the Negro a large measure of equality and then take it from him. The reason is rather simple, but it can be explained best by reviewing some post-Civil War history.

Most Negroes were unprepared for freedom in 1865. Few of them understood its meaning. "One say dis, an' one say dat, an' we don't know," an old Negro told a reporter. "After freedom a heap of people . . . went roaming round like wild, hunting cities," recalled a former slave. Many Negroes flocked to military camps seeking aid. Some freedmen actually refused to be free. They were accustomed to slavery; they were frightened and uncertain about a new way of life. "Freedom wasn't no different," said John McCoy. "I works for Marse John just the same for a long time. He say one morning, 'John, you can go out in the field iffen you wants to or you can get out iffen you wants to, cause the government say you is free. If you wants to work I'll feed you and give you clothes but can't pay you no money. I ain't got none.' Humph, I didn't know nothing what money was, nohow, but I knows I'll get plenty . . . to eat, so I stays till Old Marse die and Old Miss git shut of the place." Adeline White remembered that when "Master called us up and told us we was free, some rejoiced so they shouted, but some didn't, they was sorry. . . . I wouldn't leave my white folks. . . . I worked on for them as long as I was able to work and always felt like I belonged to 'em, and, you know, after all this long time, I feel like I am theirs."

Soon many Negroes discovered that their freedom was limited. The government "left the freedmen in a [bad] condition," said the distinguished Negro leader, Frederick Douglass. "It felt that it had done enough for him. It had made him free, and henceforth he must make his own way in the world. . . . He was free from the individual master, but the slave of society. He had neither money, property, nor friends.

He was free from the old plantation, but he had nothing but the dusty road under his feet. . . . He was . . . turned loose, naked, hungry, and destitute to the open sky."

In August, 1865, a group of disgruntled freedmen resolved by a vote of 700 to 200 that in three months of freedom they "had discovered that the prejudices of color were by no means confined to the people of the South, but . . . that it was stronger and more marked against them in the strangers from the North." They also agreed "that negroes no more than white men, can live without work, or be comfortable without homes . . . , and that . . . their true happiness and well-being required them to return to the homes which they had abandoned in a moment of excitement, and to go to work again under their old masters."

Only the exceptional freedman escaped economic bondage. Most Negroes returned to work under their old master or some new master. If the freedman could have selected his occupation, he probably would have been a planter or a businessman. Though some of the most economically successful freedmen were artisans, most blacks rejected the mechanical trades. In 1890, less than 5 per cent of all Negroes were employed in the trades. This was a natural reaction against the manual labor they had performed as slaves. Like the whites they aped in dress and manners, Negroes sought high-status employment. Their prejudices, together with those of the whites, helped fix the freedman's status. Moreover, Negroes who tried to start a business were handicapped by inexperience and inadequate capital. A Freedmen's Bureau official recounted the failure of a mercantile partnership. In 1866, four South Carolina Negroes established a store. It "was a single room in a deserted hotel, and the entire stock in trade might have been worth forty dollars. On this chance of business four families proposed to live. By the time the United States license of twenty dollars, the town license of five dollars, and certain other opening expenses had been paid, the liabilities of the firm were nearly sufficient to cover its assets." Within three weeks, two of the partners quit the business, and two others were taken in. Being ignorant of the revenue law, the freedmen formed a new partnership and were taxed for a new license. This mistake was disastrous; the business dissolved. Apparently, only one of the partners made any money from the enterprise. He sold some borrowed equipment used to start the store and absconded with the cash.

Most freedmen remained in the South, working as field laborers or sharecroppers. Usually, they received only a subsistence income. Over 82 per cent of all southern Negroes lived in rural areas in 1900, yet only 25 per cent of these owned their own farms. At the same time, 63 per cent of all southern white farmers owned their land. If a Negro managed to acquire a farm, it seldom exceeded forty acres, and he had to scratch hard to survive. He might own a cow, a few pigs, and some chickens; his farm equipment probably consisted of a ramshackle wagon, a plow, a few hoes, an axe or two, and some shovels. Very likely, his home was an unpainted, box-shaped structure of boards nailed vertically to a frame and covered with clapboards.

If not a farmer, the freedman probably was a servant. Domestic service, like agriculture, required limited skills; also, it fitted into the white man's conception of a Negro's occupation. Nearly a third of all Negroes were domestic servants in 1890.

Because the freedman was poor, ignorant, and unsophisticated, white men used him. He became their tool. When they needed his support, they wooed him; when they did not, they ignored him. Republicans as well as Democrats, northerners as well as southerners, viewed the Negro through self-interested eyes. How he could help them was far more important than how they could help him.

In 1865, Republicans vacillated on the question of Negro suffrage. A few men defended the justice of giving the black man the ballot. Other men, like George Templeton Strong, feared that "the average field hand would use political power as intelligently as would the mule he drives." A New York editor asked: "Are we expected in the light of the intelligence of the century, to believe that any body of men, be they the Congress of the United States or a body of mythological gods, can, by a simple legislative feat, lift the negro from barbarism to the summit of civilization?"

The answer to this question was that Republicans believed they could stay in power only by enfranchising and controlling the freedmen. "We need their aid," insisted a Boston editor. "We cannot expect to carry the country through the difficulties of the next twenty years without the effective assistance of Southern colored men."

Expediency, more than morality, dictated Republican policy toward the Negro. "I have never insisted," said Congressman Thaddeus Stevens, "that the franchise should be unjustly regulated so as to secure a Republican ascendancy but I have insisted and do insist that there can be no unjust regulation of that franchise which will give to any other party the power of governing." Denouncing the Democrats as the immigrant's party, Senator Ben Wade told Ohioans that Negroes were better qualified to vote than Irishmen. "I think I could easily convince any man," added Elizur Wright, "that it will probably make a difference of at least $1,000,000,000 in the . . . national debt, whether we reconstruct on the basis of loyal . . . black votes, or on white votes exclusively. . . . I am not disputing about tastes. A negro's ballot may be more vulgar than his bullet [but] . . . the question . . . is how . . . to protect my property from taxation; and I am sure . . . the victories of 1865 [will be] thrown away . . . if . . . the government allows 4,000,000 of black population to continue disfranchised."

By 1868 the Republicans had made southern Negroes voters. At first, they voted Republican almost without exception. The chief persuasive agency was the Union League. In some southern states, nearly every Negro was a member, and every member was oath-bound to vote Republican. "That's the party of my color," said a freedman. In Mississippi the Republicans could count on 90 per cent of the Negro vote.

Occasionally, the vote was used for the Negro's benefit; often, it was not. Fraud and corruption characterized many of the South's Republican regimes. One Republican governor, whose annual salary was $8,000, made over $100,000 during his first year in office. Another governor received over $40,000 in bribes. A free restaurant for state legislators cost South Carolina taxpayers $125,000. Over $300,000 was spent on legislative supplies and incidentals in one session.

Even when the freedman held high office, he seldom profited from the corruption around him. He was more the dupe than the scoundrel. Thousands of Negroes voted without knowing the names of the candidates. Enterprising Republicans sold Alabama Negroes pictures of General Grant for $2.00 each, and told them federal troops were in the South to see that all Negroes voted for him. In Florida a white Republican, who campaigned for office by kissing Negro babies, told the voters that "Jesus Christ was a Republican."

Not all Negroes were fooled. "What we call a carpet-bagger is a man who comes here . . . to occupy public position . . . and then leaves the State when he has made his money," said a Louisiana Negro. "They will associate with the negro, because they want to use him and get his vote; but as soon as they get his vote they don't care about him. They want to make money out of him and get a position."

The Republicans also followed a policy of expediency in the North. Until the adoption of the Fifteenth Amendment in 1870, only six northern states allowed the Negro to vote. In fact, the Fifteenth Amendment was intended to insure Republican political control in the South rather than to enfranchise the northern Negro. He was given a few political sops, but Republicans generally held the color line. In

1871 a white mob killed a Negro school principal in a Philadelphia election riot. "We have always known that there was a sentiment in the North strongly opposed to Negro suffrage," complained a Negro journalist. "This has never been a secret."

Of course, Republicans had no patent on expediency. Probably, most white southerners agreed with the South Carolinian who said: "For one I will never consent that when I approach the ballot-box a son of Africa shall stand by my side as my equal." But southern Democrats, like Republicans, needed the Negro's vote.

The freedman's low economic position made him particularly susceptible to Democratic persuasion. President Andrew Johnson had predicted in 1865 that former slaveowners eventually would control the freedman's ballot. In 1868 a Georgia Republican wrote the national party secretary: "The Negroes are too dependent upon their employers to be counted upon with certainty. They are without property, and cannot sustain themselves . . . without being fed by their Masters; they are without education or sufficient intelligence to appreciate the power the Ballot gives them, add to which a system of intimidation persistently practiced by the Rebels . . . , and you have a mass of poverty, ignorance, stupidity, and superstition under the influence of fears both real and imaginary, to organize and control, upon whom little reliance can be placed."

Conservative white southerners gradually drove a wedge between the Negro and the Republican party. In March, 1867, General Wade Hampton, formerly one of the South's wealthiest men, addressed a crowd of Negroes celebrating their enfranchisement at Columbia, South Carolina. Insisting that former slaveowners were the freedmen's best friends, Hampton promised to respect the Negro's right to vote. He explained his motives in a private letter: ". . . but one hope is left to us and that is to direct the Negro vote. . . . If we cannot direct the wave it will overwhelm us. Now how shall we do this? Simply by making the Negro a Southern man, . . . a Democrat."

The Hampton plan was adopted throughout the South. In April, 1867, a group of white Alabamians passed the following resolution: "We find nothing in the changed political condition of the white and black races in the South that ought to disturb the harmonious relations between them; that we are ready to accord to the latter every right and privilege to which they are entitled under the laws of the land; that we sincerely desire their prosperity and their improvement . . . ; that we are their friends, both from gratitude for their fidelity in the past . . . and because our interests in the future are inseparably connected with their well-being." Where persuasion failed, pragmatic Democrats used violence, fraud, and intimidation to capture the Negro vote and to destroy the Republican regimes.

By 1877 the conservatives had won. All attempts to keep the southern Negro voting Republican had been abandoned. Northerners had discovered that former Confederates would defend Yankee economic interests as vigorously as they had attacked Yankee armies. Besides, conservative white southerners had the Negro's vote in their pocket. They did not eliminate the Negro from public life; they merely controlled and manipulated him.

The Negro re-emerged as an important political figure in the South during the Populist period. At first, small farmers and their friends tried to win him away from the conservative Democrats. Needing the Negro's support, the Populists preached class unity. They pointed out how farmers of both races had been hurt by depressions, mortgage foreclosures, high taxes, excessive freight rates, and the increased cost of farm machinery. Leaders like Tom Watson defended Negro speakers, and encouraged black and white farmers to unite against concentrated wealth and conservative politics. The Democrats reacted with violence and intimidation. Race riots developed, and more than a dozen Negro Populists were murdered. While posing as defenders of white supremacy, the Democrats used Negro votes to beat the Populists. In the election of 1892, Populists carried every Alabama county except those twelve where Negroes constituted more than two thirds of the population. But the Democrats won the election by getting overwhelming majorities in the twelve Black Belt counties. In states where the elections were in doubt, the Democrats imported Negro voters. The Democratic vote in one Louisiana parish exceeded the total population of the parish.

The fury of the agrarian revolt convinced both Populists and Democrats that Negro voters were dangerous. No longer could they be allowed to hold the balance of political power; they must be deprived of the ballot. Mississippi led the way in 1890. Other states followed; and by the end of the nineteenth century, almost all southern Negroes had been disfranchised and barred from public office. The number of Negro legislators in South Carolina declined from eight in 1886 to none in 1900.

Anti-Negroism became a basic plank in every southern politician's platform. Mississippi's "Great White Chief," James K. Vardaman, always dressed in white and rode about the state in a wagon drawn by white oxen. He symbolized white supremacy. A contemporary said

Vardaman "stood for the poor white against the Negro—those were his qualifications as a statesman." Tom Watson, formerly a defender of Negroes, made his peace with the Georgia Democrats and turned Negro baiter. Senator Benjamin R. Tillman, the hero of South Carolina's "wool hat" and "one-gallus" boys, became the most famous anti-Negro orator of his time. In 1900, he boasted in the United States Senate: "We took the government away [from the Negro]. . . . We stuffed ballot boxes. We shot them. We are not ashamed of it." Tillman believed that dropping the caste barrier would cause the disappearance of the Caucasian, the "highest and noblest of the five races," in an orgy of miscegenation. He considered racial amalgamation the greatest of social crimes. What the Negro really wanted, Tillman insisted, was to kill all white men, marry white women, and use white children as servants. He admitted that Negroes were not baboons, but he claimed some of them were "so near akin to the monkey that scientists are yet looking for the missing link."

By 1900, there was ample proof that most northerners had deserted the Negro. Large audiences applauded Tillman everywhere he spoke in the North. In 1886 a group of New England Negroes declared: ". . . the colored citizen is discriminated against in so many depressing and injurious manners not withstanding the letter of the law. . . . No distinction is made as to intelligence, character, deportment or means among the colored people." In 1889, editor Henry W. Grady charged that in the North, six times as many Negroes as whites were in jail (one out of every 466 Negroes was behind bars); in the South, only four times as many Negroes as whites were in prison (one out of every 1,865 Negroes). "If prejudice wrongs [the Negro] in Southern courts," said Grady, "the record shows it to be deeper in Northern courts." Sophisticated Americans interpreted Darwin's theories as scientific justification for white supremacy. Moreover, the imperialism of the 1890's had brought over eight million additional "colored" people under American control. This "varied assortment of inferior races," said a northern journal, "of course, could not be allowed to vote." The Republican party no longer sought black voters. It was unnecessary; no matter what Republicans did, they could count on the Negro's vote. Northern Negroes had no other political home. In 1885 a Negro editor lamented: "No one black man in New York State enjoys the respect or confidence of the Republican politicians. . . . And this may apply to the colored leaders throughout the country in their relations to the politicians of the National Republican party."

Frustration drove Negroes in various directions. Isaiah T. Montgomery, a Negro Republican delegate to the Mississippi constitutional convention of 1890, favored the disfranchisement of over 123,000 Negroes. He thought such action would ease racial tension and improve state government. A young Negro intellectual, W. E. Burghardt DuBois, turned to historical scholarship. His purpose was to contribute "to the scientific study of slavery and the American Negro." In 1896, he published the first of his many monographs. T. Thomas Fortune, an editor, attempted to organize a black national federation (the Afro-American National League) in 1887. He hoped to unite Negroes outside the existing political parties and to use their strength to improve their status. But the Negro was unprepared educationally or financially to follow Fortune's program. Moreover, Fortune weakened his plan by suggesting that Negroes unite with poor whites. He failed to realize that race lines were more important than class lines to most white Americans.

Nineteenth-century Americans were not color-blind enough to accept racial equality. From 1860 to 1900, most Negro leaders based their plea for civil rights upon the theory of human equality expressed in the Declaration of Independence. Their argument was logical, but essentially naïve. Because most Americans gave lip service to the Declaration of Independence, Negroes made the mistake of assuming that white Americans meant what they said. They did not. Most Negroes misjudged the amount of democratic hypocrisy in America. They did not understand that white Americans who believed in equality also believed that some men were more equal than others.

Only one of the many nineteenth-century plans to improve the Negro's status seemed completely realistic. It was proposed by Booker T. Washington, the most famous Negro of his time. Instead of demanding social and political equality, he advised Negroes to strive for economic independence. "I plead for industrial education and development for the Negro not because I want to cramp him," said Washington, "but because I want to free him. I want to see him enter the all-powerful business and commercial world." Some of his ideas were outmoded—artisanship and small farming were no longer sure ways to economic independence in an industrial age—but Washington understood the whites better than most Negroes. He recognized that white opposition could doom any program for the Negro's improvement. Washington's proposal was ingeniously subtle. It appeared moderate enough for whites, North and South, to applaud.

Yet, actually, it was revolutionary in a thoroughly American and materialistic way. Washington knew that Americans measured progress in dollars. He was aware that greenbacks could not erase the color line, but he believed they could shade it. He realized that if racial prejudice ever weakened, rich Negroes had a better chance than poor Negroes of being accepted as equals by white Americans.

SUGGESTED READINGS

DE SANTIS, VINCENT P. *Republicans Face the Southern Question, The New Departure Years, 1877–1897*. Baltimore: The Johns Hopkins Press. 1959.

DuBois, W. E. BURGHARDT. *Black Reconstruction*. New York: Russell & Russell, Inc., 1935.

DURDEN, ROBERT F. *James Shepherd Pike, Republicanism and the American Negro, 1850–1882*. Durhan: Duke University Press, 1957.

FRANKLIN, JOHN HOPE. *From Slavery to Freedom*. 2d ed. New York: Alfred A. Knopf, Inc., 1956.

HIRSHON, STANLEY P. *Farewell to the Bloody Shirt, Northern Republicans and the Southern Negro, 1877–1893*. Bloomington: Indiana University Press, 1962.

LOGAN, RAYFORD W. *The Negro in American Life and Thought: The Nadir, 1877–1901*. New York: Dial Press, Inc., 1954.

MEIER, AUGUST. *Negro Thought in America, 1880–1915*. Ann Arbor: University of Michigan Press, 1963.

MYRDAL, GUNNAR. *An American Dilemma*. New York: Harper & Bros., 1944.

SPENCER, SAMUEL R., JR. *Booker T. Washington and the Negro's Place in American Life*. Boston: Little, Brown & Co., 1955.

TINDALL, GEORGE B. *South Carolina Negroes, 1877–1900*. Columbia: University of South Carolina Press, 1952.

WHARTON, VERNON L. *The Negro in Mississippi, 1865–1890*. Chapel Hill: University of North Carolina Press, 1947.

WOODWARD, C. VANN. *The Strange Career of Jim Crow*. New York: Oxford University Press, 1955.

Document 17.1

A NORTHERNER VIEWS THE NEGRO

Immediately after the Civil War, a number of northerners toured the South. One of these men was Benjamin C. Truman, a newspaper correspondent. His report to President Andrew Johnson in 1866 contained the following observation.

(From Senate Ex. Document No. 43, 39th Congress, 1st Session [Washington, D.C.: U.S. Government Printing Office, 1866], pp. 5–6)

. . . Almost the only key that furnishes a satisfactory solution to the southern question in its relations to the negro, that gives a reasonable explanation to the treatment which he receives and the estimation in which he is held, is found in the fact—too often forgotten in considering this matter—that the people from their earliest days have regarded slavery as his proper estate. . . . That a vast majority of the southern people honestly entertain this opinion no one who travels among them for eight months can doubt. . . .

Holding that the negro occupies a middle ground between the human race and the animal, they regard it as a real misfortune to him that he should be stripped of a protector, and that the immortal proclamation of President Lincoln was wicked, or at least mistaken, and a scourge to society. The persistency and honesty with which many, even of the greatest men of the south, hold to this opinion, is almost unaccountable to a northern man, and is an element of such magnitude that it cannot well be omitted from the consideration. . . .

Document 17.2

"MY PEOPLE ARE . . . BEING USED"

Hiram R. Revels, a former preacher, went to Mississippi with the Freedmen's Bureau and was elected to Jefferson Davis's old seat in the United States Senate. In 1875, Revels expressed the view of many prominent southern Negroes.

(From Walter L. Fleming [ed.], *Documentary History of Reconstruction: 1865 to the Present Time* Vol. II [Cleveland: Arthur H. Clark Co., 1907])

. . . Since reconstruction, the masses of my people have been enslaved in mind by unprincipled adventurers, who, caring nothing for country, were willing to stoop to anything, no matter how infamous, to secure power to themselves and perpetuate it. My people are naturally republicans and always will be, but as they grow older in freedom so do they in wisdom. A great portion of them have learned that they were being used as mere tools, and, as in the late election, not being able to correct the existing evil among themselves, they determined, by casting their ballots against these unprincipled adventurers, to overthrow them. . . . My people have been told by these schemers when men were placed upon the ticket who were notoriously corrupt and dishonest, that they must vote for them; that the salvation of the party depended upon it; that the man who scratched a ticket was not a republican. This is only one of the many means these unprincipled demagogues have devised to perpetuate the intellectual bondage of my people. . . .

Document 17.3

"THAT IS WHAT WE WANT"

There were many reasons for the Negro's frustration in the late nineteenth century. Doubtless, many Negroes shared the grievance against white men of J. K. Green, a carpenter in Montgomery, Alabama, in 1884.

(From Walter L. Fleming [ed.], *Documentary History of Reconstruction: 1865 to the Present Time*, Vol. II [Cleveland: Arthur H. Clark Co., 1907], pp. 445–46)

Here is the only thing that we are troubled about now, about civil rights. A colored man and his wife may go to work to get a little home, may go hungry and naked to educate a daughter, the dearest treasure that they have got, and the very moment that she begins to come up there is an inroad made upon her by the whites of this country, and we have got no redress in the world. They can't deny that. Now I want as much civil rights and rules to regulate and protect my family as any white man does, and if I catch a man under such circumstances I won't hurt him but once! . . .

That is what we want, to protect the virtue of our girls. That is the rights I want. I don't want no social equality with the white people, and I don't want them to have none with me. I see the influence of this thing every day. There has been a time when they were opposed to such things, but now that we are free the parents of the children can't even protect their children, and there ain't a white man here can deny it. That is the trouble in this country. Give the nigger a chance and he is going to till the white man's soil, and he is going to keep out of his house too. There is some fools, of course, but generally if they let the nigger alone he won't interfere with them. . . .

Document 17.4

BOOKER T. WASHINGTON'S APPEAL FOR ECONOMIC INDEPENDENCE

In a speech at the Atlanta Exposition in 1895, Booker T. Washington, Principal of the Tuskegee (Alabama) Normal and Industrial Institute, advised every member of his race to "cast down your bucket where you are." Five years later, he published a volume giving a more detailed explanation of his famous statement.

(From Booker T. Washington, *The Future of the American Negro* [Boston: Small, Maynard & Co., 1900], pp. 74–79, 84–87)

... Some time ago it was my misfortune to see a Negro sixty-five years old living in poverty and filth. I was disgusted, and said to him, "If you are worthy of your freedom, you would surely have changed your condition during the thirty years of freedom which you have enjoyed." He answered: "I do want to change. I want to do something for my wife and children; but I do not know how,—I do not know what to do." I looked into his lean and haggard face, and realised more deeply than ever before the absolute need of captains of industry among the great masses of the coloured people.

It is possible for a race or an individual to have mental development and yet be so handicapped by custom, prejudice, and lack of employment as to dwarf and discourage the whole life. This is the condition that prevails among the race in many of the large cities of the North; and it is to prevent this same condition in the South that I plead with all the earnestness of my heart. Mental development alone will not give us what we want, but mental development tied to hand and heart training will be the salvation of the Negro.

In many respects the next twenty years are going to be the most serious in the history of the race. Within this period it will be largely decided whether the Negro will be able to retain the hold which he now has upon the industries of the South or whether his place will be filled by white people from a distance. The only way he can prevent the industrial occupations slipping from him in all parts of the South, as they have already in certain parts, is for all educators, ministers, and friends of the race to unite in pushing forward in a whole-souled manner the industrial or business development of the Negro, whether in school or out of school. Four times as many young men and women of the race should be receiving industrial training. Just now the Negro is in a position to feel and appreciate the need of this in a way that no one else can. No one can fully appreciate what I am saying who has not walked the streets of a Northern city day after day seeking employment, only to find every door closed against him on account of his colour, except in menial service. It is to prevent the same thing taking place in the South that I plead. We may argue that mental development will take care of all this. Mental development is a good thing. Gold is also a good thing, but gold is worthless without an opportunity to make itself touch the world of trade. Education increases greatly an individual's wants. It is cruel in many cases to increase the wants of the black youth by mental development alone without, at the same time, increasing his ability to supply these increased wants in occupations in which he can find employment.

The place made vacant by the death of the old coloured man who was trained as a carpenter during slavery, and who since the war had been the leading contractor and builder in the Southern town, had to be filled. No young coloured carpenter capable of filling his place could be found. The result was that his place was filled by a white mechanic from the North, or from Europe, or from elsewhere. What is true of carpentry and house-building in this case is true, in a degree, in every skilled occupation; and it is becoming true of common labour. I do not mean to say that all of the skilled labour has been taken out of the Negro's hands; but I do mean to say that in no part of the South is he so strong in the matter of skilled labour as he was twenty years ago, except possibly in the country districts and the smaller towns. In the more northern of the Southern cities, such as Richmond and Baltimore, the change is most apparent; and it is being felt in every Southern city. Wherever the Negro has lost ground industrially in the South, it is not because there is prejudice against him as a skilled labourer on the part of the native Southern white man; the Southern white man generally prefers to do business with the Negro mechanic rather than with a white one, because he is accustomed to do business with the Negro in this respect. There is almost no prejudice against the Negro in the South in matters of business, so far as the native whites are concerned; and here is the entering wedge for the solution of the race problem. But too often, where the white mechanic or factory operative from the North gets a hold, the trades-union soon follows, and the Negro is crowded to the wall.

But what is the remedy for this condition? First, it is most important that the Negro and his white friends honestly face the facts as they are; otherwise the time will not be very far distant when the Negro of the South will be crowded to the ragged edge of industrial life as he is in the North. There is still time to repair the damage and to reclaim what we have lost. . . .

Not long ago I heard a conversation among three white men something like this. Two of them were berating the Negro, saying the Negro was shiftless and lazy, and all that sort of thing. The third man listened to their remarks for some time in silence, and then he said: "I don't know what your experience has been; but there is a 'nigger' down our way who owns a good house and lot with about fifty acres of ground. His house is well furnished, and he has got some splendid horses and cattle. He is intelligent and has a bank account. I don't know how the 'niggers' are in your community, but Tobe Jones is a gentleman. Once, when I was hard up, I went to Tobe Jones and borrowed fifty dollars; and he hasn't asked me for it yet. I don't know what kind of 'niggers' you have down your way, but Tobe Jones is a gentleman."

Now what we want to do is to multiply and place in every community these Tobe Joneses; and, just in so far as we can place them throughout the South this race question will disappear.

Suppose there was a black man who had business for the railroads to the amount of ten thousand dollars a year. Do you suppose that, when that black man takes his family aboard the train, they are going to put him into a Jim Crow car and run the risk of losing that ten thousand dollars a year? No, they will put on a Pullman palace car for him.

Some time ago a certain coloured man was passing through the streets of one of the little Southern towns, and he chanced to meet two white men on the street. It happened that this coloured man owns two or three houses and lots, has a good education and a comfortable bank account. One of the white men turned to the other, and said: "By Gosh! It is all I can do to keep from calling that 'nigger' Mister." That's the point we want to get to.

Nothing else so soon brings about right relations between the two races in the South as the commercial progress of the Negro. Friction between the races will pass away as the black man, by reason of his skill, intelligence, and character, can produce something that the white man wants or respects in the commercial world. . . .

18

GEORGE P. RAWICK
Wayne State University

The Corporation

THE MODERN CORPORATION is a gigantic mechanism which shapes many crucial features of our contemporary American society. It performs functions which touch directly upon every aspect of public and private life. Yet, we live in a society that still generally conceives of the corporation as the economic activity of a private individual and lacking major social responsibility. Why is this so? Was it always so? What, if any, are its alternatives? What does the history of this institution tell us about the nature of American life? How did it all come about?

The corporate form has had many different uses. Municipalities, charitable organizations, churches, trading companies, universities, business enterprises are all incorporated. In prerevolutionary America the colonies themselves were often corporations.

The diversity of corporation types tells us something important about the institution: It was used whenever the need arose for delegating authority from the sovereign to lesser bodies and investing the latter with sovereignty for certain purposes. In medieval Europe the granting of corporate authority was a way of recognizing a communal body which had developed its own inner direction. John P. Davis, an early twentieth-century student of the corporation, offers the following definition, which combines this quality of the medieval and early modern corporation with later corporate developments:

A corporation is a body of persons upon whom the state has conferred such voluntarily accepted but compulsorily maintained relations to one another and to all others that as an autonomous, self-sufficient and self-renewing body they may determine and enforce their common will, and in the pursuit of their private interest may exercise more efficiently social functions both specially conducive to public welfare and most appropriately exercised by associated persons.

What was the state of this institution, originally embodied with some function "conducive to public welfare," in the United States before 1860? In colonial America, corporations had been chartered almost exclusively for some essential public purpose. The first corporation for specifically manufacturing purposes, the Society for Useful Manufactures of New Jersey, incorporated in 1791, was part of Alexander Hamilton's deliberate policy of industrial development. Banks and insurance companies, together with companies devoted to the development of transport by canal or turnpike, to water supply, to fire fighting, and the like, comprised most of the 335 corporations chartered in the United States by 1800.

In the eighteenth century the quasi-public corporation was used sparingly. Always involving a grant of privileges, it was never considered an egalitarian institution. If the sovereign wanted something done, or if some group was strong enough to gain special favor from him, the corporate form provided a means by which the sovereign granted privileges in return for services. The corporate form was not easily available to everyone; and the state maintained the right to regulate the corporation's actions, which were always supposedly dedicated to the public interest.

In the first fifty years of American independence the position of the corporation underwent rapid change. The opening decades of the nineteenth century witnessed a great increase in incorporated businesses. For example, in New England, the chief industrial and mercantile area of the nation, some 1,900 corporations, of which some 600 were in mining and manufacturing, were created by 1830. In the other industrial states—Maryland, New Jersey, New York, Ohio, and Pennsylvania—an equal number of corporations were established in the same period. The first grants of charters to railroads came in the 1820's.

In the late 1830's, there was a steady advance in business incorporations; much of it was essentially for speculative purposes. At the height of the speculative frenzy of 1836–37, New York incorporated almost 200 companies, Ohio over 150, Pennsylvania more than 100, and New England several hundred more. The politically regnant Jacksonian Democrats were clearly not against the corporation per se; they merely opposed its control by eastern and foreign investors.

The increasing importance of the corporation was reflected in and furthered by the pre-Civil War general incorporation laws. In 1811, New York passed the first self-incorporation law, which permitted persons engaged in domestic manufacture, textiles, glass, metals, and paint to incorporate without securing special charters from the legislature. By the end of the 1830's, most of the states allowed self-incorporation for particular types of business.

General incorporation laws, largely the product of Jacksonian democracy, were the most important step in transforming Jacksonian laissez-faire agrarian democracy into post-1865 industrial *laissez-faire*. The Jacksonians fought for and often achieved general incorporation laws with provisions for low maximum capital, limited borrowing authority, and stringent protection of creditors and wage earners. The corporate form, they hoped, would prevent the creation of a special oligarchic elite. The new corporation was democratized in that, in being available to all, it led to greater social mobility, inasmuch as it permitted the merger of small capitals for both productive and speculative purposes. In the pre-Civil War period the new corporation and *laissez-faire* democracy went hand in hand.

In the process of this transformation the corporation lost much, but not all, of its character as an instrument for carrying out some particular policy of the state. Many of the attributes of the earlier corporation touching upon communal and public welfare responsibility were also lost or submerged. No longer was the corporation a subordinate body politic whose officers and members had rights and duties publicly known and socially based. Instead of representative corporate bodies being universities or companies organized for the development of canals and turnpikes, they became primarily designed to amass sufficient capital for manufacturing through the privilege of limited liability for each investor or for almost purely speculative purposes in which no product was in fact produced or any service rendered.

The struggle over the Bank of the United States from its creation in 1791 to the financial panic of 1837 was the single most important complex of events in the history of the relationship of the federal government to the corporation prior to the 1880's. By the 1840's, the main outlines of American corporation policy were set. The corporation had become and was to remain a private institution until the early twentieth century. From Andrew Jackson to Andrew Carnegie the distance was neither great nor crucial.

In the post-Civil War period, eight major new factors figured within the general framework of established corporate policy. While none involved any change in public policy, all were crucial.

First, the capitalization of corporations created during and after the Civil War was very large. Individual corporations in the new iron, steel, coal, petroleum, mining, and railroad industries generally required capitalization of tens of millions of dollars. And as these new industrial giants grew in size, so did almost all other corporations.

Second, there was the ubiquitous tendency toward both horizontal and vertical integration of industry. The era of monopoly had begun and was encouraged by the sanction of a permissive public attitude toward the corporation. Some industrial integration was undeniably beneficial in providing greater operational efficiencies. But much of it had little or nothing to do with more efficient production; rather, it was intended to limit production and to raise prices. Still other industrial integration was designed for purposes of stock market manipulation with few if any comparable economies in productive operations.

Third, the new corporate growth was accompanied by an unusual amount of political corruption. Fortunes were made and squandered on the basis of inside information. Defective equipment was sold through political connections. Legislators, bought outright, in turn granted special corporate charters. The Gilded Age had more than its share of "robber barons," although not all of the barons were legally robbers.

Fourth, the market for almost all mined and manufactured goods was truly international. Prices of such goods were heavily influenced by world market conditions. As a consequence, the United States, seeking foreign markets, had to discard its traditional isolationism.

Fifth, the modern corporation was an urban phenomenon; and many of the problems of the new cities were directly associated with it, such as crime, corrupt machine politics, and immigrant assimilation.

Sixth, the large and increasingly impersonal corporation was the source of labor-management strife and violence that erupted in the 1870's and 1880's. These decades experienced more industrial violence than any modern industrial nation was to know until the 1930's.

Seventh, the agricultural discontent of the period focused upon the corporation. Enemies of the agrarian Populists were the railroads, grain elevators, textile mills, stockyards, and banks which stood astride the arteries of commerce and exacted their toll.

Eighth, the new corporate elite, with its threateningly greater social power, displaced the old aristocracy and small-town elites—the established gentry, small-town doctors, lawyers, merchants, ministers, and schoolteachers. The power of the new corporate class posed not only political and economic threats but also put in jeopardy their social status and community leadership.

The corporation, in short, had become supreme in society. No longer could one hide from it. The corporation was socially visible, and men were forced to come to grips with it. Henry Demarest Lloyd, the journalist, understood this when he recognized that the problem for society posed by the corporation was associated with the disappearance of the world of the homestead and the frontier.

The new corporation needed one further protection to be secure from restrictive public control. This was granted by the United States Supreme Court in the due process doctrine. During the 1880's and 1890's, more and more state laws were passed to regulate corporations. But the latter, in turn, appealed to the federal courts to declare such acts unconstitutional on the grounds that the Fourteenth Amendment to the Constitution had stipulated that no "state shall deprive any person of life, liberty, or property, without due process of law." After affirming that this clause had meant only that the individual—including the legal individual, the corporation—could not be incarcerated or deprived of property without a fair trial under the established rules of law, the Supreme Court, in 1897, in the crucial case of *Allgeyer* v. *Louisiana*, declared: "The liberty mentioned . . . embraces the rights of the citizen to be free in the enjoyment of all his faculties . . . to pursue any livelihood or avocation, and for the purpose to enter into all contracts which may be proper, necessary and essential to his carrying out [these rights] to a successful conclusion." The general police powers of the state, the Court added, must be exercised in such a way as "not to infringe upon those other rights of the citizen which are protected by the Federal Constitution."

Within the next three decades the Due Process Clause was used to strike down or render ineffective much of the social welfare legislation passed by state legislatures. In 1905, for example, in *Lochner* v. *New York*, the Court declared that a New York state statute prohibiting bakers from working more than sixty hours a week was unconstitutional because the "statute necessarily interferes with the right of contract between the employer and employees. . . . The general right to make a contract . . . is part of the liberty . . . protected by the Fourteenth Amendment. . . ."

The due process decision made the corporation supreme in its domain. It gave the Supreme Court decisive powers, for the latter could decide arbitrarily which acts were or were not a violation of due process. The corporation, moreover, was left even more absolute in its rights vis-à-vis its employees. Here the Court acted in such a way as to reverse the Jacksonian policy of turning over the regulation of the corporation to the states. Consequently, the sporadic attempts of the so-called "Granger laws" of the 1870's and 1880's to regulate the state operations of corporations other than public utilities virtually came to an end. Henceforth, public control over the corporation would be through the Hamiltonian use of the federal government.

In 1911 the Supreme Court, in *Standard Oil Company of New Jersey et al.* v. *United States*, adopted the "rule of reason" which held that only "unreasonable" combinations in the restraint of trade were illegal and that it was the Court's task to establish the test of reasonableness. The high tribunal, in effect, ratified the decision of an earlier case, *United States* v. *E. C. Knight and Co.* (1895). In the Standard Oil Company decision the Court drew the teeth of the Sherman Antitrust Act of 1891, which had seemed to outlaw all combinations in restraint of trade. Moreover, it had developed a formula whereby it could not only avoid the Act's literal meaning—requiring the destruction of all monopolistic combinations—but also escape the position taken in the Knight case, which had made the law inoperative except for the regulation of railroads and other interstate utilities. It thus adopted the "good" and "bad" trust philosophy of Theodore Roosevelt which accepted the premises of a society based upon the corporation but called for regulation of those actions of a corporation that ran contrary to the best interests of society.

The general policy of the national government, then, was to regulate rather than to destroy combinations engaged in productive activities and to apply the Sherman Antitrust Act only to those corporations created for stock market speculation or to those which curtailed production in such a way as to force prices up over those prevailing in the natural market. This policy was supplemented by passage in 1914 of an act creating the Federal Trade Commission, which was empowered to regulate competitive methods and to eliminate "unfair methods of competition in commerce." The FTC has usually sought to obtain voluntary agreements among producers; it has not aimed to destroy combinations in restraint of trade but to make "self-government in industry" legal by supervising the formation of voluntary agreements among producers to eliminate certain undesirable competitive practices.

During World War I the government, through the War Industries Board, made an effort to stimulate efficiencies in production. It used coercive power to gain further rationalization of industry by obtaining agreements to abstain from certain practices and even to relinquish the production of certain items seen as wasteful. After World War I the American government resumed its role as an impartial mediator and encouraged voluntary regulation within an expanding corporate economy.

From 1914 to the present, there has been no serious threat to the position of the big corporation as the central institution of the American economy. The big corporation and the federal government, in truth, have allied to achieve the stability of the corporate system by control of the competitive activities of any of its particular parts. A crucial issue, still unresolved, is whether the government should intervene with coercive power to assure corporate self-regulation or whether it should be an impartial mediator encouraging such a development through voluntary means. Yet, either way, the corporation is secure within its assigned sphere and within the fact of the seemingly inexorable steady growth both in its size and in its importance.

In the modern corporation, shareholding has become widely dispersed. Officers and members of the boards of directors are rarely significant stockholders. And the stockholders have all but lost the power to protect themselves against decisions of management. Directors and officers have been left in a position of virtually unlimited authority.

Today, there seem to be four principal attitudes toward the corporation. The first is simply to accept the existing legal situation and to trust to the good intentions of management to act in the public interest. Advocates of this position claim that otherwise there will be no freedom in American society.

Second, there are those neoclassicist economists who look toward positive governmental action in breaking up corporate combinations both through the use of the antitrust laws and through other government programs.

A third school seeks increased and various forms of governmental regulation; the building-up of countervailing power within farmer, labor, and consumer groups; and the growth of a sense of public responsibility and social stewardship among the corporate elite. Members of this group see in present corporate practice tendencies which place increased authority in an elite of engineers, trained corporate management, economists, and other specialists. This development, they believe, will involve a more rational operation of the huge corporation.

Fourth are those who advocate some sort of public ownership. These fall into two main groups. On the one hand, there are those who want a kind of public ownership in which the state would hold legal title to and exercise regulatory power over the corporation, while actual direction would be left to the corporate management and to the operation of the market itself. On the other hand, the more radical socialists propose workers' control, in which the affairs of the productive units would be left to the direction of a combination of workers, consumers, and engineer-economist specialists under conditions in which total planning has replaced all or part of the market mechanism.

These attitudes toward the larger corporation lie at the heart of the crucial social and political decisions the American people are likely to make in the future. All of these proposals contain many variants. The American people will have to determine which of the alternative directions is most feasible and desirable.

SUGGESTED READINGS

BERLE, ADOLF A., JR. *The Twentieth Century Capitalist Revolution.* New York: Harcourt, Brace & Co., 1954.

BERLE, ADOLF A., JR., and MEANS, GARDINER. *The Modern Corporation and Private Property.* New York: Macmillan Co., 1932.

BUCHANAN, SCOTT M. *The Corporation and the Republic.* New York: Fund for the Republic, 1958.

COCHRAN, THOMAS C., and MILLER, WILLIAM. *The Age of Enterprise: A Social History of Industrial America.* Rev. ed. New York: Harper & Row, 1961.

DAVIS, JOHN P. *Corporations: A Study of the Origin and Development of Great Business Corporations and of Their Relation to the Authority of the State.* New York: Capricorn Books, 1961.

DODD, EDWIN M. *American Business Corporations until 1860, with Special Reference to Massachusetts.* Cambridge: Harvard University Press, 1954.

JOSEPHSON, MATTHEW. *The Robber Barons: The Great American Capitalists, 1861–1901.* New York: Harcourt, Brace & Co., 1934.

KIRKLAND, EDWARD CHASE. *Industry Comes of Age: Business, Labor, and Public Policy, 1860–1897.* New York: Holt, Rinehart & Winston, Inc., 1961.

LLOYD, HENRY DEMAREST. *Wealth against Commonwealth.* New York: Harper & Bros., 1894.

MASON, EDWARD S. (ed.). *The Corporation in Modern Society.* Cambridge: Harvard University Press, 1960.

SOULE, GEORGE HENRY, and CAROSSO, VINCENT P. *American Economic History.* New York: Dryden Press, 1957.

THORELLI, HANS B. *The Federal Antitrust Policy; Origination of an American Tradition.* Baltimore: The Johns Hopkins Press, 1955.

Document 18.1
LORDS OF INDUSTRY

Henry Demarest Lloyd (1847–1903) was one of the earliest popular social critics whose opposition to corporate monopoly involved a radical critique of the American corporation and corporate system. In 1894, he published *Wealth against Commonwealth,* in which he developed his analysis beyond a nonspecific radicalism and came closer to the position of the socialists of his day.

(From Henry Demarest Lloyd, "Lords of Industry," *North American Review,* Vol. CXXXVIII, No. 331 [June, 1884], pp. 535–36, 550–53)

Adam Smith said in 1776: "People of the same trade hardly meet together for merriment and diversion but the conversation ends in a conspiracy against the public, or in some contrivance to raise prices." . . . This any one may see from the reports of the proceedings of the conventions and meetings of innumerable associations of manufacturers and dealers and even producers, which are being held almost constantly. They all do something to raise prices, or hold them up, and they wind up with banquets for which we pay. . . .

On the theory of "too much of everything" our industries, from railroads to workingmen, are being organized to prevent milk, nails, lumber, freights, labor, soothing syrup, and all these other things, from becoming too cheap. The majority have never yet been able to buy enough of anything. The minority have too much of everything to sell. Seeds of social trouble germinate fast in such conditions. Society is letting these combinations become institutions without compelling them to adjust their charges to the cost of production, which used to be the universal rule of price. . . . The change from competition to combination is nothing less than one of those revolutions which march through history with giant strides. It is not likely that this revolution will go backward. Nothing goes backward in this country except reform. . . .

Society having let the individual overrun the new worlds to be conquered, is reëstablishing its lines of communication with him. Literary theorists still repeat the cant of individualism in law, politics, and morals; but the world of affairs is gladly accepting, in lieu of the liberty of each to do as he will with his own, all it can get of the liberty given by laws that let no one do as he might do with his own. The dream of the French Revolution, that man was good enough to be emancipated from the bonds of association and government by the simple proclamation of Liberty, Fraternity and Equality, was but the frenzied expression of what was called Freedom of Self-interest in a quieter but not less bloody revolution, if the mortality of the factories, the mines, and the tenements be charged to its account. A rope cannot be made of sand; a society cannot be made of competitive units. . . .

We have had an era of material inventions. We now need a renaissance of moral inventions, contrivances to tap the vast currents of moral magnetism flowing uncaught over the face of society. . . . If the tendency to combination is irresistible, control of it is imperative. Monopoly and anti-monopoly, odious as these words have become to the literary ear, represent the two great tendencies of our time: monopoly, the tendency to combination; anti-monopoly, the demand for social control of it. . . . These combinations are not to be waved away as fresh pictures of folly or total depravity. There is something in them deeper than that. The Aryan has proved by the experience of thousands of years that he can travel. "But travel," Emerson says, "is the fool's paradise." We must now prove that we can stay at home, and stand it as well as the Chinese have done. Future Puritans cannot emigrate from Southampton to Plymouth Rock. They can only sail from righteousness to righteousness. Our young men can no longer go west; they must go up or down. Not new land, but new virtue must be the outlet for the future. Our halt at the shores of the Pacific is a much more serious affair than that which brought our ancestors to a pause before the barriers of the Atlantic, and compelled them to practice living together for a few hundred years. We cannot hereafter, as in the past, recover freedom by going to the prairies; we must find it in the society of the good. . . . It may be that the coming age of combination will issue in a nobler and fuller liberty for the individual than has yet been seen, but that consummation will be possible, not in a day of competitive trade, but in one of competitive morals.

Document 18.2

LIMITING THE ANTITRUST ACT

In the decision of *United States* v. *E. C. Knight Co.*, a conservative Supreme Court attempted to limit the applicability of the Sherman Antitrust Act of 1890 to the arteries of commerce such as railroads and to exempt from the Act all combinations in the commerce in manufactured goods. Mr. Justice Harlan, in dissent, argued that all monopolies were intrinsically bad and prohibited under law. Within five years the Supreme Court clearly had departed both from the approach of the Court's majority in this case as Chief Justice Fuller affirmed it and from Mr. Justice Harlan's dissent.

(From *United States* v. *E. C. Knight and Co.* [156 U.S. (1895), 9, 12, 16–18, 22, 33–34, 42–44])

The argument is that the power to control the manufacture of refined sugar is a monopoly over a necessary of life, to the enjoyment of which by a large part of the population of the United States interstate commerce is indispensable, and that, therefore, the general government in the exercise of the power to regulate commerce may repress such monopoly directly and set aside the instruments which have created it. But this argument cannot be confined to necessaries of life merely, and must include all articles of general consumption. Doubtless the power to control the manufacture of a given thing involves in a certain sense the control of its disposition, but this is a secondary and not the primary sense; and although the exercise of that power may result in bringing the operation of commerce into play, it does not control it, and affects it only incidentally and indirectly. Commerce succeeds to manufacture, and is not a part of it. The power to regulate commerce is the power to prescribe the rule by which commerce shall be governed, and is a power independent of the power to suppress monopoly. But it may operate in repression of monopoly whenever that comes within the rules by which commerce is governed or whenever the transaction is itself a monopoly of commerce. . . .

Contracts, combinations, or conspiracies to control domestic enterprise in manufacture, agriculture, mining, production in all its forms, or to raise or lower prices or wages, might unquestionably tend to restrain external as well as domestic trade, but the restraint would be an indirect result, however inevitable and whatever its extent, and such result would not necessarily determine the object of the contract, combination, or conspiracy. . . .

. . . What the law struck at was combinations, contracts, and conspiracies to monopolize trade and commerce among the several States or with foreign nations; but the contracts and acts of the defendants related exclusively to the acquisition of the Philadelphia refineries and the business of sugar refining in Pennsylvania, and bore no direct relation to commerce between the States or with foreign nations. . . .

The Circuit Court declined, upon the pleadings and proofs, to grant the relief prayed, and dismissed the bill, and we are of opinion that the Circuit Court of Appeals did not err in affirming that decree.

Decree affirmed.

Mr. Justice Harlan, dissenting.

. . . Interstate commerce embraces something more than the mere physical transportation of articles of property, and the vehicles or vessels by which such transportation is effected. . . . It includes the purchase and sale of articles that are intended to be transported from one State to another—every species of commercial intercourse among the States and with foreign nations. . . .

It has been argued that a combination between corporations of different States, or between the stockholders of such corporations, with the object and effect of controlling not simply the manufacture but the price of refined sugar throughout the whole of the United States—which is the case now before us—cannot be held to be in restraint of "commerce among the States" and amenable to national authority, without conceding that the general government has authority to say what shall and what shall not be *manufactured* in the several States. . . .

It may be admitted that an act which did nothing more than forbid, and which had no other object than to forbid, the *mere* refining of sugar in any State, would be in excess of any power granted to Congress. But the act of 1890 is not of that character. It does not strike at the manufacture simply of articles that are legitimate or recognized subjects of commerce, but at *combinations* that unduly restrain, because they monopolize, *the buying and selling of articles* which are to go into interstate commerce. . . .

While the opinion of the court in this case does not declare the act of 1890 to be unconstitutional, it defeats the main object for which it was passed. For it is, in effect, held that the statute would be unconstitutional if interpreted as embracing such unlawful restraints upon the purchasing of goods in one State to be carried to another State as necessarily arise from the *existence* of combinations formed for the purpose and with the effect, not only of monopolizing the ownership of all such goods in every part of the country, but of controlling the prices for them in all the States. This view of the scope of the act leaves the public, so far as national power is concerned, entirely at the mercy of combinations which arbitrarily control the prices of articles purchased to be transported from one State to another State. I cannot assent to that view. In my judgment, the general government is not placed by the Constitution in such a condition of helplessness. . . .

[I]t proved—indeed, is conceded—that that object has been accomplished to the extent that the American Sugar Refining Company now controls ninety-eight per cent of all the sugar refining business in the country. . . . Now; the *mere existence* of a combination having such an object and possessing such extraordinary power is itself, . . . a direct restraint of trade in the article for the control of the sales of which in this country that combination was organized. . . .

Document 18.3

THE RULE OF REASON

In 1906 the United States government instituted a suit which sought to dissolve the Standard Oil Company of John D. Rockefeller and his associates on the ground that it was a combination in violation of the Sherman Antitrust Act. In its decision, which upheld the government's attempt to gain a court order dissolving the trust, the Court adopted the distinction between "good" and "bad" trusts that had been developed by such men as President Theodore Roosevelt. Bigness per se was not legally wrong.

(From *Standard Oil Company of New Jersey et al.* v. *United States* [221 U.S. (1911), 55–56, 60, 77, 82–84, 99–100, 104–5])

WHITE, C. J.:

. . . It is remarkable that nowhere at common law can there be found a prohibition against the creation of monopoly by an individual. This would seem to manifest, either consciously or intuitively, a profound conception as to the inevitable operation of economic forces and the equipoise or balance in favor of the protection of the rights of individuals which resulted. That is to say, as it was deemed that monopoly in the concrete could only arise from an act of sovereign power, and, such sovereign power being restrained, prohibitions as to individuals were directed, not against the creation of monopoly, but were only applied to such acts in relation to particular subjects as to which it was deemed, if not restrained, some of the consequences of monopoly might result. . . .

. . . Here as had been the case in England, practical common sense caused attention to be concentrated not upon the theoretically correct name to be given to the condition or acts which gave rise to a harmful result, but to the result itself and to the remedying of the evils which it produced. . . .

And as the contracts or acts embraced in the provision were not expressly defined, since the enumeration addressed itself simply to classes of acts, those classes being broad enough to embrace every conceivable contract or combination which could be made concerning trade or commerce or the subjects of such commerce, and thus caused any act done by any of the enumerated methods anywhere in the whole field of human activity to be illegal if in restraint of trade, it inevitably follows that the provision necessarily called for the exercise of judgment which required that some standard should be resorted to for the purpose of determining whether the prohibitions contained in the statute had or had not in any given case been violated. Thus not specifying but indubitably contemplating and requiring a standard, it follows that it was intended that the standard of reason which had been applied at the common law and in this country in dealing with subjects of the character embraced by the statute, was intended to be the measure used for the purpose of determining whether in a given case a particular act had or had not brought about the wrong against which the statute provided. . . .

The inference that no attempt to monopolize could have been intended, and that no monopolization resulted from the acts complained of, since it is established that a very small percentage of the crude oil produced was controlled by the combination, is unwarranted. As substantial power over the crude product was the inevitable result of the absolute control which existed over the refined product, the monopolization of the one carried with it the power to control the other, and if the inferences which this situation suggests were developed, which we deem it unnecessary to do, they might well serve to add additional cogency to the presumption of intent to monopolize which we have found arises from the unquestioned proof on other subjects. . . .

HARLAN, J., dissenting in part:

All who recall the condition in 1890 will remember that there was everywhere, among the people generally, a deep feeling of unrest. The Nation had been rid of human slavery—fortunately, as all now feel— but the conviction was universal that the country was in real danger from another kind of slavery sought to be fastened on the American people, namely, the slavery that would result from aggregations of capital in the hands of a few individuals and corporations. . . . Such a danger was thought to be then imminent, and all felt that it must be met firmly and by such statutory regulations as would adequately protect the people against oppression and wrong. Congress therefore took up the matter and gave the whole subject the fullest consideration. . . .

Guided . . . to the end that the people, *so far as interstate commerce was concerned*, might not be dominated by vast combinations and monopolies, having power to advance their own selfish ends, regardless of the general interests and welfare, Congress passed the Anti-trust Act of 1890. . . .

Now this court is asked to do that which it has distinctly declared it could not and would not do, and has now done what it then said it could not constitutionally do. It has, by mere interpretation, modified the act of Congress, and deprived it of practical value as a defensive measure against the evils to be remedied. . . . In effect the court says, that it will now, for the first time, bring the discussion under the "light of reason" and apply the "rule of reason" to the questions to be decided. . . .

[T]he court has now read into the act of Congress words which are not to be found there, and has thereby done that which it adjudged in 1896 and 1898 could not be done without violating the Constitution, namely, by interpretation of a statute, changed a public policy declared by the legislative department. . . .

Document 18.4

THE CORPORATION'S RESPONSIBILITY

Adolf A. Berle, Jr., formerly Professor of Law at Columbia University, was one of the key figures in the so-called "brain trust," the group of intellectuals who gathered about Franklin D. Roosevelt in the early days of the New Deal. After service to the Roosevelt administrations in various capacities, Berle devoted himself to a series of books on the structure of the American corporation and on the sociology of that increasingly all-embracing social institution. He has become one of the most significant theorists for those who believe that a highly centralized, semimonopolistic corporate economy can only be administered by increasing the social responsibility of the corporate managers.

(From Adolf A. Berle, Jr., *Economic Power and the Free Society* [New York: Fund for the Republic, December, 1957], pp. 12–16)

When power is lodged in a particular group it has no choice except either to exercise it or to try to revolutionize the system. There is no way of avoiding power. If you take it and refuse to exercise it you suffer the fate of King Lear—the king who wanted to be king but did not want to be bothered. The trust funds admit they have it but they have thus far refused to use it. This situation cannot last very much longer. Somebody is bound to use that power, of necessity. Pension trusts are so concentrated that a relatively small amount in equities outbalances any number of scattered holdings.

The private property system in production, which began with our great-grandfather's farm and forge, has almost vanished in the vast area of American economy dominated by this system. Instead we have something which differs from the Russian or socialist system mainly in its philosophical content. Under a pure socialist or Communist system, in theory, every worker has an old-age pension at the end of his labors. We are developing the same thing by "socializing" property without a revolution. It is one of our more amazing achievements. Whether one likes it or not depends on one's philosophy. . . .

Today approximately 50 per cent of American manufacturing—that is everything other than financial and transportation—is held by about 150 corporations, reckoned, at least, by asset values. If finance and transportation are included, the total increases. If a rather larger group is taken, the statistics would probably show that about two thirds of the economically productive assets of the United States, excluding agriculture, are owned by a group of not more than 500 corporations. This is actual asset ownership. . . . But in terms of power, without regard to asset positions, not only do 500 corporations control two-thirds of the non-farm economy but within each of that 500 a still smaller group has the ultimate decision-making power. This is, I think, the highest concentration of economic power in recorded history. Since the United States carries on not quite half of the manufacturing production of the entire world today, these 500 groupings—each with its own little dominating pyramid within it—represent a concentration of power over economics which makes the medieval feudal system look like a Sunday School party. In sheer economic power this has gone far beyond anything we have yet seen. . . .

Whether we like it or not, this is what has happened. As noted, it is not the product of evil-minded men. I believe that we must try to work with the system. The dangers are obvious. But history cannot usually be reversed. Until engineers and economic forces give us a way by which a man can manufacture an automobile in his back yard we will continue to have organizations the size of General Motors or Ford—as long as people want Chevrolets or Fords. We will have railroads the length of the Union Pacific as long as people want to go across the continent by railroad. In other words, until a combination of technique and organization can be invented permitting *individuals* to do the job, we are bound to try to make the best we can out of the situation. To my mind most of the results are rather surprisingly good.

This does not mean, however, that I am not afraid. I am. I believe it is the *content* of these systems rather than their *form* that matters. Their power can enslave us beyond present belief, or perhaps set us free beyond present imagination. The choice lies with the men who operate the pyramids, and with the men affected who can demand what they really want. Our Anglo-Saxon democratic liberties, after all, were beaten out, not against the framework of the personal possessory property regime, but against the background of two of the most brutal despotisms in Western history. Both the Angevin dynasty in Normandy and the Tudor dynasty in England were rank despotisms. The content of our democratic liberties from Magna Carta down was pumped in by extraneous moral processes. Our institutionalized liberties present the case of an institution conscripted into utility, rather than something that emerged full-armed from the head of Jove. It was probably better that way; the democracy of the Greeks did not work so very well.

We have to accept this power situation as, let us call it, a neutral mechanism subject to the control of the body politic as long as we *keep* it subject to that control. That control, I believe, will be essentially intellectual and philosophical, capable of being translated into legal rules when necessity arises. . . .

19

ARTHUR W. THOMPSON
University of Florida

The Gilded Age

THE GILDED AGE, a novel published in 1873 by Mark Twain and Charles Dudley Warner, depicted American society as one lacking in values and addicted to speculation, unscrupulousness, and materialism. Vernon L. Parrington reduced the motivation of this gaudy era to "Preemption, Exploitation and Progress." And Lewis Mumford, reflecting on the arts of the seventies, eighties, and nineties, settled on the drabber shade of the "Brown Decades." Yet, do not such characterizations merely reflect the veneer of American society, posing more problems than they could begin to answer? More basically, the question can be raised: Was the Gilded Age an era of transition in American development? Did long-standing values undergo significant alteration during a time when society was increasingly shaped by the forces of urbanized industrialism? Answers to such questions must involve the searcher in a consideration of changing American social values between the Civil War and the turn of the nineteenth century.

The first change to engage our attention dealt with the relationship of government to the economic order. Confusing "private enterprise" and "free enterprise," a large percentage of the population has proceeded on the assumption that the economic system which nineteenth-century socialists termed "capitalistic" was inevitably the same as that set of politico-economic relationships known as *laissez faire*.

The real beginnings of *laissez faire* in America, in a sense, can be traced to the age of Jackson. Actually, during the 1830's and 1840's, advocates of economic individualism were far less concerned with *laissez faire* than with attacking existing monopolies, real or imagined, in their pursuit of a *freer* and more genuinely competitive brand of enterprise. For some, the attack on state-chartered monopolies during the Jacksonian era was designed to achieve particular economic goals. For others, it was part of a broader onslaught against special privilege—corporate or otherwise—and directed toward the goal of creating a democratic society in which all individuals would be equal in the exercise of all rights.

Most Americans interested in scanning the half century between the age of Jackson and the Gilded Age have focused upon the Civil War. This concern with the war has obscured the growth and maturation of two significant forces: democracy and industrialism. During those years, many small, struggling Jacksonian entrepreneurs developed into relatively large and powerful industrial capitalists. And, ironically, by the 1870's and 1880's, they had contributed also to the appearance of corporate monopoly and restricted competition, the very evils against which they had fought. Not only was the Jacksonian persuasion against economic privilege undermined, but new and cynical political spoilsmen also appeared to challenge the successful operation of popular government.

How was this conflict between rampant economic individualism and expanding political democracy to be rationalized? For advocates of free enterprise, it was a matter of seeking a fresh rationale, which they soon found in the growing popularization of science, particularly the new evolutionary hypotheses. Herbert Spencer's utilization of an evolutionary universe served as a new justification of economic individualism. Cosmic evolution filled the void created by the gradual decline of a static conception of the cosmos to which Adam Smith had linked his natural economic laws. Charles Darwin's biological processes, it was concluded, had a social counterpart in which the economic struggle for existence and the survival of the fittest would best be consummated under unrestrained free enterprise.

For those seeking to use more effectively the democratic process, it was now necessary to overcome the presumption that even the peaceful utilization of majority will was contrary to science and morality. The issues in the sharply contested debate were not clearly drawn. Alternatives were not simply free enterprise versus government control. Rather, in the case of the new offending giants whose very existence precipitated the question, it was a matter of private corporate collectivism versus some kind of public action.

The situation was further complicated because social and economic critics hardly formed a solid phalanx of consistent opinion. Henry Adams, suspicious of democracy and repelled by the new industrialism, sought escape in medievalism. But most social and economic critics were willing to face up to the dilemma of the age. Some of them, like Henry George, drew inspiration from earlier egalitarian and anti-monopolist views and concocted specific remedies to cope with general economic problems. George's single-tax program gained relatively few adherents, despite its defense of private enterprise. Yet, *Progress and Poverty*, which he published in 1879, helped to dramatize the issue and to mark him as a popular figure.

Still others proposed more drastic solutions which would invoke almost total governmental intervention. Among the many and assorted socialisms advanced in those decades, the greatest response was accorded to the utopianism of Edward Bellamy, whose book *Looking Backward* appeared in 1887. In it, he attacked the excessive competitiveness, economic brutality, and social Darwinism of the day. At the same time, he unfolded for his readers a perfectly functioning socialist society. The sale of nearly a million copies of *Looking Backward* during the next decade and the appearance of 162 Nationalist clubs in twenty-seven states, organized to propagandize Bellamy's social and economic theories, was an indication that the author had struck a responsive chord among thousands of Americans.

Other dissenting voices were heard, among them those of James B. Weaver and the agrarians, Samuel Gompers and the trade unionists, and Lester Frank Ward and Richard T. Ely, who spoke for a segment of the intellectual and academic community. One of the most influential of the critics and in the long run probably the most prophetic was Henry Demarest Lloyd. A diligent scholar, skilled agitator, and provocative journalist, Lloyd wrote tirelessly for the leading reviews on reform; his book, *Wealth against Commonwealth* (1894) called for a moderate and progressive middle class to spearhead the drive toward the democratization of the economy. Such a movement, he argued, would avert the extremes of state socialism and monopoly capitalism.

Those who addressed themselves to economic reform in the Gilded Age were obviously a diverse lot. Yet, despite their differences, they were generally willing to operate within the American experience. Private enterprise would stay, but unrestrained or free enterprise should be curbed. Economic rights for the greatest number was their prime goal; in an industrialized urban society, they argued, these would best be attained by peaceful means through the instrumentality of government responsive to a free electorate.

Other questions also disturbed both individuals and institutions during the Gilded Age. Religion felt the impact of divisive forces generating change. Investigations by archaeologists, philologists, and historians had produced new studies of the Bible and brought into being the field of "higher criticism." They also unleashed a wave of skepticism which abetted the trend toward secularization. Even more disruptive in some respects were the forces of expanding science. Earlier during the nineteenth century the rapidly developing science of evolutionary geology had provoked considerable controversy. The chasm between the staunch advocates of the new science and the traditionalists regarding the nature and duration of creation was finally bridged by the patient efforts of such scholars as Edward Hitchcock. His *Religion of Geology*, which appeared in 1852, did much toward reconciling seemingly contradictory concepts of geology and Genesis.

But the breach had no sooner been mended on the geological front when Charles Darwin extended the evolutionary hypothesis to the biological world and again created conflict between science and religion. Once more, religious intransigents rejected the new science; while, contrariwise, men like Robert Ingersoll and Elizur Wright concluded that traditional religion ought to be rejected. Some men, like John Draper, made a religion of science. Religion, however, was too strong to be overthrown, and science was too important to be ignored. Ultimately, a group of outspoken theologians headed by Henry Ward Beecher and a persistent band of lecturers and writers succeeded in effecting another reconciliation.

Forces in addition to higher criticism and evolutionary science challenged religion in America. The rise of a gospel of wealth, for example, did much to weaken traditional religious values in the Gilded Age. Supported by businessmen, writers, and educators, the new gospel rapidly became a major social tenet of the churches, and received both denominational sanction and widespread ministerial endorsement.

Stripped of excess verbiage and rationalization, the gospel of wealth was a popular faith in material success, one which equated wealth and morality. Success, as measured in dollars and cents, would be achieved by hard work, thrift, frugality, and perseverance. As Episcopal Bishop William Lawrence of Massachusetts indicated, "it is only to the man of morality that wealth comes." "Godliness," he announced, "is in league with riches." For sinners the end result would be poverty. It had been suggested that the distinction made here between cause and effect had not been clearly delineated. When John D. Rockefeller explained: "The Lord gave me my money," not a few of his contemporaries pondered over the old chicken-and-egg relationship.

The gospel of wealth was no limited phenomenon. On the contrary, its influence could be perceived in many areas of American culture during the Gilded Age. Typical was Supreme Court Justice Stephen J. Field's unusual interpretations of the Fourteenth Amendment, which endowed corporations with the same liberties originally granted to persons by the Founding Fathers. In education, high schools and colleges were applauded, supported, and endowed less for the promotion of knowledge than as "a good investment." Ministers were replaced increasingly on college boards of trustees by successful businessmen whose volume of wealth was ostensibly and proportionately a barometer of their wisdom. Even literature and the arts were subject to this new pressure. The Horatio Alger success story glorified the cult of the self-made man. Elbert Hubbard's *A Message to Garcia* was an eloquent expression of the theme that unquestioning loyalty to one's superiors, perseverance, and courage marked a man for success. The same message was to be found in the writings and speeches of the Baptist clergyman Russell Conwell, whose famous lecture, *Acres of Diamonds*, provided him with fame and fortune. The "Brown Decades," moreover, produced huge mansions for the wealthy. Massive and ornate, these "tombs for the living" bore the stamp of conspicuousness which few could emulate. They were physical and artistic evidence par excellence of the gospel of wealth.

Organized religion responded to this siren call of the Gilded Age. Courting business support as a substantial source for new and larger buildings and increased ministerial salaries, clergymen of all denominations espoused the gospel of wealth. Affirming that riches, like poverty, were well deserved, they criticized labor unions and the agitation for an eight-hour day. According to some clerics, the eight-hour day would promote vice by providing too much leisure. A result of the aristocratic drift in American Protestantism, as one contemporary writer viewed the trend, was the alienation of a large part of the church's middle and lower class membership.

Not all churchmen, to be sure, adhered to these doctrines. A small but vocal and expanding minority turned to another gospel. Though still concerned with secular matters, it was not selfishly materialistic like the gospel of wealth. The welfare of the individual, rather than orthodox economic individualism, was the concern of what later came to be known as the social gospel. Emphasizing the collective moral responsibilities of Christians in an urban industrial society, it differed from pre-Cvil War evangelical movements, whose orientation was individualistic. Gilded Age evangelism, so eloquently represented by Dwight L. Moody, came to terms with the new economic order. It had not only become a bulwark of the new individualism, but it had also divorced itself from social reform, suggesting that "a heart that is right with God and man seldom constitutes a social problem."

Social gospelers, led by theologians and preachers, reinterpreted the scriptures so as to provide a humanitarian rationale to cope with problems of urbanized industrialism. Arguing for social welfare and social reform, these churchmen urged group action, including intervention by the state when necessary. Laissez-faire capitalism, they contended, was inconsistent with the basic humanistic teachings of Jesus. There was general agreement that the church should support demands of laborers for decent wages and safer working conditions, as well as the fight against such urban ills as tenements, disease, and poverty. A small but short-lived group, influenced by the British experience, insisted upon an all-out effort toward Christian socialism. But whatever their area of concern and particular solution, Washington Gladden's *Social Salvation* and Walter Rauschenbusch's *Christianizing the Social Order* reflected the dominant themes of a social gospel which challenged the gospel of wealth. Clearly, unrestrained economic individualism, as well as personalized salvation, were being questioned by an aroused social conscience which drew inspiration and respectability from its reinterpretation of Christian morality.

A change in the American attitude toward the immigrant was a third vital question which affected existing social values. A conflict of views on the desirability of immigration was hardly new. From seventeenth-century Puritan expulsion of the Quakers down to the late nineteenth-century exclusion of the Chinese, parochialism and nativism had their moments of triumph in American development. That they should begin to assume major proportions, even belatedly during the Gilded Age, was more than a little ironical for a society which itself was so completely a product of migratory forces. By and large, Americans had accepted the principle of free immigration in keeping with their traditional concepts of nationality and equality. Influenced by the cosmopolitanism of the eighteenth-century Enlightenment, early American nationalism did not bear the usual stamps of ethnic, linguistic, or religious exclusiveness. Rather, it was founded upon the conviction of being different from other nations in its establishment of a genuinely free society. It was to be a haven and, in a very real sense, the European common man's utopia. America was an idea which could conceivably embrace all men. Moreover, American acceptance of equality meant that all individuals were to be a part of the state. Instead of producing isolated individuals in an alien territory or creating a series of foreign enclaves, "immigration . . . involved the movement into a country of future citizens."[1] Liberalization of freedom of movement in Europe had released a mass of persons who made possible fulfillment of America's needs for geographic expansion and economic growth during the nineteenth century. By the Gilded Age, however, the era of free immigration began to be challenged. As the immigrant wave approached and then surpassed the half-million mark each year, many of the descendants of earlier immigrants began to look askance upon this vast influx.

Many reasons account for this shift of opinion. In part, it can be attributed to altered concepts of equality and nationality. The eighteenth- and early nineteenth-century Western view of the catholicity of human nature, which meant that men could go almost anywhere and fit in readily, had been severely impaired. Modern chauvinism and cultural nationalism clearly implied that newcomers faced a difficult problem of adjustment. Some even argued that the geographic barrier itself was an insuperable cultural obstacle. American nationalism as an idea which could absorb all who were willing to subscribe to that country's ideals was vigorously questioned. And the American idea of equality, sufficiently flexible to permit some exceptions in the past, was subjected to serious misgivings. Contributing to a cumulatively racist outlook were the growth in America of the concept of Anglo-Saxonism; the national acceptance of Jim Crowism, with its legitimation by the Supreme Court in 1896; and the capitulation of America to an imperial course of policy which brought extensive contact with non-Western peoples.

Still other factors promoted debate on free immigration. Labor unions were apprehensive of the immigrant impact on wages; business groups expressed concern over the radical tendencies of many Europeans; agrarian parties turned their backs on the immigrant in seeking popular support; and patriotic societies questioned the feasibility of properly assimilating southern and eastern Europeans. The nativist element here, of course, was a feature which readily fed the fulminations of the racists. Unfortunately, few persons suggested that the problems raised by "the new immigration" were not really new at all or that they were merely more obvious because of the larger urban concentration. Rare was the observer who indicated that the latest immigrant tide—though, like its predecessors, primarily agrarian in origin—was coming to an urban industrial society, something drastically different from past experience.

---

[1] UNESCO, *The Positive Contribution of Immigrants* (1956), p. 12.

Nevertheless, arguments grew louder, and voices became shrill. Was the immigrant making a positive contribution—providing new ideas, new skills, new demands? Or was he a menace—an inferior intruder who could never be properly assimilated? Should he be permitted to come freely, or should his entry be regulated even to the point in some cases of complete exclusion? Again, these were not entirely new issues, for nativists in the 1840's and 1850's, it should be recalled, had urged restrictions. Curtailment of immigration gained substantial momentum in the 1880's and even a sense of urgency in the nineties. Though exclusion of the Chinese was consummated in 1882, other curbs enacted in this era were relatively minor, despite efforts of assorted groups, including the Immigration Restriction League. Major obstructive legislation was to come at a later date.

There were, indeed, other movements and forces which altered the outlook and perspective of Americans during the late nineteenth century. But clearly, the three points discussed had something in common. The challenge to *laissez faire*, the questioning of the gospel of wealth, and the attack on free immigration all involved a larger measure of group action, in which the government was to be a positive and manipulative factor. However, not many had as yet perceived the significant difference between what the majority would define as *its general welfare* and what a few would decide was *the national welfare*. The distinction between state welfare and the welfare state was still to be made.

What, then, of the original question? Was the Gilded Age an era in which older social values were changed by the impact of urban industrialism? To some degree, yes! Substantially revised economic and social conditions suggested that many aspects of older values were not always suitable. Newer ideas and newer methods seemingly would achieve traditional goals far more effectively. More and more, it was argued that governmental regulation would protect far more effectively the economic rights of the majority than would ruthlessly competitive economic individualism. The individual continued to be the prime concern of American socety; and perhaps it was no accident that even though *free* enterprise was beginning to be curbed, *private* enterprise remained as strong as ever.

Basic values, then, were faced with the need to change, but resistance was encountered on all fronts. In nearly every area of American culture, fundamentally opposing forces could be uncovered, as the three questions discussed earlier amply illustrate. But in very few areas did the new ideas and the new values achieve immediate fruition. Rugged economic individualism had hardly disappeared by

1900, although state and even federal activity foreshadowed events of the Progressive era. The gospel of wealth was a force still to be reckoned with, though the social gospel would gain considerable backing in the period after 1900. And finally, immigration curbs in the name of patriotism and for the specific welfare of certain groups attained few successes as compared with those which came after the first World War.

The old order was changing. In a very real sense, the Gilded Age was an *era of transition* in the development of American civilization.

SUGGESTED READINGS

AARON, DANIEL. *Men of Good Hope: A Story of American Progressives.* New York: Oxford University Press, 1951.

CURTI, MERLE E. *Growth of American Thought*, Part VI. New York: Harper & Bros., 1943.

DORFMAN, JOSEPH. *The Economic Mind in American Civilization*, Vol. III. New York: Viking Press, Inc., 1949.

FINE, SIDNEY. *Laissez-Faire and the General Welfare State: A Study of Conflict in American Thought, 1865–1901.* Ann Arbor: University of Michigan Press, 1956.

HANDLIN, OSCAR. *The Uprooted: The Epic Story of the Great Migrations That Made the American People.* Boston: Little, Brown & Co., 1951.

HIGHAM, JOHN. *Strangers in the Land: Patterns of American Nativism, 1860–1925.* New Brunswick: Rutgers University Press, 1955.

HOFSTADTER, RICHARD C. *Social Darwinism in American Thought.* Philadelphia: University of Pennsylvania Press, 1944.

HOPKINS, CHARLES H. *The Rise of the Social Gospel in American Protestantism, 1865–1915.* New Haven: Yale University Press, 1940.

KIRKLAND, EDWARD CHASE. *Dream and Thought in the Business Community, 1860–1900.* Ithaca: Cornell University Press, 1956.

MAY, HENRY F. *Protestant Churches and Industrial America.* New York: Harper & Bros., 1949.

MORGAN, H. WAYNE (ed.). *The Gilded Age: A Reappraisal.* Syracuse: Syracuse University Press, 1963.

WITTKE, CARL. *We Who Built America*, Part III. New York: Prentice-Hall, Inc., 1939.

Document 19.1

AN ARGUMENT FOR LAISSEZ FAIRE

Among the staunchest advocates of unrestricted free enterprise was Yale University's William Graham Sumner. A specialist in both economics and sociology, his essays on contemporary problems made him a nationally known figure. In the excerpts which follow from "The Challenge of Facts," written about 1880, Sumner offers some of his reasons for defending *laissez faire*.

(From William Graham Sumner, *The Challenge of Facts and Other Essays* [New Haven: Yale University Press, 1914], pp. 25, 27–28, 49–50)

Private property, also, which we have seen to be a feature of society organized in accordance with the natural conditions of the struggle for existence produces inequalities between men. The struggle for existence produces inequalities between men. The struggle for existence is aimed against nature. It is from her niggardly hand that we have to wrest the satisfactions for our needs, but our fellow-men are our competitors for the meager supply. Competition, therefore, is a law of nature. Nature is entirely neutral; she submits to him who most energetically and resolutely assails her. She grants her rewards to the fittest, therefore, without regard to other considerations of any kind. If, then, there be liberty, men get from her just in proportion to their works, and their having and enjoying are just in proportion to their being and their doing. Such is the system of nature. If we do not like it, and if we try to amend it, there is only one way in which we can do it. We can take from the better and give to the worse. We can deflect the penalties of those who have done ill and throw them on those who have done better. We can take the rewards from those who have done better and give them to those who have done worse. We shall thus lessen the inequalities. We shall favor the survival of the unfittest, and we shall accomplish this by destroying liberty. Let it be understood that we cannot go outside of this alternative: liberty, inequality, survival of the fittest; not-liberty, equality, survival of the unfittest. The former carries society forward and favors all its best members; the latter carries society downwards and favors all its worst members. . . .

It follows from what we have observed that it is the utmost folly to denounce capital. To do so is to undermine civilization, for capital is the first requisite of every social gain, educational, ecclesiastical, political, æsthetic, or other.

It must also be noticed that the popular antithesis between persons and capital is very fallacious. Every law or institution which protects persons at the expense of capital makes it easier for persons to live and to increase the number of consumers of capital while lowering all the motives to prudence and frugality by which capital is created. Hence every such law or institution tends to produce a large population, sunk in misery. All poor laws and all eleemosynary institutions and expenditures have this tendency. On the contrary, all laws and institutions which give security to capital against the interests of other persons than its owners, restrict numbers while preserving the means of subsistence. Hence every such law or institution tends to produce a small society on a high stage of comfort and well-being. It follows that the antithesis commonly thought to exist between the protection of persons and the protection of property is in reality only an antithesis between numbers and quality. . . .

Popular institutions have their own abuses and dangers just as much as monarchical or aristocratic institutions. We are only just finding out what they are. All the institutions which we have inherited were invented to guard liberty against the encroachments of a powerful monarch or aristocracy, when these classes possessed land and the possession of land was the greatest social power. Institutions must now be devised to guard civil liberty against popular majorities, and this necessity arises first in regard to the protection of property, the first and greatest function of government and element in civil liberty. . . .

Document 19.2

FALSE NOTIONS OF GOVERNMENT

Lester Frank Ward, author of several pioneer volumes in the United States on sociology, viewed the relationship between government and the economy in a light very different from Sumner. Asserting the need for man to play a more positive role in the evolutionary scheme of things, Ward attacked what he felt to be some of the false notions of government held by many of his contemporaries.

(From Lester Frank Ward, "False Notions of Government," *Forum*, Vol. III [June, 1887], pp. 367–68, 370–72)

The old idea of government was that it was a power essentially hostile to the people, but fastened upon them by fate. The modern survival of this idea contemplates government as a "necessary evil." No matter how representative it may be it is still looked upon to a great extent as an arbitrary personality, with great power and evil intent, requiring the exercise of "eternal vigilance" to prevent it from destroying all liberty. Many who know better are unable to divest themselves of this view, and entertain it as a mere hereditary instinct. In fact, it is one of those late social instincts of self-preservation, which persist, as all instincts do, long after the conditions under which they were developed have passed away. . . .

The most disastrous effect of this false public sentiment is that it deprives government itself of its chief element of usefulness to the people, viz., its power to protect society.

Without going back over the history and reputed origin of government, it will not be disputed that its primary purpose is protection. In the earlier and more primitive types of society the chief protection required was that against the crude physical elements of human nature that perpetually conflicted and destroyed all peace. These still exist, perhaps undiminished, and it is not denied that they are fairly and effectually held in check by government. But besides these, in the modern epoch of vast undertakings and complicated civilization, there has grown up another class of social evils against which protection should be secured, which is far more dangerous than that of brute force, sporadic passion, and low animal cunning. I refer to the evils of organized aggrandizement, the abuse of wealth, and the subtle processes by which the producer of wealth is deprived of his share in it. These evils have grown up with civilization, and are simply the organized expression of human acquisitiveness. They are the natural products of an advancing intelligence without moral restraint. . . .

In view of all this, it becomes clear that nothing is so much needed at the present time as the removal of the popular error on this point. It is the duty of all those who have the true reform of society at heart to point out in the most convincing manner that the people are no longer in any danger from governmental oppression, that their present danger lies in an entirely different direction, that what they really need is more government in its primary sense, greater protection of the exposed masses from the rapacity of the favored few, and that, instead of distrusting and crippling government, they should greatly enlarge its power to grapple with these evils. Let it be insisted upon that this is nothing but the reclothing of government with its original power to protect society. It was for this that it was instituted, and unless it does this it has no right to exist. . . .

Above all, the working people should realize that the government is their own and will be just what they make it. They should learn to look upon it as a creature of their will. They should cease to fear and distrust it, and should seek to mold and shape it. They should turn a deaf ear to those who seek to use it as a scarecrow to frighten them into inaction. If they are to secure from government that protection which forms its only claim to exist, they must throw off all party allegiance, and demand of all candidates the strongest pledges of fidelity to their interests, and sustain none who do not honestly and earnestly fulfill those pledges. They need no revolutionary schemes of socialism, communism, or anarchy. The present machinery of government, especially in this country, is all they could wish. They have only to take possession of it and operate it in their own interest. . . .

Document 19.3

THE GOSPEL OF WEALTH

William Lawrence, born in Boston in 1850, rose to prominence as an outspoken cleric during a long ministry in the Episcopal Church. In 1893, he became Bishop of Massachusetts. His following comments are taken from an article published in a popular journal in 1901.

(From William Lawrence, "The Relation of Wealth to Morals," *World's Work*, Vol. I [January, 1901], pp. 286–87)

There is a certain distrust on the part of our people as to the effect of material prosperity on their morality. We shrink with some foreboding at the great increase of riches, and question whether in the long run material prosperity does not tend toward the disintegration of character. . . .

History tells us that, while riches have been an item and an indirect cause of national decay, innumerable other conditions entered in. Therefore, while wealth has been a source of danger, it has not necessarily led to demoralization.

That leaders have sprung from the ranks of the poor is true and always will be true, so long as force of character exists in every class. But there are other conditions than a lack of wealth at the source of their uprising.

And as to the Bible :—while every word that can be quoted against the rich is as true as any other word, other words and deeds are as true ; and the parables of our Lord on the stewardship of wealth, His association with the wealthy, strike another and complementary note. Both notes are essential to the harmony of His life and teachings. His thought was not of the conditions, rich or poor, but of a higher life, the character rising out of the conditions—fortunately, for we are released from that subtle hypocrisy which has beset the Christian through the ages, bemoaning the deceitfulness of riches and, at the same time, working with all his might to earn a competence, and a fortune if he can.

Now we are in a position to affirm that neither history, experience, nor the Bible necessarily sustains the common distrust of the effect of material wealth on morality. Our path of study is made more clear. Two positive principles lead us out on our path.

The first is that man, when he is strong, will conquer Nature, open up her resources, and harness them to his service. This is his play, his exercise, his divine mission. . . .

The other principle is that, in the long run, it is only to the man of morality that wealth comes. We believe in the harmony of God's Universe. We know that it is only by working along His laws natural and spiritual that we can work with efficiency. Only by working along the lines of right thinking and right living can the secrets and wealth of Nature be revealed. We, like the Psalmist, occasionally see the wicked prosper, but only occasionally.

Put two men in adjoining fields, one man strong and normal, the other weak and listless. One picks up his spade, turns over the earth, and works till sunset. The other turns over a few clods, gets a drink from the spring, takes a nap, and loafs back to his work. In a few years one will be rich for his needs, and the other a pauper dependent on the first, and growling at his prosperity.

Put ten thousand immoral men to live and work in one fertile valley and ten thousand moral men to live and work in the next valley, and the question is soon answered as to who wins the material wealth. Godliness is in league with riches.

Document 19.4

THE SOCIAL GOSPEL

Born in the Midwest, George D. Herron became a Congregational minister and Grinnell College professor. His religious view of social problems not only carried him to the radical wing of the social gospel movement, but also led to the publication of several books on the subject. An excerpt from *The New Redemption*, which appeared in 1893, follows.

(From George D. Herron, *The New Redemption* [New York, 1893], pp. 29–31, 37–38)

The social problem is the call of the state to become Christian. The state can save itself only by believing in the Lord Jesus Christ as the supreme authority in law, politics, and society. The state is the social organ. . . . It is the business of the state to develop and shield the common manhood and happiness, the physical and moral health, of men as sons of God. Government has a right to existence and authority for no other end than that for which God sent his only begotten Son into the world. It is the vocation of the state, as the social organ, to so control property, so administer the production and distribution of economic goods, as to give to every man the fruit of his labor, and protect the laborer from the irresponsible tyranny of the passion of wealth. It is the duty of the state to so reconstruct itself as to procure for every man full opportunity to develop all his powers, and to see that no member of society suffers for the want of work and bread. . . .

The love that moved God to give his only begotten Son to save the world must be the law that shall govern wealth, and move its possessors to consecrate themselves to the creation of a Christian society and Christian state. It lies within the power of the American capitalists who call themselves Christian, by taking the Sermon on the Mount and patiently working it into the foundations of industry, to be the creators of a new and divine civilization that would surpass all our apprehensions of the Revelation of John. If they would take the Sermon on the Mount as economic law, as a revelation of the nature of things, as the safest basis upon which the market of the world could stand, they would lift the commerce and industry of the world above the chance and strife of competing interests, and make the moving trains of merchandise, the toil of the mills and echo of the mines, the barter and exchange of the markets, all accordant parts of a harmony of divine justice. I do not believe there can ever be peace between man and man, between interest and interest, between class and class, by any other mode than through the belief of capital, the belief of industry, the belief of the market, in the naturalness, in the wisdom, in the safety, of the moral law of Jesus. . . .

Document 19.5

IMMIGRATION RESTRICTION

Henry Cabot Lodge was one of the prominent political figures favoring immigration restriction during this era. Staunch nationalist, Anglophile, and close friend of Theodore Roosevelt, the Massachusetts Republican leader set down his views on the matter in 1891:

(From Henry Cabot Lodge, "The Restriction of Immigration," *North American Review*, Vol. CLII, No. 410 [January, 1891], pp. 32–35)

Thus it is proved, first, that immigration to this country is increasing, and, second, that it is making its greatest relative increase from races most alien to the body of the American people and from the lowest and most illiterate classes among those races. In other words, it is apparent that, while our immigration is increasing, it is showing at the same time a marked tendency to deteriorate in character. . . .

As one example of the practical effect of unrestricted immigration the committee cite the case of the coal-mining country.

"Generally speaking, the class of immigrants who have lately been imported and employed in the coal regions of this country are not such, in the opinion of the committee, as would make desirable inhabitants of the United States. They are of a very low order of intelligence. They do not come here with the intention of becoming citizens; their whole purpose being to accumulate by parsimonious, rigid, and unhealthy economy a sum of money and then return to their native land. They live in miserable sheds like beasts; the food they eat is so meagre, scant, unwholesome, and revolting that it would nauseate and disgust an American workman, and he would find it difficult to sustain life upon it. Their habits are vicious, their customs are disgusting, and the effect of their presence here upon our social condition is to be deplored. They have not the influences, as we understand them, of a home; they do not know what the word means; and, in the opinion of the committee, no amount of effort would improve their morals or 'Americanize' this class of immigrants. They have been brought here in such numbers, and have been employed at such low wages, that it has resulted in their replacing the American citizens who formerly performed this class of labor, until now there are comparatively few Americans engaged in mining coal in Pennsylvania." . . .

In a word, the continued introduction into the labor market of four hundred thousand persons annually, half of whom have no occupation and most of whom represent the rudest form of labor, has a very great effect in reducing the rates of wages and disturbing the labor market. This, of course, is too obvious to need comment, and this tendency to constantly lower wages by the competition of an increasing and deteriorating immigration is a danger to the people of the United States the gravity of which can hardly be overestimated. Moreover, the shifting of the sources of the immigration is unfavorable, and is bringing to the country people whom it is very difficult to assimilate and who do not promise well for the standard of civilization in the United States—a matter as serious as the effect on the labor market.

The question, therefore, arises,—and there is no more important question before the American people,—What shall be done to protect our labor against this undue competition, and to guard our citizenship against an infusion which seems to threaten deterioration? We have the power, of course, to prohibit all immigration, or to limit the number of persons to be admitted to the country annually, or—which would have the same effect—to impose upon immigrants a heavy capitation tax. Such rough and stringent measures are certainly neither necessary nor desirable if we can overcome the difficulties and dangers of the situation by more moderate legislation. These methods, moreover, are indiscriminate; and what is to be desired, if possible, is restriction which shall at the same time discriminate. . . .

Document 19.6

THE IMMIGRANT IN PERSPECTIVE

Robert Louis Stevenson, the eminent Scottish writer, married an American in 1880 after following her across the Atlantic. His observations on the American scene have been set forth in several books, among them *Across the Plains*, which contains the following sensitive observations.

(From Robert Louis Stevenson, *Across the Plains* [New York, 1896], pp. 62–66)

Of all stupid ill-feelings, the sentiment of my fellow-Caucasians towards our companions in the Chinese car was the most stupid and the worst. They seemed never to have looked at them, listened to them, or thought of them, but hated them *a priori*. The Mongols were their enemies in that cruel and treacherous battle-field of money. They could work better and cheaper in half a hundred industries, and hence there was no calumny too idle for the Caucasians to repeat, and even to believe. They declared them hideous vermin, and affected a kind of choking in the throat when they beheld them. . . . Again, my emigrants declared that the Chinese were dirty. I cannot say they were clean, for that was impossible upon the journey; but in their efforts after cleanliness they put the rest of us to shame. . . .

These judgments are typical of the feeling in all Western America. The Chinese are considered stupid, because they are imperfectly acquainted with English. They are held to be base, because their dexterity and frugality enable them to underbid the lazy, luxurious Caucasian. They are said to be thieves; I am sure they have no monopoly of that. They are called cruel; the Anglo-Saxon and the cheerful Irishman may each reflect before he bears the accusation. . . .

Awhile ago it was the Irish, now it is the Chinese that must go. Such is the cry. It seems, after all, that no country is bound to submit to immigration any more than to invasion: each is war to the knife, and resistance to either but legitimate defence. Yet we may regret the free tradition of the republic, which loved to depict herself with open arms, welcoming all unfortunates. And certainly, as a man who believes that he loves freedom, I may be excused some bitterness when I find her sacred name misused in the contention. . . .

For my own part, I could not look but with wonder and respect on the Chinese. Their forefathers watched the stars before mine had begun to keep pigs. Gunpowder and printing, which the other day we imitated, and a school of manners which we never had the delicacy so much as to desire to imitate, were theirs in a long-past antiquity. They walk the earth with us, but it seems they must be of different clay. They hear the clock strike the same hour, yet surely of a different epoch. They travel by steam conveyance, yet with such a baggage of old Asiatic thoughts and superstitions as might check the locomotive in its course. Whatever is thought within the circuit of the Great Wall; what the wry-eyed, spectacled schoolmaster teaches in the hamlets round Pekin; religions so old that our language looks a halfling boy alongside; philosophy so wise that our best philosophers find things therein to wonder at; all this travelled alongside of me for thousands of miles over plain and mountain. Heaven knows if we had one common thought or fancy all that way, or whether our eyes, which yet were formed upon the same design, beheld the same world out of the railway windows. . . .

20

HERBERT GUTMAN
State University of New York at Buffalo

Labor's Response to Modern Industrialism

THE UNITED STATES industrialized between 1840 and 1900. Although the process was slow and uneven, industrialism, once started, proved irrevocable and appeared irresistible. All aspects of human experience felt its consequences: where people worked, the tools they used, how they traveled, what they ate and wore, their leisure habits, their thoughts about themselves and the world in which they lived, and the pace of life itself. In many ways the industrialization of a modern nation is the most significant set of social and economic changes affecting a people—and perhaps the most difficult to analyze. Compare the problem of evaluating the impact of industrialization upon a people with, let us say, the successes of John Adams as a diplomat or Andrew Jackson's motives in attacking the Second Bank of the United States or, better still, the causes of the Mexican War. Once done, the relative difficulty of appraising the effect of industrial development and the responses to it become self-evident. The *process* of industrialization extends over a greater length of time and has many more indirect consequences than the influence of a single great leader or of particular events surrounding a momentary political and diplomatic crisis. For this reason, among others, analysis of the industrial process and the responses to it is important. Our own United States, after all, has as its central quality the fact that it is an industrial nation.

Industrialization meant many things to nineteenth-century Americans: the process by which investment capital poured into the building of new railroads and factories as well as into the development of mines; the widespread application of new sources of nonanimal power to the productive process; the application of new machinery to agriculture in an effort to increase productivity; the introduction of new systems of mechanized production. And it meant more, too. Indus-

71

trialization also accelerated the movement of people from farm to city. Centers of trade, manufacturing, and commerce grew rapidly, as did a laboring population dependent on others for work and income.

Part of the industrial process is revealed in the simple reporting of elementary statistical trends and the wondrous fashion in which contemporaries viewed such data. A few examples suffice. The number of Cincinnati workers engaged in manufacturing increased from 9,040 in 1840 to 58,508 in 1872. In the latter year, 350,000 wage earners lived in New York City, and more than 200,000 crowded into Philadelphia. Pittsburgh, center of the iron and steel industry, impressed one contemporary as a city "like 'hell with the lid taken off.' The entire landscape seems ablaze. . . . The factories are so continuous on the various streets that if placed in a . . . row they would reach thirty-five miles." Steam-propelled machinery became increasingly important. In 1870, 2,346,142 horsepower was used in manufacturing; thirty years later the figure stood at 11,300,081. Coal production soared from 14,610,042 tons in 1860 to 513,525,477 tons in 1914. "One horse power," a prominent Philadelphia manufacturer declared in 1872, "equals the labor-power of ten able-bodied men. . . . This is wealth—embodied wealth in its most advanced form. . . . Human labor is economized; the ingenuity of man has devised labor-saving machinery by which vast economies are affected, and none need labor sixteen hours a day. . . ." Industrial production rose spectacularly, and four industries led the way: iron and steel and allied manufactures, food and kindred processed goods, textiles, and lumber and its finished products. In 1890, for the first time, the value of manufactured products exceeded that of agricultural goods; ten years later, it had doubled. No less a personage than Horace Greeley paid glowing tribute to this industrial progress. Together with Albert Brisbane and others, he penned a 1,300-page paean in 1872 entitled *The Great Industries of the United States.* Characterizing leading inventors and manufacturers as men who led the people "out of the plodding ways which the feudal age . . . imposed upon the race," Greeley and his associates cheerfully concluded: "Though prompted in the main by the spirit of self-aggrandizement, these men have proved themselves the chief philanthropists of the time and have borne the standard of progress. . . ."

Yet the industrial process cannot be measured simply by statistics indicating economic growth. Industrialism also meant a new way of life for whole sectors of the population. In 1859 the nation counted

1,311,346 wage earners. By 1914, more than 7,000,000 persons depended on wages for income. In these years, and even earlier, the skilled craftsman declined in importance, and the factory worker replaced him as the symbol of the new industrial order. The commissioners of the Massachusetts Bureau of Labor Statistics admitted the importance of economic growth in the early postbellum years; but significantly, they asked if it was "logical to reason" that the building of a railroad, itself a sign of unquestioned progress, meant that "the laborers who excavate . . . the grade . . . , dig the ore . . . , and cast the rails," automatically were "prosperous and growing rich."

A critical aspect of the industrial process is its effect on the standard of comfort. But even more is involved, for much of the history of industrialization between 1840 and 1900 is the story of the painful process by which an old way of life gave over to a new one. And in this context, the central issue was the rejection or modification of a traditional set of "rules" and "commands" that no longer fit the more modern industrial context. What did it mean to work in a factory for the first time after one was used to the routine of a small shop or, better still, of agricultural life? How could an employer, himself uneasy in his new position of power, impose discipline on persons unaccustomed to the demands of factory labor? What did unemployment mean to persons entirely dependent for the first time on others for income with which to purchase necessities? Although he spoke in language peculiar to nineteenth-century America, Carroll D. Wright, the first Commissioner of Labor for the United States, put it well in 1878: "The divine economy takes neither the old machine nor the discarded operator of it into account, but puts in the place of one a more perfect piece of mechanism, and in the place of the other an intellect of a much higher order, and contemplates the general results to humanity, and not the loss to the individual. . . . An examination, carried in any direction, demonstrates the proposition that all progress, every step in advance, is over apparent destruction, and, like every pioneer who has startled the world by his discoveries, and by them benefited his kind, is over the graves of men."

Stripped to its essence, Wright's words capsuled a central dilemma inherent in the industrial process: The new social order, serviced by steam and coal and rails, and centering around the factory and the mine, exacted a heavy price from those who surrendered an earlier and less complex way of life. The craftsman's pride in his work lost its meaning as he was overwhelmed by specialization and the machine.

The New York Wood Carvers' Union, for example, complained that "unlimited competition" meant lower prices and forced the manufacturer to seek cheaper productive methods. "Ingenious machinery has then to be used to such a degree that skilled workingmen . . . become superfluous. All mechanics become *factory workmen* and [all] production *machine work*. There is no escape from that." Similarly, a cigar maker complained of the revolutionary effects of the cigar mold on his craft: "The mode by which most segars . . . are produced to-day is so divided that skilled labor is no longer required. The inventive genius has superseeded [*sic*] skill. . . ."

The growing importance of unskilled and semiskilled labor also altered the status of women and children. Always useful on the farm, they proved equally valuable in the factory. New England's early cotton mills illustrated this development. But it was intensified by the ethos of the entire period—by the emphasis placed on investment capital and cheap production. The Massachusetts Bureau of Labor Statistics found that factory labor proved that a woman could operate machinery and perform manual labor out of her home. Not surprisingly, one of every three factory workers in Philadelphia in 1870 was a woman. Child labor also increased in these years. Horace Greeley and his associates insisted that "the pride of the nation is in its children, and in none so much as in those who pre-eminently distinguish themselves in the arts of peace—domestic manufacturing. . . ." A New York daily advised its readers that "a bright twelve year old girl" easily could be "taught to make a cap in four weeks." And so it went. In addition to a new status for skilled craftsmen in the bustling factories, there was a new kind of labor for women and children who worked to supplement the meager wages of unskilled fathers.

New conditions of work and life tell much about the impact of the industrial order upon the wage earner, but his response to these conditions is an equally important part of the story. At times the wage earner was passive. Was his silence the result of satisfaction? Or was protest made difficult by the very conditions of the new industrial order? At other times the wage earner protested. Bitter strikes and lockouts—most usually caused by the demand for labor organization or for better wages, hours, and working conditions—characterized innumerable industrial disputes. The violence that accompanied the great railroad strikes in 1877 and the bitterness on all sides during the Homestead strike and the Pullman boycott in the 1890's were outstanding illustrations, but there were countless unrecorded and lesser disputes between workers and employers between 1840 and 1900. What explained the bitterness of industrial conflict at that time? Were skilled workers more discontented than unskilled? Were immigrant workers more satisfied than native-born laborers? Did the violence in the United States during its prime years of industrialization, as some historians argue, far exceed that of any European nation? How does one account for such bitterness and violence?

One clue to the answer to these questions about the social behavior of wage earners rests in understanding just *who* the workers were, *what* they did *before* they entered the factory, and the *frame of mind* they carried with them into the new industrial order and used to interpret it. In general, four kinds of persons became wage earners in the United States between 1840 and 1900. Two of them already were accustomed to urban experience but knew little of factory life. One consisted of the urban skilled craftsmen, who surrendered independence and skill to the factory and the machine. Unskilled urban day laborers, so numerous in preindustrial cities, made up the other. Rural Americans, most often sons and daughters of farmers—familiar at best with the small town—were a third important element drawn to the industrial city by the dynamism of shop and factory. The fourth group—the foreign-born—came mostly from Europe and, to a much lesser extent, from the Orient. Immigrants, largely from Ireland, Germany, Great Britain, and the Scandinavian countries, totaled about one third of all workers in the mining, mechanical, and manufacturing industries in the late nineteenth century. Furthermore, an increasing number of newcomers were pouring in from southern and eastern Europe. British immigrants excepted, few of the foreign-born brought industrial experience with them to the United States.

How did each of these groups react to the industrial order in America? Persons sensitive to the process *and* the problems of social change most often view the former in one of two ways. They compare the present with the past and judge what is becoming by what has been. Or they criticize the present by comparing it to a utopian order that lies in the future. Several problems of analysis emerge. Did those workers who questioned the direction of the industrial order use the past or the future as their point of reference? If they judged primarily by past experience, did they tend to romanticize it? If the future served as the point of reference, what ideal of social reconstruction most appealed to what group: co-operatives, socialism, abolition of the "wages system," or simple trade unions that sought through organization to improve living conditions without changing the structure of the new order?

Whatever their point of reference or particular criticism, wage earners who questioned the industrial order often shared a general revulsion against the quality of *dependence* that characterized the new way of life. Each element had its own reasons for resenting dependence. With high expectations, the immigrant came in search of opportunity, which he viewed as the fulfillment of the dream of independent ownership and self-sufficiency. The urban skilled worker, on the other hand, witnessed a genuine decline in his status and self-image. Native-born persons who entered the labor force experienced a *new* quality of dependence for the first time. What did the factory mean to the son of a farmer who moved from a western New York farm to work in a Cleveland iron mill or oil refinery? How did a person accustomed to the rigors and simplicity of a small New England or Pennsylvania town react to the regimen imposed by a Fall River textile mill or a Pittsburgh coal mine? And how did the native-born worker, a citizen *before* he became a worker and in this sense unique in the nineteenth-century world, react to his new dependent status?

Before the coming of industrialism, the American dream (or ideal) had abjured a dependent status. In the early years of the republic, Thomas Jefferson warned: "Dependence begets subservience and venality, suffocates the germ of virtue, and prepares fit tools for the designs of ambition." Years later, Abraham Lincoln, shortly before winning the nomination as candidate for the presidency on the Republican ticket, asserted the ideal in positive terms. During a strike of shoe workers, Lincoln spoke in New Haven, Connecticut:

. . . What is the true condition of the laborer? I take it that it is best for all to leave each man free to acquire property as fast as he can. Some will get wealthy. I don't believe in a law to prevent a man from getting rich; it would do more harm than good. So while we do not propose any war upon capital, we do wish to allow the humblest man an equal chance to get rich with everybody else. When one starts poor, as most do in the race of life, free society is such that he knows he can better his condition; he knows that there is no fixed condition of labor, for his whole life. . . . I want every man to have a chance . . . in which he *can* better his condition—when he may look forward and hope to be a hired laborer this year and the next, work for himself afterward, and finally hire men to work for him! That is the true system. . . .

Here, then, was the dream—independence, self-sufficiency, and upward mobility based largely on merit and personal talent.

The industrial way of life tested this ideal in many ways. It is instructive to compare Lincoln's statement with that of Terence V. Powderly less than three decades later. In his memoir, *Thirty Years of Labor*, this head of the Knights of Labor eloquently lamented the passing of the old order. He described the new obstacles to the old ideal and revealed a characteristic response to dependent status:

> . . . With the introduction of machinery, large manufacturing establishments were erected in the cities and towns. . . . The village blacksmith shop was abandoned, the road-side shoe shop was deserted, the tailor left his bench, and all together these mechanics turned away from their country homes and wended their way to the cities wherein the large factories had been erected. . . . They no longer carried the keys of the workshop, for workshop, tools, and keys belonged not to them, but to their master. . . . Competition between man and man is healthy to both, but competition between man and the machine is injurious to the former. He who offered to sell his labor after the introduction of machinery, could not hope to compete with a fellowman in the work he proposed to do; he was forced to compete with a machine, or a whole row of machines, being managed by boys or girls who worked for inadequate wages. . . . Beneath the shadow of machinery, merit went for naught so far as man's natural ability to perform labor was concerned.

In this light, can one argue that the individualist and "entreprenurial" tradition, which encouraged rapid capital accumulation and, at times, a ruthless insensitivity to others, also shaped the embittered response of workers to the condition of dependence?

Response to dependence took many forms. Often, it was little more than a lament. In other instances, it was sheer anger and frustration. At times, it revealed a deep sense of betrayal. Some workers sought only a means of escape from city and factory. Others were aggrieved that an ostensibly democratic government should support only one group, the new industrial capitalists, or merely stand by and watch the "natural laws" of social development unfold. Still others questioned the morality and ethics of the new era. And finally, some argued that dependence best could be overcome by self-organization among the wage earners. Here, too, many problems for analysis arise. In these years, unions collapsed almost as quickly as they came into being. E. L. Godkin, editor of *The Nation*, insisted in 1868 that "the trades-unions . . . have, in reality, put the laborer and the capitalist for the first time on equal terms, economically considered." Unions, Godkin explained, "have rendered, and are rendering, to the working classes, one essential service—by enabling them, for the first time in their history, to contract with masters as free agents and on equal terms." What, then, explained the rapid rise and fall of unions? Was it the rapid growth of the economy? Was it the changing composition of the labor force? Was it the attitude of employers and their power, supported by a sympathetic government? Or was it the very dream itself of independent proprietorship?

SUGGESTED READINGS

BRUCE, ROBERT V.   *1877: Year of Violence.* Indianapolis: Bobbs-Merrill Co., Inc., 1959.

COMMONS, JOHN R., AND ASSOCIATES.   *History of Labour in the United States.* 4 vols. New York: Macmillan Co., 1918–35.

DAVID, HENRY.   *The History of the Haymarket Affair.* New York: Russell & Russell, Inc., 1958.

DESTLER, CHESTER M.   *American Radicalism, 1865–1901.* New London: Octagon, 1946.

ERICKSON, CHARLOTTE.   *American Industry and the European Immigrant, 1860–1885.* Cambridge: Harvard University Press, 1957.

FONER, PHILIP S.   *History of the Labor Movement in the United States.* 2 vols. New York: International Publishers Co., Inc., 1947–55.

GINGER, RAY.   *The Bending Cross: A Biography of Eugene Victor Debs.* New Brunswick: Rutgers University Press, 1949.

GROB, GERALD N.   *Workers and Utopia: A Study of Ideological Conflict in the American Labor Movement, 1865–1900.* Evanston: Northwestern University Press, 1961.

GROSSMAN, JONATHAN.   *William Sylvis: Pioneer of American Labor.* New York: Columbia University Press, 1945.

HANDLIN, OSCAR.   *The Uprooted: The Epic Story of the Great Migrations That Made the American People.* Boston: Little Brown & Co., 1951.

KIRKLAND, EDWARD C.   *Industry Comes of Age: Business, Labor, and Public Policy 1860–1897.* New York: Holt, Rinehart and Winston, 1961.

MADISON, CHARLES.   *American Labor Leaders.* New York: Harper & Bros., 1950.

QUINT, HOWARD H.   *The Forging of American Socialism: Origins of the Modern Movement.* Columbia: University of South Carolina Press, 1953.

TAFT, PHILIP.   *The A. F. of L. in the Time of Gompers.* New York: Harper & Bros., 1957.

WARE, NORMAN J.   *The Industrial Worker, 1840–1860.* Gloucester, Mass.: Peter Smith, 1958.

WARE, NORMAN J.   *The Labor Movement in the United States, 1860–1895.* New York: D. Appleton Co., 1929.

Document 20.1

THE PASSING OF THE OLD ORDER AND THE RECOGNITION OF DEPENDENCE

Soon after the Civil War ended, the Massachusetts Bureau of Labor Statistics compiled data and drew conclusions about the transition from a craft-oriented to a factory-dominated economy.

THE MACHINE

(From Massachusetts Bureau of Labor Statistics, *Annual Report, 1872* [Boston, 1873], pp. 341–42)

Skill, once the strong defence of the artisan, is now trembling in the balance, to-day of value, to-morrow of none, rapidly retiring, with its apprenticed pupils before the advance of machinery. In fact, it is about conquered. Men of skill in trades which it was never supposed invention would reach, have been compelled to enlist into the service of machinery, or turned adrift to learn new trades, or gone to swell the ranks of unskilled laborers—nothing save the increased demand for articles manufactured, coming in to their rescue. . . . As the machine is the embodiment of skill, there is small need of skill on the part of the machine-tender. He is transformed from an adept to be the servant of automatic apparatus, and the sub-division of labor renders this service simple and easily acquired. But few trades remain, in all departments of which a man can become an adept, and wherein he has opportunity to exercise his constructive faculties, for he knows that the machinery he tends will adjust its work with the needed precision. He needs neither to calculate nor to make allowance; his principle function is "to feed the thing he tends," and if properly fed, the machine works up its food and digests it to the expected result, with unfailing certainty.

Charles Litchman's father manufactured shoes. For six years, Litchman worked as a salesman for his father. Between 1870 and 1874, he owned his own shoe factory. He then studied law, worked "at the bench" in a shoe factory, and became Grand Servitor of the Knights of St. Crispin, a labor union of shoe workers. In November, 1879, he testified before a Congressional committee investigating labor conditions and the causes of industrial depression.

SPECIALIZATION

(From "Testimony of Charles H. Litchman," *Causes of the General Depression in Labor and Business, Investigation by a Select Committee of the House of Representatives*, 46th Congress, 2d Session, Miscellaneous House Document No. 5 [Washington, D.C.: U.S. Government Printing Office, 1879], pp. 422–33)

Mr. Litchman: . . . . The first effect of the introduction of labor-saving machinery is the degradation of the labor.

The Chairman: How so?

Mr. Litchman: By the sub-division of labor a man now is no longer a tradesman. He is a part of a tradesman. In my own trade of shoe-making, twenty years ago the work was done almost entirely by hand, and the man had to learn how to make a shoe. Now with the use of machines of almost superhuman ingenuity, a man·is no longer a shoemaker, but only the sixty-fourth part of a shoemaker, because there are sixty-four sub-divisions in making shoes ; and a man may work forty years at our trade and at the end of forty years he will know no more about making a whole shoe than when he commenced business.

The Chairman: He would only know how to make a peg or a waxed end?

Mr. Litchman: Yes ; or he would be a laster, or a beveler, or heeler, or nailer, or he would be running and using a machine, or a peg-measure, or attending to any one of the sixty-four sub-divisions into which the trade is parceled out. . . . You cannot turn back the hands upon the dial of human progress and say that all machinery must be banished. You would not take up the rails, destroy the locomotive, and break up the railroad cars, and go back to stage-coaches and horses. . . . Yet all these improvements, while in the abstract they benefit mankind, have as their first result the degradation of labor by the sub-division of labor. Under our present wage-labor system, capital gets the whole advantage of the introduction of [the] human brain into human labor.

.   .   .   .

The Chairman: How many of [the] 48,000 [Massachusetts] shoemakers can make a shoe?

Mr. Litchman: I have no means of knowing, but I would venture to assert that not one-tenth of them can make a shoe, and the shoe that they could make would be the old kind of a turned shoe. I cannot make a machine shoe. My sixty-fourth part of making shoes is standing at the bench and cutting the uppers.

The Chairman: Still you might hang out a sign, "Boots and shoe made"; but the man who only makes pegs cannot say to the world, "Here is a shoemaking shop."

Mr. Litchman: No, Sir. Of course, the man who makes pegs would not be called a shoemaker anyhow. . . .

The Chairman: Does this rule which you have applied to the manufacturing of shoes apply to all other branches of manufacturing industry?

Mr. Litchman: It does substantially. I have no hesitation in saying that. It applies to every trade, not even excepting stone cutting. . . .

Document 20.2

THE CONDITION OF DEPENDENCE: UNEMPLOYMENT

Unemployment at different times resulted from technological change, seasonal patterns of work, and cyclical fluctuations.

SEASONAL WORK

(From Massachusetts Bureau of Labor Statistics, "Testimony of Unidentified Worker," *Annual Report, 1870–1871* [Boston, 1871], pp. 242–43)

. . . Since the old system of working in little shops was abandoned for that of large manufactories, there has been a steady diminution in the length of the working season per year. Before the time of factories, there would be a steady run of employment for from seven to ten years, only interrupted by commercial depressions or revulsions. The working hours would be from twelve to fifteen. The season for lighting up was from September 20 to May 20. Since that time, there has never been a year of steady work. At first a month only would be lost; now it has got so that we lose over four months' time every year. The system is worse here than elsewhere because machinery has been thoroughly introduced.

In January, 1874, the Federal Council of the International Workingmen's Association urged Congressman Benjamin Butler to support a bill that would "provide for all citizens who desire to settle on the public lands with transportation for themselves and families, and also lumber, seed, tools, food and all other necessaries for their establishment as farmers on the public lands for the term of one year, cost of same . . . to be a mortgage on their farm." This petition appeared in the *New York Sun* and caused Emanuel Richards to write to that newspaper.

CYCLICAL UNEMPLOYMENT

(From Emanuel Richards to the editor, *New York Sun*, January 15, 1874)

Sir: The petition . . . to the Government to settle the poor on public lands . . . [is] what I have long desired and hoped for. I am a good mechanic with a family of seven children. I have no work and no hope of anything better for myself than a life of dependence, crime, or hard hand-to-mouth labor. I would like to take my children out of the city. I can till the ground. I hope you will be in this . . . the friend of the people, and help us to an independent, useful life on the great prairies of the West.

Document 20.3

THE CONDITION OF DEPENDENCE: WORK CONTRACTS

Located in Johnstown, Pennsylvania, the Cambria Iron Works, according to the *New York Times,* was the "finest iron works in the country and one of the glories of Pennsylvania industry." The *Times* made its observation because the mill included four modern blast furnaces, forty-two double-turn puddling furnaces, and more than five thousand workers. In April, 1874, after a bitter dispute with its coal miners, the Cambria managers introduced a new contract, and the trade journal *Iron Age* admonished its readers: "If every employer in the country would adopt the same policy as that adopted by the Cambria Company and a few other large works, we would soon have an end of this whole wretched business of trade union tyranny."

RULES ADOPTED BY THE CAMBRIA IRON WORKS, APRIL 6, 1874

(From "Rules Adopted by the Cambria Iron Works, April 6, 1874," printed in *Iron Age*, December 31, 1874)

. . . .

9. Any person or persons known to belong to any secret association or open combination whose aim is to control wages or stop the works, or any part thereof, shall be promptly and finally discharged. Persons not satisfied with their work or their wages can leave honorably by giving the required notice; and persons quitting work, or inducing, or attempting to induce others to quit work other than in the manner prescribed in

these rules and regulations, shall forfeit whatever may be due or owing to such person or persons absolutely.

10. Any person going to work intoxicated, or absenting himself from work, without having previously given notice and obtained leave, will be discharged or fined, at the option of the company. Any person failing to do his work in a proper manner, or failing to do a satisfactory amount, may expect to be dismissed whenever it may suit the convenience of the company.

11. Quarreling or rioting about the works, or on the company's premises, shall be punished by a fine of not less than $5 nor more than $10, or the discharge of the offender, who may also be prosecuted for violation of the law.

12. All money collected as fines and penalties will be set apart and reserved for those workers injured by accident.

. . . .

14. Persons detected in stealing coal will be charged the price of a load of coal for every lump so stolen . . . and for a repetition of the offense will be discharged.

15. Persons living in the company's houses will be charged for all damages done to the houses beyond the ordinary wear and tear, and will be compelled to leave at once upon ceasing to be employed by the company. In renting the houses, preference will always be given to those whose business requires them to live near the works.

. . . .

19. In hiring, promoting, and discharging workmen, superintendents and foremen must regard only the interest of the company and the merits of employees.

P. Lorillard & Company, the largest tobacco manufacturer in the country, had its works in Jersey City, New Jersey, and employed nearly four thousand men, women, and children, including large numbers of recent immigrants, in the manufacture of smoking tobacco, chewing tobacco, and snuff. In 1880, it offered these workers a new contract.

A TOBACCO FACTORY, 1880

(From contract enclosed in Dick ———— to the editor, n.d., *Fall River Labor Standard*, June 5, 1880)

I, the undersigned, in consideration of employment being furnished to me and wages agreed to be paid me, by the firm of P. Lorillard & Co., do hereby agree and covenant with the said firm, its survivors, successors and assigns, to allow the said firm, or its proper agent or agents for the purpose appointed, to search and examine my person, clothing or other personal effects and property, at any and all times while I am upon the premises of said firm, or while leaving the said premises; and also to allow the said firm, or its proper agents, to enter and search my house or place of abode, without suit, let, hinderance, or molestation, with a view to detect and ascertain whether I have taken or secreted any of the goods, wares, tools or any other property of the said firm; and law, custom, or enactment to the contrary notwithstanding. And I do further, for the consideration above named, agree that all injury to life, limb, body, or health, by reason of my employment by said firm shall be at my own risk, and I . . . will not use or prosecute said firm for damage by reason of any such injury that may occur to me, in or upon the premises of the said firm or when about the business of the said firm. And I hereby covenant that I will faithfully observe and keep the rules of said firm, for the government of employees, which said rules are hereby made a part of this agreement; and will promptly obey the orders of my foreman, and other superiors in said employment. Witness my hand this _____ day of _____ 18__.

Document 20.4

THE CONDITION OF DEPENDENCE: HEALTH AND THE FACTORY SYSTEM

Five hundred cigar workers and their supporters met in Germania Hall, New York City, in September, 1874, to protest against tenement-house cigar manufacturing. This meeting started a long campaign for legislation to abolish work of this kind in the home. The following resolution was passed.

TENEMENT-HOUSE MANUFACTURING

(From the *New York Sun*, September 28, 1874)

. . . It has become the custom of many cigar manufacturers in this city to rent tenement houses, fill them with families of cigar makers, and carry on the trade of cigar making therein. These houses are used to serve as a workshop, a packing, sleeping, and dwelling room without an opportunity to purify the locality from the odor of moist tobacco. It has been proven by physicians and a committee of investigation that small pox and other contagious diseases have infected some of these tenement houses. The neighborhood and the city are threatened by disease, and are in constant danger thereof . . . [because] these poison-breeding shops are permitted to exist. The consumers of these articles, when made by workmen so affected, are likewise threatened with infection, and their health endangered in an alarming way. It is the sacred and bounden duty of the Board of Health to remove all shops of this kind because the Board has been created solely to protect the inhabitants of the city in their health. . . .

Constant contact with the cotton factory workers in Fall River led Dr. John B. Whitaker to write the following letter to the Massachusets Bureau of Labor Satistics in 1871.

A MEDICAL REPORT

(From Dr. John B. Whitaker, Fall River, 1871, to the gentlemen of the Massachusetts Bureau of Labor Statistics, printed in Massachusetts Bureau of Labor Statistics, *Annual Report, 1870–1871* [Boston, 1871], pp. 504–6)

. . . 1. Accidents and casualties are very numerous, partly owing to the exposed machinery and partly owing to carelessness. . . . It is really painful to go round among the operatives and find the hands and fingers mutilated, in consequence of accidents. 2. Unnatural or monotonous working positions . . . in some cases [make the worker] round-shouldered, in other cases producing curvature of the spine and bow-legs. 3. Exhaustion from overwork. In consequence of the long hours of labor, the great speed the machinery is run at, the large number of looms the weavers tend, and the general overtasking, so much exhaustion is produced, in most cases, that immediately after taking supper, the tired operatives drop to sleep in their chairs. . . . 4. Work by artificial light. It is very injurious to the eyes. The affections consist principally in conjunctiviti, opacity of cornea, granulations of the lids, &c. 5. The inhalation of foreign articles. . . . I have been called to cases where I suspected this to be the cause of trouble in the stomach. After giving an emetic, they have in some cases vomited little balls of cotton. . . . 10. Predisposition to pelvic diseases . . . among the female factory operatives produces difficulty in parturition. The necessity for instrumental delivery has very much increased within a few years, owing to the females working in the mills while they are pregnant and in consequence of deformed pelvis. . . . 11. . . . Predisposition to sexual abuse. There is no doubt that this is very much increased, the passions being excited by contact and loose conversation. . . . They are, also, as a general thing, ignorant—at least to the extent that they do not know how to control their passions nor to realize the consequences. . . . 12. Predisposition to depression of spirits. . . . Factory life predisposes very much to depression of spirits. Hence you see the careworn haggard look, the dull expression of the eye. . . . Hypochondria and hysteria are quite common amongst the females. . . . 15. Connection between continuous factory labor and premature old age. . . . Very few live to be old that work in a factory. . . . With regard to provision on the part of the operative, for sickness there is none, they having about as much as they can do to live while they are able to work. When sickness comes, they have either to assume debts they will never be able to pay, or call upon the city or State to take care of them. . . .

Document 20.5

THE CONDITION OF DEPENDENCE: CHILD LABOR

A Fall River textile worker criticized the use of children in factories before a special investigating committee appointed by the Massachusetts legislature in the 1860's.

A SEVEN-YEAR-OLD

(From "Testimony of John Wild," *Massachusetts Report of Special Committee on the Hours of Labor and the Condition and Prospects of the Industrial Classes*, Massachusetts House Document No. 98 [Boston, n.d.], p. 6)

Question: How old are the children? *Answer:* Seven and eight. *Question:* Have you a child of seven working in the mills? *Answer:* Yes, I have. . . . *Question:* Does he get any schooling now? *Answer:* When he gets done in the mill, he is ready to go to bed. He has to be in the mill ten minutes before we start up, to wind spindles. Then he starts about his own work and keeps on till dinner time. Then he goes home, starts again at one and works till seven. When he's done he's tired enough to go to bed. Some days he has to clean and help scour during dinner hour. . . . Some days he has to clean spindles. Saturdays he's in all day.

The overseer who gave this testimony had seventeen years' experience in the Massachusetts cotton mills.

A KINDLY OVERSEER

(From Massachusetts Bureau of Labor Statistics, *Annual Report, 1870–1871* [Boston, 1871], p. 126)

. . . Six years ago I ran night work from 6:45 P.M. to 6 A.M. with 45 minutes for meals, eating in the room. The children were drowsy and sleepy. [I] have known them to fall asleep standing up at their work. I have had to sprinkle water in their faces to arouse them after having spoken to them till hoarse; this was done gently and without any intention of hurting them.

Otis G. Lynch, superintendent of the Enterprise Manufacturing Company, which employed 100 children between the ages of 10 and 15 years among its 485 workers in an Augusta, Georgia, cotton mill, explained his attitude toward child labor to a United States Senate committee in 1883.

A SOUTHERN FACTORY

(From "Testimony of Otis G. Lynch, Augusta, Georgia," *Report of the Committee of the Senate upon the Relations between Labor and Capital,* Vol. IV [Washington, D.C.: U.S. Government Printing Office, 1885], pp. 748–58)

Q. Is it a good thing according to your experience that children of from ten to fifteen years of age should work in the factories?—*A.* I think it would be better for them if they were not compelled to work at all, but,—

Q. (Interposing). You would want them to work a part of the time in order to learn a business for life, would you not?—*A.* Yes, sir. Circumstances now force them into the mill. They come in with their mothers.

. . . .

Q. You think, I suppose, that it would be better for the children to have a chance to be outdoors?—*A.* Yes, sir.

Q. But the testimony is that many of those children seem to enjoy their work in the factory.—*A.* Oh, yes. It is not laborious work, and it is not continuous; there is more or less rest as they go along.

Q. Not much play, I suppose?—*A.* Some little; not much. Of course, we have discipline in the mill, but the labor is not continuous or excessive.

Q. Do the children remain in the mill during the whole eleven hours as the older operatives do?—*A.* Yes.

. . . .

Q. . . . If you lost your present supply of white labor you think that you would be compelled to substitute foreign white labor rather than negro labor?—*A.* Yes.

Q. For some reason or other the negro is not well adapted to cotton manufacturing, I take it?—*A.* He is not adapted to the management of intricate machinery.

Q. But this intricate machinery is not so troublesome but what ten-year-old white people can take care of it and run much of it?—*A.* Oh, the colored people can be used in factories if circumstances should make it necessary.

Document 20.6

THE CONDITION OF DEPENDENCE: LIFE OUTSIDE THE MILL OR MINE

In 1877 the Ohio Commissioner of Labor asked for detailed descriptions from coal and iron ore miners about the prevalence and the character of store pay, scrip money, and "company stores" in the coal and iron ore regions. The responses printed below are by a coal miner in Athens County and an ore digger in Lucas County.

THE "COMPANY STORE"

(From Ohio Bureau of Labor Statistics, "The Payment of Wages," *Annual Report, 1877* [Columbus, 1878], pp. 156–92)

Lucas County.   Store pay is our ruin. . . . The store keeps no meat, no potatoes, no lard, and the most of the time this summer no flour, no butter, no eggs; but we can get hominy at 5 cents per pound, crackers at 10 cents per pound, and rice at 10 cents per pound. Now, it must be evident, that if I work for store-pay, and the store has no meat, I must go without it; and if they have no flour, I must buy crackers. If we were paid in cash, we could go to Toledo, and save, at least, 40 per cent. . . . How can a man be a moral, liberty-loving citizen, when he can not send his children to school for want of clothes, or take his wife to church in decent attire?

Athens County.   . . . When a man's work is done, it is money that is due him, yet he must take just what he can get, or do without. If he sues for it a stay is taken, and his family can starve. There should be no stay on the wages of labor, and the man or company should be compelled under penalty to pay wages every two weeks, in currency. . . . We cannot exchange . . . [the store money] with farmers or others. A farmer comes to my door. He has produce, just what I need. He sells for thirty cents. He also wants something out of the store, and would willingly give me the produce and take the "check" on the store, but the store will not receive the check from him, so he is obliged to sell his produce to the store, and I am forced to pay the store forty cents for the article I could have bought for thirty cents. . . .

Document 20.7

THE REAFFIRMATION OF INDIVIDUAL RESPONSIBILITY IN AN INDUSTRIAL SOCIETY

Employers vigorously defended their prerogatives and criticized efforts by trade unions and city or state governments to interfere with their freedom of action. They often drew support from eminent social theorists. Henry V. Rothschild manufactured wholesale clothing in New York City, and J. H. Walker owned a shoe factory in Worcester, Massachusetts. William Graham Sumner was Professor of Political and Social Science at Yale College. All three testified before a Congressional committee in 1878.

HENRY V. ROTHSCHILD

(From *Investigation by a Select Committee of the House of Representatives Relative to the Causes of the General Depression in Labor and Business,* 45th Congress, 3d Session, Miscellaneous House Document No. 29 [Washington, D.C.: U.S. Government Printing Office, 1879], pp. 131–36)

. . . .

Q. Your remedy is, for the moral improvement of the working classes, to keep them so busy that they cannot indulge in dissipation?—*A.* That is a most significant point, and it is the only form in which the workingman can be improved. . . . I say the legislature has no right to encroach upon me as to whether I shall employ men eight hours, or ten, or fifteen hours. It is a matter of mutual agreement, and the legislature has no right, according to the principles of the Declaration of Independence, to impose upon me what hours of labor I shall have between myself and my employes. . . . Political economy teaches us that the laborers and the capitalists are two different forms of society. . . . The laborer should do as good as he can for himself, and the capitalist should do as good as he can for himself; it is a matter between the laborer and the capitalist.

Q. You think the community have no interest in that question at all?—*A.* They have an interest so far as if an unprincipled employer tyrannizes in some way over the laborer; that is a different thing.

Q. How would you interfere in that case—by legislation or not?—*A.* If a tyranny arises, from which we are not amply protected at the present day, the legislature can always interfere, without a doubt. But this is no tyranny, if the contract arises between a laborer and the employer. The horse-car drivers of New York are employing their hands

14 and 16 hours a day. They are all willing to work; they are not bound to accept the labor; it is a matter between themselves and their employers.

Q. But do they want to work that length of time?—A. All labor is irksome.

J. H. WALKER

(From *Investigation by a Select Committee of the House of Representatives Relative to the Causes of the General Depression in Labor and Business*, 45th Congress, 3d Session, Miscellaneous House Document No. 29 [Washington, D.C.: U.S. Government Printing Office, 1879], pp. 181–208)

Q. The most important fact before this committee is that we have in this country a large amount of unemployed labor.—A. A man might just as well hang himself because he has a boil, as to talk about changing our laws or institutions because the country has a local ache just now.

Q. What remedy are we to take for this surplus population?— A. Leave them alone; that is the remedy.

Q. You think they will take care of themselves?—A. Let them alone. "The man who will not work shall not eat."

.   .   .   .

Q. Are we to have these panics in the future as we have had them? Can they be avoided?—A. Nothing will prevent "panics" until human nature is radically changed. Their comparative severity will increase with advancing civilization, unless the disposition to protect themselves . . . by saving a portion of their earnings is more universal among the people than it now is. . . . The laws and institutions of the country can no more be adjusted to them than they can be to the condition of yellow fever. . . .

WILLIAM GRAHAM SUMNER

(From *Investigation by a Select Committee of the House of Representatives Relative to the Causes of the General Depression in Labor and Business*, 45th Congress, 3d Session, Miscellaneous House Document No. 29 [Washington, D.C.: U.S. Government Printing Office, 1879], pp. 310–21)

Q. What is the effect of machinery on those laborers whom for the time being it turns out of employment?—A. For the time being they suffer, of course, a loss of income and a loss of comfort. . . .

Q. Is there any way to help it?—A. Not at all. There is no way on earth to help it. The only way is to meet it bravely, go ahead, make the best of circumstances; and if you cannot go on in the way you were going, try another way, and still another until you work yourself out as an individual. . . .

Q. Do you admit that there is what you call distress among the laboring classes of this country?—*A*. No sir; I do not admit any such thing. I cannot get evidence of it. . . . I do not know of anything that the government can do that is at all specific to assist labor—to assist noncapitalists. The only things that the government can do are generally things such as are in the province of a government. The general things that a government can do to assist the non-capitalist in the accumulation of capital (for that is what he wants) are two things. The first thing is to give him the greatest possible liberty in the directing of his own energies for his own development, and the second is to give him the greatest possible security in the possession and use of the products of his own industry. I do not see any more than that that a government can do. . . . Society does not owe any man a living. In all cases that I have ever known of young men who claimed that society owed them a living, it has turned out that society paid—in the State prison. I do not see any other result. . . . The fact that a man is here is no demand upon other people that they shall keep him alive and sustain him. He has got to fight the battle with nature as every other man has; and if he fights it with the same energy and enterprise and skill and industry as any other man, I cannot imagine his failing—that is, misfortune apart. . . .

Document 20.8

THE RESPONSE TO DEPENDENCE: THE RAILROAD STRIKES OF 1877

The railroad strikes of 1877 affected the entire nation and, for the first time, made the labor question a national one. The destruction of life and property in several cities brought home to many the impact of the industrial order on the wage-earning classes. Responses varied. Henry Ward Beecher, the prominent Protestant minister, addressed his followers in Brooklyn's Plymouth Church. A. C. Buell was special correspondent in New York City for the *New Orleans Daily Democrat*.

THE REVEREND HENRY WARD BEECHER

(From the *New York Times*, July 30, 1877)

. . . It is true that $1 a day is not enough to support a man and five children, if the man insists on smoking and drinking beer. Is not a dollar a day enough to buy bread? Water costs nothing. Men cannot live by bread, it is true; but the man who cannot live on bread and water is not fit to live. When a man is educated away from the power of self-denial, he is falsely educated. A family may live on good bread and water in the morning, water and bread and midday, and good water and bread at night. Such may be called the bread of affliction, but it is fit that man should eat the bread of affliction. . . . The great laws of political economy cannot be set at defiance.

A. C. BUELL

(From A. C. Buell, special correspondent, New York, July 30, 1877, *New Orleans Daily Democrat*, August 4, 1877)

. . . The most striking fact developed by this movement is the terrible antipathy which has grown up among the poor and laboring classes against those who possess great wealth. . . . John Jones and William Smith, laborers, regard William H. Vanderbilt, Jay Gould, and Tom Scott, capitalists, as their natural enemies, whose welfare means their loss and whose downfall would redound to their gain. . . . To-day, Tom Scott could not get through Pittsburgh, or Vanderbilt through Buffalo, alive! . . . You may call it whatsoever name you please—Communism, Agrarianism, Socialism, or anything else— . . . in the estimation of the vast majority of the American people the millionaire has come to be looked upon as a public enemy! . . . We have just now had a foretaste of real Civil War; of that conflict of classes, which is the most terrible of all species of war. . . . The inadequacy of the present governmental system to combat servile insurrections has been forced home upon the capitalistic classes as a fact that can no longer be evaded. . . . The average citizen may forget the danger as soon as it is past, but not the man of millions. He has seen the ghost of the Commune, and it will stalk his dreams every night until he can feel with his prototype of the old world the security of mercenary bayonets enough to garrison every considerable town. . . .

Document 20.9

OPPOSITION TO DEPENDENCE

Martin A. Foran, President of the Coopers' International Union in the early 1870's and later an Ohio Congressman, disputed the popular contention that the government could not interfere in relations between employers and their workers. He spoke in Indianapolis in December, 1873, a few months after the start of a severe depression.

MARTIN A. FORAN

(From speech by Martin A. Foran printed in *Coopers' New Monthly*, Vol. I [January, 1874], pp. 5–6)

. . . We hear a great deal about the presumptuous absurdity of asking the government to interpose its protecting arm in behalf of the people in emergencies and crises of the nature through which we are now passing. We are told that doing so is a strange and unusual proceeding in free America, . . . that to do so would recognize a principle at variance with the spirit and genius of our institutions. . . . What, permit me to ask, is the object of government? Why do we form governments? Is it not for the purpose of having each citizen protected in all his social rights and privileges? Why give up, surrender a portion of our natural rights, those rights which God has given in *ventre sa mere*, unless it be for the purpose of having the balance of them more securely and safely protected? Certainly, the object of a true Democratic government is not to confer exclusive privileges and artificial rights upon a very small portion of the people. . . . It is the conferring of such exclusive rights, powers, and priviliges upon corporate monopolies, national banks, especially, that has brought upon us the present panic. . . . Should we not demand, are we not justified in demanding from the sovereign power a revocation of the laws that have entailed upon us these evils? If not, then, it were better we had no government at all. . . . How shall the people be saved? Simply by repealing bad or class legislation, and by enacting wise, salutary laws, such laws, and such only, as will beneficially affect, not banks or railroads, not any special class, but such as will beneficially affect the whole people. . . .

Craft workers often argued that the principle of *scarcity* would work to their advantage and maintain or improve their status and condition. At times, such arguments meant the exclusion of ethnically different groups. The following circular was distributed by Atlanta workers in 1875. Similar documents urged the exclusion of immigrants, especially Chinese workers. The principle of scarcity was put forth in all parts of the country.

ATLANTA WORKERS

(From petition printed in *Iron Age*, July 22, 1875, p. 14)

We, the undersigned mechanics and working men, appreciating the difficulties that beset us on every hand, and which, through the cupidity of certain proprietors, contractors, and capitalists, whose greed of gain would force us into hopeless poverty, and thus virtually enslave us and our children forever, hereby, individually and collectively, pledge our sacred honor that from and after this date—

1. We will not deal in a business way, or support for public office, any man or men (whether grocer, dry goods, provision or other dealer) who oppresses us by employing negro instead of skilled white labor.

2. We will not trade with any retail dealer who purchases his supplies from a man or men who employ negro instead of skilled white labor.

3. We will not rent a house or houses owned by persons who employ negro to the exclusion of skilled white labor in their construction or repairs.

In 1883, Adolph Strasser and Samuel Gompers, leaders of the cigar workers, offered broader justifications for trade unions to a committee of the United States Senate.

ADOLPH STRASSER

(From *Report of the Committee of the Senate upon the Relations between Labor and Capital, 1883*, Vol. I [Washington, D.C.: U.S. Government Printing Office, 1885], pp. 294–95, 373–75)

. . . We have no ultimate ends. We are going on from day to day. We are fighting only for immediate objects—objects that can be realized in a few years. . . . We want to dress better and to live better, and become better off and better citizens generally. . . . No well-organized trade [union] can be riotous. New organizations having no funds to back them may become desperate and may do damage to property, but when a trade is well organized you will find that no violence will be committed under such conditions. . . .

SAMUEL GOMPERS

(From *Report of the Committee of the Senate upon the Relations between Labor and Capital, 1883*, Vol. I [Washington, D.C.: U.S. Government Printing Office, 1885], p. 460)

. . . If you wish to improve the condition of the people, you must improve their habits and customs. The reduction of the hours of labor reaches the very root of society. It gives the workingmen better conditions and better opportunities, and makes of him what has been too long neglected—a consumer instead of a mere producer. . . . A man who goes to his work before the dawn of the day requires no clean shirt to go to work in, but is content to go in an old overall or anything that will cover his members; but a man who goes to work at 8 o'clock in the morning wants a clean shirt; he is afraid his friends will see him, so he does not want to be dirty. He also requires a newspaper; while a man who goes to work early in the morning and stays at it late at night does not need a newspaper, for he has no time to read, requiring all the time he has to recuperate his strength sufficiently to get ready for his next day's work. . . . The general reduction of the hours per day . . . would create a greater spirit in the working man; it would make him a better citizen, a better father, a better husband, a better man in general. . . . The trades unions are not what too many men have been led to believe they are, importations from Europe. . . . Modern industry evolves these organizations out of the existing conditions where there are two classes in society, one incessantly striving to obtain the labor of the other class for as little as possible . . . ; and the members of the other class being, as individuals, utterly helpless in a contest with their employers, naturally resort to combinations to improve their condition, and, in fact, they are forced by the conditions which surround them to organize for self-protection. Hence trade unions. . . . Wherever trades unions have organized and are most firmly organized, there are the rights of the people respected. . . . I believe that the existence of the trades-union movement, more especially where the unionists are better organized, has evoked a spirit and a demand for reform, but has held in check the more radical elements in society. . . .

21

THEODORE SALOUTOS
University of California in Los Angeles

Populism Re-examined

POPULISM HAS MEANT different things to different people. To its more hostile critics, it was the sponsor of the wildest monetary schemes of the day. To the Populists themselves, Populism was a crusade in behalf of political and economic democracy that was entitled to the respect of all righteous citizens. Sympathetic scholars have viewed it as a reminder of the passing of the frontier and a warning for the federal government to adopt a more positive role in economic affairs. Still others consider it as the agrarian response to an emerging industrial order. Within recent years a handful of writers have claimed that in Populism are to be found the roots of American Fascism.

Which of these analyses should one accept? Since the heyday of Populism, our experiences would indicate that it was a more involved effort, one that attempted to get to the roots of the problems of the day. It has become patently evident that the Populists were more constructive and farsighted in their approach than their harshest critics would have us believe.

Basically, Populism was a dramatic protest against those sweeping changes of the post-Civil War decades that were downgrading agriculture and upgrading the profit-making nonagricultural interests of the nation. It was middle-class in its orientation and sectional in its appeal. It sought to cushion the effects of these changes, to right the imbalance, and restore agriculture to its position of pre-eminence by sponsoring a program of direct political action built chiefly upon the aims and aspirations of the Grangers, Farmers Alliance men, and lesser groups. Its principles, although born and bred in rural America, were found adaptable to the needs of urban America.

The Populists were practical people who grappled with problems demanding immediate solutions instead of with justifications for some theoretical position they had assumed. They recognized that farmers were fighting with backs to the wall in an effort to preserve their way of life from forces that threatened to uproot it. From the one side, farmers were being pressed by a disappearing agricultural frontier, the unprofitableness of farming, and the breaking-up of the farm family; from the other, by a dynamic industrialism, growing cities, mammoth corporations, corrupt political machines, and swarms of immigrants. The America they knew, or believed they knew, was being ground to bits by a new, foreign, and frightening America they did not understand.

The more immediate grievances of the Populists are a matter of common knowledge. Farmers in the West complained of a long procession of low prices, heavy debts, high interest rates, farm foreclosures, and tenancy. Droughts, blizzards, grasshoppers, insects, and floods compounded their woes. Farmers in the South, too, were weighed down by these burdens, plus sharecropping, the crop-liens system, and the petty tyrannies of the country merchants.

Even the concept of "economic growth," which has become a major concern to our economists, did not escape the probing minds of the Populists. One of their more perceptive philosophers observed that the growth of agriculture lagged behind that of railroading, banking, and manufacturing. One may quibble with the accuracy of their statistics and the rate at which the various sectors of the economy grew, but certainly not with the idea of contrasting the rate of growth. The Populist Senator William A. Peffer of Kansas found that from 1850 to 1880, railroading had grown by more than 700 per cent, which was far above the general average of 500; banking by more than 900 per cent; and manufacturing by more than 800 per cent. Agriculture' s rate of growth did not exceed 200 per cent. In short, the Senator was showing the "railroad builder, the banker, miner, and manufacturing growing richer, . . . the farmer and his co-worker poorer as the years pass."

All this had a painful effect on the farmers, who had always believed that they were the mainstay of the American economy. For these ailing agriculturists comprised the bulk of the population, paid most of the taxes, produced the food and raw materials that sustained life, and kept going the wheels of industry, commerce, and finance. And unless these farmers, who were struggling for their economic life, were rescued, the agricultural America which nurtured them and so many of their leaders in government, business, and industry was in jeopardy.

For these reasons, rural society had to be cleansed and provision made for training of future farmers and leaders. Agriculture needed to regain its economic health. The Populists were convinced that farming was the most fundamental of all occupations—so fundamental that survival of the nation and civilization hinged upon its prosperity and prestige. As the farmers fared, so fared America.

Whether one agrees with the Populists' rationale is beside the point. They believed they were right; so did many of their disciples, who accepted the tenets of Populism in the spirit in which they accepted the teachings of the Bible. In the final analysis, what they believed was more important than the truth itself.

By the late nineteenth century, many, if not most, farmers had been cured of their pathological distrust of a strong central government. Low farm prices, high production costs, mortgage indebtedness, rising tenancy, dry summers, severe winters, and poor crops had left thousands of them in dire straits. Their inability to strike a good bargain with merchants, buyers, bankers, and large corporations caused them to look to the federal government as an ally.

The Populists, in charting their course of action, surveyed the agrarian strategy of the recent past and found it wanting. Farmers and their leaders erroneously had assumed that voluntary economic action such as group buying and selling, better farming practices, diversified production, and cheaper credit facilities would bring the necessary relief and correct the imbalance. What farmers needed was vigorous, well-directed, and assertive leadership, not half-measures, balance-of-power politics with apologetic overtones. These goals had to be reinforced with a vigorous program of political action by the farmers themselves.

But to influence the government and control it, the farmers had to build a People's party comprised of rank-and-file producers. They had to buttress their economic program with a political crusade aimed at the extermination of those elements that preyed on them. And the farmers were the logical ones to head this crusade, for they were the most numerous, suffered the most, and had the experience to guide them in their quest for justice.

Populist leaders were a striking and colorful lot. The ferocious, acid-tongued Tom Watson of Georgia was one of the more eloquent. Champion of the underdog and then a friend of the Negro, Watson spoke endlessly about the money question, monopolies, and the sham of reform from within the major parties. Obstinate and strong-minded Davis H. Waite of Colorado concentrated on railroad legislation and the silver question. To his foes, he was known as "Bloody Bridles" Waite, as a result of a speech in which he said: "It is better, infinitely better, that blood should flow to the horses' bridles rather than our national liberties should be destroyed."

An interesting triumvirate came from Kansas. "Sockless Jerry"

Simpson, according to one account, got his sobriquet during the Congressional campaign of 1890 when he accused his opponent of wearing "silk stockings." Subsequently, someone retorted that Simpson wore no socks at all; hence the "Sockless Jerry." A dynamic speaker with a large following, Simpson's chief grievance was the railroads and their influence. Senator William A. Peffer, or "Whiskers" Peffer, was a learned and capable man who wrote and spoke on a wide variety of subjects. Although described as "a well-meaning, pin-headed anarchistic crank," Peffer was far better informed than his critics believed. The most unusual was the Irish-born and Irish-tempered Mary Elizabeth Lease. A tall, slim, attractive woman with a flair for oratory, she went up and down Kansas telling farmers to "raise less corn and more hell." The appearance of this "Patrick Henry in petticoats" on the Populist platform was evidence that women were finding their way in the reform movement and that the farmers were advocates of women's rights.

Populism was built on more than the shopworn argument that the producers were a sound and virtuous people. It was founded, in part, on a felt need for articulate spokesmen of agrarian democracy. Its leaders argued with a high degree of indignation that farmers and wage earners deserved and had to have greater representation in a government hitherto dominated by lawyers, millionaires, financiers, and their allies. The basic needs of the people must be satisfied and the integrity of the government restored.

If virtuous and industrious farmers filled the legislative chambers, they would find themselves strategically placed to challenge those self-seeking interests that obstructed the channels of economic and social justice. They might even gain control of the government and marshal its resources—that is, the resources of the people—and regulate the corporations and financial empires which had a strangle hold on the economic life of the nation. They might eliminate fraudulent business practices, assure honest elections, preserve competition, restrict immigration, block alien and corporate land controls, and perhaps revive most of the prosperity that had been choked off.

Although high in praise of the virtues and values of an agrarian order, the Populists had no intention of turning the clock backward, stifling industrialism, and checking material progress. They wanted reforms within the framework of a democratic capitalism, reforms that would give producers a fairer share for their labors and a greater voice in the government. They asked only for prosperity in place of privation, and representation in place of misrepresentation.

The Populists considered solution of the money crisis a prime requisite to recovery. With undeniable sincerity, if not always with learned accuracy, they argued that the population, industry, commerce, and transportation of the country had been increasing at a faster pace than money in circulation. This disparity, in turn, precipitated a fierce competitive struggle among borrowers for the limited quantities of money, forced up interest rates, and made it difficult for the small producers to borrow. Shortage of money placed the farmer in particular in a disadvantageous position, depressed his prices, and forced him to give more products for less money.

The Populist solution was for the federal government to pump more money into circulation and to assume the initiative in liberalizing the nation's credit. A judicious amount of inflation, Populists believed, was good not only for debtors but also for business elements in need of finances to expand their operations. More money in circulation promised to raise farm prices, enable the farmers to pay their debts, bring down interest rates, and make it easier to borrow. In due time, this was expected to produce a chain reaction that would have a healthy and invigorating effect on the entire economy. The farmers would be able to buy more goods, produce more employment; farm surpluses would move into the market; wheels of prosperity would hum again. In effect, this was a form of Keynesianism before Keynes.

The Populists wanted a flexible financial system that would place money in the hands of farmers at harvesttime, when they needed it the most. Given their way, the Populists would have demolished the national banking structure and restricted the money-issuing power to the federal government, where it rightfully belonged. They would have authorized free and unlimited coinage of silver until it rose to $50 per capita, a sum considered sufficient to transact the business of the country on a cash basis.

Despite an emotional attachment to silver, Populist theoreticians actually were less concerned with the support that money had behind it than they were in having the federal government issue it. Such a responsibility could not be taken lightly, for only a government responsive to the needs of the people was truly responsible. Money, argued the Populists, obtained its value from the strength and prestige of the government that issued it, not from precious metals stored in government vaults. Paper money issued by a strong government was as sound as silver or gold money.

The Populists would pump this money into circulation through the Farmers' Alliance subtreasury plan, a land-loan scheme, or any other acceptable device. The subtreasury plan was viewed as a moneylending scheme by some and as a price-influencing mechanism by others.

Both the subtreasury and the land-loan ideas were based on the simple fact that farmers had two kinds of property to offer as collateral: their farmlands and their nonperishable products, such as cotton, wheat, oats, barley, and tobacco.

The subtreasury plan was a forerunner of numerous credit-issuing and price-influencing devices that gained popularity after the first World War. But in the 1890's, it was viewed as a harebrained scheme that could be supported only by the worst kind of money cranks. It called for creation of subtreasuries—which for all practical purposes amounted to government lending agencies and warehouses—where farmers could borrow at a nominal rate of interest up to as much as 80 per cent of the market value of the stored commodity.

A singular advantage of the plan, apart from its lending features, was that it would enable farmers to keep their products off the market during the rush season when prices could be forced down to unreasonable levels. The government could, if it chose, sell these products at any time during the year as a means of obtaining more favorable prices. This, too, was the germ of the orderly marketing philosophy that attracted widespread support after the first World War.

The land-loan idea likewise anticipated plans sponsored by various groups during the twentieth century. One Populist proposal asked for the granting of loans not in excess of $3,000 or more than 80 per cent of the cash value of the property offered as security. The loan was to mature within fifty years and carry no more than 2 per cent interest; applications for loans were to be received until the amount of money in circulation climbed to $50 per capita.

Here, in essence, was the Populist program for adjusting the nation's money and credit to an expanding economy: Confine the money-issuing power to the federal government, and issue money generously through a combination of loans on the land and crops of farmers. Within a reasonable time the prices the farmer received would begin rising; he would then pay his debts, increase his purchases, create jobs for city people, promote commerce, force interest rates to drop, and accelerate the recovery of the general economy, which was so dependent upon a healthy agriculture.

The Populists also had some positive views on landownership. According to their creed, man was placed on earth by the laws of God and nature, not by those of any political or economic system. Hence, man was entitled to as much land as he needed to make a living, and the government was obligated to see to it that he got it. Farmers, as producers, created all wealth; yet, they had little or no voice in the distribution of the land. Far too much land had fallen into the hands of railroads, corporations, and financiers, who preyed on the producers.

This prodigality had to be supplanted by a policy of responsibility. Among other things, the federal government was obligated henceforth to reserve all lands recovered from corporations as a consequence of their failure to abide by the provisions of their grants. It was also to safeguard remnants of the public lands for homesteads by actual settlers. Ownership by corporations had to be limited to legitimate business needs. Finally, ownership by aliens had to be eliminated, for as one Farmers Alliance paper wrote: "By allowing aliens to own the lands of the country the way is open for them to own the whole country."

Adequate transportation at reasonable rates was an important part of the Populist agenda. Since state and federal regulation allegedly had failed to provide it at reasonable rates, the Populists espoused government ownership of the railroads, and even of the telephone and telegraph lines.

The Populists likewise pleaded for a more equitable system of taxation, which would shift some of the farmers' burden to the recipients of large incomes. The general property tax, source of the bulk of the local and state revenues, was virtually a real property tax, except in the farming districts, where personal property was in view of the assessors and taxed. But in the cities, much, if not most, of the wealth in intangibles escaped taxation, since it was concealed from tax assessors. Consequently, a disproportionate share of the load fell on the shoulders of the farmers. Enactment of an income tax would help transfer a greater part of the tax burden to those who could afford to carry it: rich urban holders of securities, wealthy businessmen, and well-to-do members of the professional classes. And still one other change had to be inaugurated: Improvements on the land had to be exempted from taxation. Levies, according to the Populists, ought to be made in terms of the assessed value of the land, without reference to improvements added by labor.

In keeping with agrarian tradition, the Populists insisted that government expenditures be cut to the bone by a policy of honesty in public office and reduction in the salaries of all state and federal officials. This policy could be counted on to bring relief to the overburdened taxpayers.

Populism further sought to broaden the base of American democracy by bringing the people closer to their government, in the hope of checking the encroachment of special interests on their economic rights. This they would help accomplish through the direct election of United States senators. In theory, the direct election of senators would encourage more people to take a genuine interest in the affairs of government, weaken party domination over the Senate, lessen the influence of the privileged interests, and enhance that of the people. Moreover, it would make it far more difficult to corrupt the citizenry than the existent system, which confined the power of election to a few men in the state legislature. Finally, it would eliminate the evil of a deadlock in making selections, which in the past had sometimes left states unrepresented in the Senate. Certainly, if the people had the intelligence to choose judges, state legislatures, and congressmen, they could choose senators.

Adoption of the Australian ballot was still another vehicle for bringing the government closer to the people. Such would enable the citizen to take his ballot into the polling booth, where he could make his choice and cast it without anyone knowing how he voted.

Obviously, Populism held that society suffered from too little instead of too much democracy, and that the surest way of extending its scope was by distributing political and economic power over as many people as possible. The Populists believed in the ultimate goodness of man, the very premise on which democracy was based; that honesty and decency would ultimately triumph in a society that was money-mad. And Populism sought not the eradication of the profit system, but its reform, so that its benefits could be shared by more people. It sought all this through gradual, constitutional means, and within the framework of the existing social economy. It sought to make the profit system function in a more equitable fashion, not to destroy it.

The Populists have come under attack for embracing what is referred to as the conspiratorial philosophy of history, which viewed financiers, railroad owners, middlemen, and others as partners in a cabal to rob the common people, i.e., the producers, of their just rewards. The truth of the matter is that this was a widely held view over which the Populists had no monopoly. Civil service reformers, trade unionists, preachers of the social gospel, urban humanitarians, and others bemoaned the antisocial influences that the monied interests wielded over social and political institutions. Much, if not most, of the social legislation proposed by the Populists in the 1890's and by the Progressives in the following decade was geared to the undoing of these antisocial forces.

Populism hardly was encased in the class philosophy frequently ascribed to it by its critics and some of the ungrateful Progressives who borrowed copiously from its ideas. As spokesmen for agriculture, long the dominant occupation and source of wealth, the Populists were hardly more class-oriented than were the leaders of industry, finance, commerce, and labor. Unconcerned with and unschooled in the art of public relations, the Populists often used coarse and brutal language, but they spoke with sincerity. They believed that what was good for the farmers was good for the nation in the very same spirit that labor leaders claimed that what was good for the wage earner was good for the country, or as a corporation executive later more bluntly put it: "What is good for General Motors is good for America."

The ideology of Populism lived long after the movement itself had disintegrated and passed from the political scene. Many of its ideas were absorbed lock, stock, and barrel by the more adept Progressives, who benefited from the years of agitation and economic prosperity denied the Populists. "Might-have-beens" do not fall properly within the scope of the historian, but one may wonder how far Wilsonian liberalism would have progressed if during the New Freedom period the business cycle had been on the downgrade instead of the upgrade.

The Wilsonian elements, with roots in the agrarian past, more so than any other segment of the Progressive movement, strengthened Populism. By 1912, much, if not most, of what the Populists espoused had gained respectability and a larger following. The income tax, for example, was placed on the statute books; it began to place some of the tax burden on those who could best afford to bear it and made available useful data to the lawmakers. The Federal Reserve Act, the most important piece of financial legislation enacted since Civil War years, was designed in part to meet the money and credit needs of the farmers. In this respect, it was a disappointment, but its defects were partly overcome with the passage of the Federal Farm Loan Act and the Federal Warehouse Act. Both had familiar Populist overtones. The former offered mortgage facilities to those who otherwise might have had difficulties in obtaining them; the latter enabled farmers to store their products, obtain loans on them, and even anticipate higher prices.

Populism may be properly considered the political forebear of the Nonpartisan League, the farmer-labor party idea, and even of LaFollette Progressivism. Long-standing grievances against middlemen, financiers, corporations, and special interests temporarily stirred farmers and trade unionists to adopt a common course of action.

Yet, there were notable differences in general strategy and tactics, and even in the source of leadership. Populism favored formation of a new party, adoption of its own platform, and nomination of its own candidates. It drew heavily from the leadership of the Farmers Alliance. The Nonpartisan League, on the other hand, discarded the new party strategy, preferred playing balance-of-power politics from within one of the major parties, and relied for leadership in part on ex-socialists and members of the American Society of Equity. The League's strategy was one of political expediency: obtaining a favorable bargaining position within the party or even controlling it. It also went several steps beyond the Populists in demanding that the state government of North Dakota take a more direct hand in the economic life of the farmer by building state-owned mills, elevators, banks, and industries. Despite these differences, the Populists and the Nonpartisan Leaguers were agreed on the need for farmers to take a more active role in politics.

The farmer-labor party idea was more a lineal descendant of the Populists than was the Nonpartisan League, even though it was inspired by Nonpartisan Leaguers who had become disenchanted with balance-of-power politics and belatedly felt the need for a new party. Unlike the Populist party, this new coalition appealed more to trade unionists than to farmers, giving indication that the spearhead of liberalism had become urban-industrial. But its sponsors believed that farmers and wage earners had sufficient interests in common to wage successful campaigns in behalf of public utility regulation, progressive income taxes, government assistance to farmers, and shorter hours and better wages for employees.

The LaFollette Progressives, frequently treated in the Populist tradition, sought unsuccessfully to build a party on an amorphous middle-class base in which occupational lines were blurred. The principal difference between the LaFollette Progressives and the farmer-laborites was that the platform of the former had less of a doctrinaire quality about it.

Echoes of the Populist philosophy were heard in other quarters as well during the 1920's and 1930's, when Old Dealers and New Dealers stressed the benefits to be had by farmers from storing their crops in warehouses, obtaining credit from the government, and marketing their products in an orderly manner. Populist philosophy affected the various commodity pools of the 1920's, the Federal Farm Board of Herbert Hoover, and the Ever-Normal Granary Plan of Henry A. Wallace. Even more graphic was the revival of the old Populist war cry for the free and unlimited coinage of silver at the ratio of sixteen to one during the closing days of the Hoover administration and the early hours of Franklin D. Roosevelt's New Deal. Finally, the inflationary agricultural programs of the New Deal were evidence that the Populist argument had not been in vain.

Although the Populists did not win many elections, they challenged the two major parties. They agitated, argued, discussed, and demanded; for the most part, they appealed to the rank and file, though they also attracted some intellectuals. For good or for ill, they helped popularize the idea of the federal government serving as an agency of social reform and may even be considered as precursors of the "welfare state." Racism and antiforeignism hardly were the cornerstone of their thinking, as some historians seem to insist; they were incidental and probably less concentrated than in urban quarters.

Populism occupies a conspicuous place in the history of American liberalism. It helped replenish the liberal reservoir with ideas that were appropriated to great advantage by the Progressives and public policy makers of the future. Populism, with its program for a broad popular participation in the affairs of the government and the benefits of the American economy, helped inject more democracy into American society.

SUGGESTED READINGS

ARNETT, ALEX MATHEWS. *The Populist Movement in Georgia.* New York: Columbia University Press, 1922.

FERKISS, VICTOR C. "Populist Influences on American Fascism," *Western Political Quarterly,* Vol. X (June, 1957), pp. 350–73.

GOLDMAN, ERIC F. *Rendezvous with Destiny: A History of Modern American Reform.* New York: Alfred A. Knopf, Inc., 1953.

HICKS, JOHN D. *The Populist Revolt.* Minneapolis: University of Minnesota Press, 1931.

HOFSTADTER, RICHARD C. *The Age of Reform: From Bryan to F.D.R.* New York: Alfred A. Knopf, Inc., 1955.

NOBLIN, STUART. *Leonidas LaFayette Polk.* Chapel Hill: University of North Carolina Press, 1949.

NUGENT, WALTER T. K. *The Tolerant Populists.* Chicago: University of Chicago Press, 1963.

POLLACK, NORMAN. *The Populist Response to Industrial America.* Cambridge: Harvard University Press, 1962.

RIDGE, MARTIN. *Ignatius Donnelly.* Chicago: University of Chicago Press, 1962.

ROCHESTER, ANNA. *The Populist Movement in the United States.* New York: International Publishers Co., Inc., 1943.

SALOUTOS, THEODORE. *Farmer Movements in the South, 1865–1933.* Berkeley and Los Angeles: University of California Press, 1960.

SALOUTOS, THEODORE, and HICKS, JOHN D. *Agricultural Discontent in the Middle West, 1900–1939.* Madison: University of Wisconsin Press, 1951.

WOODWARD, C. VANN. *Tom Watson: Agrarian Rebel.* New York: Macmillan Co., 1938.

Document 21.1

THE FARMER: SOURCE OF AMERICAN LIFE

The importance of agriculture to the national well-being was a favorite Populist propaganda argument. The agrarian origins of the nation's leaders were constantly brought to public attention. The following selection by N. B. Ashby is a succinct statement of agricultural fundamentalism.

(From N. B. Ashby, *The Riddle of the Sphinx* [Des Moines, 1890])

. . . But suppose drought or mildew should claim the whole land for a single year, and the earth would refuse her increase; or suppose the whole farming world would simultaneously go out upon a strike and refuse to market any portion of their entire products for a year—what would happen? Panic, calamity, ruin. First, the country merchant would close up store—like Othello, his occupation gone; then the country banker would close the doors of his loan-shop and retire to one of his farms secured by foreclosure, and the town would hang out the sign so frequently seen upon the wagons of returning '49ers. The freight departments of the railways would now suspend, weary and bankrupt from transporting "emptys." Next the great elevators and the stock-yards would go to the wall, and the packing-houses would close. Panic would seize the whole country. The banks in the great centers would suspend, railroad stocks would collapse, the Goulds and Vanderbilts would be paupers, factories and mines would close down, trade and transportation in every line would cease, and the cities would be full of a hungry, panic-stricken, famishing mob, for whom there would be no bread, and who would re-enact the scenes in Paris in 1791. Agriculture is so inseparably connected with the whole business structure of the country as a first cause that such direful ruin would necessarily follow upon its suspension. . . .

Man began civilized life as a farmer, and the industrial army is ever returning to the farm for recruits. The farm constantly furnishes the brain and the brawn to the nations. The leading men in journalism, medicine, ministry, finance, law, transportation, and trade are the sons of farmers, or, at farthest remove, grandsons. A generation or two removed from the invigorating influences of the farm wears out both mental and bodily vigor. Hence, the leaders in the great moral, social, intellectual, and political movements of the race come continually from the descendants of the sturdy yeomen. And thus the farm sustains the forum and the mart in fully as substantial a way as in the furnishing of products for the shop and factory. . . .

Document 21.2

PASTORAL VISION AND PLUTOCRATIC REALITY

Decrying the influence of the new plutocracy in the social and political life of the nation, the Populists singled out the United States Senate for special criticism. By the 1890's, the Senate was already gaining the reputation as a club for retired millionaires. The following selection by Populist historian N. A. Dunning is typical of such criticism.

(From N. A. Dunning, *The Farmers' Alliance History* [Washington, D.C., 1891], pp. 3–4, 4–5)

. . . One of the relics of aristocracy that has been handed down to us is the United States Senate, a branch of our government whose uselessness is only equalled by its aristocratic notions. In connection with this old-time, blue-blooded aristocracy, and supplemental to it, has sprung into existence, in almost every part of our country, another species of aristocracy, which follows the acquirement of large fortunes. It has come to be an accepted idea, that the accumulation of money will, in some manner, divorce its possessors from the taint of plebeian birth, obscure beginnings, or former social relations, and at once change the inner as well as the outer individual.

Aristocratic ideas, backed up by intelligence and refinement, may serve a good purpose in toning down the untamed spirit, and broadening the nature of a native American; but when this station in society is reached through the medium of a bank account, human nature revolts, and the average person becomes disgusted. This spirit of avarice, or desire to make money, has become the bane of our social relations, and threatens the perpetuity of the government itself. The desire for wealth is increased as the power and privileges which it brings become more clearly understood. When the brains of a Webster or a Calhoun must wait unnoticed in the anteroom, while the plethoric pocket-book of some conscienceless speculator, monopolist, or trickster, brings to its owner the privileges of the parlor, and the softest seat at the feast, intelligence and moral rectitude will always be at a discount, while fraud and corruption will bring a premium. In order that such conditions may exist, some portions of the people must suffer. . . .

It was to satisfy the American farmer that his calling had either become obsolete, or his environment unnatural, that agricultural organizations, for political or economic purposes, were brought into existence. Up to 1860 the economic privileges of the farmer were somewhat near a parity with other branches of productive industry. The systematic spoliation of the present was, to a large extent, practically unknown. Special laws and privileges, which operated directly against the national interests of agriculture, existed only in a mild degree. At that period immense fortunes were almost unknown, and aristocracy was confined to the better educated and more refined. Neither poverty nor crime existed in the same proportion as now, and the general trend of events was toward conservatism in all economic conditions. Moderate fortunes, moderate sized farms, and moderate business enterprises, were not only the rule of the times, but were maintained under the protecting care of society's consent. Of course there were exceptions, but not in the offensive and disturbing sense in which they now exist. All must admit that the parasitic age had not begun at this date, and that labor in production paid less tribute than at the present time. Emerson says: "The glory of the farmer is that, in the division of labors, it is his part to create. All trade rests at last on his primitive activity. He stands close to Nature; he obtains from the earth the bread and the meat. The food which was not he causes to be." It is because of the truth contained in this statement that the farmer complains. It is because he simply creates for others, with but a feeble voice, if any, in determining the measure of his remuneration, that he has at last been compelled to enter an earnest protest. Willing as he is to create, and anxious to serve all other classes with the fruits of his industry and skill, yet the farmer has learned, by sad experience, that his toil has gone unrequited, and his anxiety has been construed into servility. The American farmer, in his present condition, is a living example of the folly and disaster which inevitably follow, where one class of citizens permits another class to formulate and administer all economic legislation. In other words, he is the victim of misplaced confidence, and has at last undertaken to regain his lost advantages and rights. . . .

Document 21.3

THE PARTIES HAVE FORGOTTEN THE PEOPLE

The Populists had little faith in the leadership of the Republican and Democratic parties. As one of their supporters saw it: "The capital of the Republican party consists in the virtues of its ancestry, and the capital of the Democratic party consists in the faults of its opponents." W. A. Morgan, in his *History of the Wheel and Alliance*, tells of the deterioration of the two major parties.

(From W. A. Morgan, *History of the Wheel and Alliance* [Fort Scott, Kansas, 1889], pp. 715–17)

The Republican party was born of the spirit of opposition to chattel slavery. It was this principle that gave it life, vitality and power. While this contest was waging it was grand in its conception of right and justice. It taught the inconsistency of slavery growing on the tree of liberty; that the two could not be blended in one harmonious setting; that the cries of the mother who was compelled to part with her child did not harmonize with the songs of heaven; that the groans of the woman compelled to become a mother without being a wife, were not consistent with the teachings of Christianity; that this was intended by the fathers of American liberty to become, indeed and in truth, a free land; that it was a Union of States having a common interest, that it was a land of free churches, free schools and free men. When the contest for these principles was over, and chattel slavery went down amid the boom of artillery, the rattle of musketry and groans of the dying, the Republican party emerged from the conflict with a prestige and glory that commanded the admiration of the world. Flushed with victory, they said in the pride of their heart—like the king of Babylon—see, we have done all this.

Then the work of despoiling began. . . . The glory of the Republican party has departed. Their bright sun has set in the hopeless misery which their financial policy has entailed upon an enterprising people. Their record on contraction of the currency, national banks, back salary steals, credit strengthening act, funding schemes and demonetization tendencies should have consigned them to political oblivion long ago, and would, but there was no power that promised any better, and the people were in the hands of corporations and combinations. . . .

. . . Since the war [the Democratic Party has] aped the policy of the

Republican party on every issue of vital interest to the great masses of the people. They have voted for contraction; they have favored national banks; they have aided the Republicans in their funding schemes; they have voted and worked to strike down silver; they have bowed to Baal; they have worshipped Mammon; they have built unto themselves false Gods, and set them on the hill-tops of freedom; they have courted aristocratic establishments; they have partaken of the spoils; they have received bribes; they have neglected the people; they have forsaken their principles, and their glory is departed from them forever. . . .

Document 21.4

"THE AMOUNT OF MONEY NEEDED"

A major complaint of the Populists was the shortage of circulating money. In fact, by 1894, it became their major political issue, overshadowing all others. An eloquent speaker on the "money problem" was William A. Peffer, United States Senator from Kansas. The following selection is extracted from his book, *The Farmer's Side*.

(From William A. Peffer, *The Farmer's Side* [New York, 1891], pp. 227–29)

If the functions of money be public functions, the people, as a body politic, ought to provide money enough for the use of the people, and regulate its use in such a way as to make it most serviceable and least expensive. It is on this theory and reason that the plan herein set forth is based. It is universally agreed among workers that the amount of circulating money needed by the people is such amount as is sufficient for our business if transacted on a cash basis. That necessarily is indefinite. Whenever definiteness is attempted, the amount is put at $50 per capita. That is the amount named by the Ohio farmers at a State meeting in May, 1891. The same figures have been given frequently by other public bodies. This particular amount is agreed upon, probably, because when our great war ended and when business was prosperous, our money circulation was above that. On careful examination, however, it will be found that population alone is not a proper basis for estimating money volume. The amount of money needed in any community depends not on population, but on the amount of business done and the density of population—in other words, on the necessities of the people, not on their number. One community requires more money than another, though the number of its inhabitants may be less. If a rule must be found and applied, why should it not be the same as that adopted in the case of coffee, sugar, shoes, or axes? Let the people themselves determine the quantity they need. . . .

. . . In this case, then, suppose we adopt a rule somewhat like this: Ascertain the amount of pressing indebtedness now resting upon the people for which their homes are mortgaged as security, and which debts are due and subject to *immediate collection*. If it be ascertained that that particular class of indebtedness is $1,000,000,000, then that amount of money is needed at once to relieve the people. Besides paying the debts of this particular class of persons, the money would immediately go into circulation, and within thirty days afterward pay as many more debts, and within another thirty days as many more debts, and so on; so that by the time a year had passed the money would have paid off twelve times as much indebtedness as it did at first. Upon a plan something of that kind the people may be relieved of their debt burdens in the course of twelve or fifteen years by the practice of a very simply policy, one which has been practiced ever since money was invented. . . .

Document 21.5

GOVERNMENT CONTROL OF FISCAL AFFAIRS

The issuance of money ought to be confined exclusively to the federal government and not to private bankers, according to the Populists. Senator William A. Peffer here uses an argument that thousands of Americans heard from the stentorian voice of William Jennings Bryan.

(From N. A. Dunning, *The Farmers' Alliance History* [Washington, D.C., 1891], pp. 262–63)

Is there anything unreasonable or dangerous in the request that money be issued by the government directly to the people? It must be remembered that the money of every nation is issued by the governing power. In this country Congress is authorized to "coin money and regulate the value thereof," and no other body is so empowered. Every American coin, every piece of money, whether of metal or of paper, which has been given to the people as money, was made and issued to them by authority and direction of Congress. Four hundred million dollars in treasury notes were so made and issued in 1862, and the national banking law was enacted one year later for the express purpose of giving more money to the people. At one time the aggregate amount of treasury notes (greenbacks) and national bank notes in use as money, was more than $700,000,000 dollars. Besides these, some of the bonds were used as money. The government issuing money to the people is not a new or untried proceeding. But what the farmers object to is, that the government unnecessarily uses a very costly channel through which to effect the distribution, and the people are charged with the expense; that is to say, the money is passed to the people through banks, and they—the banks—charge anywhere from ten per cent to twenty-four per cent per annum for making the transfer; whereas, if it were issued to the people directly, without the intervention of the banks or any other private agency demanding profit on the work, the expense would not exceed one to three per cent. If the money is intended for the people (and it is), why not give it to them at once through government hands, as postage stamps, for example, are given? In the first place, money belongs to the people; the people's general agent, the government, makes the money, every dollar of it, by authority of the people and for them; why, then, should banks or any trafficking agency be permitted to trade in it before it reaches the people to whom it belongs, and for whose use it is intended? That practice is not adopted with respect to anything else which the government does for the people. Whatever else it delivers to them passes through government hands only. What reason can be assigned for delivering treasury notes to the people through banks, that would not apply with equal force to the issuing and delivering to them of patents to public lands, or postage stamps? The object in making and issuing money is, that the people shall have it to use in their business affairs. It would reach them quite as easily and early if sent out through direct channels from the treasury as it does by passing through banks, and it would not cost the people more than from one-tenth to one-eighth as much as the banks and loan agencies compel them to pay. It is believed that this exorbitant charge for the use of money, more than any other one thing, is responsible for the general depression of agriculture. . . .

22

NORMAN A. GRAEBNER
University of Illinois

American Imperialism

CONTEMPORARIES sensed—and historians have since agreed—that 1898 was a turning point in the history of the American republic. The events of that year, culminating in Commodore George Dewey's victory at Manila, ushered the United States onto the international stage as a world power. Yet, neither the concept of world power nor that of national expansion represented anything new or unique in the nation's history. Significant changes in a country's power position never occur overnight. From the moment of its birth the United States had been a world power, a nation important enough to influence the decisions of the great nations of Europe. During the nineteenth century, especially after the American Civil War, Europe's leaders recognized increasingly that the United States had become the equal of the traditional powers in its ability to sustain a war.

To be sure, acquisition of the Philippine Islands was a clear departure from established national precedent. If expansion had been a recurrent concern of the American people, it had been limited to regions contiguous to the United States. The only exception had been Alaska. With the annexation of the Philippines the nation abandoned for the first time its strategy of hemispheric isolation in favor of a major strategic commitment in the western Pacific. Also, for the first time, the United States established its sovereignty over territories that were never intended for self-government under the aegis of the United States Constitution. Instead, the Philippine population, ethnically and culturally remote from American society, was destined from the beginning for the imposition of minority white rule.

What mattered in the events of 1898 was not that the United States had become a world power or an imperialistic nation but that, in acquiring the Philippine Islands, it had deserted those principles of statecraft which had determined important decisions throughout the previous century. The defiance of diplomatic tradition lay in the determination of American officials to anchor the nation's imperialistic behavior to abstract moral principles rather than to the political wisdom of the past. Neither war against Spain nor acquisition of the Philippines resulted from any recognizable or clearly enunciated national interest. They emanated, rather, from a sense of moral obligation. In a large measure the critical decisions of 1898 were totally incompatible with assumptions and methods upon which earlier generations of Americans had attempted to defend the national interest abroad. For this reason, they inaugurated a new age for the United States in world affairs.

American diplomacy prior to 1898 had been rooted firmly in the realistic tradition of the modern world. It had followed the precepts of President Washington expressed in 1795: "In every act of my administration I have sought the happiness of my fellow citizens. My system for the attainment of this objective has uniformly been to overlook all personal, local, and partial consideration; to contemplate the United States as one great whole, . . . and to consult only the substantial and permanent interest of our country." In 1796, in his farewell address, he warned the nation to expect no more of others, declaring that "it is a maxim, founded on the universal experience of mankind, that no nation is to be trusted further than it is bound by its interest; and no prudent statesman or politician will venture to depart from it."

Of necessity those who believed that American policy abroad should seek fulfillment of the nation's democratic mission challenged Washington's realistic position. During the debates on the French alliance in 1793 and 1794, the Greek revolt of the early 1820's, and the European revolutions of 1848, American idealists pleaded that the United States underwrite the cause of liberty abroad. But without exception, these pleas emanated from men who had no direct responsibility for American action. Their appeals to idealism generally had less a diplomatic purpose overseas than a political purpose at home. The energy and determination with which every administration, including that of Grover Cleveland, countered all pressures to involve the nation in humanitarian movements abroad measured the true depth of the country's tradition of realism. The Spanish American War of 1898 shattered this nineteenth-century tradition of diplomacy.

Historians generally agree that the United States had no legitimate cause for declaring war against Spain. The Spanish government had recognized its failure in Cuba and was doing all within its power, short of granting independence, to relieve conditions on the island. Conscious of their complete incapacity to wage a successful war, Spanish officials sought to avoid open conflict with the United States; they moved as rapidly as Spanish opinion would permit to meet American demands. But the "yellow press" of the United States insistently clamored for war, especially after the destruction of the *Maine* in Havana harbor. The conviction of most Republican editors and politicians, that Cuban liberty was popular and just, mobilized both the GOP majority in Congress and the McKinley administration behind the clamor for action. Warning the Republican leadership that Democratic ambition would permit no postponement of the decision to intervene in Cuba, the *Chicago Times-Herald* declared: "Let President McKinley hesitate to rise to the just expectation of the American people, and who can doubt that 'war for Cuban liberty' will be the crown of thorns that Free Silver Democrats and Populists will adopt at the elections this fall. . . . The President would be powerless to stay any legislation, however ruinous to every sober honest interest of the country." Two days after McKinley learned of the Spanish government's extensive concessions to his demands, he nonetheless permitted the Congress to decide the whole question, knowing full well it would vote for war.

Few Americans justified the Spanish-American War in terms of the security and well-being of the United States. Theodore Roosevelt observed in his *Autobiography:* "Our own interests [in Cuba] were great. . . . But even greater were our interests from the standpoint of humanity. Cuba was at our very doors. It was a dreadful thing for us to sit supinely and watch her death agony." Walter Hines Page termed the war "a necessary act of surgery for the health of civilization." To Senator John T. Morgan, the United States had been drawn into the war by a sense of humanity and the "duty we owe to Christian civilization." That the United States achieved its initial goal of freeing Cuba and thus fulfilling its great moral purpose at little national expense merely confirmed the growing conviction that policy anchored primarily to national interest was no longer legitimate for a nation so fortunate in its institutions and so militarily and economically powerful.

Traditional political considerations played no greater role in the decision to acquire the Philippines than in the declaration of war itself. If the solemnly declared purpose of the war did not transcend the simple liberation of Cuba, even this limited objective necessitated some degree of military victory over Spain. To destroy Spanish sea power in the Pacific and thereby protect American commerce, the administration ordered Commodore Dewey to Manila Bay. On May 1, 1898, he destroyed the Spanish squadron anchored there with loss of but one American life—through a heat stroke. No one suspected this victory would lead to the acquisition of the Philippines except, perhaps, a few administration zealots. Most Americans thought the problems of order and security in the Islands sufficient to demand the American expeditionary force which occupied Manila in August.

The crisis then arose. The sudden reduction of Spanish power in the Philippines confronted the United States with an unanticipated dilemma. What was to be the disposition of the Islands, now largely in American hands? Doubts and confusion within the administration were profound, for prior to Dewey's naval victory there was no apparent sentiment for acquisition of any portion of the Philippine archipelago. Finley Peter Dunne's Mr. Dooley remarked that the American people "did not know whether the Philippines were islands or canned goods." President McKinley himself had to resort to a globe to discover their location; he could not, he admitted, have described their position within two thousand miles! On May 16 the *New York Times* reported that "neither in the White House nor the State Department is there any definite conviction or determination concerning the future direction of the national policy with respect to the disposal of those oversea possessions, over which the American flag will be flying when the war is over."

But the nation's mood, excited by persuasive arguments of a small but determined group of Republican expansionists and by dreams of empire, increasingly accepted the inevitability of acquiring the Philippines. The philosopher William James sensed the changing national spirit. In June, 1898, he acknowledged a genuine sincerity in the American effort to base policy on philanthropic duty, but he also warned that "once the excitement of action gets loose, the taxes levied, the victories achieved . . . the old human instincts will get into play with all their old strength, and the ambition and sense of mastery which our nation has will set up new demands. . . . We had supposed ourselves . . . a better nation than the rest, safe at home, and without the old savage ambition, destined to exert great international influence by throwing in our 'moral weight' . . . Dreams! Human Nature is everywhere the same; and at the least temptation all the old military passions rise, and sweep everything before them." The perceptive James knew whereof he spoke, for during the summer months of 1898, imperialist sentiment rolled across the nation, capturing the support of newspaper editors and businessmen who wanted nothing less than the retention of Manila, which, according to Senator Henry Cabot Lodge, was "the thing which will give us the Eastern trade."

Slowly, a national policy emerged. At the end of July, 1898, President McKinley, responding to expansionist pressure, announced that any truce with Spain must stipulate that the United States continue to occupy Manila until the conclusion of a treaty. Then, on September 16, the administration clarified its intentions more precisely in its instructions to the peace commissioners. The President wrote:

Without any original thought of complete or even partial acquisition, the presence and success of our arms at Manila imposes upon us obligations which we cannot disregard. The march of events rules and over-rules human action. . . . We cannot be unmindful that without any desire or design on our part the war has brought us new duties and responsibilities which we must meet and discharge as becomes a great nation on whose growth and career from the beginning the Ruler of Nations has plainly written the high command and pledge of civilization.

Except for a vague suggestion that American responsibility and interests might require a cession of the island of Luzon, the President assigned to the American commissioners in Paris the task of determining the actual terms of the treaty with Spain.

The commissioners, unable to agree among themselves, sought the advice of officers knowledgeable in Far Eastern affairs. William R. Day, recently Secretary of State, believed retention of Luzon, Mindoro, and Palawan sufficient for a naval base; but strategically, it appeared inescapable that the United States acquire either the entire archipelago or no portion of it. Although Senator George Gray, the lone Democratic member of the commission, opposed any acquisitions in the Philippines, the majority favored the retention of all the islands. With this decision, McKinley eventually concurred.

That the United States perhaps acquired the Philippines reluctantly does not mean it lacked freedom of choice. But that freedom had literally become extinguished with the initial decision to conquer the Islands. Once liberated, their restoration to Spain would have defied the will of the vast majority of Filipinos. Clearly, the Islands lacked the power and resources to sustain their own independence; to cast them adrift seemed nothing less than a total negation of responsibility. The order to destroy Spanish authority in Manila was crucial. Thereafter, all avenues of escape from a self-imposed dilemma appeared closed. Like the Spanish-American War itself, the ultimate decision to annex the Islands was then rationalized in terms of humanitarianism. There was no alternative, President McKinley is said to have explained to a group of visiting clergymen, "but to take them all, and to educate the Filipinos, and uplift and Christianize them, and by

God's grace do the very best we could by them, as our fellowmen, for whom Christ also died. . . ."

Opponents of expansion—and they were legion—placed powerful intellectual obstacles in the path of the imperialists. Any acquisition of territory in the Philippine archipelago, they held, would defy the spirit of both the Declaration of Independence and the Constitution. Neither of these documents, they said, provided for the government of peoples not designated for statehood. Nor was it clear how the American people could assimilate a population that was so racially and culturally different. If granted political equality, the Filipinos would merely corrupt the American democratic system. Secretary of State John Hay, who had warmly supported "the splendid little war," told McKinley in August, 1898, that "the more I hear about the state of the Tagalog population and their leaders the more I am convinced of the seriousness of the task which would devolve upon us if we made ourselves permanently responsible for them."

Even more sobering was the observation that the Philippines were so distant, exposed, and defenseless that they would constitute a hostage which other world powers could employ in bargaining with the American government. Senator Alexander Clay of Georgia put his colleagues on notice of the price which might be exacted of the nation for its new involvement in the Far East. "We want no complications or war with England, France, Germany, Russia, China, Japan, or any other foreign power," he declared. "We want no territory or population liable and likely to involve us in complications which may lead to war with any of these powers. The danger of frequent and almost constant wars between foreign nations in the Far East . . . should be a warning against the acquisition of this foreign territory and population. . . . The United States has heretofore been solid, compact, contiguous, and impregnable. . . . When we go out into the seas beyond the Western Hemisphere and acquire other countries, we increase our responsibilities, weaken our defenses, and enormously increase the expenses of our Army and Navy. We must not come to the conclusion because we destroyed the Spanish fleets, that we could so easily cope with the navies of the European powers."

For most Americans and even members of Congress, such warnings passed unnoticed. So remote were the burdens of empire that many assumed that the acquisition of the Philippines actually strengthened the nation.

Yet, unless the Islands themselves possessed sources of power which equaled or exceeded that required for their defense, they would be-

come a strategic liability. As the English *Saturday Review* saw it, the
new American commitment in the Far East was so extensive that the
reliance of the United States on British naval power was greater than
ever before. Thereafter, London officials would expect the United
States to deal generously with Canada on the matter of tariffs and to
support the British in the approaching conflict over China occasioned
by European encroachment and rivalry. The United States, declared
the *Review,* had a growing need for a stout friend, namely, Great
Britain.

United States policy in 1898 extended the Monroe Doctrine to the
western Pacific and thereby destroyed the nation's traditional isolation
from the eastern hemisphere. Only the ridiculously easy victory over
the Spanish squadron at Manila obscured the magnitude of the new
obligations. The Islands were acquired so painlessly that the strategic
commitment involved scarcely disturbed American isolationist habits
of mind. For this challenge to the national behavior, no obvious precedent existed in the American experience. The political wisdom of the
past, which had guarded carefully the concept of limited objectives
and limited power, had been forgotten. After the events of 1898, it
would become increasingly difficult for American officials to employ
the nation's nineteenth-century tradition in their perennial efforts to
carry out policy. Occasional warnings that the United States possessed
neither the required naval forces to maintain an empire nor the intention of building them were largely ignored. The suddenness and
completeness of the changes wrought by expansion measured the extent to which illusions emanating from easy success had supplanted
analysis in the conduct of the nation's external affairs.

What was especially disturbing to thoughtful Americans at the turn
of the century was the widespread conviction that victory would always reward the nation's efforts abroad. Senator George Turner of the
state of Washington pointed disapprovingly at the "vain and boastful
spirit which seems to be abroad in the land, that we of this day and
age and generation are entirely sufficient unto ourselves; that there
are no problems which we can not solve unaided; that there is no danger which it is not cowardly and un-American for us to fear." No
longer did it appear essential that American leadership obey the principles of the past that ends be limited by means and that the long-
term interests of the nation be defined in a coherent fashion. If the
United States had experienced success in the past at no inordinate
cost, it would continue to do so.

This baseless assumption that American will was unlimited underlay the promulgation of the open-door policy toward China in the summer of 1900. The McKinley administration's intention to oppose any moves by the European powers to restrict permanently the commerce of China and to endanger that nation's territorial integrity appeared feasible enough. And the magnificent undertaking of saving China from dismemberment—through mere circulation of the famous first open-door. notes, to which all interested European powers gave their equivocal approval—merely intensified the illusion that great achievements abroad required little but the proper motivation. Ignoring the skepticism of other countries, the American press hailed the open-door policy as one of the most brilliant diplomatic achievements in the nation's history. For the Republican leadership, facing an election year, it was highly welcome. The bold stroke in China satisfied the demand for protection of American commercial interests. Moreover, by guaranteeing Chinese rights against foreign encroachment, it supported the cause of freedom.

As had happened with regard to the Philippines in 1898, the American policy toward China overlooked the enormity of the resulting commitment. In the Boxer Rebellion crisis, China was "saved" less by American intention than by the rivalries of the European forces. Despite the momentary success of American leadership in sustaining the Manchu empire, it was soon clear to Secretary Hay, with whose name the open door was identified, that the United States was not prepared to defend Chinese political and territorial integrity with force. In the wake of the Boxer Rebellion, Hay was confronted by a series of Russian maneuvers in Manchuria which clearly defied the open-door principle. The Secretary began to recognize the fallacy of building policy on high-minded declarations alone. "The talk of the papers about our 'pre-eminent moral position giving us the authority to dictate to the world,' " he observed, "is mere flap-doodle." Yet, for Hay, there was no avenue of retreat. To the popular mind, his concept of the open door appeared so laudable in objective and so sound in precept that no later administration dared retract it.

Thus, in the fourth-of-July atmosphere of the closing years of the nineteenth century, the United States entered an age of overcommitment in the Far East. In the long run, the acquisition of the Philippines and the open door in China could prove disastrous. The Japanese assault on Manchuria in 1931 and the subsequent war in the Pacific demonstrated the ultimate price that must be paid for sustaining imperial designs with appeals to humanitarian sentiment rather than precise assessments of the national interest. From the beginning, both the Philippines and China rendered the nation vulnerable; both regions lay across the Pacific in a vast area where other powers deployed greater military strength than did the United States. It was only the temporary absence of any direct challenge to these distant commitments that permitted the United States to escape for a long generation the normal penalty of creating ends of policy without sufficient consideration of means.

SUGGESTED READINGS

DENNIS, A. L. P. *Adventures in American Diplomacy, 1866–1906.* New York: E. P. Dutton & Co., Inc., 1928.

DULLES, FOSTER RHEA. *The Imperial Years.* New York: Thomas Y. Crowell Co., 1956.

GRISWOLD, A. WHITNEY. *The Far Eastern Policy of the United States.* New York: Harcourt, Brace & Co., 1938.

KENNAN, GEORGE F. *American Diplomacy, 1900–1950.* Chicago: University of Chicago Press, 1951.

MAY, ERNEST R. *Imperial Democracy.* New York: Harcourt, Brace & World, Inc., 1961.

MILLIS, WALTER. *The Martial Spirit.* Boston: Houghton Mifflin Co., 1931.

PRATT, JULIUS W. *The Expansionists of 1898.* Baltimore: Johns Hopkins Press, 1936.

VARG, PAUL A. *Open Door Diplomat: The Life of W. W. Rockhill.* Urbana: University of Illinois Press, 1952.

WISAN, J. E. *The Cuban Crisis as Reflected in the New York Press, 1895–1898.* New York: Columbia University Press, 1934.

Document 22.1

ANTI-IMPERIALISM: THE ARGUMENT AGAINST EXPANSIONISM

Among the many arguments leveled at American expansion into the western Pacific at the turn of the century, one—presented by Andrew Carnegie—appeared especially significant. It challenged the popular notion that the new acquisitions would require no special military expenditures and that the new commitments would not unduly expose the United States to embarrassment or attack.

(From Andrew Carnegie, "Distant Possessions—The Parting of the Ways," *North American Review,* Vol. CLXVII [August, 1898], pp. 239–48)

Let another phase of the question be carefully weighed. Europe is today an armed camp, not chiefly because the home territories of its various nations are threatened, but because of fear of aggressive action upon the part of other nations touching outlying "possessions." France resents British control of Egypt and is fearful of its West African possessions; Russia seeks Chinese territory, with a view to expansion to the Pacific; Germany also seeks distant possessions; Britain, who has acquired so many dependencies, is so fearful of an attack upon them that this year she is spending nearly eighty millions of dollars upon additional warships, and Russia, Germany and France follow suit. Japan is a new element of anxiety; and by the end of the year it is computed she will have 67 formidable ships of war. The naval powers of Europe, and Japan also, are apparently determined to be prepared for a terrific struggle for possessions in the Far East, close to the Philippines—and why not for these islands themselves? Into this vortex the Republic is cordially invited to enter by those powers who expect her policy to be of benefit to them, but her action is jealously watched by those who fear that her power might be used against them.

It has never been considered the part of wisdom to thrust one's hand into the hornet's nest, and it does seem as if the United States must lose all claim to ordinary prudence and good sense if she enter this arena, and become involved in the intrigues and threats of war which make Europe an armed camp.

It is the parting of the ways. We have a continent to populate and develop; there are only 23 persons to the square mile in the United States. England has 370, Belgium 571, Germany 250. A tithe of the cost of maintaining our sway over the Philippines would improve our internal waterways; deepen our harbors; build the Nicaraguan Canal; construct a waterway to the ocean from the Great Lakes; an inland canal along the Atlantic seaboard; a canal across Florida, saving 800 miles distance between New York and New Orleans; connect Lake Michigan with the Mississippi; deepen all the harbors upon the lakes; build a canal from Lake Erie to the Allegheny River; slackwater through movable dams the entire length of the Ohio River to Cairo; thoroughly improve the Lower and Upper Mississippi, and all our seaboard harbors. All these enterprises would be as nothing in cost in comparison to the sums required for the experiment of possessing the Philippine Islands, 7,000 miles from our shores. If the object be to render our Republic powerful among nations, can there be any doubt as to which policy is the better? To be more powerful at home is the surest way to be more powerful abroad. To-day the Republic stands the friend of all nations, the ally of none; she has no ambitious designs upon the territory of any power upon another continent; she crosses none of their ambitious designs, evokes no jealousy of the bitter sort, inspires no fears; she is not one of them, scrambling for "possessions"; she stands apart, pursuing her own great mission, and teaching all nations by example. Let her become a power annexing foreign territory, and all is changed in a moment.

If we are to compete with other nations for foreign possessions we must have a navy like theirs. It should be superior to any other navy, or we play a second part. It is not enough to have a navy equal to that of Russia or of France, for Russia and France may combine against us just as they may against Britain. We at once enter the field as a rival of Britain, the chief possessor of foreign possessions, and who can guarantee that we shall not even have to measure our power against her?

What it means to enter the list of military and naval powers having foreign possessions may be gathered from the following considerations. First, look at our future navy. If it is only to equal that of France it means 51 battleships; if of Russia, 40 battleships. If we cannot play the game without being at least the equal of any of our rivals, then 80 battleships is the number Britain possesses. We now have only 4, with 5 building. Cruisers, armed and unarmed, swell the number threefold, Britain having 273 ships of the line built or ordered, with 308 torpedo boats in addition; France having 134 ships of the line and 269 torpedo boats. All these nations are adding ships rapidly. Every armor and gun making plant in the world is busy night and day. Ships are indispensable, but recent experience shows that soldiers are equally so. While the immense armies of Europe need not be duplicated, yet we shall certainly be too weak unless our army is at least twenty times what it has been—say 500,000 men. . . .

To-day two great powers in the world are compact, developing themselves in peace throughout vast coterminous territories. When war threatens they have no outlying "possessions" which can never be really "possessed," but which they are called upon to defend. They fight upon the exposed edge only of their own soil in case of attack, and are not only invulnerable, but they could not be more than inconvenienced by the world in arms against them. These powers are Russia and the United States. . . . Britain, France, Germany, Belgium, Spain, are all vulnerable, having departed from the sagacious policy of keeping possessions and power concentrated. Should the United States depart from this policy, she also must be so weakened in consequence as never to be able to play the commanding part in the world, disjointed, that she can play whenever she desires if she remains compact.

Whether the United States maintain its present unique position of safety or forfeit it through acquiring foreign possessions, is to be decided by its action in regard to the Philippines; for, fortunately, the independence of Cuba is assured, for this the Republic has proclaimed to the world that she has drawn the sword. But why should the less than two millions of Cuba receive national existence and the seven and a half millions of the Philippines be denied it? The United States, thus far in their history, have no page resting self-sacrifice made for others; all their gains have been for themselves. This void is now to be grandly filled. The page which recites the resolve of the Republic to rid her neighbor Cuba from the foreign "possessor" will grow brighter with the passing centuries, which may dim many pages now deemed illustrious. Should the coming American be able to point to Cuba and the Philippines rescued from foreign domination and enjoying independence won for them by his country and given to them without money and without price, he will find no citizen of any other land able to claim for his country services so disinterested and so noble.

We repeat there is no power in the world that could do more than inconvenience the United States by attacking its fringe, which is all that the world combined could do, so long as our country is not compelled to send its forces beyond its own compact shores to defend worthless "possessions." If our country were blockaded by the united powers of the world for years, she would emerge from the embargo richer and stronger, and with her own resources more completely developed. We have little to fear from external attack. No thorough blockade of our enormous seaboard is possible; but even if it were, the few indispensable articles not produced by ourselves (if there were any such) would reach us by way of Mexico or Canada at slightly increased cost. . . .

Document 22.2

ANTI-IMPERIALISM: THE APPEAL TO CONSERVATIVE TRADITION

A major position taken by antiexpansionists challenged the new American habit of rationalizing national action with appeals to patriotism and democratic ideology. William Graham Sumner, the Yale sociologist, urges his countrymen to remember the true sources of national greatness and idealism.

(From William Graham Sumner, "The Conquest of the United States by Spain," *Yale Law Journal*, Vol. VIII, No. 4 [January, 1899], pp. 168–93)

. . . The war with Spain was precipitated upon us headlong, without reflection or deliberation, and without any due formulation of public opinion. Whenever a voice was raised in behalf of deliberation and the recognized maxims of statesmanship, it was howled down in a storm of vituperation and cant. Everything was done to make us throw away sobriety of thought and calmness of judgment, and to inflate all expressions with sensational epithets and turgid phrases. It cannot be denied that everything in regard to the war has been treated in an exalted strain of sentiment and rhetoric very unfavorable to the truth. At present the whole periodical press of the country seems to be occupied in tickling the national vanity to the utmost by representations about the war which are extravagant and fantastic. There will be a penalty to be paid for all this. Nervous and sensational newspapers are just as corrupting, especially to young people, as nervous and sensational novels. The habit of expecting that all mental pabulum shall be highly spiced, and the corresponding loathing for whatever is soberly truthful, undermines character as much as any other vice. Patriotism is being prostituted into a nervous intoxication which is fatal to an apprehension of truth. It builds around us a fool's paradise, and it will lead us into errors about our position and relations just like those which we have been ridiculing in the case of Spain. . . .

. . . The laws of nature and of human body are just as valid for Americans as for anybody else, and if we commit acts, we shall have to take consequences, just like other people. Therefore prudence demands that we look ahead to see what we are about to do, and that we gauge the means at our disposal, if we do not want to bring calamity on ourselves and our children. We see that the peculiarities of our system of government set limitations on us. We cannot do things which a great centralized monarchy could do. The very blessings and special advantages which we enjoy, as compared with others, bring disabilities with them. That is the great fundamental cause of what I have tried to show throughout this lecture, that we cannot govern dependencies consistently with our political system, and that, if we try it, the state which our fathers founded will suffer a reaction which will transform it into another empire just after the fashion of all the old ones. That is what imperialism means. That is what it will be, and the democratic republic, which has been, will stand in history as a mere transition form like the colonial organization of earlier days.

And yet this scheme of a republic which our fathers formed was a glorious dream which demands more than a word of respect and affection before it passes away. . . .

. . . Our fathers would have an economical government, even if grand people called it a parsimonious one, and taxes should be no greater than were absolutely necessary to pay for such a government. . . .

... No adventurous policies of conquest or ambition, such as, in their belief, kings and nobles had forced, for their own advantage, on European states, would ever be undertaken by a free democratic republic. Therefore the citizen here would never be forced to leave his family, or to give his sons to shed blood for glory and to leave widows and orphans in misery for nothing. Justice and law were to reign in the midst of simplicity, and a government which had little to do was to offer little field for ambition. In a society where industry, frugality and prudence were honored, it was believed that the vices of wealth would never flourish.

We know that these beliefs, hopes and intentions have been only partially fulfilled. We know that, as time has gone on, and we have grown numerous and rich, some of these things have proved impossible ideals, incompatible with a large and flourishing society, but it is by virtue of this conception of a commonwealth that the United States has stood for something unique and grand in the history of mankind, and that its people have been happy. It is by virtue of these ideals that we have been "isolated," isolated in a position which the other nations of the earth have observed in silent envy, and yet there are people who are boasting of their patriotism, because they say that we have taken our place now amongst the nations of the earth by virtue of this war. My patriotism is of the kind which is outraged by the notion that the United States never was a great nation until in a petty three months campaign it knocked to pieces a poor, decrepit bankrupt old state like Spain. To hold such an opinion as that is to abandon all American standards, to put shame and scorn on all that our ancestors tried to build up here, and to go over to the standards of which Spain is a representative.

Document 22.3

"THE ANGLO-SAXON AND THE WORLD'S FUTURE"

Josiah Strong, a gifted young Congregational minister, was Secretary of his denomination's Home Missionary Society. A leading religious journalist, he also was a pioneer in the social gospel movement. The selection below is characteristic of his belief in the future destiny and God-given "mission" of the United States.

(From Josiah Strong, *Our Country* [New York, 1885], pp. 159, 161, 165, 174–76)

Every race which has deeply impressed itself on the human family has been the representative of some great idea—one or more—which has given direction to the nation's life and form to its civilization. . . . The Anglo-Saxon is the representative of two great ideas, which are closely related. One of them is that of civil liberty. . . . The noblest races have always been lovers of liberty. That love ran strong in early German blood, and has profoundly influenced the institutions of all the branches of the great German family; but it was left for the Anglo-Saxon branch fully to recognize the right of the individual to himself, and formally to declare it the foundation stone of government.

The other great idea of which the Anglo-Saxon is the exponent is that of a pure *spiritual* Christianity. . . .

It is not necessary to argue to those for whom I write that the two great needs of mankind, that all men may be lifted up into the light of the highest Christian civilization, are, first, a pure, spiritual Christianity, and, second, civil liberty. Without controversy, these are the forces which, in the past, have contributed most to the elevation of the human race, and they must continue to be, in the future, the most efficient ministers to its progress. It follows, then, that the Anglo-Saxon, as the great representative of these two ideas, the depositary of these two greatest blessings, sustains peculiar relations to the world's future, is divinely commissioned to be, in a peculiar sense, his brother's keeper. Add to this the fact of his rapidly increasing strength in modern times, and we have well nigh a demonstration of his destiny. . . .

It is not unlikely that, before the close of the next century, this race will outnumber all the other civilized races of the world. Does it not look as if God were not only preparing in our Anglo-Saxon civilization the die with which to stamp the peoples of the earth, but as if he were also massing behind that die the mighty power with which to press it? My confidence that this race is eventually to give its civilization to mankind is not based on mere numbers—China forbid! I look forward to what the world has never yet seen united in the same race; viz., the greatest numbers, *and* the highest civilization.

There can be no reasonable doubt that North America is to be the great home of the Anglo-Saxon, the principal seat of his power, the center of his life and influence. . . .

. . . It seems to me that God, with infinite wisdom and skill, is training the Anglo-Saxon race for an hour sure to come in the world's future. Heretofore there has always been in the history of the world a comparatively unoccupied land westward, into which the crowded countries of the East have poured their surplus populations. But the widening waves of migration, which milleniums ago rolled east and west from the valley of the Euphrates, meet to-day on our Pacific coast. There are no more new worlds. The unoccupied arable lands of the earth are limited, and will soon be taken. The time is coming when the pressure of population on the means of subsistence will be felt here as it is now felt in Europe and Asia. Then will the world enter upon a new stage of its history—*the final competition of races, for which the Anglo-Saxon is being schooled.* Long before the thousand millions are here, the mighty *centrifugal* tendency, inherent in this stock and strengthened in the United States, will assert itself. Then this race of unequaled energy, with all the majesty of numbers and the might of wealth behind it—the representative, let us hope, of the largest liberty, the purest Christianity, the highest civilization—having developed peculiarly aggressive traits calculated to impress its institutions upon mankind, will spread itself over the earth. If I read not amiss, this powerful race will move down upon Mexico, down upon Central and South America, out upon the islands of the sea, over upon Africa and beyond. And can any one doubt that the result of this competition of races will be the "survival of the fittest"? . . .

. . . "At the present day," says Mr. Darwin, "civilized nations are everywhere supplanting barbarous nations, excepting where the climate opposes a deadly barrier; and they succeed mainly, though not exclusively, through their arts, which are the products of the intellect." Thus the Finns were supplanted by the Aryan races in Europe and Asia, the Tartars by the Russians, and thus the aborigines of North America, Australia and New Zealand are now disappearing before the all-conquering Anglo-Saxons. It would seem as if these inferior tribes were only precursors of a superior race, voices in the wilderness crying: "Prepare ye the way of the Lord!" . . .

Document 22.4

"GOD'S COMMAND IS ON US"

Senator Albert J. Beveridge was a Progressive Republican from Indiana. Like Josiah Strong, he was an uninhibited spokesman for Anglo-Saxon racism and also invoked the American century; but he did not omit profits from the divine mission of the United States.

(From Albert J. Beveridge, "The March of the Flag," in Thomas B. Reed [ed.], *Modern Eloquence*, Vol. II [Philadelphia: John D. Morris & Co., 1903], pp. 224–43)

. . . It is a noble land that God has given us; a land that can feed and clothe the world: a land whose coast lines would inclose half the countries of Europe; a land set like a sentinel between the two imperial oceans of the globe; a greater England and a nobler destiny. It is a mighty people that He has planted on this soil; a people sprung from the most masterful blood of history; a people perpetually revitalized by the virile workingfolk of all the earth; a people imperial by virtue of their power, by right of their institutions, by authority of their heaven-directed purposes, the propagandists and not the misers of liberty. It is a glorious history our God has bestowed upon His chosen people; a history whose keynote was struck by Liberty Bell; a history heroic with faith in our mission and our future; a history of statesmen, who flung the boundaries of the Republic out into unexplored lands and savage wildernesses; a history of soldiers, who carried the flag across blazing deserts and through the ranks of hostile mountains, even to the gates of sunset: a history of a multiplying people, who overran a continent in half a century; a history divinely logical, in the process of whose tremendous reasoning we find ourselves to-day.

Therefore, in this campaign the question is larger than a party question. It is an American question. It is a world question. Shall the American people continue their resistless march toward the commercial supremacy of the world? Shall free institutions broaden their blessed reign as the children of liberty wax in strength until the empire of our principles is established over the hearts of all mankind? Have we no mission to perform—no duty to discharge to our fellow-man? Has the Almighty Father endowed us with gifts beyond our deserts, and marked us as the people of His peculiar favor, merely to rot in our own selfishness, as men and nations must who take cowardice for their companion and self for their deity—as China has, as India has, as Egypt has? Shall we be as the man who had one talent and hid it, or as he who had ten talents and used them until they grew to riches? And shall we reap the reward that waits on the discharge of our high duty as the sovereign power of earth; shall we occupy new markets for what our farmers raise, new markets for what our factories make, new markets for what our merchants sell,— aye, and please God, new markets for what our ships shall carry? Shall we avail ourselves of new sources of supply of what we do not raise or make, so that what are luxuries to-day shall be necessities to-morrow? Shall we conduct the mightiest commerce of history with the best money known to man or shall we use the pauper money of Mexico, China, and the Chicago platform? Shall we be worthy of our mighty past of progress, brushing aside, as we have always done, the spider webs of technicality, and march ever onward upon the highway of development, to the doing of real deeds, the achievement of real things, and the winning of real victories?

In a sentence, shall the American people endorse at the polls the American administration of William McKinley, which, under the guidance of Divine Providence, has started the Republic on its noblest career of prosperity, duty and glory; or shall the American people rebuke that administration, reverse the wheels of history, halt the career of the flag. . . ?

. . . William McKinley is continuing the policy that Jefferson began, Monroe continued, Seward advanced, Grant promoted, Harrison championed. Hawaii is ours; Porto Rico is to be ours; at the prayer of its people Cuba will finally be ours; in the islands of the East, even to the gates of Asia, coaling stations are to be ours; at the very least the flag of a liberal government is to float over the Philippines, and it will be the stars and stripes of glory. And the burning question of this campaign is whether the American people will accept the gifts of events; whether they will rise, as lifts their soaring destiny; whether they will proceed along the lines of national development surveyed by the statesmen of our past, or whether, for the first time, the American people doubt their mission, question their fate, prove apostate to the spirit of their race, and halt the ceaseless march of free institutions?

The opposition tells us that we ought not to govern a people without their consent. I answer, the rule of liberty that all just government derives its authority from the consent of the governed, applies only to those who are capable of self-government. We govern the Indians without their consent; we govern our Territories without their consent; we govern our children without their consent. I answer, would not the natives of the Philippines prefer the just, humane, civilizing government of this Republic to the savage, bloody rule of pillage and extortion from which we have rescued them? Do not the blazing fires of joy and the ringing bells of gladness in Porto Rico prove the welcome of our flag? And regardless of this formula of words made only for enlightened, self-governing peoples, do we owe no duty to the world? Shall we turn these peoples back to the reeking hands from which we have taken them? Shall we save them from those nations, to give them to a self-rule of tragedy? It would be like giving a razor to a babe and telling it to shave itself. It would be like giving a typewriter to an Esquimau and telling him to publish one of the great dailies of the world. . . .

. . . To-day, we are making more than we can use. Therefore, we must find new markets for our produce, new occupation for our capital, new work for our labor. And so, while we did not need the territory taken during the past century at the time it was acquired, we do need what we have taken in 1898, and we need it now. Think of the thousands of Americans who will pour into Hawaii and Porto Rico when the Republic's laws cover those islands with justice and safety. Think of the tends of thousands of Americans who will invade the Philippines when a liberal government shall establish order and equity there. Think of the hundreds of thousands of Americans who will build a soap-and-water, common school civilization of energy and industry in Cuba, when a government of law replaces the double reign of anarchy and tyranny. . . .

. . . . The resources of the Philippines have hardly been touched by the finger tips of modern methods. And they produce what we cannot, and they consume what we produce—the very predestination of reciprocity. And William McKinley intends that their trade shall be ours. It means an opportunity for the rich man to do something with his money, besides hoarding it or lending it. It means occupation for every workingman in the country at wages which the development of new resources, the launching of new enterprises, the monopoly of new markets always brings. . . .

. . . Why mumble the meaningless phrases of a tale that is told when the golden future is before us, the world calls us, its wealth awaits us and God's command is on us? . . .

Fellow-Americans, we are God's chosen people. Yonder at Bunker Hill and Yorktown His providence was above us. At New Orleans and on ensanguined seas His hand sustained us. Abraham Lincoln was His minister, and His was the altar of freedom the boys in blue set up on a hundred smoking battlefields. His power directed Dewey in the east, and He delivered the Spanish fleet into our hands on Liberty's natal day as He delivered the elder Armada into the hands of our English sires two centuries ago. His great purposes are revealed in the progress of the flag, which surpasses the intentions of Congresses and Cabinets, and leads us, like a holier pillar of cloud by day and pillar of fire by night, into situations unforeseen by finite wisdom and duties unexpected by the unprophetic heart of selfishness. The American people cannot use a dishonest medium of exchange; it is ours to set the world its example of right and honor. We cannot fly from our world duties; it is ours to execute the purposes of a fate that has driven us to be greater than our small intentions. We cannot retreat from any soil where Providence has unfurled our banner; it is ours to save that soil for liberty and civilization. For liberty and civilization and God's promises fulfilled, the flag must henceforth be the symbol and the sign to all mankind.

Document 22.5

THE ADVANTAGES OF NAVAL AND TERRITORIAL EXPANSION

Alfred Thayer Mahan was an Annapolis graduate who served in the United States Navy during the Civil War, was appointed to the Naval War Board in the Spanish-American War, and subsequently advanced to the rank of Rear Admiral. A "big navy" man and a leading exponent of expansionism, he was admired by the entire bloc of imperialist spokesmen, Theodore Roosevelt in particular. Mahan argued that the national security demanded a growing naval force, an Isthmian canal, and Caribbean and Pacific island possessions. He presented his message within the social Darwinian framework, his central thesis being that international competition was a naked struggle for power—with control of the sea being an indispensable factor.

(From Alfred Thayer Mahan, "The United States Looking Outward," in *The Interest of America in Sea Power* [New York: Harper & Bros., 1897], pp. 3–27)

Indications are not wanting of an approaching change in the thoughts and policy of Americans as to their relations with the world outside their own borders. For the past quarter of a century, the predominant idea, which has asserted itself successfully at the polls and shaped the course of the government, has been to preserve the home market for the home industries. . . .

. . . Within, the home market is secured; but outside, beyond the broad seas, there are the markets of the world, that can be entered and controlled only by a vigorous contest, to which the habit of trusting to protection by statute does not conduce. . . .

. . . The interesting and significant feature of this changing attitude is the turning of the eyes outward, instead of inward only, to seek the welfare of the country. To affirm the importance of distant markets, and the relation to them of our own immense powers of production, implies logically the recognition of the link that joins the products and the markets,—that is, the carrying trade; the three together constituting that chain of maritime power to which Great Britain owes her wealth and greatness. Further, is it too much to say that, as two of these links, the shipping and the markets, are exterior to our own borders, the acknowledgment of them carries with it a view of the relations of the United States to the world radically distinct from the simple idea of self-sufficingness? We shall not follow far this line of thought before there will dawn the realization of America's unique position, facing the older worlds of the East and West, her shores washed by the oceans which touch the one or the other, but which are common to her alone.

Coincident with these signs of change in our own policy there is restlessness in the world at large which is deeply significant, if not ominous. It is beside our purpose to dwell upon the internal state of Europe, whence, if disturbances arise, the effect upon us may be but partial and indirect. But the great seaboard powers there do not stand on guard against their continental rivals only; they cherish also aspirations for commercial extension, for colonies, and for influence in distant regions, which may bring, and, even under our present contracted policy, already have brought them into collision with ourselves. The incident of the Samoa Islands, trivial apparently, was nevertheless eminently suggestive of European ambitions. America then roused from sleep as to interests closely concerning her future. At this moment internal troubles are imminent in the Sandwich Islands, where it should be our fixed determination to allow no foreign influence to equal our own. All over the world German commercial and colonial push is coming into collision with other nations. . . .

. . . In a general way, it is evident enough that this canal [through the Central American Isthmus], by modifying the direction of trade routes, will induce a great increase of commercial activity and carrying trade throughout the Caribbean Sea; and that this now comparatively deserted nook of the ocean will become, like the Red Sea, a great thoroughfare of shipping, and will attract, as never before in our day, the interest and ambition of maritime nations. Every position in that sea will have enhanced commercial and military value, and the canal itself will become a strategic centre of the most vital importance. Like the Canadian Pacific Railroad, it will be a link between the two oceans; but, unlike it, the use, unless most carefully guarded by treaties, will belong wholly to the belligerent which controls the sea by its naval power. In case of war, the United States will unquestionably command the Canadian Railroad, despite the deterrent force of operations by the hostile navy upon our seaboard; but no less unquestionably will she be impotent, as against any of the great maritime powers, to control the Central American canal. Militarily speaking, and having reference to European complications only, the piercing of the Isthmus is nothing but a disaster to the United States, in the present state of her military and naval preparation. It is especially dangerous to the Pacific coast; but the increased exposure of one part of our seaboard reacts unfavorably upon the whole military situation.

Despite a certain great original superiority conferred by our geographical nearness and immense resources,—due, in other words, to our natural advantages, and not to our intelligent preparations,—the United States is woefully unready, not only in fact but in purpose to assert in the Caribbean and Central America a weight of influence proportioned to the extent of her interests. We have not the navy, and, what is worse, we are not willing to have the navy, that will weigh seriously in any disputes with those nations whose interests will conflict there with our own. We have not, and we are not anxious to provide, the defence of the seaboard which will leave the navy free for its work at sea. We have not, but many other powers have, positions, either within or on the borders of the Caribbean which not only possess great natural advantages for the control of that sea, but have received and are receiving that artificial strength of fortification and armament which will make them practically inexpugnable. On the contrary, we have not on the Gulf of Mexico even the beginning of a navy yard which could serve as the base of our operations. . . .

. . . Though distant, our shores can be reached; being defenceless, they can detain but a short time a force sent against them. . . .

Yet, were our sea frontier as strong as it now is weak, passive self-defence, whether in trade or war, would be but a poor policy, so long as this world continues to be one of struggle and vicissitude. All around us now is strife; "the struggle of life," "the race of life," are phrases so familiar that we do not feel their significance till we stop to think about them. Everywhere nation is arrayed against nation; our own no less than others. What is our protective system but an organized warfare? . . .

23

EDWIN C. ROZWENC
Amherst College

The Progressive Era

AMERICANS in the years before the first World War understood that they were living in a time of great excitement and change. William Allen White, the noted newspaper editor from Emporia, Kansas, expressed this awareness of new directions in a book published in 1910, entitled *The Old Order Changeth* (New York: The Macmillan Co.): "During the recent years . . . that movement has been unmistakable. It is now one of the big self-evident things in our national life. It is called variously: Reform, the Moral Awakening, the New Idea, the Square Deal, the Uplift, Insurgency . . . but it is one current in the thought of the people."

The question inevitably arises: When did this movement for reform begin? What are the sources of the ideas, aspirations, and modes of behavior that are to be thought of as part of the progressive movement?

The progressive movement has been seen by some historians as little more than an extension of the Populist revolt of the 1890's, which reached its climax in the Free Silver crusade of 1896, when William Jennings Bryan led the combined forces of the Democratic and Populist parties to defeat in the presidential campaign. Populists and progressives were lumped together as a continuous movement of reform from 1890 to 1917. This progressive revolt, it was asserted, had a leadership decidedly moralistic in character—as exemplified by men such as Bryan, LaFollette, Roosevelt, Wilson. Progressivism was Jeffersonian rather than Hamiltonian in outlook; it was liberal rather than radical, optimistic rather than desperate. While it seemed to be romantic in its philosophical implications, it certainly was tinged with a sense of realism, in that it recognized the economc bases of politics.

For a time, this interpretation seemed reasonable. Everyone remembered William Allen White's often-quoted comment that the Republican progressives of 1912 "caught the Populists in swimming and stole all their clothing except the frayed underdrawers of free silver." Yet the inadequacy of an interpretation which conceives of progressivism simply as an extension of the Populist revolt has become obvious. Actually, the differences between Populism and progressivism are more crucial than the similarities.

Comparisons of the leadership of the two movements show that the majority of progressive leaders had been opposed to Bryan and to Populist principles. Theodore Roosevelt, for example, had made the menacing remark in the 1890's: "I know the Populists and the laboring man well and their faults. . . . I like to see a mob handled by the regulars, or by good State-Guards, not overscrupulous about bloodshed." Woodrow Wilson was revolted by the "crude and ignorant minds" of the Populists and privately remarked that he would like to "knock Bryan into a cocked hat."

These attitudes of Roosevelt and Wilson were not unique. Other progressive Republican leaders had been McKinley Republicans in the 1890's, and many progressive Democrats had been anti-Bryanites. Moreover, voting statistics indicate that urban areas, which had been against Bryan, were giving support to progressive leaders a decade later. Why, then, should middle-class Americans living in cities, who had been largely unmoved by the Populist revolt, support the progressive movement with considerable emotional fervor? William Allen White had sensed this change in the manners and style of the reform movement when he wrote that Populism had "shaved its whiskers, washed its shirt, put on a derby, and moved up into the middle class."

Alfred D. Chandler's examination of the social, political, and occupational backgrounds of 260 leaders of the progressive party in the campaign of 1912 makes impressively clear that these progressive leaders came from middle-class, urban backgrounds, and most of them had been McKinley Republicans in the 1890's. Of these leaders, 95 were businessmen, principally of large businesses; 75 were lawyers; 36 were editors; 19 were college professors; seven were authors; and six were professional social workers. Among the 260, there were no farmers, no laboring men, and only one labor union leader. Nor were there any white-collar workers or salaried managers of large industrial concerns ("The Origins of Progressive Leadership" in Elting Morison [ed.], *The Letters of Theodore Roosevelt*, Vol. VIII [Cambridge, 1954], pp. 1462–65).

Most of the leaders had been and continued to be their own bosses. As lawyers, businessmen, and professional men, they had worked for themselves during most of their adult lives. On the whole, they were unacquainted with the institutional discipline of the emerging corporate economy. Presumably, they still preferred America's historic values of individualism and equality of economic opportunity.

The middle-class preconceptions of the progressives led them to attack the new plutocracy which had come into being with the consolidation of American business. Theodore Roosevelt's attacks on the "malefactors of great wealth" stirred a sympathetic response from this group. At the same time, however, progressive leaders were as frightened by the rise of labor unions as they were by the growth of corporate combinations. To many small businessmen and professionals, labor unions were just another form of monopoly, created for the same results as industrial monopoly. "Every step in trade unionism has followed the steps that organized capital has laid down before it," Clarence Darrow declared in 1903 in a speech to the Henry George Association of Chicago. The typical progressive abhorred the ideas of class warfare or class politics. " 'I am for capital,' or 'I am for labor' substitutes something else for the inimitable laws of righteousness," Theodore Roosevelt remarked to Jacob Riis in 1904. "The one and the other would let the class man in, and letting him in is the one thing that will most quickly eat out the heart of the Republic."

At times, the progressive seemed to exhibit a nostalgia for the values of the older, more rural America. Some of this was expressed in a dislike for the city as a center of crime, vice, and human degradation. The typical progressive was a native-born Protestant, descended from older American immigrant stock. He often felt threatened by the alien character of the swarms of new immigrants pouring into the country— Poles, Italians, Greeks, Russians, east European Jews, Hungarians, Slovaks, and Czechs, who overwhelmed whole sections of American cities with strange tongues, strange religions, and strange customs. Edward A. Ross, a leading sociologist and a progressive, charged that the new immigrants, with their "pigsty mode of life," would lower the standards of American civilization.

In his view of the social problems of America the typical progressive probably agreed wholeheartedly with the *California Weekly*, which proclaimed in 1908: "Nearly all the problems which vex society have their source above or below the middle class man. From above come the problems of predatory wealth. . . . From below come the problems of poverty and of pig-headed and brutish criminality." In between was the middle-class progressive, who sought to replace class politics and class selfishness with a crusade for moral abstractions like "good government" and "responsible citizenship" or a "square deal."

If progressivism was urban, middle-class, and nationwide, whereas Populism had been rural and provincial, why should the urban middle classes have chosen to take part in a reformist crusade during the first decades of the twentieth century? Why should agitation rather than apathy have been the mood of those prosperous years? Why should reform rather than the enjoyment of higher levels of consumption have attracted the American middle class?

Leaning heavily on the observations of Walter Weyl, a gifted progressive writer, Richard Hofstadter argues that middle-class types who supported the progressive movement did so not because of economic deprivations but because they were victims of an upheaval of status. Weyl, in his book, *The New Democracy* (New York: The Macmillan Co., 1912), elaborated this sense of psychic loss: "Our industrial development (of which the Trust is but one phase) has been towards a sharpening of the angle of progression. Our eminences have become higher and more dazzling. . . . Although lawyers, doctors, engineers, architects, and professional men generally, make larger salaries than ever before, the earning of one hundred thousand dollars a year by one lawyer impoverishes by comparison the thousands of lawyers who scrape along on a thousand a year."

Weyl concluded that America was developing new types of destitutes—"the automobileless, the yachtless, the Newport cottage-less. The subtlest of luxuries become necessities, and their loss is bitterly resented. The discontent of today reaches very high in the social scale."

Up to about 1870 the small merchant or manufacturer, the distinguished lawyer, editor, or preacher was a person of local eminence in an age when local eminence mattered a great deal. The building of giant industrial empires and the emergence of the corporation as the dominant form of enterprise, however, transformed the old society and revolutionized the distribution of power and prestige. The newly rich, the new captains of industry, were by-passing the old gentry, the merchants and manufacturers of long standing, the established professional men and the civic leaders of an earlier era.

Operating with this conception of the psychology of the progressives, it is possible to assume that the typical progressive leader was likely to be a "Mugwump type"—resembling the liberal Republican of 1872, or those self-styled "Mugwumps" who bolted the Republican ticket to vote for Cleveland in 1884. The Mugwump had taken the stand for clean government and the long-established ideas of business morality as opposed to the ruthless code of the new bosses of politics and industry. But can we really say that progressivism was an extension of the Mugwumpery of the seventies and eighties?

The philosophy and the spirit of the progressives was quite divergent from that of the Mugwumps. The progressive leaders had dropped much of the ideological baggage of the Mugwumps. The Mugwumps had been committed to notions of aristocratic leadership as the most appropriate for the Republic; the progressives worked actively for the development of democratic reforms which would return the government to the people. Indeed, the direct primary, the initiative, and the referendum were devices which tended to give effective power to the least common denominator in democratic politics. The Mugwumps had also been dogmatically committed to the prevailing economic theories of laissez faire. The progressives, on the other hand, were ready to embrace ideas of state intervention and limited collectivism to accomplish their objectives.

Progressives were far more successful in politics than the Mugwumps had ever been. This was true because, despite their moral approach to politics, progressives were willing to seek popular support and to deal with the demands of the socially discontented. They did not cut themselves off from political intercourse with agrarian rebels, labor leaders, and leaders of minority groups. Progressives could and did work together with agrarian rebels on national issues. Labor leaders were given recognition by the White House and Congressional committees. And Theodore Roosevelt did invite Booker T. Washington to lunch at the White House! The typical progressive had also made a radical break with the fundamental assumptions about man and society which had been held by his putative Mugwump ancestors. By and large, the Mugwump accepted a view of the world in which man was the agent of the natural laws that controlled the forces operating in the free market according to the model of laissez-faire economic theories. In other areas of life besides the market place, man was thought of as a captive of natural laws of development and of the will of a benevolent Providence. The great popularity of the writings of Herbert Spencer in America and the widespread acceptance of his form of social Darwinism had reinforced this notion of man as the passive receptor of natural and social forces.

The progressive, on the other hand, thought of man as a creator and a change maker rather than a mere captive of natural and social forces. Henry George had broken through the iron bands of classical economic theory with his attack on the "fixed and eternal laws" of laissez-faire doctrines as rationalizations of greed and selfish interests. Many progressive leaders had been jolted into the way of reform after reading *Progress and Poverty*, even though they could not accept Henry George's proposed solutions for the social evils he described.

But by the end of the nineteenth century a new generation of academic economists and social scientists was beginning to challenge the assumptions of Spencer and Adam Smith. Lester Frank Ward, a pioneer American sociologist, made the most fundamental attack upon the conservative formulations of social Darwinism in his *Dynamic Sociology* and *Psychic Factors of Civilization*. Ward was a thoroughgoing Darwinian in his social theories, but he distinguished between two forms of evolution: physical evolution, which moved by natural laws over which man had little or no control, and social evolution, which could be controlled by man through the rational techniques of technology and social planning. Similar ideas were developed by other social scientists—Richard T. Ely, John R. Commons, Simon Patten, Thorstein Veblen. And before the progressive era was over, John Dewey had codified this belief in the efficacy of socialized intelligence into a philosophy of instrumentalism.

Hence the progressive had a faith in progress so strong as to seem naïve to our disillusioned and skeptical generation. In the rhetoric of progressivism, phrases like "the upward spiral of human development" and "permanent progress" appear again and again. "Only the man whose hand never touches the realities of life," Senator Albert J. Beveridge declared in 1900, "despairs of human progress or doubts the providence of God."

The progressive, therefore, was predisposed to social tinkering. He was committed to a belief in the efficacy of human effort in reshaping the social environment. He was the first political type in American history to conceive of the possibility of applying social science to the affairs of government. "Before progressive legislation can become a success," wrote Lester Frank Ward, "every legislature must become . . . a laboratory of philosophical research into the laws of human society and human nature. Every true legislator must be a sociologist, and have his knowledge of that most intricate of all sciences founded upon organic and inorganic science."

The Populists had also advocated various forms of governmental control and government intervention in economic affairs; but while the Populist was much more at home in stating grievances and envisioning the goals of a society freed of greed and oppression, he was less interested in *techniques* of social organization and social science. Indeed, with William Jennings Bryan, he was likely to be suspicious of the "aristocracy of learning" and to "thank God for the democracy of the heart."

The progressive, on the other hand, began to use the appointive commission or bureau, manned by experts, to administer public affairs in a more scientific manner. Robert LaFollette's Wisconsin was a progressive laboratory in the sense that Ward had urged. During LaFollette's governorship, Wisconsin had Tax, Railroad, Conservation, Insurance, Banking, Public Service, and Industrial commissions, a State Bureau of Efficiency, a Legislative Reference Service for the drafting of bills, and other similar commissions and bureaus staffed by economists, scientists, and engineers from both academic and private life.

Theodore Roosevelt sensed the need for a more scientific approach to the trust problem in his first message to Congress when he called for the creation of a Bureau of Corporations to investigate the facts of corporate concentration. "The mechanism of modern business is so delicate that extreme care must be taken not to interfere . . . in a spirit of rashness or ignorance." Roosevelt's more complex approach to the regulation of railroad rates and his efforts in the field of conservation represented a movement in the direction of more sophisticated administrative techniques. Roosevelt's policies as President often lacked clarity and coherence; but in the campaign of 1912, he was fully committed to conceptions of government regulation and social welfare which required the use of the expert on a large scale.

Woodrow Wilson was suspicious of Roosevelt's New Nationalism, as outlined in the campaign of 1912, but he could escape neither the logic of events nor the logic of progressive preconceptions. The champion of the New Freedom was forced to accept the tenets of the New Nationalism in the Federal Trade Commission Act of 1914 and the reform legislation of 1916.

One may say also that the passion for a scientific approach to the problems of American society was nourished for the public at large by the muckraking journalists, writing in such magazines as *McClure's*, *Collier's*, *Everybody's*, *Munsey's*, etc. Of course, the exposures of political corruption and of the machinations of monopolists were written in a tone of moral exhortation and appealed to sentiments of responsibility, indignation, and guilt. Yet, much of the work of such journalists as Lincoln Steffens and Ida Tarbell, was analogous to the social scientist's patient investigation of social data.

The moral rhetoric of the progressives must not be overemphasized. The progressives had two vocabularies; they were also developing a vocabulary of social planning and social efficiency. LaFollette taught audiences of the Middle West to accept and appreciate a new vocabulary and a new style in politics. Unlike that of Bryan, LaFollette's appeal to the public was rational rather than emotional. He was not satisfied with moral preachments. He spoke instead in a rapid and intense fashion, piling up statistics and examples. The fact that he could keep a crowd of farmers on the edges of their seats for three hours reciting tariff schedules is not only a tribute to his unique or oratorical skill, but also is evidence of the higher levels of sophistication to which political discourse had been raised by the progressives and their academic allies.

The progressive era, in retrospect, is one of the brightest in American political history. We may scorn the naïveté of progressives, but they did establish a fruitful relation between the practical affairs of politics and the higher forms of intellection in the various disciplines of human knowledge of their time. Not since the days of Washington and Jefferson had rationality and politics been in such a close and happy relationship.

SUGGESTED READINGS

COMMAGER, HENRY S. *The American Mind: An Interpretation of American Thought and Character since the 1880's.* New Haven: Yale University Press, 1950.

FAULKNER, HAROLD U. *The Decline of Laissez-Faire, 1897–1917.* New York: Rinehart & Co., Inc., 1951.

FILLER, LOUIS. *Crusaders for American Liberalism.* Yellow Springs: Antioch College Press, 1950.

GOLDMAN, ERIC F. *Rendezvous with Destiny: A History of Modern American Reform.* New York: Alfred A. Knopf, Inc., 1952.

HOFSTADTER, RICHARD C. *The Age of Reform: From Bryan to F.D.R.* New York: Alfred A. Knopf, Inc., 1955.

LINK, ARTHUR S. *Woodrow Wilson and the Progressive Era.* New York: Harper & Bros., 1954.

MANN, ARTHUR. *Yankee Reformers in the Urban Age.* Cambridge: Harvard University Press, 1954.

MOWRY, GEORGE S. *The California Progressives.* Berkeley: University of California Press, 1951.

MOWRY, GEORGE S., *The Era of Theodore Roosevelt.* New York: Harper & Bros., 1958.

NOBLE, DAVID W. *The Paradox of Progressive Thought*. Minneapolis: University of Minnesota Press, 1958.

NYE, RUSSEL B. *Midwestern Progressive Politics: A Historical Study of Its Origins and Development, 1870–1950*. East Lansing: Michigan State University Press, 1951.

WHITE, MORTON G. *Social Thought in America: The Revolt against Formalism*. Boston: Beacon Press, 1949.

Document 23.1

PROGRESSIVE TECHNIQUES OF REGULATION

The following selection from Robert M. LaFollette's *Autobiography* is an account of the regulatory laws passed when he was Governor of Wisconsin. Wisconsin was often cited as a model of progressive government during this period, and this selection illustrates LaFollette's conception of the proper role of a progressive government as well as the techniques to be employed in achieving progressive goals.

(From Robert M. LaFollette, *LaFollette's Autobiography* [Madison: University of Wisconsin Press, 1960], pp. 149, 151–53)

As soon as the legislature passed our regulation law I appointed the three commissioners. I had contended all along for an appointive rather than an elective commission. I felt that the state should have the best experts in the country in these positions, whether residents of Wisconsin or not, for much would depend upon the way in which our new law was administered. They would have to match wits with the highly skilled, highly paid agents of the railroads, and they would have to make their work pass the critical consideration of the courts. Now, the men best equipped by study and experience for such work might, if the commission were elective, prove very poor campaigners. If pitted against brilliant talkers or good "mixers" they might stand no show at all. The submission also of a large number of candidates to the voter to be selected at a time when his mind is occupied with the consideration of questions under discussion, as well as candidates, tends still further to lessen the chances of the selection of the best man for particular service. For these reasons I have always strongly advocated the appointive method for filling all places requiring the services of trained experts. . . .

The Railroad Commission keeps accurate account of all the business of every railroad and public utility in the state. It has jurisdiction over property whose total value amounts to $450,000,000. The books are kept exactly as the commission orders them to be kept. These accounts show that while during the first five years of its existence the commission reduced rates by more than $2,000,000 a year, the *net earnings* of the railroads of Wisconsin increased relatively just a little more than the net earnings for all railways in the United States. The increase in Wisconsin was 18.45 per cent., and in the United States it was 18.41 per cent. . . .

Other public utilities besides railroads were not brought under the control of the Railroad Commission until 1907, and it was not until 1909 that the commission was able to get their accounts into such shape as to be reliable. But, for the year 1910, compared with 1909, notwithstanding reductions in rates and improvements in service, the water utilities increased their net earnings 7.1 per cent., the telephone utilities 7.1 per cent., gas utilities 7.4 per cent., and electric utilities 25 per cent. These utilities have even exceeded the railroads in the rate at which they have made cash investments for new construction. While the increase in railroad construction has averaged 2½ per cent. a year for six years, the water utilities in 1910 increased their new construction of property 2.5 per cent. over what it had been in 1909; the telephone utilities 5.4 per cent., gas utilities 1.6 per cent., and electric utilities 35.5 per cent. For the year 1911 compared with 1910 the water utilities increased their net earnings 4.3 per cent., the telephone utilities 15.9 per cent., gas utilities 5.7 per cent., and electric utilities 24.2 per cent. The water utilities in 1911 increased their property by new construction 4 per cent. over that of 1910; the telephone utilities 5.7 per cent., gas utilities 6.1 per cent., and electric utilities, 22.1 per cent.

Wisconsin is certainly not driving capital out of the state when the electrical business in the single year 1910, after two years of regulation by the state, made *bona fide* new investments 35 per cent. greater than it had done in 1909. All of this has been accomplished notwithstanding the fact that the Railroad Commission has reduced the rates charged by public utilities $250,000 a year, and has required improvements in the quality of service amounting to $125,000 a year—a total saving to the consumers of gas, water, and electricity of $375,000 a year. . . .

How has it been possible that both the people of Wisconsin and the investors in public utilities have been so greatly benefited by this regulation? *Simply because the regulation is scientific.* The Railroad Commission has found out through its engineers, accountants, and statisticians what it actually costs to build and operate the road and utilities. Watered stock and balloon bonds get no consideration. On the other hand, since the commission knows the costs, it knows exactly the point below which rates cannot be reduced. It even raises rates when they are below the cost, including reasonable profit. . . .

Document 23.2

ROOSEVELT ASKS FOR REGULATION

In his years in the presidency, Theodore Roosevelt had aligned himself with many progressive ideas and, in particular, had sought after new methods of dealing with the problem of concentrated corporate power. The selection below is taken from an article written for *Outlook* magazine as Theodore Roosevelt was preparing to make a bid for another term in the presidency in the exciting campaign of 1912. The selection is an interesting combination of moral language mixed with proposals for new techniques of administration.

(From Theodore Roosevelt, "The Trusts, the People and the Square Deal," *Outlook*, Vol. XCIX [November 18, 1911], pp. 653, 655–56)

Business cannot be successfully conducted in accordance with the practices and theories of sixty years ago unless we abolish steam, electricity, big cities, and, in short, not only all modern business and modern industrial conditions, but all the modern conditions of our civilization. The effort to restore competition as it was sixty years ago, and to trust for justice solely to this proposed restoration of competition, is just as foolish as if we should go back to the flintlocks of Washington's Continentals as a substitute for modern weapons of precision. The effort to prohibit all combinations, good or bad, is bound to fail, and ought to fail; when made, it merely means that some of the worst combinations are not checked and that honest business is checked. Our purpose should be, not to strangle business as an incident of strangling combinations, but to regulate big corporations in thoroughgoing and effective fashion, so as to help legitimate business as an incident to thoroughly and completely safeguarding the interests of the people as a whole. Against all such increase of Government regulation the argument is raised that it would amount to a form of Socialism. This argument is familiar; it is precisely the same as that which was raised against the creation of the Inter-State Commerce Commission, and of all the different utilities commissions in the different States, as I myself saw, thirty years ago, when I was a legislator at Albany, and these questions came up in conection with our State Government. . . .

This Nation should definitely adopt the policy of attacking, not the mere fact of combination, but the evils and wrong-doing which so frequently accompany combination. The fact that a combination is very big is ample reason for exercising a close and jealous supervision over it, because its size renders it potent for mischief; but it should not be punished unless it actually does the mischief; it should merely be so supervised and controlled as to guarantee us, the people, against its doing mischief. We should not strive for a policy of unregulated competition and of the destruction of all big corporations, that is, of all the most efficient business industries in the land. Nor should we persevere in the hopeless experiment of trying to regulate these industries by means only of lawsuits, each lasting several years, and of uncertain result. We should enter upon a course of supervision, control, and regulation of these great corporations—a regulation which we should not fear, if necessary, to bring to the point of control of monopoly prices, just as in exceptional cases railway rates are now regulated. Either the Bureau of Corporations should be authorized, or some other governmental body similar to the Inter-State Commerce Commission should be created, to exercise this supervision, this authoritative control. . . .

It is not necessary in an article like this to attempt to work out such a plan in detail. It can assuredly be worked out. Moreover, in my opinion, substantially some such plan must be worked out or business chaos will continue. Wrong-doing such as was perpetrated by the Standard Oil Trust, and especially by the Tobacco Trust, should not only be punished, but if possible punished in the persons of the chief authors and beneficiaries of the wrong, far more severely than at present. But punishment should not be the only, or indeed the main, end in view. Our aim should be a policy of construction and not one of destruction. Our aim should not be to punish the men who have made a big corporation successful merely because they have made it big and successful, but to exercise such thoroughgoing supervision and control over them as to insure their business skill being exercised in the interest of the public and not against the public interest. Ultimately, I believe that this control should undoubtedly indirectly or directly extend to dealing with all questions connected with their treatment of their employees, including the wages, the hours of labor, and the like. Not only is the proper treatment of a corporation, from the standpoint of the managers, shareholders, and employees, compatible with securing from that corporation the best standard of public service, but when the effort is wisely made it results in benefit both to the corporation and to the public. The success of Wisconsin in dealing with the corporations within her borders, so as both to do them justice and to exact justice in return from them toward the public, has been signal; and this Nation should adopt a progressive policy in substance akin to the progressive policy not merely formulated in theory but reduced to actual practice with such striking success in Wisconsin. . . .

. . . We need to formulate immediately and definitely a policy which, in dealing with big corporations that behave themselves and which contain no menace save what is necessarily potential in any corporation which is of great size and very well managed, shall aim not at their destruction but at their regulation and supervision, so that the Government shall control them in such fashion as amply to safeguard the interests of the whole public, including producers, consumers, and wageworkers. This control should, if necessary, be pushed in extreme cases to the point of exercising control over monopoly prices, as rates on railways are now controlled; although this is not a power that should be used when it is possible to avoid it. . . .

Document 23.3

THE OLD ORDER CHANGETH

The following selection is taken from one of Woodrow Wilson's New Freedom speeches in the presidential campaign of 1912. Although much of the speech is very general in language and moralistic in tone, Wilson's remarks are an illustration of the way in which a Progressive understood the changing forces of his day and the political demands which progressive leadership must accept.

(From William E. Leuchtenburg [ed.], *The New Freedom: A Call for the Emancipation of the Generous Energies of a People—Woodrow Wilson* [Englewood Cliffs, N.J.: Prentice-Hall, Inc., 1961], p. 29)

The old order changeth—changeth under our very eyes, not quietly and equably, but swiftly and with the noise and heat and tumult of reconstruction.

I suppose that all struggle for law has been conscious, that very little of it has been blind or merely instinctive. It is the fashion to say, as if with superior knowledge of affairs and of human weakness, that every age has been an age of transition, and that no age is more full of change than another; yet in very few ages of the world can the struggle for change have been so widespread, so deliberate, or upon so great a scale as in this in which we are taking part.

The transition we are witnessing is no equable transition of growth and normal alteration; no silent, unconscious unfolding of one age into another, its natural heir and successor. Society is looking itself over, in our day, from top to bottom; is making fresh and critical analysis of its very elements; is questioning its oldest practices as freely as its newest, scrutinizing every arrangement and motive of its life; and it stands ready to attempt nothing less than a radical reconstruction, which only frank and honest counsels and the forces of generous co-operation can hold back from becoming a revolution. We are in a temper to reconstruct economic society, as we were once in a temper to reconstruct political society, and political society may itself undergo a radical modification in the process. I doubt if any age was ever more conscious of its task or more unanimously desirous of radical and extended changes in its economic and political practice.

We stand in the presence of a revolution,—not a bloody revolution; America is not given to the spilling of blood,—but a silent revolution, whereby America will insist upon recovering in practice those ideals which she has always professed, upon securing a government devoted to the general interest and not to special interests.

We are upon the eve of a great reconstruction. It calls for creative statesmanship as no age has done since that great age in which we set up the government under which we live, that government which was the admiration of the world until it suffered wrongs to grow up under it which have made many of our own compatriots question the freedom of our institutions and preach revolution against them. I do not fear revolution. I have unshaken faith in the power of America to keep its self-possession. Revolution will come in peaceful guise, as it came when we put aside the crude government of the Confederation and created the great Federal Union which governs individuals, not States, and which has been these hundred and thirty years our vehicle of progress. Some radical changes we must make in our law and practice. Some reconstructions we must push forward, which a new age and new circumstances impose upon us. But we can do it all in calm and sober fashion, like statesmen and patriots.

I do not speak of these things in apprehension, because all is open and above-board. This is not a day in which great forces rally in secret. The whole stupendous program must be publicly planned and canvassed. Good temper, the wisdom that comes of sober counsel, the energy of thoughtful and unselfish men, the habit of co-operation and of compromise which has been bred in us by long years of free government, in which reason rather than passion has been made to prevail by the sheer virtue of candid and universal debate, will enable us to win through to still another great age without violence.

24

HOWARD H. QUINT
University of Massachusetts

Socialism and Communism in Modern America

SOCIALISM AND COMMUNISM have had strange and spectacularly unsuccessful careers in the United States. Why this has been so has been the basis for countless self-congratulatory books, articles, and speeches by Americans who have maintained that we are too wise to be taken in by the siren appeals of Marxism, whether in its more moderate or extreme forms. Yet, there are, of course, those among us who insist that we already have taken the road to socialism, or even worse, to communism. They reinforce their gloomy forebodings with the invariable warning that unless government, both national and local, stops concerning itself with broad "welfare" measures and regulating the "free enterprise" system, we shall arrive at a Marxist destination far sooner than we think.

We need not deal with the failure of socialism and communism in the United States in terms of our collective intelligence to eschew them; it may be doubted that as a people we possess any such inherent wisdom. The arguments of self-styled conservatives that welfare and economic regulatory measures are leading us to a Marxist society hardly deserve the privilege of debate, for, in fact, what these measures represent is the response of a twentieth-century democracy to the pervasive social and economic problems that stem from a modern industrial society. To avoid facing up to these problems might well invite the demand for a drastic change in the nature of our political and economic institutions. Certainly, socialism's golden day in the United States came early in this century, when social and economic inequities resulting from the new and still raw industrial capitalism cried out for correction. But today, a decade and a half after mid-century, there is perhaps no better evidence of the over-all success of these welfare measures and economic regulation in terms of our demo-cratic-capitalistic system than the virtual absence in the United States of either a socialist or a communist political organization dedicated to a general societal reconstruction. It was the New Deal, with its eco-nomic reforms and its concern for mass security, that finished off the Socialist party. As Norman Thomas, the distinguished socialist leader, sadly acknowledged: "What cut the ground out pretty completely from under us was . . . Roosevelt."

Previously, the American socialist movement had almost been wrecked by World War I when the Socialist party, which had taken an adamant antiwar stand, was deserted by a large segment of its membership supporting President Wilson's crusade "to make the world safe for democracy." It was hobbled shamefully by the govern-ment's policy of repression, condoned by the President at the expense of his reputation as a liberal. Although the party limped on through the twenties and was briefly rejuvenated in the early years of the Great Depression, it died a lingering death in the 1950's, with only a few of the faithful left to mourn it. It was in the post-World War I years that the Communist party appeared on the scene, took up some of the slack in the radical movement, and after a decade of some influ-ence (1935–45) entered also into a period of rapid decline, culmi-nating in its present-day moribundity.

It is important at this point to do what the average man on the street too often fails to do, namely, to discriminate between the so-cialist and communist movements in America. The socialists, what-ever one may think of their social and economic philosophy, sought to operate and to achieve their ends within the framework of the Ameri-can constitutional system. True, they wanted to make substantial structural revisions in the system with the end, in their opinion, of democratizing it, but at no time did they ever suggest scrapping it completely. Most important of all, their basic loyalty was always to the United States, even though fraternally they were linked to so-cialists in others parts of the world through the Second International.

Not so the communists. Unlike any other previous radical group in America, they took their orders from a foreign power; either they obeyed these orders, or they were expelled. They gave to the Soviet Union their first and only allegiance. They operated clandestinely and never gave the American constitutional system serious consideration except to invoke its guarantees for their own protection or enhance-ment. And they were at constant war with the socialists, who early recognized the undemocratic nature of both their political organization and their ultimate goals. Only during the late 1930's, when the communists were able to identify themselves with anti-Fascism and social and economic reform (at the expense of doctrinal purity), could they obtain a hearing and a following, though by no means a large one, in the United States.

We know today how enormously wrong was Karl Marx's prediction that a socialist society would emanate only from an advanced form of industrial capitalism. This prediction had the sanctity of law in Marxian doctrine. Yet the truth of the matter is that wherever thoroughgoing socialist societies have come into being during the last half century, aside from those imposed by the force of Soviet political and military power, they have been in economically backward countries. And the reason for this is clear to us, if it was not to Marx: In their drive for quick industrialization the people of these countries have turned to the state because it, and it alone, possesses sufficient capital —and sometimes not too much, at that—to mobilize economic resources and to undertake ambitious production programs. The human cost of such industrialization under state auspices has come high, as witness the experience of the Soviet Union; but this has not lessened its appeal, particularly in those countries where the great mass of poverty-stricken people have had everything to gain and very little or nothing to lose.

In the late nineteenth and early twentieth centuries, socialists throughout the world were under the spell of Marx's seemingly impregnable analysis. And this essentially was why they were hard pressed to explain the pronounced weakness of the socialist movement in the United States, where it should have been strong. The United States was undeniably a rising industrial colossus with a pronounced tendency toward industrial monopoly. Marx's theory of capitalistic accumulation and concentration surely applied to the American republic. Yet, other components of Marx's dialectical materialism did not fit the American pattern. There had not come into being, for example, a sizable class-conscious proletariat dedicated to the overthrow of capitalism; the economic well-being of American industrial workers was not deteriorating but improving; the middle class, contrary to Marx's prognosis, was not being ground down into the proletariat but expanding; and the Socialist party, which was to be the political vehicle for anticapitalist discontent, had not made a significant dent in the traditional party loyalties of American voters. The Socialist party's best showing came in 1912, at the very crest of the progressive era, when Eugene V. Debs, its perennial candidate for the presidency, received 897,011 votes, or 5.97 per cent of the total number cast. The Socialists never elected a United States senator nor a state governor; the best they could claim were two lonely congressmen, Victor Berger of Wisconsin and Meyer London of New York. Both men served in the second decade of the century.

The organization of a vigorous, united socialist movement in the United States was complicated by widely differing and strongly held beliefs as to what socialism involved. But more pertinent, perhaps, than the question of ideology, though not divorced from it, was the method by which socialism was to be attained. Here the socialists ran head on into formidable socioeconomic, political, and institutional barriers imposed by a successful American capitalism and a triumphant American democracy.

The pre-World War I socialist movement, both in Europe and in the United States, was plagued by a duality of doctrine which resulted in a kind of schizophrenia and simultaneously created bitter internecine conflicts. On the one hand, the scientific socialists aimed at a revolutionary new order and were pledged to eradicate capitalism, if and when they ever came to power. But to hew close to the line of doctrinal purity, to give short shrift to contemporary issues, and to emphasize only the glory day of socialist salvation—the delivery date of which could not be guaranteed—was to limit socialism's appeal to the pragmatically minded American wage earners and middle class. On the other hand, if the socialists were to seek to mitigate conditions of the existing order and to improve the lot of those living under it, they would have to accept the major premises of a capitalistic society and ultimately be forced to play the game of social reformers. According to hard-shelled Marxists, this would have the effect of making them socialists in name only and blur socialism's grand vistas. To sum up the problem, the scientific socialists were torn between ends and means, between millenial hopes and everyday actualities.

The Marxist "pitch" to American proletarians was made along orthodox lines of class solidarity and increasing misery. But this appeal lacked the magnetism that it held for European workers. As all students of the labor movement know, the United States at the turn of the century was hardly a worker's paradise. Yet the American industrial worker was well aware of and constantly reminded that the nation's capitalistic system had achieved higher real wages and living standards and greater occupational opportunities and mobility than were to be found elsewhere in the world. On the basis of the mass-production system, low prices, and generous credit, most Americans could enjoy consumption goods that were far beyond the reach of foreign workers.

This latter factor bears attention in the light of repeated claims by cultural nationalists that the vista of the "American dream" classless society, a fervently embraced idea of "uniqueness" and "giveness," and a frontier tradition of individualism were together responsible for counteracting socialism's appeal to the country's wage earners. Folk beliefs, of course, have an amazing persistency and an undeniable importance in the shaping of the national character. But what was it in the new industrial society if not the availability of consumption goods that gave to the older tradition of individualism the necessary material underpinnings? If the American worker did not qualify for membership in the middle class either by job or by income status, still the fact that he could obtain, or even think of acquiring, most of the material comforts of life placed him psychologically in the middle class, as had been true under the older agrarian order. There is a certain irony in the fact that whereas American middle-class social reformers have invariably maintained that they have been *for* but not *of* the working class, members of the latter just as consistently have considered themselves as being *of* though not necessarily *for* the middle class.

Economically speaking, the success of capitalism offers the best general answer to the query of the failure of socialism, as an ideology, to win more American adherents. There was little cause to accept a gospel of social and economic salvation emanating from a Europe already at the point of being surpassed by Yankee drive, technology, and ingenuity. In so far as socialism as an organized movement was concerned, however, its essential weakness was the failure of socialists themselves to "bore from within" and to gain control of the trade-union movement. Without trade-union foundations, as the early-day Marxists had maintained, the socialists could have little hope of either immediate or future success in the United States.

Socialists were active in both the National Labor Union and the Knights of Labor, though by no means did they play a controlling role in either. Efforts to bore from within and capture control of the American Federation of Labor encountered formidable difficulties, since several of its founders had been at one time confirmed Marxists. These men, while not hesitating to present as their own much of the Marxist critique of modern capitalism, nevertheless had deserted socialism's standard because they had become convinced that labor's trade-union goals and socialism's objectives could be neither identified nor harmonized. Accepting the permanency of industrial capitalism, they were subsequently willing to operate within its assumptions and to accept that very same stratified class society which the socialists wished to eliminate.

Socialism's high-water mark within the American Federation of Labor and within the American labor movement came amidst the panic and depression of 1893 and 1894. During the latter year, one Federation affiliate followed another in voting favorably on a political program calling for the "collective ownership by the people of all of the means of production and distribution." But the Federation's 1894 convention, taking its lead from Samuel Gompers, jettisoned the political program. It was a galling defeat for the socialists; and thereafter, as the nineties wore on, the so-called "pure and simple" forces gained control until Gompers was literally unchallenged and the Federation committed irrevocably to co-operation with capital. And why, it may quite properly be asked, did the socialists in the AFL acquiesce to Gompers' determined leadership? Perhaps the best answer is that, as trade unionists, they were more concerned with maintaining an organization dedicated to securing bread-and-butter objectives than, as socialists, in adhering unswervingly to a policy that offered the proverbial "pie in the sky."

Failure of the socialists to gain control of the trade-union movement had the effect of sharpening their interest in political action. But here, they encountered even greater difficulties than in the field of trade unionism. For one thing, there has been a traditional disinclination in the United States to support absolutist and abstract theories of society and government. To gain mass acceptance, socialism had to originate in and grow out of the institutional fabric of American society. Such was hardly the case. Although it had many distinct American ramifications, socialism was ideologically a foreign importation, and the great mass of Americans never ceased to regard it as such. Equally if not more important, the fact that Marxist theory condoned ultimate resort to force and violence not only stigmatized "scientific socialism" but also placed it outside the then still honorable tradition of native American radicalism. Marxist leaders, always painfully conscious of the high percentage of immigrants within their ranks, stressed the need to "Americanize" the movement, but it was not until the collapse of the People's party after 1896 that the memberships of socialist political organizations began to be sprinkled generously with native-born Americans.

The two-party system and tradition constituted the greatest single political obstacle to the socialists as well as to other third parties. Spokesmen for the orthodox parties, when they did not ignore the socialists completely, never failed to point out the futility of throwing away one's vote on socialist candidates who were destined to certain defeat. Socialism's objectives might be alluring, but they were of little concrete value if the means of achieving them were not at hand. Under the circumstances, the socialists and their sympathizers were often unable to resist voting for the less objectionable of the Republican or Democratic candidates. And political victories over and above the local level *were* important, despite the contentions of socialist leaders that elections under the existing capitalistic system were significant only as propaganda opportunities for the general enlightenment of the American public. Constant political setbacks proved more discouraging than educational to the socialist rank and file. In the face of such defeats, party morale was difficult to maintain, and converts were seldom made on the basis of political impotence.

In those places where socialism, as a political movement, has enjoyed a modicum of success, it has been largely because of the support of members of the middle class who were convinced that the socialists would bring about increased economic efficiency and greater social justice. During the 1890's, the vogue of Edward Bellamy's *Looking Backward* caused thousands of middle-class Americans to take an interest in socialism and gave it a thin veneer of respectability hitherto completely lacking. Yet, as with the working class, only a very small segment of the American middle class was attracted to socialism. A few mavericks threw in their lot with the Marxists and in some instances, notably in the progressive era, rose to positions of leadership. But most middle-class radicals, even those who were willing to label themselves "Fabian socialists," eschewed association with the Marxists and the political parties they dominated. First and foremost, they rejected the emphasis of the Marxists on the class struggle doctrine. But they were also understandably irritated by the allocation of all of humanity's virtues to the proletarians who toiled with sweat and brawn.

In any consideration of the relationship of the middle class to socialism, one must bear in mind the difficulties that confronted socialist leaders in their efforts to win over that particular hard core of the American *bourgeoisie*, the farmers. In the Midwest and in some parts of the South the socialists received some of the legacy of the agrarian discontent generated by Populism, but their appeal was fundamentally one of negative protest against the existing social and economic order rather than of positive adherence to the principles of the cooperative commonwealth. The socialists faced the same very real bugaboo that had confronted Henry George when he sought to enlist the support of farmers in his crusade against land rents. In the last analysis, socialism meant the expropriation of land, and that could not be explained away. American farmers, furthermore, were far more concerned with preserving competitive capitalism than in extirpating it. Some had been willing to go along with the mild collectivist proposals of the Populists, not because they condoned state ownership per se but because it gave promise of eliminating the private monopolist. Only the most despairing saw in socialism a solution to their own personal problems.

Socialism needs a favorable disposition in the national temperament to permit it an unbiased hearing and perhaps a trial of its claims. This it has lacked in the United States, where all of the institutional cards have been thoroughly stacked on the side of the existing order. From those cradles of ideas and ideals, the public schools, the young have been early inculcated with the inherent superiority of American democracy and American capitalism. Nor have the nation's colleges and universities been seminaries of socialist sedition, as frightened conservatives have always complained. American students have been on the whole conservative, if not completely socially and politically apathetic. Further, it is also a matter of public record that university administrators, spurred on by determined boards of trustees, have shown on occasion a zeal in purging their faculties of instructors who have held mildly unorthodox, let alone socialist views.

Religious institutions, too, have been bulwarks of the *status quo*. Few will deny their important role in shaping the national mind; and in this regard, it is perhaps well to re-emphasize the traditional social conservatism of American churches of all denominations. In recent years, historians have been prone to overplay the importance of the social gospel movement in American Protestantism. One needs rather to remember that only a very meager part of the Protestant clergy was tinged with radical social Christianity. Much the same can be said of the Catholic counterpart of the social gospel. The Catholic church in America, dominated by a conservative Irish-American hierarchy, has been an important factor in immunizing Catholic workingmen against socialism. Karl Marx himself had given the kiss of death to socialism in America. For try as they might, the American socialists could not live down his famous statement that religion was the "opiate of the people." To millions of Americans, socialism was identified with atheism and automatically an anathema.

One other molder of public attitude, the press, merits a word. Even those papers which boasted their objectivity and impartiality rarely extended press coverage to the socialists. And when, by chance, they did, there was usually a perceptible effort made to denigrate them. Nor were editorials on socialism the epitome of intellectual honesty, as socialist doctrines were consistently and—one cannot help but believe, purposely—misrepresented.

In broad and highly general terms, then, these have been the principal reasons for the present bankruptcy of socialism in the United States. Undoubtedly, there are others which may be equally significant, particularly in the context of specific situations. The failure of an ideological and political movement can hardly be intellectually packaged and explained in a neat and all-inclusive formula.

From an institutional point of view, the causes for the failure of socialism in the United States apply also to communism. Again, most important of all, communism, like socialism, has been overwhelmed by American economic abundance. This has been notably true since the end of World War II. David A. Shannon, an astute historian of American communism, has observed: "The era of the picture window and the tail-finned automobile has produced its own dissatisfactions and frustrations but not the kind that leads one to seek salvation in Left Wing politics."

But American communism also has provided its own unique causes for its checkered history and current agonies. No political movement that is ancillary to a foreign power and blindly follows its dictates can hope to retain for long the allegiance of any sizable portion of the American people. While many of us may be deceived some of the time, only a few, who purposely choose not to see, can be fooled all of the time.

The Communist party of today has thousands of disloyal and disillusioned alumni. For such persons, it usually was a way station in their political and economic education; and for one reason or another, they learned that it was not where they wished to stay for the remainder of their lives. Consequently, they got out—quietly in most cases; with rancor, recrimination, and bitterness in others. During the depression years, when the communists were at the pinnacle of their strength, they were able to attract followers because of their support of social reform measures and their aggressive trade-union activity. That they were engaged in labor and reform movements for their own ends, sometimes even to wreck them, was frequently overlooked by those who did not have to deal intimately with them. With few exceptions, American liberals during the 1930's were willing to extend to the communists a broad band of tolerance.

During the same years the communists seemed to stand almost courageously alone in their opposition to Nazi aggression in Europe. As a consequence, the Communist party ranks were swollen by new members, men and women dismayed by the appeasement policies of the Western democracies toward the Axis powers. The Soviet Union's aid to the Spanish republic in the bloody civil war—although given at a high price—was reflected to the advantage of the American communists. But any gain thus obtained was obliterated almost overnight by the announcement of the Soviet-Nazi pact of 1939. Those who had joined the party because of its opposition to Fascism deserted it en masse in disgust.

Since the end of World War II the very real menace of Soviet and Chinese imperialism has destroyed whatever little favor the communists still enjoyed in the United States. No longer were they looked upon tolerantly by liberals and labor organizations. On the contrary, there was a strong revulsion against them, and the rest of the *non-communist* left became what the socialists had been from almost the very beginning, an *anticommunist* left. The brutal Soviet suppression of the Hungarian uprising in 1956 added the finishing touch to demoralization that had already set in among the comrades.

Except for professional anticommunists, who make a living from exposing the "red menace" and other forms of official and unofficial bogeymen, the communist movement is largely a memory in the United States. Only a tiny group of communist die-hards continue to bray in the wilderness. Speaking editorially of "the virtually non-existent internal Communist threat," the *New York Times* declared on June 7, 1961: "The real Communist challenge is from abroad; and the sooner Americans get over the idea that we can solve the problem by persecuting the tattered remnants of American communism at home, the better able we will all be to face the really hard decisions and hard problems posed by the genuine menace of communism pushing outward from China and the Soviet Union."

Americans need not fear any domestic form of communism, social-ism, or any other "ism" so long as they maintain an economy that is capable of abundance, a political system that makes democratic the-ory a living reality, and a social order that assures both mass security and equality of opportunity to all, irrespective of race, color, creed, or social status. All these are still part of the nation's unfinished business.

SUGGESTED READINGS

AARON, DANIEL. *Writers on the Left: Episodes in American Literary Com-munism.* New York: Harcourt Brace & World, Inc., 1961.

BELL, DANIEL. "The Background and Development of Marxian Socialism in the United States," in DONALD EGBERT and STOW PERSONS (eds.), *Socialism and American Life,* Vol. I. Princeton: Princeton University Press, 1952.

DRAPER, THEODORE. *American Communism and Soviet Russia.* New York: Viking Press, Inc., 1960.

DRAPER, THEODORE. *The Roots of American Communism.* New York: Viking Press, Inc., 1957.

GINGER, RAY. *The Bending Cross: A Biography of Eugene Victor Debs.* New Brunswick: Rutgers University Press, 1949.

HILLQUIT, MORRIS. *History of Socialism in the United States.* New York: Beacon Press, 1903.

HOWE, IRVING and COSER, LEWIS. *The American Communist Party.* Boston: Beacon Press, 1957.

KIPNIS, IRA. *The American Socialist Movement, 1897–1912.* New York: Co-lumbia University Press, 1952.

QUINT, HOWARD H. *The Forging of American Socialism: Origins of the Modern Movement.* Columbia: University of South Carolina Press, 1953.

SHANNON, DAVID A. *The Decline of American Communism.* New York: Har-court, Brace & Co., 1959.

SHANNON, DAVID A. *The Socialist Party of America.* New York: Macmillan Co., 1955.

Document 24.1

SOCIALISM AND INDIVIDUALISM

Nicholas Paine Gilman (1849–1912), a Harvard-trained Unitarian cler-gyman and Professor of Sociology and Ethics at the Meadville Theologi-cal School, was one of America's leading critics of socialism at the turn of the twentieth century. A spokesman for "enlightened conservatism,"

Gilman strongly advocated profit sharing, which he believed would reconcile labor and management and give the worker a just share of the rewards of business enterprise.

(From Nicholas Paine Gilman, *Socialism and the American Spirit* [Boston, 1896], pp. 342–48)

No more ingenious scheme, however, than scientific socialism has ever been imagined by the perverse intellect of partial thinkers for diminishing the progress of civilization. The philosophic thinker is repelled by the exaggerated emphasis which they place on the material comfort of the least successful part of the human race. The palace of the multi-millionaire, whose conscience does not forbid his assailing legislators with every argument in his power, is not, indeed, a spectacle to afford comfort to the enlightened observer of contemporary life; but a proposal to strike a dead level for all men between the palace and the poorhouse would not, therefore, be agreeable to him. The palace is an incident in general progress, the phalanstery would be an accompaniment of widespread stagnation. The full-fledged socialist, in America and elsewhere, commonly indulges in unmitigated denunciation of all the rich. He improves upon the motto of Terence so far that nothing human is alien to him, except the man of wealth. Now if we remember the relativity of the notion of wealth and consider that, as a simple fact, the vast majority of the rich people of this country at least have acquired their fortunes by honest and legitimate effort, and that their wealth, in a rough way, corresponds to the amount of actual capacity which they have shown; if we consider, still further, that in acquiring this wealth they have contributed greatly, and of necessity, to the welfare of thousands upon thousands of their fellowmen, we shall incline to a more rational socialism that has some sympathy with the honest rich as well as with the honest poor.

The great body of the American people are neither rich nor poor. They are not exposed to the temptations or disadvantages of extreme wealth or extreme poverty. They are capitalists, to the extent of knowing in some degree what the possession of private property means. They are all the more highly developed human beings because of this possession of capital, —for capital, rightly interpreted, means power and opportunity. With this mass of people the solution of every industrial and social problem finally rests in this country. They are not making an outcry, or clamoring for the discontinuance of many existing institutions. They feel, quite strongly enough, a discontent with their own lot; but their condition renders them quite incapable of such indiscriminate denunciation of the rich as the socialist usually falls into. They are only too ready to perceive the advantages, rather than the disadvantages, of wealth, as compared with that modest competence which leaves personal exertion of a regular character essential. These American citizens, possessed of American ambition, have no desire to level things down to their own standard of comfort; on the contrary, they are determined to level up their own lot to the highest attainable point. Just so fast and so far as this great class, neither rich nor poor, receives the cultivation and refinement of the higher education (and it desires nothing more ardently than the best educational opportunities), will the material and moral problems of advanced civilization obtain satisfactory solution. No socialism, we may be sure, will commend itself to them which virtually denounces leadership by the men who have fully shown their capacity. Where, indeed, is the religion or the philosophy which has ever led men to trust themselves long to guidance by the incompetent?

The fundamental antecedent to any form of rational social betterment must be a willingness on the part of the individual to think upon the lot of other men with a lively and sympathetic interest. Experience shows that a certain degree of material comfort is almost indispensable, with the great mass of mankind, for the manifestation of any considerable degree of such interest. When the simple effort to obtain bread for the day or the year requires the full strength and ability of the individual, there is little room for altruism and small chance of one's putting himself, imaginatively, in the other man's place. So great is the number, however, of the well-to-do in our country, as compared with the number of the positively indigent, that the appeal to the comfortable and prosperous classes to interest themselves, individually and cooperatively, in the welfare of their weaker brethren is, as it should be, incessant. It may be impossible to improve civilization in that extreme geometrical proportion which the eager philanthropist often imagines. None the less do we need to combat steadfastly the native tendency of the prosperous man to be satisfied with himself. He is only too prone to consider the comfort of others as of little consequence if that large self which includes his family is luxuriously appareled, royally housed, and gratified with the obsequiousness mankind is ever ready to exhibit to wealth. But here we have to deal, not with any transient or superficial phenomenon of a passing year or generation, but with that "old Adam," as the theologians once delighted to call it, of selfishness. Yet while the preacher denounces "self" and "sin" as equivalent, the man of science and even the man of philosophy more contentedly recognize that human nature is as it is, and must be taken as it is, and that, in all probability, the theologian, the philan-thropist and the preacher would fail miserably in making it over, even according to the highest and brightest ideal in their earnest minds. Con-descension and superciliousness toward actual human nature, groping its way toward something better and higher, are out of place. Human nature, as the main feature in the social situation, must be recognized without praise or blame. Its multiformity and complexity forbid the acceptance of the depressing pictures of a monotonous future which socialism has thus far presented.

The scientific temper, both as respects calmness in observation and sobriety in expectation, is one of the factors on which we may safely rely for the rationalization of socialism and individualism alike. The cool and deliberate spirit which, first of all, inquires carefully into the facts of the situation, whether in the world of physics or in the world of human nature, and then infers the lines on which movement may be initiated with profit, in conformity with the past evolution, is an excellent corrective of the temper of the ordinary socialist. He almost invariably gives a very one-sided and unjust picture of our industrial civilization; he contem-plates with a jaundiced eye all the unpromising phenomena of the present, despising the happier mood which a fuller view would authorize. The man of scientific spirit will think better of the existing situation, as he compares it with the past; at the same time, he will have a more moderate conception of the possibilities of progress in the immediate future,—the only future concerning which he cares to occupy himself much. He offers us a far brighter prospect of probable achievement in this near future than the socialist. It is curious, indeed, in this century of discovery and invention that the socialist should put so largely to one side the possibili-ties of social improvement which we may rationally expect from the progress of applied science and inventive skill. He is strangely biased by his propensity to rely upon legislation as an instrument of progress. Surely, one need consider but briefly the history of the last hundred years, to see how small a part legislation has played in the tremendous development of modern society, compared with science, invention and discovery. The merest allusion to the great steps in the amazing scientific and industrial development will here suffice. We may confidently trust ourselves for much of our salvation to further advance in man's mastery over the powers of nature. The first step in such mastery has ever been a submission of the mind to the facts of a universe of law and order. The plainest note of the socialistic agitation of our time is, on the con-trary, an obstinate desire to impose on our complicated society—the result of thousands of years of evolution—an ideal scheme, not even thought out with theoretical consistency, and never yet presented in such a practical form as to assure careful thinkers that it would keep in running order for a year in any civilized nation. In the very different prophetic strain to which old Experience hath attained, one may feel safe in anticipating that, however the pace may be accelerated, the future development of civilization will be essentially on the same lines which it has followed in the last hundred years.

One must risk the charge of cant in the discussion of social reform by saying that, after all, the difficulty with the men and women of to-day, rich or poor, is moral rather than economic. More than once, of late years, it has been declared with great reason, that if men and women were morally fit for socialism,—morally good enough to give such a scheme a chance to work,—there would be no need of setting up the socialistic state, because every advantage which it promises would have been already secured, through the moral elevation of the men and women who would have to constitute that state. The assertion is quite unanswerable, as a calculation of the probabilities, moral and economic. We cannot be sure that any socialistic scheme ever yet outlined would succeed in practice. Socialists who admit this, believe in the necessity for a long preliminary period, largely given to a preparation of the heart and conscience. But it is altogether probable that, in the course of such a preparation, the full benefits of the fanciful industrial and political scheme would be anticipated. Despite its enthusiasm for equality in comfort and possessions among the citizens of the ideal State, socialism lays little stress upon morals. The monotonous emphasis of its advocates is upon the material side of life, and upon legislation rather than upon that slow moral advancement which in fact conditions all lasting material progress. There is no small force in the declaration that "Socialism is individualism run mad." The saying implies that a scheme is irrational which holds that the main matter is the greatest amount of material comfort for the individual.

Human society has not been ruled by such a law. Whoever is responsible for the fact,—God, or Nature, or mankind,—the advance of the race in knowledge, wisdom and righteousness has been the far more exigent standard. . . . The one right and reasonable attitude of man is to bend his mind to patient study of the facts and laws of a God-ordained universe, seeking to derive strength and mastery by submission to the forces of nature and of the spirit, very sure that social betterment lies on the difficult line of obedience and righteousness, not over the flowery paths of the assertion, comfort and indulgence of the lower self. . . .

Document 24.2

CLASSES IN AMERICA

Probably only a very few residents of present-day Los Angeles are aware that the city's best-known artery of commerce is named after a man who spent nearly his entire adult life predicting the downfall of capitalism, namely, H. Gaylord Wilshire (1861–1927). Renowned in the first decade of the twentieth century as "the millionaire socialist," he was the publisher of *Wilshire's Magazine*, which had a large circulation both in the United States and in Great Britain. Wilshire, never completely orthodox in his socialist beliefs, was frequently at odds with his fellow socialists; and after 1912, he gave up socialism for syndicalism.

(From "Classes in America," *Wilshire's Magazine*, March 1903, pp. 5–6)

We Americans have a great advantage over other nations in our unconsciousness of classes. That we have rich and poor is not denied, but that we have classes and class feeling is almost as vigorously denied by the poor as by the rich. And this denial of the palpable has an effect upon the social consciousness that it is hard to over-estimate.

In Europe classes are a recognized institution. The peasant never thinks that he is anything but a peasant, nor does the nobleman ever think he is anything but a nobleman. Even the very rich capitalist feels that he is hardly as good as the poor aristocrat.

In America, while differences in wealth have really made very distinct class cleavages, we refuse to recognize this condition; and there is no doubt that this refusal will sooner or later have a considerable political effect. We deny that Mr. Rockefeller's money was ever given to him except for the benefit of the whole people, and we have been insisting that the wealth of such men would be distributed by natural laws in the course of time, and the sons of other men would be quite as liable to own Rockefeller's wealth as his own descendants. This, indeed, is the stock argument of almost all opponents of Socialism. They insist that while there is great wealth in a few hands, this is simply an ephemeral condition of affairs, and that no one family will hold great wealth any length of time. So long as people generally believe this, it is not difficult to understand why it is they refuse to consider any change of society which would aim at preventing the concentration of wealth, feeling, as they do, that it will regulate itself automatically. However, we are now realizing that this concentration of wealth, and the holding of the natural resources of the country by a few immensely rich families, not only gives no sign of being an ephemeral state of affairs, but has every indication of being a permanency. Every year the very rich are becoming more and more strongly intrenched behind their ramparts of gold, and the public are generally recognizing that under our existing social system there is no possible remedy for the inequality of wealth. It is true we have anti-Trust bills galore introduced in our Houses of Congress, having for their object the levelling of the great fortunes, but these bills are felt by everyone to be of no possible avail in that direction. Concentration of wealth is an inevitable result of our economic system, and we can no more make effective laws to prevent it than we can make laws to prevent the sun shining. However, the introduction of these anti-Trust bills year after year in our Congress indicates strongly the wish of the people to level wealth and to abolish conditions which make classes. They are also a very reluctant confession that there is such a thing as a class cleavage in the United States. Our sentiments are too strongly democratic to allow any classes to remain if we can possibly prevent it, because we are fundamentally opposed to classes, and to this extent Socialism, which aims to abolish classes, will have a spiritual significance to the people of the United States which it has not in European countries where aristocracy is a recognized institution. There has never been a nation of free people, such as we Americans are, resolving year after year that they wished to do a certain thing, and having every reason to get their wish, and also having every means for carrying it into effect, but what finally succeeded in their desires. While we scoff at the anti-Trust laws as being ridiculous, yet we can see behind them the determination of the people to accomplish the establishment of an economic equality among the people of this country. One hundred years or more ago, in colonial days, and before we separated from England, there was a long period of time in which we kept on passing resolutions and having meetings, and even having physical encounters with her. It was with the greatest reluctance we ever finally considered the possibility of separation from the mother country. In fact, it was once considered rank treason to refer to independence as an ultimate outcome of the agitation against England's tyranny. We expected to make some sort of a compromise by which we would still remain colonies and yet participate in all the advantages of an independent country. It is the same today. We expect to allow the Rockefellers and Morgans to own us, and yet we expect to have all the luxuries of complete independence which can only accompany self-ownership. It will finally be found to be just as impossible for us to remain free and independent under King Morgan as it was for us to remain free and independent under King George. In fact, theoretically, as has been proven by the English colonies—Canada and Australia, New Zealand, etc.—it would have been much more possible for us to remain under King George than it will be for us to remain under King Morgan. King George did not need to have been even a benevolent despot to have kept the American colonies; he needed but to have been sane. King Morgan, with all his benevolence, can never keep his American colonies, simply because the economic system will prevent him from devising a plan which can avert the great unemployed problem. He cannot feed us. Under King George the economic problem was how we could produce *enough* to give us the luxuries and comforts of life. Under King Morgan the problem is:—How can we prevent ourselves producing too much? Our fear is that we will be swamped in a rising sea of wealth.

What we must do is not to try and prevent the sea of wealth from rising, but to construct the bark of Socialism which will float us safely upon it, so that instead of wealth being a menace to us we will be borne forward upon it to the Golden Age of Man.

Document 24.3

"THE SOVIET UNION HAS SET A GLORIOUS EXAMPLE"

The American communist "line" on the Soviet-Nazi pact of August 23, 1939, and the subsequent carving-up of Poland are reflected in the *Daily Worker*, which spoke for the Communist party, U.S.A. Following are brief editorial excerpts and a portion of an interview with the party's Secretary General, Earl Browder, which reveal how the American communists were caught unprepared for the announcement of the pact and how they sought to explain away both the pact and the Soviet invasion of eastern Poland.

HITLER THREATENS WAR

(From the *Daily Worker*, August 11, 1939)

Hitler's mobilized army of 2,000,000 soldiers are ready to be plunged against Poland in order to make Danzig a part of the Nazi Reich. . . .

For the sake of world peace every firm stand of Poland—especially of the Polish people and those in the Warsaw government who show they are sincere—should be supported. . . .

THE SOVIET UNION AND NONAGRESSION

(From the *Daily Worker*, August 23, 1939)

In the recent period the masses of the American people have come to realize better than they ever did before what a true friend the Soviet Union is for America as well as for all non-aggressor countries. Every true American and sincere opponent of reaction will rejoice together with the Chinese people at the fact that the Soviet Union in entering negotiations for this non-aggression treaty with Germany does so in the interest of curbing fascist aggression and promoting world peace. . . .

BROWDER REFUTES ISOLATION THEORY

(From the *Daily Worker*, August 24, 1939)

. . . Browder: I do not see any reason to expect any departure in the Soviet Union's peace policy. The principle of the Soviet Union has always been to provide against aggression, not to attack any other nation, and it always provided against complicity in the aggression of any other nation. . . .

FOR NATIONAL FREEDOM AND WORLD PEACE

(From the *Daily Worker*, September 18, 1939)

With the total collapse of the treacherous and semi-fascist Polish government, the Polish people—including the White Russian and Ukrainian minorities—were left completely at the mercy of the Nazi invaders. On the one hand, these unhappy people were faced with brutal Nazi aggression; on the other, they were being stabbed in the back by the Chamberlain Munichmen, with whom the Polish ruling circles were in league. As Hitler's hordes advanced further into Poland, the atrocities against the Jewish people and other minorities exceeded some of fascism's goriest deeds.

In this situation the Soviet government sent in the Red Army, as an army of liberation, to protect the Ukrainian and White Russian minorities, after the semi-fascist Polish government had ceased to exist and had left them to the ravages of war and fascist enslavement. More than a million Jews living in Western Ukraine and Western Byelo-Russia are now beyond the pale of fascist anti-Semitism.

Freed from tyrannical rule of the greedy landlords and the corrupt nobility, all these minorities for the first time can chart for themselves a life of freedom, happiness and peace as have their brothers in the land of socialism. Freed from the chains of exploitation, they can now enjoy real self-determination, a chance to choose their own future, and decide their own fate.

Truly the Soviet Union has scored another triumph for human freedom—destined for the brightest page of world history. It is in accordance with her steadfast unshakable peace policy and with her policy of neutrality already clearly proclaimed in the present imperialist war in Europe. . . .

Faced with the war of imperialist rivalries now going on in Europe, the main concern of the American people is to stay out of it. They want no part of imperialist wars hatched by Chamberlain and his fascist intrigues. They want real neutrality from imperialist conflicts. In this the Soviet Union has set a glorious example. It is by proclaiming her neutrality that the Soviet Union has been able to help a people threatened by fascist slavery. In her own interest, America will greet peace and freedom.

25

HAROLD W. CARY

University of Massachusetts

The United States Rejects the League of Nations

TWENTY YEARS after the expansionists of 1898 had led the United States to embark upon their "large policy" in foreign relations, the country was again face to face with another challenge to responsibility in the course of world events. Both occasions were marked by sudden involvement in war; and in each instance, Americans were impelled into closer relations with peoples whose affairs they had previously ignored. Moreover, both wars were followed by serious debate regarding the future course of the nation's foreign policy.

But there the similarity ends. Where the war of 1898 had been followed by adoption of the so-called "large policy," World War I was to end in the Senate's refusal to advise and consent to the terms of peace drawn up by representatives of the associated powers at Paris. And with this denial came rejection of membership in the new League of Nations and responsibility for the future peace of the world. Why, then, did the United States turn its back upon the League? What led to the rejection of the work of its diplomats? Was no hope of compromise possible among the differing groups in America? What consequences would flow from this debate?

A variety of explanations has been offered to these questions. To some historians the answer lies in the anti-League sentiment of American liberals, who saw betrayal of their hopes for a more equitable peace settlement. Other scholars have found the answer in the intricacies of the political processes which surround the conduct of America's foreign relations—the Senate's jealousy of its prerogatives, failure of rapport between the White House and the Department of State, and ineptitude of presidential leadership. And still others have come to believe that defeat of the new program resulted primarily from the clash of internal political forces spearheaded by two intransigent leaders, both jealous of their reputations as "scholars in politics"—Democratic President Woodrow Wilson and Massachusetts Republican Senator Henry Cabot Lodge.

When war burst upon the world in 1914, Americans understandably fixed their attention upon the unfolding events in Europe. As the war dragged on, with mounting carnage and inconclusive results, more and more of them became concerned with finding means of eliminating its curse forever. By mid-1915, responsible men and women were beginning to talk of a league to enforce the peace; Republicans and Democrats alike accepted the new idea. Ex-President William Howard Taft and President Wilson lent it their prestige. And Senator Lodge, who even then was convinced that Wilson was, with one exception, the worst President in American history, agreed with them. Speaking at Union College in June, 1915, the Massachusetts Senator asserted: "There is no escape from the proposition that the peace of the world can be maintained only by the force which united nations are willing to put behind it." A year later, Wilson and Lodge defended the proposed league from the same platform, an event described as "one of the great dramatic moments in American and world history."

The impact of this new policy upon the American people is impossible to measure; but by January, 1917—some three months before the country's entrance into the war—it clearly had become a major part of Wilson's program for the national well-being. Addressing the Senate on January 22, he urged American co-operation with the other world powers. "It is inconceivable that the people of the United States should play no part in that great enterprise. . . . They can not with honor withhold the service to which they now are about to be challenged. . . . It will be absolutely necessary that a force be created as a guarantor of the permanency of the settlement so much greater than the force of any nation now engaged or any alliance hitherto formed or projected that no nation . . . could face or withstand it."

Up to this point, few publicly stated objections to a league to enforce the peace had been heard. But when the President formally proposed this idea to the Senate, it immediately became a prickly political issue. Initially leading the opposition were Senators Porter J. McCumber, a Republican from South Dakota, and the erstwhile proponent of the league idea, Senator Lodge. In January, Lodge refused an invitation to address a meeting of league supporters; privately, he regretted "ever getting mixed up with it."

January, 1917, was a momentous month for the United States. On the twenty-second the President had offered—specifically to the Senate and generally to the world—his estimate of the essential terms of peace. Moreover, he called upon the nation to prepare itself to champion them. Within the week the German ambassador had delivered the note that made American entry into the military struggle inevitable. And on the following day, February 1, Senator Lodge delivered in the Senate his first antileague speech, one which was to become the basic text both for a denial of league membership and for a thoroughgoing American isolationism.

It was a biting speech, combining caustic criticism of Wilson's understanding of history with a frontal assault upon his latest proposal for national policy. Wilson's suggestions for a peace without victory and the requisites of democracy and freedom in international relations were termed unrealistic and illogical, "soft concealments to cover up realities." But Lodge's tour de force, couched in a series of rhetorical questions, aimed at the proposals for enforcing peace. Was the United States ready, he asked, to merge its armed forces into a league army, commanded by league-appointed officers? Would it be willing to enter a war which easily might be precipitated by some irresponsible small nation? Should this nation bind itself to fight at the command of any body other than Congress? Was it ready to pass beyond the voluntary stage of world peace?

Once the country became involved in war, debate over future collective policy was suspended in Congress. During the hostilities the President continued to develop his program for peace. In the famous Fourteen Points, which he outlined in another address to Congress in January, 1918, he included a proposal for a league of nations. Subsequent Allied and German acceptance of the Fourteen Points as a basis for the armistice agreement of November 11, 1918, served as a warrant of the world's approval.

The forces of opposition in the United States, however, were not permanently silenced. In the first week of November, 1918, the Republican party, victorious in the Congressional elections, gained control of the Senate, and Senator Lodge was soon busy organizing it. By seniority, he was to become Chairman of the Committee on Foreign Relations, a strategic post from which to oppose a league.

The battle to defeat Wilson began early. Even before the peace conference had assembled, Lodge delivered to Henry White, the sole Republican member of the American peace delegation, his own list of acceptable peace terms. In subsequent conferences with ex-President Theodore Roosevelt, ex-Senator Albert J. Beveridge, and Senator William E. Borah (R.) of Idaho, Lodge settled on the lines of political strategy. If Wilson's terms involved "control of our legislation, of our armies and navies, or the Monroe Doctrine or an international peace force. . . ," Lodge wrote to Beveridge, "our issue is made up and we shall win."

Strategy thus planned, tactics remained to be perfected. The first maneuver was to put the President under pressure as early as possible. Wilson's decision to return to the United States in February, 1919, offered the opportunity.

Once back in Washington, the President invited members of the Senate Foreign Relations Committee to a White House dinner meeting for a briefing on the treaty. Two days later, on the Senate floor, Lodge made a frontal attack on the treaty. He repeated essentially the same arguments he had made in 1917: (1) The warnings of Washington, Jefferson, and Monroe against foreign entanglements were invoked; (2) pledges to protect the independence and integrity of member nations were held as mere steps to involvement of the United States in foreign questions; and (3) submission of disputes to an international body threatened loss of sovereignty, particularly if the nation's immigration policy were ever to be challenged. In short, Lodge charged that what Wilson had proposed at Paris constituted a revolution in traditional American foreign policy.

Lodge's speech set the tone for the Republican leadership; and a few days later, its famous "round robin" letter began to circulate in the Senate. It called on that body to reject the proposed Covenant of the League of Nations, and on the President to omit the League from the treaty of peace currently being drafted.

A second aspect of Republican strategy related to amendments. This process was discussed at the White House conference in February and hinted at by Lodge in his speech to the Senate. The administration was ready to meet some of the objections to the treaty by this method, but Lodge was in no mood to reach an agreement with Wilson. Soon, he had committed Senator Borah to presenting amendments which would either obtain the treaty he desired or defeat it entirely by making it completely unacceptable to the President. Efforts by Henry White in Paris to elicit from Lodge proposals which might be written into the treaty at the conference proved unavailing. Still later, when Wilson announced that the Covenant had been so modified as to allow members the right of withdrawal, exemption of domestic questions, option in acceptance of mandates, and freedom of the Monroe Doctrine, Lodge rejected these changes as inadequate.

The road to compromise through amendments obviously would not be easy—perhaps not even possible.

The stage had thus been carefully set for the great debate. The final draft of the Treaty of Versailles, which contained the Covenant of the League of Nations, was presented to the Senate in July, 1919. The history of the subsequent contest, of Wilson's ill-fated attempt to carry the League issue to the country, of the refusal of the Senate to consent to the treaty in any form—all are well known. The process of events, however, was slow and, on the part of the League's opponents, deliberate. "Delay," said Lodge, "is one of our strongest weapons." The issue was thoroughly aired, first in a series of hearings by the Committee on Foreign Relations which ran on for two months, and secondly in a Senate debate of equal duration. After the Treaty and the League had been roundly defeated on November 19, 1919, a decision to reconsider led the participants through a second debate which lasted for three more months without altering the result.

In all this protracted argument, few fresh ideas were added by either side to those previously presented. Opponents placed the President and his supporters uncomfortably on the defensive. Their tactics emerged clearly in the record of the three-hour interview which the Senate Committee held with Wilson at the White House on August 19, 1919. The Committee members objected mainly to what they called "commitments." Senator Borah found the pledges under Article X too binding, while Senator McCumber deplored provisions for economic sanctions. When the President urged the national conscience and moral duty as obligations for action, his foes discovered snares in the Covenant's legality. The essence of the opposition was tersely stated in a question posed by Senator Frank Brandegee (R.) of Connecticut : "If we have rescued our fellow belligerents from the German peril voluntarily and without any charge, and if we prefer not to have any entanglements or connections with European powers, but to pursue our course as we did before the war, where is the moral obligation to merge ourselves with Europe forever?" The debate over the Covenant divided the Senate into three groups so closely knit as to render the usual processes of compromise completely ineffective. Standing adamantly opposed to entrance into the League on any terms was a small group of fourteen "irreconcilable" senators. The remainder favored ratification in some form. Unfortunately, this large majority divided over the wording of pro-League reservations which all acknowledged to be necessary. In the end, *every* senator voted against ratifying the Covenant in one form or another, while four fifths of them also voted in favor of such action, but with differing amendments. Why could not such a preponderant majority have found a meeting ground?

Defenders of the treaty took their cue from the President. The League was expected to eliminate the causes of war through control of armaments, prevention of artificial channeling of trade, and elimination of secret agreements which might tip the balance of power. Small nations would meet their larger neighbors upon a basis of equality, while the moral force of the organized world would be brought to bear in defense of the sovereignty of all.

Objections differed little from those raised by Lodge early in 1917, although supplemented with a new note of disillusionment coming from the alleged betrayal of liberal hopes for a more just peace. Criticism of the "defects" of the Paris settlement were secondary, however, to the departure from the traditional foreign policy of the United States.

In the last analysis, the Senate was *not* making a choice between entering or not entering the League of Nations. Rather, it was a choice of approving the Covenant with the fourteen reservations dictated by Lodge or with the five presented by the administration stalwart, Senator Gilbert M. Hitchcock (D.) of Nebraska. Study of the two lists of reservations indicates the limits of the willingness of the two sides to compromise, as well as the degree of hesitancy with which senators desired to commit the United States to collective action in international affairs. Agreement in principle seemed to have been reached between the two major Senate groups. Significantly, issues crucial to American freedom of action—the right to withdraw from the League, the right to withhold matters relating to the Monroe Doctrine and to domestic affairs, the privilege of increasing armaments beyond fixed limits when national defense was imperiled—were demanded by both groups. Parting of the ways came over the nine points (after subtraction of Hitchcock's five) which remained on Senator Lodge's list. In several of these the issue rested in definition of prerogatives of the Senate and Congress in the conduct of American foreign relations. The others focused upon dangers supposedly lurking in plans for distribution of mandates, collection of international debts and reparations payments, and operation of economic sanctions. Were the problems which would be crucial in the future of American diplomacy to be found primarily in these issues? Were these provisions of such complexity as to make compromise impossible? Was it better that the League be rejected?

Fear of commitments such as those mentioned above was to be the mainspring of isolationism in American foreign policy for the next twenty years. Quickly, the spirit captivated the press, which previously had given loyal support to Wilson's "new internationalism." By the spring of 1920, there was a heavy swing of leading newspapers to the opposition. And in the elections of that fall, the voters appeared to give their mandate to the point of view expressed by President-elect Warren G. Harding. "If the United States ever did join an association of nations," he remarked, "it must be one which would definitely safeguard our sovereignty and recognize our ultimate and unmortgaged freedom of action."

At various times during the ensuing two decades, from 1921 to 1941, the United States made efforts to achieve some of the objectives for which Wilson had designed the League of Nations. Limitation of armaments, renunciation of war, pledge of the open door in China and Manchuria, as well as the *status quo* in the Pacific—all seemed within the scope of legitimate American concern. Several attempts were made to write them into active policy. In every case the United States government insisted upon freedom of action, either by specific reservations of the 1919 variety or by omission of commitment to action if violence threatened. Thus, President Harding had no objection to the treaties drawn at Washington in 1921–22. "Nothing in them commits the United States . . . to any kind of alliance, entanglement or involvement," he confidently told the Senate. And Senator Borah, he who had labeled the League as "the gathered scum of the nations organized into a conglomerate international police force," waxed enthusiastic in 1929 over the recently signed Kellogg-Briand pact for the renunciation of war. "When the treaty is broken the United States is absolutely free," he observed. "It is just as free to choose its course as if the treaty had never been written." In similar vein, President Herbert Hoover recommended in 1930 that the Senate ratify the protocols for adherence to the World Court because "the provisions of the protocols free us from any entanglement in the diplomacy of other nations. We cannot be summoned before this court, we can from time to time seek its services with other nations. These protocols permit our withdrawal from the court at any time without reproach or ill will."

Persistence of this national reserve constantly hampered friends of the United States in efforts to defend world peace against aggression in the postwar era. The early stages of the Manchurian crisis of 1931 provided a case in point. The United States had ratified formal promises to protect the sovereign rights of China; yet, in the autumn of 1931, she chose to reserve her own action and to urge the League of

Nations to seek a solution. When that body uncertainly sought the co-operation of the United States, American unwillingness to enter any concerted action became painfully apparent. To the world, the United States announced that it would not interfere with the efforts of the League; but Secretary of State Henry L. Stimson hoped the League would not ask his co-operation. Thus the idea of reservation of America's responsibility in the world, which in 1919 suggested precautionary wisdom, later hardened into conviction that promises of active assistance to friendly foreign powers in their crises were immoral. The new internationalism had been supplanted by the new neutrality.

SUGGESTED READINGS

ADLER, SELIG. *The Isolationist Impulse.* New York: Abelard-Schuman Ltd., 1957.

BAILEY, THOMAS A. *Woodrow Wilson and the Lost Peace.* New York: Macmillan Co., 1944.

BAILEY, THOMAS A. *Woodrow Wilson and the Great Betrayal.* New York: Macmillan Co., 1945.

BARTLETT, RUHL J. *The League to Enforce Peace.* Chapel Hill: University of North Carolina Press, 1944.

BUEHRIG, E. C. *Woodrow Wilson and the Balance of Power.* Bloomington: Indiana University Press, 1955.

FLEMING, DENNA F. *The United States and the League of Nations, 1918–1920.* New York: G. P. Putnam's Sons, 1932.

GARRATY, JOHN A. *Henry Cabot Lodge.* New York: Alfred A. Knopf, Inc., 1953.

GELFAND, LAWRENCE. *The Inquiry.* New Haven: Yale University Press, 1963.

HOLT, W. STULL. *Treaties Defeated by the Senate.* Baltimore: Johns Hopkins Press, 1933.

LINK, ARTHUR S. *Wilson, the Diplomatist.* Baltimore: Johns Hopkins Press, 1957.

LODGE, HENRY CABOT. *The Senate and the League of Nations.* New York: Charles Scribner's Sons, 1925.

WALWORTH, ARTHUR. *Woodrow Wilson.* New York: Longmans, Green & Co., Inc., 1958.

Document 25.1

THE LODGE RESERVATIONS

Senator Lodge felt that the interests of the United States demanded that the Covenant of the League of Nations should be ratified only after reservations had been made a part of the agreement.

(From *Congressional Record*, 66th Congress, 1st Ssession, Vol. LVIII, Part 9, 1919, pp. 8777–78)

The Lodge resolution of ratification containing the 14 reservations follows:

Resolved (two-thirds of the Senators present concurring therein), That the Senate advise and consent to the ratification of the treaty of peace with Germany concluded at Versailles on the 28th day of June, 1919, subject to the following reservations and understandings, which are hereby made a part and condition of this resolution of ratification, which ratification is not to take effect or bind the United States until the said reservations and understandings adopted by the Senate have been accepted by an exchange of notes as a part and a condition of this resolution of ratification by at least three of the four principal allied and associated powers, to wit, Great Britain, France, Italy, and Japan:

1. The United States so understands and construes article 1 that in case of notice of withdrawal from the league of nations, as provided in said article, the United States shall be the sole judge as to whether all its international obligations and all its obligations under the said covenant have been fulfilled, and notice of withdrawal by the United States may be given by a concurrent resolution of the Congress of the United States.

2. The United States assumes no obligation to preserve the territorial integrity or political independence of any other country or to interfere in controversies between nations—whether members of the league or not—under the provisions of article 10, or to employ the military or naval forces of the United States under any article of the treaty for any purpose, unless in any particular case the Congress, which, under the Constitution, has the sole power to declare war or authorize the employment of the military or naval forces of the United States, shall by act or joint resolution so provide.

3. No mandate shall be accepted by the United States under article 22, part 1, or any other provision of the treaty of peace with Germany, except by action of the Congress of the United States.

4. The United States reserves to itself exclusively the right to decide what questions are within its domestic jurisdiction and declares that all domestic and political questions relating wholly or in part to its internal affairs, including immigration, labor, coastwise traffic, the tariff, commerce, the suppression of traffic in women and children, and in opium and other dangerous drugs, and all other domestic questions, are solely within the jurisdiction of the United States and are not under this treaty to be submitted in any way either to arbitration or to the consideration of the council or of the assembly of the league of nations, or any agency thereof, or to the decision or recommendation of any other power.

5. The United States will not submit to arbitration or to inquiry by the assembly or by the council of the league of nations, provided for in said treaty of peace, any questions which in the judgment of the United States depend upon or relate to its long-established policy, commonly known as the Monroe doctrine; said doctrine is to be interpreted by the United States alone and is hereby declared to be wholly outside the jurisdiction of said league of nations and entirely unaffected by any provision contained in the said treaty of peace with Germany.

6. The United States withholds its assent to articles 156, 157, and 158, and reserves full liberty of action with respect to any controversy which may arise under said articles between the Republic of China and the Empire of Japan.

7. The Congress of the United States will provide by law for the appointment of the representatives of the United States in the assembly and the council of the league of nations, and may in its discretion provide for the participation of the United States in any commission, committee, tribunal, court, council, or conference, or in the selection of any members thereof and for the appointment of members of said commissions, committees, tribunals, courts, councils, or conferences, or any other representatives under the treaty of peace, or in carrying out its provisions, and until such participation and appointment have been so provided for and the powers and duties of such representatives have been defined by law, no person shall represent the United States under either said league of nations or the treaty of peace with Germany or be authorized to perform any act for or on behalf of the United States thereunder, and no citizen of the United States shall be selected or appointed as a member of said commissions, committees, tribunals, courts, councils, or conferences except with the approval of the Senate of the United States.

8. The United States understands that the reparation commission will regulate, or interfere with exports from the United States to Germany, or from Germany to the United States, only when the United States by act or joint resolution of Congress approves such regulation or interference.

9. The United States shall not be obligated to contribute to any expenses of the league of nations, or of the secretariat, or of any commission, or committee, or conference, or other agency, organized under the league of nations or under the treaty or for the purpose of carrying out the treaty provisions, unless and until an appropriation of funds available for such expenses shall have been made by the Congress of the United States.

10. If the United States shall at any time adopt any plan for the limi-

tation of armaments proposed by the council of the league of nations under the provisions of article 8, it reserves the right to increase such armaments without the consent of the council whenever the United States is threatened with invasion or engaged in war.

11. The United States reserves the right to permit, in its discretion, the nationals of a covenant-breaking State, as defined in article 16 of the covenant of the league of nations, residing within the United States or in countries other than that violating said article 16, to continue their commercial, financial, and personal relations with the nationals of the United States.

12. Nothing in articles 296, 297, or in any of the annexes thereto or in any other article, section, or annex of the treaty of peace with Germany shall, as against citizens of the United States, be taken to mean any confirmation, ratification, or approval of any act otherwise illegal or in contravention of the rights of citizens of the United States.

13. The United States withholds its assent to Part XIII (articles 387 to 427, inclusive) unless Congress by act or joint resolution shall hereafter make provision for representation in the organization established by said Part XIII, and in such event the participation of the United States will be governed and conditioned by the provisions of such act or joint resolution.

14. The United States assumes no obligation to be bound by any election, decision, report, or finding of the council or assembly in which any member of the league and its self-governing dominions, colonies, or parts of empire, in the aggregate have cast more than one vote, and assumes no obligation to be bound by any decision, report, or finding of the council or assembly arising out of any dispute between the United States and any member of the league if such member, or any self-governing dominion, colony, empire, or part of empire united with it politically has voted.

Document 25.2

"A TREATY . . . WHICH RENDERS PEACE IMPOSSIBLE"

Senator Lodge and that little group of extremists led by senators Borah and Johnson, who gathered about him, represented the chief opposition to the League, but they were not the only hostile elements. Antagonism to the proposed settlement also came from a heterogenous group which included the Hearst press, the liberals, German-Americans, and Italian-Americans. Progressives had followed Wilson during wartime and shared his noble dream; but becoming disillusioned by his compromises at Versailles, they joined the Congressional opposition in the fight over treaty ratification.

(From the *New Republic*, Vol. XIX [May 24, 1919], pp. 100–102)

. . . Americans who are deeply troubled by the proposed treaty of peace are feeling for a way out which does not imply outspoken and uncompromising opposition. Just as four and one-half years ago they shrank from breaking down the traditional aloofness of this country from European political and military controversies, so now they shrink from parting company with their recent companions in arms. The bonds forged by their fight against a common enemy are hard to break. If they reject the treaty they are afraid of looking to themselves and to their European friends like quitters. They are longing for peace and are tempted to accept it at any price.

Yet if they connive at this treaty they will, as liberal and humane American democrats who seek by social experiment and education to render this country more worthy of its still unredeemed national promise, be delivering themselves into the hands of their enemies, the reactionaries and the revolutionists. The future of liberal Americanism depends upon a moral union between democracy and nationalism. Such a union is compromised so long as nationalism remains competitive in policy, exclusive in spirit and complacently capitalist in organization. Liberals all over the world have hoped that a war, which was so clearly the fruit of competition and imperialist and class-bound nationalism, would end in a peace which would moralize nationalism by releasing it from class bondage and exclusive ambitions. The Treaty of Versailles does not even try to satisfy these aspirations. Instead of expressing a great recuperative effort of the conscience of civilization, which for its own sins has sweated so much blood, it does much to intensify and nothing to heal the old and ugly dissensions between political nationalism and social democracy. In so far as its terms are actually carried out, it is bound to provoke the ultimate explosion of irreconcilable warfare. It weaves international animosities and the class conflict into the very fabric of the proposed new system of public law. The European politicians who with American complicity have hatched this inhuman monster have acted either cynically, hypocritically or vindictively, and their handiwork will breed cynicism, hypocrisy or vindictiveness in the minds of future generations. The moral source of the political life of modern nations remains polluted.

The authors of the Treaty of Versailles are the victims of the blind interests and the imperious determinism of an inhumane class economy. . . . They themselves are the unconscious servants of the cupidity and the vindictiveness which infect the psychology of an inhumane and complacent capitalist society. They crave at any cost the emotional triumph of imposing on the German nation the ultimate humiliation of solemnly consenting to its own abdication as a self-governing and self-respecting community. To satisfy this craving they are so far as possible depriving the German people by public law of the status of economic citizens with rights which other nations are bound to respect. Thus they are deliberately raising the question of working-class solidarity. They are defying the community of interest and the feeling of brotherhood which unites the socially alert workers of all the European peoples. They are subsidizing the growth of class-conscious and class-bound proletarian internationalism dominated by the conviction of the incorrigible inhumanity of a capitalist national economy. They are demonstrating by example what a perfidious protectorate nationalism exercises over the common human interests of all peoples. . . .

In our opinion the Treaty of Versailles subjects all liberalism and particularly that kind of liberalism which breathes the Christian spirit to a decisive test. Its very life depends upon the ability of the modern national state to avoid the irreconcilable class conflict to which, as the Socialists claim, capitalism condemns the future of society. In the event of such a conflict, liberalism is ground, as it is being ground in Russia, between the upper and lower millstones of reaction and revolution. The treaty in so far as it commits the national democracies to a permanent policy of inhumane violence does weave this conflict into the fabric of international law. It is the most shameless and, we hope, the last of those treaties which, while they pretend to bring peace to a mortified world, merely write the specifications for future revolution and war. It presents liberalism with a perfect opportunity of proving whether or not it is actually founded in positive moral and religious conviction. If a war which was supposed to put an end to war culminates without strenuous protest by humane men and women in a treaty of peace which renders peace impossible, the liberalism which preached this meaning for the war will have committed suicide. That such a protest on the part of national liberals may not have much immediate success in defeating the ratification of the treaty is not essential. The Treaty of Versailles, no matter under what kind of compulsion it is ratified by the nations, is impossible of execution and will defeat itself. But it is essential that the ratification should not take place with the connivance of the sincerely liberal and Christian forces. . . .

The calamity of the war descended on the western nations because of the existence of one crying weakness in western civilization. The organized Christian nations could never agree upon an effective method of subordinating the exercise of political and economic power to moral and humane purposes. Many liberals have hoped that at the end of the war the enlightened conscience of the western people would arise and exert itself to cure this weakness. The Treaty of Versailles is damned because it does nothing to moralize the future exercise of political and economic power. On the contrary, it conceives the victors who exercise the power as possessing only rights and the vanquished who have lost the power as possessing only duties. The powerful are permitted to abuse it as much as they please, ... The treaty does not embody either the spirit or method even of punitive justice. What it does embody and strain to the breaking point is the pagan doctrine and spirit of retaliation. What it treats with utter ignorance is the Christian doctrine of atonement and redemption. At a crisis in the history of civilization, the rulers of the victorious Christian states conclusively demonstrate their own contemptuous disbelief in the practical value of Christian moral economy.

Just as the acceptance of the Treaty of Versailles without protest will undermine the moral foundation of nationalism and menace civilization with an uncontrollable class conflict, so its defeat or discredit will clearly and emphatically testify to a formative connection between religion and morals and economics and politics. It would begin the cure of the spiritual anarchy in western civilization which the recent war and the proposed peace both exemplify. It would constitute the first step in the moral preparation of the western democracies for a League of Nations. For the possibility of any vital League of Nations does not depend, as so many liberals seem to suppose, on the ratification of the treaty. It depends on the rejection of the treaty. The League is not powerful enough to redeem the treaty. But the treaty is vicious enough to incriminate the League. It would convert the League into the instrument of competitive imperialist nationalism whose more disinterested members would labor in vain to mould it into a cooperative society. Liberal democrats cannot honestly consent to peace on the proposed terms. If it was wrong when confronted by the imperialist aggression of Germany to tolerate peace by conniving at such an attack, it is equally wrong when confronted by a treaty which organizes competitive imperialism into an international system to pay so high a price for the ending of the war. This above all others is the time and the occasion to repudiate the idea of peace at any price, to reject immediate peace at the price of permanent moral and economic warfare.

Document 25.3

WILSON DEFENDS THE PEACE SETTLEMENT

The chief architect of American intervention in the first World War, Wilson served the cause of peace in much the same manner. He envisioned the League of Nations as a first step on the road to world peace, and saw the fight for the League's successful establishment as part of a noble crusade for liberty, democracy, and mankind. Such convictions spurred him, in the face of rising opposition, to take his cause to the people, and counter the arguments of Henry Cabot Lodge and the irreconcilables. No decision during his presidency so dramatically demonstrated Wilson's integrity, for it was taken with the knowledge of poor health and medical injunctions about the dangers of a long speaking tour. In Phoenix (September 25, 1919), a week before the stroke that nearly took his life, Wilson explained why Americans had a vital stake in his proposed world organization.

(From Ray Stannard Baker and William E. Dodd [eds.], *The Public Papers of Woodrow Wilson*, Vol. II: *War and Peace* [New York: Harper & Bros., 1927], pp. 399–415)

The chief pleasure of my trip has been that it has nothing to do with my personal fortunes, that it has nothing to do with my personal reputation, that it has nothing to do with anything except great principles uttered by Americans of all sorts and of all parties which we are now trying to realize at this crisis of the affairs of the world. But there have been unpleasant impressions as well as pleasant impressions, my fellow citizens, as I have crossed the continent. I have perceived more and more that men have been busy creating an absolutely false impression of what the treaty of peace and the Covenant of the League of Nations contain and mean. I find, moreover, that there is an organized propaganda against the League of Nations and against the treaty proceeding from exactly the same sources that the organized propaganda proceeded from which threatened this country here and there with disloyalty, . . . My fellow citizens, it is only certain bodies of foreign sympathies, certain bodies of sympathy with foreign nations that are organized against this great document which the American representatives have brought back from Paris. Therefore, in order to clear away the mists, in order to remove the impressions, in order to check the falsehoods that have clustered around this great subject, I want to tell you a few very simple things about the treaty and the Covenant.

Do not think of this treaty of peace as merely a settlement with Germany. It is that. It is a very severe settlement with Germany, but there is not anything in it that she did not earn. Indeed, she earned more than she can ever be able to pay for, and the punishment exacted of her is not a punishment greater than she can bear, and it is absolutely necessary in order that no other nation may ever plot such a thing against humanity and civilization. But the treaty is so much more than that. It is not merely a settlement with Germany; it is a readjustment of those great injustices which underlie the whole structure of European and Asiatic society. This is only the first of several treaties. They are all constructed upon the same plan. . . . They are based upon the purpose to see that every government dealt with in this great settlement is put in the hands of the people and taken out of the hands of coteries and of sovereigns who had no right to rule over the people. It is a people's treaty, that accomplishes by a great sweep of practical justice the liberation of men who never could have liberated themselves, and the power of the most powerful nations has been devoted not to their aggrandizement but to the liberation of people whom they could have put under their control if they had chosen to do so. Not one foot of territory is demanded by the conquerors, not one single item of submission to their authority is demanded by them. The men who sat around that table in Paris knew that the time had come when the people were no longer going to consent to live under masters, but were going to live the lives that they chose themselves, to live under such governments as they chose themselves to erect. That is the fundamental principle of this great settlement. . . .

At the front of this great treaty is put the Covenant of the League of Nations. It will also be at the front of the Austrian treaty and the Hungarian treaty and the Bulgarian treaty and the treaty with Turkey. Every one of them will contain the Covenant of the League of Nations, because you cannot work any of them without the Covenant of the League of Nations. Unless you get the united, concerted purpose and power of the great Governments of the world behind this settlement, it will fall down like a house of cards. There is only one power to put behind the liberation of mankind, and that is the power of mankind. It is the power of the united moral forces of the world, and in the Covenant of the League of Nations the moral forces of the world are mobilized. . . . And what do they unite for? They enter into a solemn promise to one another that they will never use their power against one another for aggression; that they never will impair the territorial integrity of a neighbor; that they never will interfere with the political independence of a neighbor; that they will abide by the principle that great populations are entitled to determine their own destiny and that they will not interfere with that destiny; and that no matter what differences arise amongst them they will never resort to war without first having done one or other of two things—either submitted the matter of controversy to arbitration, in which case they agree to abide by the result without question, or submitted it to the consideration of the council of the League of Nations, laying before that council all the documents, all the facts, agreeing that the council can publish the documents and the facts to the whole world, agreeing that there shall be six months allowed for the mature consideration of those facts by the council, and agreeing that at the expiration of the six months, even if they are not then ready to accept the advice of the council with regard to the settlement of the dispute, they will still not go to war for another three months. In other words, they consent, no matter what happens, to submit every matter of difference between them to the judgment of mankind, and just so certainly as they do that, my fellow citizens, war will be in the far background, war will be pushed out of that foreground of terror in which it has kept the world for generation after generation, and men will know that there will be a calm time of deliberate counsel. . . .

Let us sweep aside all this language of jealousy. Let us be big enough to know the facts and to welcome the facts, because the facts are based upon the principle that America has always fought for, namely, the equality of self-governing peoples, whether they were big or little—not counting men, but counting rights, not counting representation, but counting the purpose of that representation. . . .

When you come to the heart of the Covenant, my fellow citizens, you will find it in Article X, and I am very much interested to know that the other things have been blown away like bubbles. There is nothing in the other contentions with regard to the League of Nations, but there is something in Article X that you ought to realize and ought to accept or reject. Article X is the heart of the whole matter. What is Article X? I never am certain that I can from memory give a literal repetition of its language, but I am sure that I can give an exact interpretation of its meaning. Article X provides that every member of the League covenants to respect and preserve the territorial integrity and existing political independence of every other member of the League as against external aggression. . . .

But you will say, "What is the second sentence of Article X? That is what gives very disturbing thoughts." The second sentence is that the council of the League shall advise what steps, if any, are necessary to carry out the guarantee of the first sentence, namely, that the members will respect and preserve the territorial integrity and political independence of the other members. I do not know any other meaning for the word "advise" except "advise." The council advises, and it cannot advise without the vote of the United States. Why gentlemen should fear that the Congress of the United States would be advised to do something that it did not want to do I frankly cannot imagine, because they cannot even be advised to do anything unless their own representative has participated in the advice. It may be that that will impair somewhat the vigor of the League, but, nevertheless, the fact is so, that we are not obliged to take any advice except our own, which to any man who wants to go his own course is a very satisfactory state of affairs. Every man regards his own advice as best, and I dare say every man mixes his own advice with some thought of his own interest. Whether we use it wisely or unwisely, we can use the vote of the United States to make impossible drawing the United States into any enterprise that she does not care to be drawn into.

Yet Article X strikes at the taproot of war. Article X is a statement that the very things that have always been sought in imperialistic wars are henceforth forgone by every ambitious nation in the world. I would have felt very lonely, my fellow countrymen, and I would have felt very much disturbed if, sitting at the peace table in Paris, I had supposed that I was expounding my own ideas. Whether you believe it or not, I know the relative size of my own ideas; I know how they stand related in bulk and proportion to the moral judgments of my fellow countrymen, and I proposed nothing whatever at the peace table at Paris that I had not sufficiently certain knowledge embodied the moral judgment of the citizens of the United States. . . .

Now, the other specification is in the Covenant. The Covenant in another portion guarantees to the members the independent control of their domestic questions. There is not a leg for these gentlemen to stand on when they say that the interests of the United States are not safeguarded in the very points where we are most sensitive. You do not need to be told again that the Covenant expressly says that nothing in this Covenant shall be construed as affecting the validity of the Monroe Doctrine, for example. You could not be more explicit than that. And every point of interest is covered, partly for one very interesting reason. This is not the first time that the Foreign Relations Committee of the Senate of the United States has read and considered this Covenant. I brought it to this country in March last in a tentative, provisional form, in practically the form that it now has, with the exception of certain additions which I shall mention immediately. I asked the Foreign Relations Committees of both

Houses to come to the White House and we spent a long evening in the frankest discussion of every portion that they wished to discuss. They made certain specific suggestions as to what should be contained in this document when it was to be revised. I carried those suggestions to Paris, and every one of them was adopted. What more could I have done? What more could have been obtained? The very matters upon which these gentlemen were most concerned were, the right of withdrawal, which is now expressly stated; the safeguarding of the Monroe Doctrine, which is now accomplished; the exclusion from action by the League of domestic questions, which is now accomplished. All along the line, every suggestion of the United States was adopted after the Covenant had been drawn up in its first form and had been published for the criticism of the world. There is a very true sense in which I can say this is a tested American document. . . .

Again and again, my fellow citizens, mothers who lost their sons in France have come to me and, taking my hand, have shed tears upon it not only, but they have added, "God bless you, Mr. President!" Why, my fellow citizens, should they pray God to bless me? I advised the Congress of the United States to create the situation that led to the death of their sons. I ordered their sons oversea. I consented to their sons being put in the most difficult parts of the battle line, where death was certain, as in the impenetrable difficulties of the forest of Argonne. Why should they weep upon my hand and call down the blessings of God upon me? Because they believe that their boys died for something that vastly transcends any of the immediate and palpable objects of the war. They believe, and they rightly believe, that their sons saved the liberty of the world. They believe that wrapped up with the liberty of the world is the continuous protection of that liberty by the concerted powers of all civilized people. They believe that this sacrifice was made in order that other sons should not be called upon for a similar gift—the gift of life, the gift of all that died—and if we did not see this thing through, if we fulfilled the dearest present wish of Germany and now dissociated ourselves from those alongside whom we fought in the war, would not something of the halo go away from the gun over the mantelpiece, or the sword? Would not the old uniform lose something of its significance? These men were crusaders. They were not going forth to prove the might of the United States. They were going forth to prove the might of justice and right, and all the world accepted them as crusaders, and their transcendent achievement has made all the world believe in America as it believes in no other nation organized in the modern world. There seems to me to stand between us and the rejection or qualification of this treaty the serried ranks of those boys in khaki, not only these boys who came home, but those dear ghosts that still deploy upon the fields of France.

My friends, on last Decoration Day I went to a beautiful hillside near Paris, where was located the cemetery of Suresnes, a cemetery given over to the burial of the American dead. Behind me on the slopes was rank upon rank of living American soldiers, and lying before me upon the levels of the plain was rank upon rank of departed American soldiers. Right by the side of the stand where I spoke there was a little group of French women who had adopted those graves, had made themselves mothers of those dear ghosts by putting flowers every day upon those graves, taking them as their own sons, their own beloved, because they had died in the same cause—France was free and the world was free because America had come! I wish some men in public life who are now opposing the settlement for which these men died could visit such a spot as that. I wish that the thought that comes out of those graves could penetrate their consciousness. I wish that they could feel the moral obligation that rests upon us not to go back on those boys, but to see the thing through, to see it through to the end and make good their redemption of the world. For nothing less depends upon this decision, nothing less than the liberation and salvation of the world. . . .

Document 25.4

THE SEARCH FOR A COMPROMISE

When the Senate had refused to advise and consent to the ratification of the treaty of peace, including the League of Nations, as modified by Lodge's fourteen reservations, Senator Gilbert M. Hitchcock presented the following five points, attempting to effect a compromise between the two groups of senators who were favorable to approval.

(From the *Congressional Record*, 66th Congress, 1st Session, Vol. LVIII, 1919, Part 9, p. 8800)

That any member nation proposing to withdraw from the league on two years' notice is the sole judge as to whether its obligations referred to in article 1 of the league of nations have been performed as required in said article.

That no member nation is required to submit to the league, its council, or its assembly, for decision, report, or recommendation, any matter which it considers to be in international law a domestic question such as immigration, labor, tariff, or other matter relating to its internal or coastwise affairs.

That the national policy of the United States known as the Monroe doctrine, as announced and interpreted by the United States, is not in any way impaired or affected by the covenant of the league of nations and is not subject to any decision, report, or inquiry by the council or assembly.

That the advice mentioned in article 10 of the covenant of the league which the council may give to the member nations as to the employment of their naval and military forces is merely advice which each member nation is free to accept or reject according to the conscience and judgment of its then existing Government, and in the United States this advice can only be accepted by action of the Congress at the time in being, Congress alone under the Constitution of the United States having the power to declare war.

That in case of a dispute between members of the league if one of them have self-governing colonies, dominions, or parts which have representation in the assembly, each and all are to be considered parties to the dispute, and the same shall be the rule if one of the parties to the dispute is a self-governing colony, dominion, or part, in which case all other self-governing colonies, dominions, or parts, as well as the nation as a whole, shall be considered parties to the dispute, and each and all shall be disqualified from having their votes counted in case of any inquiry on said dispute made by the assembly.

26

NORMAN F. FURNISS

Late of Colorado State University

The Fundamentalist Controversy in the Twenties

SOME STUDENTS of history have suggested that the church, eager to protect creeds from any re-examination, has been the enemy of man's knowledge in every age since ecclesiastical authorities anathematized the theories of Copernicus and Galileo. In the post-Civil War years, this ancient argument was reopened in the United States when several new concepts, both scientific and theological, collided with traditionally held religious beliefs. There ensued approximately seventy years of bitter controversy in which some defenders of the Christian faith felt that preservation of their religion demanded suppression of hostile ideas.

These fundamentalists, as they came later to be called, subscribed to the so-called "Five Points." The first tenet, basic to the rest, was the infallible Bible, inerrant because it had been inspired by God. The others forming the irreducible minimum of the faith concerned Jesus Christ—His virgin birth, His substitutionary atonement for all men's sins upon the cross, His resurrection from the dead, and His second coming. Orthodox men joined in resolute alliance against anyone who might question these dogmas.

With great alarm, therefore, the fundamentalists discovered that not one, but two currents of thought contradicted their Five Points. Both challenges had appeared in America before the Civil War and had caused discussion. Modernism, making use of "higher criticism" of the scriptures and seeking to re-evaluate inherited doctrines, assumed that the Bible was a collection of humanly written documents. Thomas Paine had been merely one of many who had analyzed the Bible from this point of view; more eminent scholars after Paine had studied different translations and earlier sources in an effort to understand who had written the Bible and why. The orthodox were incensed. To question that God Himself had inspired the Bible was to shake the basis of their faith, leaving them a mutilated scrapbook rather than the keys to heaven. Characteristically seeing issues as black or white, they believed that the Bible was either God's work or a colossal fraud, that Jesus must either be the Savior or a "Jewish bastard, born out of wedlock, and stained forever with the shame of His mother's immorality."

The theory of evolution posed an even more direct threat to conservative religious beliefs than did modernism. The Civil War and other factors had impeded the popularization of Charles Darwin's ideas in the United States after the publication of *On the Origin of Species* (1859) and *The Descent of Man* (1871), yet the fundamentalists reacted soon enough. They could see no room in Darwin's writings for the fiat creation of man by God, for a Garden of Eden, or for a miraculous Savior, as their Bible preached. The development of species through an age-long process of intense struggle for limited sustenance had absolutely no point of contact with Jesus' gospel of love. If Darwinism was right, their faith was vain. They embarked upon a crusade against it.

The warfare between science and religion in nineteenth-century America was stormy but brief. The northern Presbyterians suspended or expelled three professors from their denominational colleges for unsound thinking. The Methodist church accused the geologist Alexander Winchell of "untamed speculation" in 1878 and drove him from Vanderbilt University. The Protestant Episcopal church had some quarrels, especially during the heresy trial of the Reverend Algernon S. Crapsey in 1905. The fundamentalists succeeded in precipitating other incidents in their defense of the Five Points. But by the turn of the century, most of these alarums had faded. In their first battle the orthodox had based their opposition to Darwinism and higher criticism generally upon argument from fact; since fact supported their opponents, their cause was doomed. Ultimately, they either found a way to reconcile the old faith with the new knowledge, assisted by the philosopher John Fiske and the clergyman Henry Ward Beecher, or they turned to other vineyards more suitable for their labors. This arrangement, however, brought only a truce.

The resumption of the controversy after 1918 following several years of quiet was due to a number of forces. At bottom was the incompatibility of inherited and still unmodified religious beliefs with theories of evolution and modernism. Many devout people still clung to the Five Points. Unaware of the argument which had previously taken place, they had certainly not been a party to any compromise reached by a retreat from orthodoxy. Gradually awakening to the fact that their faith was challenged, they struck back.

World War I was itself another cause of the conflict's revival. Hatreds and anxieties loosed in this holocaust were impossible to dispel completely once peace had come. Although the country subsequently enjoyed a security which would never return, men still felt that agents of some evil power were sapping the bastions of goodness. The postwar changes in sexual mores, the increase in the number of divorces, and the antics of the "flappers" convinced many that the United States was indeed morally sick. During these worried times, there was no dearth of professional bigots capable of naming dangers felt but not seen. While leaders of the Ku Klux Klan turned national attention to certain racial and religious groups, fundamentalist spokesmen identified other foes. The Darwinist and the "creeping critic," both mockers of the old-time religion, were singled out as the real enemies.

The decade of the 1920's was an era marked by intolerance. It was a time when men, instead of refuting their opponents, sought to suppress them. The period opened with the "red scare," a witch-hunting hysteria promoted by Attorney General A. Mitchell Palmer. The period was characterized by the Sacco-Vanzetti trial, the depredations of the Ku Klux Klan, and the American Legion's attack upon "unsafe" textbooks. The fundamentalist crusade was part and parcel of this intolerance. Although the defenders of orthodoxy did not use faggot and hemp against their intellectual adversaries, as their ideological ancestors had once done, they tried to silence them by any means at hand.

The characteristic ignorance of the fundamentalists was another factor in the resumption of the controversy. Old dogmas were difficult to reconcile with evolution and modernism, but the fact that the orthodox never clearly grasped these teachings made reconciliation impossible. Although they pretended to study the writings of their opponents, and William Jennings Bryan at times boasted about his many honorary degrees, the fundamentalists studied only to reinforce preconceived ideas. Thus, their understanding was cloudy. If the giraffe's neck had stretched because of the need to browse on tree leaves during a prolonged drought, why had it not snapped back to its original length once the rains had returned? Since King Tutankhamen's mummy was that of a human being and not a monkey—despite the fact that he had lived long ages ago—Bryan insisted that man could

not have descended from the ape. In their confused way the fundamentalists seized upon these "question marks about evolution"; one of
the less literate among them triumphantly cried: "Like Bancho's ghost,
they will not down."

Did scientists and modern theologians bear the blame for this ignorance and for the controversy it helped to precipitate, since they
failed to popularize their findings? Was their task finished when
they announced the truths they had isolated, or did they also have
the equally important obligation of assisting the people to adjust their
inherited ideas to these discoveries? Perhaps the intellectuals had
become tongue-tied, unable to communicate with anyone other than
their own colleagues, as was to be the case when later they discovered
the power of atomic fission but could offer no coherent suggestion concerning its control. At any rate, after 1918, no John Fiske or Henry
Ward Beecher helped men understand the new currents of thought.

Another important cause of the conflict's revival was the appearance of Bryan in the arena. Before 1918, he had been too busy with
campaigns against the gold standard, strong drink, and other scourges
of mankind to grasp the threat of Darwinism to his religious faith. But
when the war had ended, Bryan suddenly became aware of this menace and turned his attention to propagandizing fundamentalism. Conceivably, his declining importance in politics made him seek adulation
in another field. A middle-aged man whose organlike voice had once
inspired the devotion of millions could hardly be content to promote
real estate in Florida but must find another campaign to attract followers. Whatever his motive, Bryan set fire to the fundamentalist
cause. He brought to the orthodox side not only the still significant
army of his partisans, but also his phrasemaking ability. His aphorisms
seemed to many to explain truth itself. "If a man believes that he is a
descendant of the ape," Bryan warned, "he can go to a zoological
garden and speculate on how far he has come. If he believes the Bible
he goes to church and considers how far he has to go." Or, more simply: "I have no use for any man who prefers the blood of the beast
to the Blood of the Lamb."

The sincerity of most fundamentalists could not be questioned.
Deeply alarmed at Darwinism and modernism, they convinced themselves that these concepts had produced "defalcations and robberies,
and murders, and infanticides, and adulteries, and drunkenness, and
every form and degree of social dishonor." Yet, it is also true that some
"Elmer Gantrys" joined their crusade for purely selfish reasons.

Fundamentalism attracted its share of scoundrels. Despite a distinguished lineage, Edgar Young Clarke had had constant trouble with the law. In his earlier years, he was accused of several indiscretions, from mishandling church funds to violation of the Mann Act. Later, Clarke joined the Ku Klux Klan, primarily to make money, and soon became dominant in it. Eventually, he lost control of this lucrative organization when a revolt among the Grand Goblins ousted him in 1921, but he quickly learned that even more money was available in fundamentalism. Worried conservatives, he came to see, would contribute generously to the overthrow of Darwinism and modernism. To facilitate collection of such donations, he formed a society called the Supreme Kingdom. Other such persons scuttled into the movement, among them the popular preacher in Fort Worth, J. Frank Norris, who had shot an unarmed man to death, and John Roach Straton, the New York City "fundamentalist pope," who was guilty of unbecoming if less lethal conduct.

Even where financial reward was not a motive, desire for prestige may have assisted revival of the conflict. Certain forces had interrupted the march of faith in America, thereby causing a decline in church attendance and contributions. To overcome this indifference, some ministers resorted to flamboyant methods, including sermons with such arresting titles as "Back Home and Dead Broke" (the parable of the prodigal son), "Eventually, Why Not Now?" (conversion), and "Three-in-One Oil" (the Trinity). Others discovered in fundamentalism a topic both popular and compelling enough to return backsliders to their pews.

A final source of fundamentalism may be found in the rural-urban conflict, a problem which became acute in the 1920's. The tug of war between the city and the country had gone on at least since the days when Jefferson praised the farmers as the chosen people of God. With the explosion of the city after the Civil War the dispute grew more intense. Worried agrarians deplored the fact that both parties fell more and more under the dominance of urban machines and politicians. In American literature, country folk no longer received adulation, but instead were pictured by Hamlin Garland, Edgar Lee Masters, Sherwood Anderson, and Sinclair Lewis as ignorant, bigoted, and backward. When rural forces demanded prohibition, they met with the organized power of the urban "wets"; when they sought to keep American white and Protestant, they were motivated by their distaste for the melting-pot nature of the city. This unhappy division bore bitter fruit in the Democratic convention of 1924 and the national election of 1928, when Al Smith, with his flat accent and his derby hat, won little favor among the people in the rural South and Midwest.

The split between city and country intensified the fundamentalist controversy. Although fundamentalists had considerable strength in cities, especially where they found militant spokesmen, their power lay primarily in the country. Their opponents, the evolutionists and modernists, seemed to fundamentalists the vicious products of the city seminaries and universities. Fundamentalist leader William Jennings Bryan had considered the city as the enemy's camp ever since his first campaign. Rural isolation produced certain characteristic weaknesses of the fundamentalists—lack of formal education and an ignorance of new currents of thought in science and theology. The fundamentalists' greatest triumphs came in rural states—Tennessee, Mississippi, and Arkansas—where they mustered enough votes to put antievolution statutes on the books.

The impact of World War I, the power of Bryan, the machinations of unscrupulous or misguided men, and the rural-urban antagonism combined to bring about resumption of the controversy. With increasing determination, conservatives fought against Darwinism and modernism, until the argument reached its climax in the mid-1920's. Two lines of attack were followed: antievolution laws to insure safe teaching in the schools and measures to drive heretics from pulpits.

Fundamentalists felt no sense of guilt when they demanded laws to bar the teaching of evolution in public schools. Such legislation, they insisted, did not abridge freedom of speech or any other basic constitutional right. A Darwinist or an atheist (to fundamentalists the two were indistinguishable) could say what he pleased on the street or in private institutions. But in state-supported schools and colleges, he must not teach anything objectionable to his employers, the taxpayers. Do not the people have the right, the fundamentalists asked, to decide what will be taught in the schools which their own money built? Using another argument, Bryan also pointed out that the courts had prohibited the reading of the Bible in the schools on the ground that such practice violated separation of church and state. If the ruling was correct, he demanded, should not anti-Christian instruction also be outlawed? If one teacher could not read from Genesis in the classroom, could another with impunity discuss a theory which denied the accounts in Genesis?

Such arguments brought up an abiding issue confronting any democracy, that is, the validity of majority rule in the control of education. Bryan had the great ability to make complex issues seem amazingly simple: "The hand that writes the paycheck rules the school." Such a position insisted that truth could be determined by majority decision, a not intolerable assertion in a democracy. The eminent jurist Oliver Wendell Holmes, Jr., had even declared that if an idea could succeed in competition with others in being accepted by the majority, it was as near to truth as man could get. Others, however, rejected this proposition. Arthur Garfield Hays, a liberal New York lawyer, insisted that while the people could decide what courses were to be taught in public schools, they could not then determine *how* subject matter was to be explained. In short, they could not order a subject to be taught falsely. Still others would go farther than Hays. They would question whether the voters should have *any* control over curricula. To this thinking, education, to be of value, must be free of all restraints.

Antievolution laws raised an even more pertinent issue than control of public education, namely, the viability of democracy itself. Among many other political philosophers, Hamilton and Jefferson had debated whether the common man possessed the wisdom to govern himself. Jefferson had won the argument, at least in the election of 1800; but had he been right, after all? In 1925 a commentator in *The Nation* used fundamentalism to question "the ultimate value of democracy." In his mind the antievolution law "was a triumph of the will of the people. It is the logical outcome of the application of the principle that the mediocre majority are capable of dealing more wisely than the educated minority." The criticism had merit. In approving this law, the people had created a monstrosity. True, the statute could be undone or evaded—there was time for that. But the people might commit other acts of folly when the urgency of cold wars left no margin for error.

Whatever side of the argument had the better case, freedom of teaching ran afoul of the American faith in the law as a powerful specific for any trouble. One state legislature had previously tried to make pi equal four; another had settled upon the number three as the proper value. Antivivisectionists wrote their ideas into Maine law in 1919; many more voters decreed that drunkenness would disappear forever when they approved the Eighteenth Amendment. It was not odd, therefore, that when John Washington Butler became worried about Darwinism, he should place his faith in the law as the remedy. He won election to the Tennessee legislature and in 1925 introduced his bill. Within a short time, it became illegal "for any teacher in any of the universities, normal, and all other public schools of the state, to teach any theory that denies the story of the divine creation of man as taught in the Bible and to teach instead that man has descended from a lower order of animals."

Tennessee was not the only state to bar the teaching of evolution, nor was it the first. After 1922, temporary laws or decrees of limited application were approved in Oklahoma, Florida, North Carolina, Texas, and Louisiana. Two more, Mississippi in 1925 and Arkansas in 1928, followed Tennessee's example by enacting a definite antievolution statute. Between 1921 and 1929, fundamentalists presented thirty-seven bills, riders, or resolutions to some twenty legislatures. Yet, Tennessee has remained the state popularly identified with this peculiar form of thought control. It should now be asked why the Butler Bill was approved there, and so easily at that.

The same forces which precipitated the controversy in the United States undoubtedly operated in Tennessee when Butler introduced his measure. But one reason for the fundamentalists' victory was more apparent here than elsewhere, and that was the lack of any firm opposition. A contemporary observer, Joseph Wood Krutch, felt that cowardice had paralyzed the forces which should have done battle.

The administration and faculty of the University of Tennessee had much to lose by the passage of the Butler Bill; if obeyed conscientiously, it would have prevented instruction in many disciplines. Yet, as Krutch contemptuously pointed out, no man from the University fought it openly during the legislature's deliberations or denounced it after its approval. Presumably, this silence arose from prudence rather than cowardice. Until World War I the institution had been a small one, with some six hundred students enrolled and a very modest endowment. After the war the state became more generous, first with loans and then with appropriations that reached $800,000 in one year. Buildings sprang up, faculty salaries increased, and able young instructors joined the staff. Even greater things lay ahead, since in 1925 the legislature had before it another large appropriation bill. Vigorous opposition to the antievolution bill by the University at this precise time might have stunted this growth. The fundamentalists, who comprised probably much more than half of the voters, would have been quick to disown a Godless university.

In another decade and in another dispute the chancellor of the University of Pittsburgh gave his faculty some advice: "Gentlemen, we dare not challenge the ingrained prejudices of this community upon which the university depends for financial and moral support.

On the other hand, I realize that you have your obligations as scholars to the subjects you teach. But, gentlemen, may I beg you in God's name, exercise a little tact!" Tact and prudence, not cowardice, may thus have operated in Tennessee in 1925. And this line of conduct appeared successful. Lecturers could dwell at any length upon evolution, only being careful to use the word "development." Meanwhile the University continued to grow, cherished by a benign legislature and, behind it, approving taxpayers. The handsome new library, opened in 1931, was only one indication that the University of Tennessee was gaining a national reputation for excellence.

Krutch's criticism, however, would not die away. The thought returned that if the intellectual leaders had opposed the Butler Bill resolutely, they might have brought about its defeat and at the same time persuaded the fundamentalists to accept evolution. In other states, brave men fought the orthodox faction openly, imperiling both their institutions and their own academic careers. And they won the battle. In North Carolina, President Harry W. Chase of the University opposed passage of an antievolution measure introduced in 1925. When warned that his actions might draw financial reprisals, he answered unequivocally: "If this university doesn't stand for anything but appropriations, I, for one, don't care to be connected with it." Antievolution bills were defeated in North Carolina. They also failed in other states—Virginia, Georgia, and Kentucky among them—where educators took an uncompromisingly hostile stand. Even if the contest had been lost in Tennessee, what good was the new library if men hesitated to teach frankly?

The high-water mark of the fundamentalist controversy came in the summer of 1925 in the little Tennessee town of Dayton. There a high school teacher and his friends decided to test the Butler law in court. Accordingly, John T. Scopes, biology teacher and athletic instructor, deliberately lectured on evolution and in time was brought to trial. The case, so modestly begun, drew national attention. The great Bryan joined the locally recruited prosecution, and freethinking Clarence Darrow, Arthur Garfield Hays, and other distinguished attorneys served as Scopes's counsel. The climax of the trial came when Darrow subjected Bryan to a pitiless cross-examination which broke the Peerless Leader's spirit even if it did not force him to abandon the doctrines of his faith. In the end the case failed to test the antievolution law. Scopes was convicted, as the defense had expected, but appeal to the United States Supreme Court was thwarted because of a technicality.

While Darwinism was agitating the politics of the states, modernism precipitated equally heated controversies in the churches. The northern Baptists, worrying about unsoundness in their educational institutions and foreign missions, reached the point of anxiety at which they even considered adoption of a creedal statement. Methodists and Presbyterians also wrangled over heresy. The Protestant Episcopal church suffered through another ecclesiastical trial, not of a mere priest, as in the case of Algernon S. Crapsey, but this time of a bishop. Modernist ministers had to face much the same decisions thrust upon university presidents in Tennessee. If their denominations or congregations were ultraorthodox, they were compelled to decide whether to avow their beliefs openly or keep a discreet silence. Some took the latter course, justifying their actions on the ground that they did not wish to split Protestantism into even more sects or to shake their congregations with doctrines which they were not ready to accept. Critics could not distinguish this line of thought from cowardice.

After 1925 the fundamentalist movement began to falter; and by 1930, it had lost national importance. Several factors brought about this decline. The death of Bryan, either from gluttony or perhaps from Darrow's savage treatment at Dayton, left the fundamentalists without a leader. Other men tried to put on his mantle—or in this case, his alpaca coat—but lacked either his stature or his integrity. The impact of the depression after 1929 caused churchmen to forget differences of faith. The spread of knowledge, presumably correcting fundamentalist ignorance, helped men accept both evolution and modernism. Thus the controversy was quieted, if not completely settled.

And yet, some questions raised in the dispute remained unanswered. Should one fight intolerance by retreat, accommodation, or defiance? Do taxpayers have the right to ban from public school curricula any instruction which is hostile to their ingrained beliefs, whether it be Darwinism, Marxism, or other concepts? Must religious crusades, or any movement relying more upon emotion than reason, inevitably attract the unscrupulous? Are all advances in man's knowledge won only in the face of unremitting hostility from entrenched institutions, among them the churches?

Could one more question be asked—were the fundamentalists right, after all? They had warned that any relaxation of beliefs, any retreat from orthodoxy, must lead to destruction of the people's moral fiber. Men must have security and guidance, they insisted; take from them the comfort of the Five Points, and they will turn elsewhere. It

may have happened just that way. For in thirty years and more after
the fundamentalist crusade had passed, Americans faced one emergency after another—a depression, a world war, a period of endless
international tension. In other ages, people might have withstood
these tests serenely, comforted by their Five Points. Is the faith of
today, without the Five Points, so pallid and eviscerated that men
cannot live by it? Finding no help in the churches, with their creeds
possibly reduced to the idea that it is good form to agree with one's
neighbors, the people may have turned to the psychiatrist's couch or
to the state instead of the Savior. Or they may have turned to luxury,
a hedonism symbolized by the outboard motor, to dull whatever terror
they feel within themselves.

SUGGESTED READINGS

BRYAN, WILLIAM JENNINGS. *Seven Questions in Dispute*. New York: Fleming H.
Revell Co., 1924.

COLE, STEWART G. *The History of Fundamentalism*. New York: R. R. Smith,
1931.

FURNISS, NORMAN F. *The Fundamentalist Controversy, 1918–1931*. New Haven: Yale University Press, 1954.

GINGER, RAY. *Six Days or Forever? Tennessee v. John Thomas Scopes*. Boston:
Beacon Press, 1958.

LOEWENBERG, BERT J. "Darwinism Comes to America, 1859–1900," *Mississippi
Valley Historical Review*, Vol. XXVIII (1941).

NIEBUHR, H. R. "Fundamentalism," *Encyclopedia of Social Science*, Vol. III
(1937).

RILEY, WILLIAM BELL. "The Faith of the Fundamentalists," *Current History*,
Vol. XXVI (1927).

SHIPEY, MAYNARD. *The War on Modern Science: A Short History of the Fundamentalist Attacks on Evolution and Modernism*. New York: Alfred A. Knopf,
Inc., 1927.

VANDERLAAN, E. D. (ed.). *Fundamentalism versus Modernism*. New York:
H. W. Wilson Co., 1925.

*The World's Most Famous Court Trial—Tennessee Evolution Case: A Complete
Stenographic Report*. Cincinnati: National Book Co., 1925.

Document 26.1

BRYAN DEFENDS THE FAITH

William Jennings Bryan produced many books, articles, and speeches
in defense of his religious beliefs. *The Menace of Darwinism*, one of the
most popular of his efforts, appeared in all three forms. The very ortho-

dox Albert A. Murphree, President of Florida State University, was so impressed with it that in 1922 he asked Bryan for two hundred copies, to be distributed "where they will do the most good."

THE ORIGIN OF MAN

(From William Jennings Bryan, *The Menace of Darwinism* [New York: Fleming H. Revell Co., 1922], pp. 15–17, 22–23, 49–51)

When the mainspring is broken a watch ceases to be useful as a time-keeper. A handsome case may make it still an ornament and the parts may have a market value, but it cannot serve the purpose of a watch. There is that in each human life that corresponds to the mainspring of a watch—that which is absolutely necessary if the life is to be what it should be, a real life and not a mere existence. That necessary thing is *a belief in God*. . . .

. . . If there is at work in the world to-day anything that tends to break this mainspring, it is the duty of the moral, as well as the Christian, world to combat this influence in every possible way.

I believe there is such a menace to fundamental morality. The hypothesis to which the name of Darwin has been given—the hypothesis that links man to the lower forms of life and makes him a lineal descendant of the brute—is obscuring God and weakening all the virtues that rest upon the religious tie between God and man. . . .

Science has rendered invaluable service to society; her achievements are innumerable—and the hypotheses of scientists should be considered with an open mind. Their theories should be carefully examined and their arguments fairly weighed, but the scientist cannot compel acceptance of any argument he advances, except as, judged upon its merits, it is convincing. Man is infinitely more than science; science, as well as the Sabbath, was made for man. It must be remembered, also that all sciences are not of equal importance. Tolstoy insists that the science of "How to Live" is more important than any other science, and is this not true? It is better to trust in the Rock of Ages, than to know the age of the rocks; it is better for one to know that he is close to the Heavenly Father, than to know how far the stars in the heavens are apart. And is it not just as important that the scientists who deal with matter should respect the scientists who deal with spiritual things, as that the latter should respect the former? If it be true, as Paul declares, that "the things that are seen are temporal" while "the things that are unseen are eternal," why should those who deal with temporal things think themselves superior to those who deal with the things that are eternal? Why should the Bible, which the centuries have not been able to shake, be discarded for scientific works that have to be revised and corrected every few years? The preference should be given to the Bible.

The two lines of work are parallel. There should be no conflict between the discoverers of *real* truths, because real truths do not conflict. Every truth harmonizes with every other truth, but why should an hypothesis, suggested by a scientist, be accepted as true until its truth is established? Science should be the last to make such a demand because science to be truly science is classified knowledge; it is the explanation of facts. Tested by this definition, Darwinism is not science at all; it is guesses strung together. There is more science in the twenty-fourth verse of the first chapter of Genesis (And God said, let the earth bring forth the living creature after his kind, cattle and creeping things, and beast of the earth after his kind; and it was so.) than in all that Darwin wrote. . . .

. . . At the University of Wisconsin (so a Methodist preacher told me) a teacher told his class that the Bible was a collection of myths. When I brought the matter to the attention of the President of the University, he criticized me but avoided all reference to the professor. At Ann Arbor a professor argued with students against religion and asserted that no thinking man could believe in God or the Bible. At Columbia (I learned this from a Baptist preacher) a professor began his course in geology by telling his class to throw away all that they had learned in the Sunday school. There is a professor in Yale of whom it is said that no one leaves his class a believer in God. (This came from a young man who told me that his brother was being led away from the Christian faith by this professor.) A father (a Congressman) tells me that a daughter on her return from Wellesley told him that nobody believed in the Bible stories now. . . .

I submit three propositions for the consideration of the Christians of the nation:

First, preachers who break the bread of life to lay members should believe that man has in him the breath of the Almighty, as the Bible declares—not the blood of the brute, as the evolutionists affirm. He should also believe in the virgin birth of the Saviour.

Second, none but Christians in good standing and with a spiritual conception of life should be allowed to teach in Christian schools. Church schools are worse than useless if they bring students under the influence of those who do not believe in the religion upon which the Church and church schools are built. Atheism and agnosticism are more dangerous when hidden under the cloak of religion than when they are exposed to view.

Third, the tax-payers should prevent the teaching in the public schools of atheism, agnosticism, Darwinism, or any other hypothesis that links man in blood relationship with the brutes. Christians build their own colleges in which to teach Christianity; let atheists and agnostics build their own schools in which to teach their doctrines—whether they call it atheism, agnosticism, or a scientific interpretation of the Bible.

If it is contended that an instructor has a right to teach anything he likes, I reply that the tax-payers must decide what shall be taught. The hand that writes the pay check rules the school. To continue the illustration used on preceding page, a person can expose himself to the smallpox if he desires to do so, but he has no right to communicate it to others. So a man can believe anything he pleases but he has no right to teach it against the protest of his employers. . . .

Document 26.2

TENNESSEE AND ITS "MONKEY LAW"

Joseph Wood Krutch, a distinguished academician, essayist, and dramatic critic, graduated from the University of Tennessee in 1915. In this article, he discusses Tennessee's reaction to the antievolution law and the impact of developments in Dayton upon the state.

(From Joseph Wood Krutch, "Tennessee: Where Cowards Rule," *The Nation*, Vol. CXXI [1925], pp. 88–89)

. . . At Dayton no one is afraid to tell me what he thinks. But when I go to Knoxville, seat of the State University and one of the three largest cities in Tennessee, I enter a different world. One of the most important members of the university board of trustees takes me aside to whisper in my ear; the president of that institution, telling me I am a good fellow, takes me confidentially by the arm; the editor of one of the leading newspapers, distinguished by the safe piety of its editorials upon the subject, closes the door of his office; and the remarks of all might be summarized in what were the actual words of one: "Of course it's a damn-fool law— but I won't be quoted." . . .

Not even those who voted for the bill wanted it to pass. As a member of the legislature told me, he thought he might as well win the favor of a few fundamentalist constituents by saying "aye" because he felt sure the Senate would reject so preposterous a measure; the Senate, following the same admirable political logic, decided to put the burden upon the Governor, who, as the last responsible party, would hardly dare write himself down an ass; but the Governor, so it is said, remarked only: "They've got their nerve to pass the buck to me when they know I want to be United States Senator" before he signed the bill. . . .

. . . The president of the university, who ought to know better, can think of no plan more courageous than weakly to disobey the law when necessary, while pretending to the legislature that he approves of its acts or, more accurately, gives it to understand that he will not embarrass it by publicly stating his opinion of the law which both he and it know to be asinine. Concerned above all else with his precious appropriations, it never occurs to him to ask whether his chief duty might not possibly be something other than wangling money from a cowardly legislature. He does not realize that this first duty might be to prove himself worthy to spend the educational funds he is so eager to get, to show some sign of that zeal for truth and that intellectual honesty which it is, presumably, the function of education to inculcate, and he is anxious only to defend himself to everybody. . . .

Document 26.3
THE BATTLE FOR THE MINNESOTA MIND

The antievolution campaign was not limited to Tennessee, or even to the South. It had adherents in every section of the United States, including the Midwest, and eventually mingled with the dark currents of racism. To a simple constituency nursed in evangelical Protestantism, rejection of Darwinism was as inevitable as acceptance of the fundamentalist campaign against urban immorality. Such a constituency naturally believed evolution must be kept out of the schools, and it disregarded the threat to academic freedom implicit in this position.

(From Bruce Tarrant, "Minnesota: Modern or Mediaeval?" *The Independent,* January 1, 1927, pp. 8–9, 28)

Minnesota will probably be the scene of the next great battle between Fundamentalist theology and modern science. Rev. William B. Riley, pastor of the First Baptist Church of Minneapolis and president of the World's Christian Fundamentalist Association, has taken the offensive against the evolutionists of the Gopher State. Dr. Riley is the recognized head of the antievolution movement in the United States. One might almost add that he alone is the movement in Minnesota. . . .

The central feature of Fundamentalist strategy seems to be to make it appear that this is a fight, not between Fundamentalism and science, but

between true and false science. So Dr. Riley boasts that he is a member
of the American Association for the Advancement of Science, and
strenuously maintains that science is verified knowledge, a definition by
which he neatly brands as false science all evidences, theories, and hypotheses which have not been demonstrated with the certainty of the
multiplication table. His personal knowledge of science is well shown by
his reply to Professor Metcalfe's question regarding vestigial organs, "I
have no vestigial organs in my body"; and by the response which he made
last year to a student who asked him about the facts of parthenogenesis:
"I know only one Genesis, and that is good enough for me!" . . .

. . . The history of Dr. Riley's recent tilt with the administration of
the University of Minnesota is interesting. Last year, at his own request,
the doctor was invited to speak at the university. Later, when he undertook to advertise the meeting, the university withdrew the invitation.
This was, of course, playing into the hands of the Fundamentalists. It
gave them a promptly embraced opportunity to fill the papers with complaints of persecution and discrimination. This fall Dr. Riley again asked
to be invited to speak on the campus, this time to deliver a series of four
lectures. The faculty gasped, recovered itself, and said, "Give him the
four hours, before he asks for fourteen!"

So the administration invited Dr. Riley to speak at a series of meetings, on subjects of his own choosing. Tall, gray, vigorous, and of commanding presence, he seemed to the two thousand students who thronged
the armory a speaker who would certainly enlighten them. In these an-
ticipations they were disappointed. Dr. Riley was fluent in delivery and
keen in sarcasm, but his logic was not that of the university. Though he
condemned scientists for their alleged assumption that evolution is true,
he himself made the tremendous assumption of the literal interpretation
of the Bible, an inconsistency which the students were quick to note.

Dr. Riley's method of dealing with his lecture audiences suggested
that he had learned well the formula for controlling the crowd which is
offered in "Social Psychology" by his old antagonist, Prof. Edward
Allsworth Ross. "Vigorously affirm and reiterate with fire and passion,"
says Ross. "Cut out facts, statistics, valid proof and evidence. . . . Never
argue out painstakingly the links of a logical chain. . . . Address passions,
but not rational interests." Dr. Riley followed this advice admirably. He
quoted freely from scientists, especially eminent evolutionists, such as
Darwin and Wallace, though he had to wrench their statements from
the context in order to make them serviceable. One could not help thinking of the man who undertook to prove the case for atheism from the
Bible by solemnly quoting the four words, "There is no God." . . .

In later addresses Dr. Riley explained what all mature students know, that the nature of the remains known as *Pithecanthropus erectus* and *Eoanthropus dawsoni* is highly controversial. Then he made his astounding leap to the conclusion, "Therefore, evolution is false." Just as if scientists had not accepted the theory of evolution thirty years before *Pithecanthropus* was discovered! Among arguments such as these, Dr. Riley interspersed edifying anecdotes to the effect that King Tutankhamen did not have a tail, and that a dentist once camouflaged a woman's tooth so that certain scientists were led to believe that it had once belonged to a prehistoric man.

As usual, Dr. Riley repeated his challenge to debate on evolution. The challenge was not general. No professional radicals need apply. Last year at a meeting of the campus Liberal Discussion Club, a scrappy little radical dared Dr. Riley to debate him, saying, "This is the sixth time that I have challenged you"; but the Fundamentalist champion was silent. Dr. Riley wants to debate only the head of a university department. This is clever. He knows that his followers will early pack the house to the doors if such a debate is staged, and that when a popular vote is taken he will be credited with defeating a scientist. No wonder, then, that he has won fourteen out of fifteen such debates, and no wonder that no professor is willing to engage in such a mock contest.

Document 26.4

"HE WAS, IN FACT, A CHARLATAN"

The great critic of American life in the 1920's, H. L. Mencken, found in Bryan all the weaknesses he so loved to ridicule. On the day after the Peerless Leader died, he wrote a bitter essay on Bryan which contained the following passages.

(From H. L. Mencken [ed.], *A Mencken Chrestomathy* [New York: Alfred A. Knopf, Inc., 1949], pp. 243–47)

There was something peculiarly fitting in the fact that his last days were spent in a one-horse Tennessee village, beating off the flies and gnats, and that death found him there. The man felt at home in such simple and Christian scenes. He liked people who sweated freely, and were not debauched by the refinements of the toilet. Making his progress up and down the Main street of little Dayton, surrounded by gaping primates from the upland valleys of the Cumberland Range, his coat laid aside, his bare arms and hairy chest shining damply, his bald head sprinkled with dust—so accoutred and on display, he was obviously happy....

. . . Talk of sincerity, I confess, fatigues me. If the fellow was sincere, then so was P. T. Barnum. The word is disgraced and degraded by such uses. He was, in fact, a charlatan, a mountebank, a zany without sense or dignity. His career brought him into contact with the first men of his time; he preferred the company of rustic ignoramuses. It was hard to believe, watching him at Dayton, that he had traveled, that he had been received in civilized societies, that he had been a high officer of state. He seemed only a poor clod like those around him, deluded by a childish theology, full of an almost pathological hatred of all learning, all human dignity, all beauty, all fine and noble things. He was a peasant come home to the barnyard. Imagine a gentleman, and you have imagined everything that he was not. What animated him from end to end of his grotesque career was simply ambition—the ambition of a common man to get his hand upon the collar of his superiors, or, failing that, to get his thumb into their eyes. He was born with a roaring voice, and it had the trick of inflaming half-wits. His whole career was devoted to raising those half-wits against their betters, that he himself might shine. . . .

When I first encountered him, on the sidewalk in front of the office of the rustic lawyers who were his associates in the Scopes case, the trial was yet to begin, and so he was still expansive and amiable. I had printed in the *Nation*, a week or so before, an article arguing that the Tennessee anti-evolution law, whatever its wisdom, was at least constitutional—that the yahoos of the State had a clear right to have their progeny taught whatever they chose, and kept secure from whatever knowledge violated their superstitions. . . .

But that was the last touch of amiability that I was destined to see in Bryan. The next day the battle joined and his face became hard. By the end of the week he was simply a walking fever. Hour by hour he grew more bitter. What the Christian Scientists call malicious animal magnetism seemed to radiate from him like heat from a stove. From my place in the courtroom, standing upon a table, I looked directly down upon him, sweating horribly and pumping his palm-leaf fan. His eyes fascinated me; I watched them all day long. They were blazing points of hatred. . . .

27

E. DAVID CRONON
University of Wisconsin

The Great Crash

ONE OF THE really memorable years in American history is 1929—a landmark from which we may survey the end of one era and the beginning of another. The year opened with the nation enjoying a period of unprecedented prosperity. Never before had so many Americans lived so well. The United States, so the new President, Herbert Hoover, had predicted in the recent political campaign, was "nearer to the final triumph over poverty than ever before in the history of any land." And few Americans, as Hoover's landslide victory attested, were inclined to dispute this optimistic appraisal in the early months of 1929. Economists and businessmen alike were agreed that the country had entered upon a New Era in its economic development, an era characterized by general economic well-being and ever-expanding material abundance. True, some ominous signs of a runaway speculative boom appeared in the stock market, but outgoing President Calvin Coolidge offered comforting reassurance that conditions were "absolutely sound" and that stocks were "cheap at current prices." Yet, by late autumn the great bull market had collapsed; and 1929 closed with the nation slipping into a decade of depression, the worst in its history.

It is far easier to determine *what* happened during those fateful months of 1929 than it is to arrive at a definitive answer as to *why* the speculative boom developed and then collapsed with such devastating results. Nevertheless, some questions come immediately to mind. (1) Just how prosperous, really, were the "golden twenties"? Was the prosperity soundly based and widely diffused, or was it more apparent than real? (2) What caused the speculative mania that led to the great bull market of 1929? (3) What role did the political and financial leaders of the country play in stimulating this speculative boom? (4) Why did the stock market crash, and why did this collapse trigger a disastrous depression?

Unquestionably, the twenties were a period of rapid economic growth that brought a rising standard of living to a substantial part of the American people. One authority has estimated that national income, measured in current prices which fluctuated only slightly, rose from $60.7 billion in 1922 to $87.2 billion in 1929, or a gain of over 43 per cent. Probably the chief reason for this striking increase was the extraordinary rise in productivity during the decade. American industry and agriculture literally shifted into high gear as businessmen installed laborsaving machinery and farmers retired Old Dobbin in favor of the new gasoline tractors. Between 1919 and 1929, for example, horsepower per worker in manufacturing jumped 50 per cent, and output per man-hour rose 72 per cent. The rising national income was reflected in higher wages for many workers, though this was partially offset by a slight decline in the average work week. If one also includes the marked expansion of public services—better schools, more libraries, parks, playgrounds, and health facilities—the signs of a prosperous society are clearly evident.

Yet, at the same time, not all Americans shared in the general well-being. A few industries—notably coal, textiles, leather, ship building, and some railroads—were economically sick throughout the twenties. Faced with mounting competition and slackening demand, they limped through the decade scarcely touched by the over-all prosperity. Agriculture, too, slumped after the boom years of the first World War. Farm prices tumbled in 1920 and 1921, and except for some specialized areas of agriculture, they remained depressed throughout the decade. The farmers' share in the national private production income dropped from 22.9 per cent in 1919 to only 12.7 per cent in 1929. No doubt, partly because of this, nearly twenty million people left the land for the city during the decade, though the remaining farmers continued to produce more than ever in a futile effort to improve their worsening economic position.

As the twenties progressed, moreover, it was plain that the fruits of prosperity were being distributed with growing inequality. By 1929 the economy was clearly top-heavy, and such a disproportionate share of the national income was going to a small minority of the population that it was problematical how much longer the workers on American farms and assembly lines could continue to consume all the goods they were producing. A study in 1929 revealed the existence of nearly 27,500,000 families in the United States. Of these, nearly 6,000,000, or over 21 per cent, received an income of less than $1,000 a year, or less than what many authorities calculated as the minimum subsistence level. Nearly 20,000,000 families, or 71 per cent, had incomes of under $2,500, the sum estimated as necessary for a decent living standard. The distortion was even clearer with respect to savings. Over three quarters of American families were listed as having no significant savings at all, while the 2.3 per cent with incomes over $10,000 possessed two thirds of the $15 billion of savings. In short, as productivity in industry rose, costs fell, and profits mounted. Instead of being shared more equitably with the labor force through higher wages, these profits were retained by management or dispensed as dividends, which jumped 110 per cent between 1922 and 1929. This encouraged the high level of investment that lay behind the booming productivity; but by the late twenties, it was also nourishing the speculative mania that gripped Wall Street.

One reason why industrial workers did not share more fully in the prosperity of the 1920's was the steady decline and growing paralysis of organized labor. The dominant force in the labor movement at this time was the American Federation of Labor, a loose grouping of national craft unions. Ever since its establishment in 1886 the AFL had considered itself the aristocracy of labor; and indeed, it was. It had concentrated on organizing the highly skilled workers, whose superior bargaining power as contrasted with the unskilled gave their craft unions necessary strength and stability. On the other hand, the AFL had never tried very hard to organize the semiskilled mass-production industries that were becoming ever more characteristic of American industrial society. Sensing the mood of the business-minded twenties, AFL leaders sought to convince the country of their conservatism, respectability, and sturdy devotion to capitalism. Unfortunately, this policy neither impressed those employers who wanted no independent unions in their plants nor imbued the rank-and-file union membership with the militancy needed to combat an aggressive open-shop campaign by management early in the decade. Nor were union leaders successful in counteracting the so-called "welfare capitalism"—recreational programs, pensions, stock ownership schemes, employee representation plans, etc.—introduced by some employers to reduce industrial unrest and undercut the appeal of independent unions. As a result, from 1920 to 1929, total union membership declined from 5.1 million to 3.4 million. Although wages in unionized industries remained higher than in the unorganized industries, the great mass of industrial workers had no effective voice and no bargaining strength to remind employers that perhaps a larger proportion of the rising profits ought to go into wages rather than dividends.

One of the most remarkable developments of the twenties was the speculative mania that seized a substantial minority of the American people. Never before in the country's history had so many Americans tacitly abandoned the old values of hard work and thrift in favor of the seductive lure of the "fast buck." Perhaps this was a natural accompaniment of the good times and the cheery optimism preached by the hucksters of the New Era. After all, if the nation had entered upon a New Era of rising abundance, why not participate more actively in the prosperity? Why not invest in the rosy future (especially when a rising market enabled one to cash in tomorrow at a handsome profit)?

The first signs of speculative fever came in the form of a boom in real estate. As ownership of automobiles became more commonplace—another revolutionary aspect of the twenties—more Americans began moving to the suburbs. Suburban land values accordingly began to rise, along with the expectations of that always optimistic fraternity, the real estate promoters. Lots were subdivided with lavish abandon on the outskirts of every city. Each town had its Babbittlike boosters, who argued convincingly that the economic future of Zenith City or Gopher Prairie or Podunk was limitless. Each town also had its quota of land speculators, some of whom soon cast their eyes abroad for more exciting ventures.

They found the excitement they sought in Florida, which, by the mid-twenties, had become the center of the real estate boom. Florida had long been the playground of the rich, but improved transportation and higher incomes gave rise to hopes that it could be turned into a vacation land for the growing middle class. Sunny Florida, the land of balmy tropic breezes, chanted the promoters, would soon be an American Riviera. We know now that such expectations were not entirely unreasonable, given several decades of prudent growth and development. But the credo of the twenties was one of boundless optimism, and thousands of Americans lost their heads completely over the siren call of Florida. From Jacksonville to Miami and westward to Tampa and beyond, almost overnight, once worthless swampland began to command fantastic prices. By 1925, inside lots within forty miles of Miami were selling for as much as $20,000, and seashore sites were bringing up to $75,000.

Many of the purchasers of Florida land were not interested in living in the state or even in developing their land. They merely expected to hold it long enough to be able to sell at a profit. At the peak of the boom, this might be only a matter of a fortnight or so. But the rising prices of a speculative boom are dependent upon an ever-expanding supply of buyers who are willing to pay the ever-fancier prices. And by early 1926, buyers were becoming more wary. Then, in the autumn, Florida was devastated by two hurricanes, which demonstrated, as Frederick Lewis Allen has neatly phrased it, "what a Soothing Tropic Wind could do when it got a running start from the West Indies." Wind velocity at the height of the second storm, it might be noted, reached 138 miles per hour and tossed steam yachts all over the streets of Miami. Hundreds were killed, and many thousands more made homeless. Overnight, interest in the American Riviera had literally gone with the wind, and the Florida land boom collapsed, with real and paper losses totaling millions of dollars.

Rather surprisingly, the painful lesson of Florida did not kill the current appetite for speculation. Major interest shifted to the stock market, which had already begun the historic rise that would culminate in the great bull market of 1929. Since the early twenties, stock prices had been gradually increasing. For this, there were sound reasons, for—as we have seen—corporate earnings were good and seemed likely to get better. In fact, at the beginning of the decade, stock prices were comparatively low in relation to earnings, and many issues offered attractive yields. But during 1927, stock prices began to advance substantially and with monotonous regularity, thereby leading many Americans to forget that even in a New Era, what goes up may also come down.

The advance continued even more strongly in 1928. In March the average of industrial stocks rose nearly 25 points (dollars), with some speculative favorites jumping 10 or 15 points in a single day. Prices declined in June, leading to premature predictions that the boom was over, but by late summer the market was surging ahead once more. In September, Secretary of the Treasury Andrew Mellon, one of the richest men in the country, advised the nation not to worry. "The high tide of prosperity," he declared expansively, "will continue." If this were not reassurance enough, the election of Herbert Hoover in November, with its promise of four more years of Republican good times, set off a further wave of buying. Despite some setbacks the following month, the *New York Times'* list of industrial stocks showed an overall increase of 86 points for the year. Some individual stocks, moreover, had made Florida-size gains. Radio Corporation of America skyrocketed from 85 to 420 (though it had never paid a dividend); Montgomery Ward went from 117 to 440, DuPont from 310 to 525.

If the gains of 1928 were impressive, those that followed in the spring and summer of 1929 were even more so. And as the bull market continued its boiling advance, additional thousands of speculators rushed to get in on what seemed to be the quickest way to turn a dollar since the invention of money. There seemed to be little risk, for as 1929 wore on, the market scarcely ever hesitated in its upward climb. During June the *New York Times'* list of industrials went up 52 points; in July, another 25. In August, it rose still another 33 points, making an incredible gain of 110 points in three months. In other words, during the summer, values had risen nearly 25 per cent on the average. Small wonder that the stock market dominated the news in the summer of 1929 or that Wall Street had become an exciting symbol of the promise of the New Era.

Why had the runaway boom in stock developed, and what did the leaders in government and finance attempt to do about it? It is difficult, of course, to explain just why the speculative fever built up in 1928 and 1929 to the point where otherwise prudent men and women decided to gamble their savings in what was clearly an inordinately high and presumably unsound market. One important reason, certainly, was the pervasive mood of confidence and optimism. To most Americans the future appeared good. The affairs of government and business were being looked after by men the country trusted. Never before or since were the businessmen and bankers more respected and admired figures of society. Hence, why not rely on the judgment of these leaders, who constantly reiterated that conditions were sound and prosperity was here to stay? Furthermore, savings had been growing rapidly during the decade and, as has been noted, in a lopsided pattern. A sizable minority of the population had more money than ever before and was accordingly more inclined to risk some of it in stock speculation.

Still another factor in the boom was the ease with which speculative ventures could be launched and pyramided to dizzy heights in the unregulated markets of the twenties. Buying on margin—speculating with borrowed money—was one popular technique. Margin buying was admirably suited to the needs of the speculator. He merely bought his stock by paying a certain percentage of the purchase price in cash —the margin—and then took out a loan through his broker for the remainder, using the stock itself as collateral. In this way, he could stretch his funds to finance much broader purchases. The banks which put up the money for these brokers' loans found the arrangement advantageous, too. The loans were protected not only by the buyer's cash margin, but also by stocks that were normally instantly salable. If the market declined, the loans could be called (hence the synonyms "call loans" or "call money"), or the stock collateral could be sold to protect the lender. On a rising market the speculator did not mind paying a high interest rate on his loan, since he was counting upon much larger capital gains in the stocks he bought. At the end of 1928 the interest rate on call money had risen to 12 per cent. But what was this to a man who was speculating in RCA stock, which had increased in value over the year by 500 per cent? The volume of brokers' loans rose enormously during the bull market, a measure of the frantic speculation in progress. At the end of 1927, brokers' loans totaled $3.4 billion; by September 30, 1929, they amounted to an unprecedented $8.5 billion. As the interest rate on call money edged upward, funds from all over the world began to flow to Wall Street to take advantage of the high return on these comparatively risk-free loans. Some American corporations began lending their surplus funds in this fashion, their officials concluding that such was more profitable than investing in new plants or equipment. At least one company, Cities Service, even sold a new stock issue and loaned the proceeds in the stock market.

Other factors also stimulated the boom. One was the extraordinary growth in the number of investment trusts in 1928 and 1929, which gave the unwary investor a comforting assurance that his funds were being looked after by professionals, yet whose stocks demonstrated nice speculative gains. Certainly, the large commercial banks played an important role as well, not only in financing the large volume of brokers' loans but also by establishing investment affiliates which traded stocks actively, underwrote speculative issues, and launched high-pressure sales campaigns to lure more investors into the market.

A few Americans recognized by early 1929 that the stock market was dangerously high. One was the incoming President, Herbert Hoover, who was faced with an exceedingly painful dilemma. He could either try to prick the speculative bubble gently, or he could sit tight and let the inevitable collapse come in its own good time. The first course was risky, for it might fail in its aim of gradual retardation, leaving the new administration to face certain public wrath and perhaps an unwanted depression. The second course invited an even more devastating collapse but at least avoided any direct responsibility for a deliberate deflation of the boom. Some of Hoover's advisers—Secretary of the Treasury Andrew Mellon for one—counseled a policy of inaction. Ironically, Mellon's own fiscal policies during the twenties—cutting income taxes at the highest levels—were partly responsible for the administration's dilemma, since the Secretary's largesse had provided several extra billions of the savings that now were flowing into the bull market. In the end, Hoover's commitment to *laissez faire* triumphed over his immediate and well-grounded fears. While the stock market faltered and then declined in late March out of uncertainty over what the new administration would do, Hoover hesitated, and lost his best and perhaps only real chance to apply the brakes. From then on, the sky was the limit.

Nor was the Federal Reserve Board, the semiautonomous guardian of the nation's banking structure, much more aggressive in curbing the dangerous stock speculation through bank loans. Early in 1929 the Board began selling some of its holdings of government bonds in an effort to deny funds to the stock market, but it pursued the policy hesitantly and with little result. In February the Board addressed a mild warning to the individual Federal Reserve banks cautioning against the common practice of loaning money to the commercial banks for relending in the stock market. This, too, had little effect and was widely disregarded. When the New York Federal Reserve Bank suggested raising the rediscount rate from 5 to 6 per cent as a means of tightening the reins on credit, both the Board and President Hoover were reluctant to take a step that might hurt legitimate business borrowers. As a result, the rediscount rate was not increased until late summer, when the boom had nearly run its course.

Probably what was needed most in the early months of 1929 was a clear and unmistakable public warning from some unimpeachable authority of the dangers of the current speculative boom. Such a warning might have come from President Hoover or the Federal Reserve Board, either of whom could have asked Congress for authority to curb margin trading by giving the Board power to set margin requirements. (This was done eventually in the Securities Exchange Act of 1934.) Or some of the great private bankers could have spoken out against further stock speculation and taken steps to cut back the volume of brokers' loans. Surely, these or other moves would have broken the spell and started a downturn. Yet, precisely because no one knew where such a downturn would lead, everyone feared to act. Those few who did warn publicly of a possible crash and depression were roundly denounced as spoilsports whose pessimism had no place in the New Era.

Obviously, stock prices could not go on climbing forever at the mad pace of the summer of 1929. And the crash, when it came, was even more spectacular than the boom. There were a few setbacks in September, enough to give pause to a few wise operators, though the volume of brokers' loans continued to increase. But by mid-October, even the most optimistic could see that the stock market was behaving badly. Margin traders discovered that stock prices could decline suddenly and precipitously, wiping them out almost without warning. Many tried to hang on by increasing their cash margins, only to learn that in a falling market, this was an extraordinarily efficient way to send good money after bad. Confidence gradually eroded. Then, on October 24, 1929—"Black Thursday"—blind panic set in as thousands of investors all over the country rushed to unload at any price. Before the day was out, an incredible 12,894,650 shares had been sold, many at prices that represented utter ruin to their owners. In the afternoon the panic was checked momentarily by a group of leading Wall Street bankers, who pooled their resources to bolster the market by bidding up the price of a number of key stocks. It was a futile gesture. For investors generally, Black Thursday represented the end—literally the end of the line for many speculators, and for all the end of confidence in the New Era. On October 29 the bottom again dropped out of the market, with a record 16,410,030 shares traded in what was certainly the wildest day in the history of the New York Exchange. This time the bankers recognized their inability to stem the tide. The great bull market was over.

Nor was this all. The crash, with its 40 per cent decline in stock values in a few terrible weeks, could not be whistled away, despite a paean of rosy statements about the essential soundness of the country's economic health. The financial and psychological shock was too great, and it soon began to affect the rest of the economy. Businessmen cut back inventories and postponed plans for expansion. American investments abroad dried up. This, in turn, forced foreigners to curtail purchases of American goods and resulted in a severe financial crisis in Europe by 1931 that further weakened key American banks. As business conditions worsened, unemployment mounted steadily, until it reached staggering proportions and exhausted the relief resources of private philanthropy and local governments. For more than three years after the crash the economy spiraled downward, until by early 1933 the disaster was so complete and far-reaching that many believed the nation's basic political and economic institutions might be at stake.

While the boom lasted, the "golden twenties" seemed aptly named, and the New Era seemed to be everything its prophets promised. Perhaps for some investors the illusion for a time of sudden wealth was worth the subsequent hardships. But the country as a whole paid a heavy price for the speculative orgy in Wall Street. And in retrospect, it seems clear that the era that ended in October, 1929, was not really new. That term might better be applied to the developments of the next decade, when a chastened nation sought to rebuild its shattered economy.

SUGGESTED READINGS

ADAMS, SAMUEL HOPKINS. *Incredible Era: The Life and Times of Warren Gamaliel Harding.* Boston: Houghton Mifflin Co., 1939.

ALLEN, FREDERICK LEWIS. *Only Yesterday: An Informal History of the Nineteen-Twenties.* New York: Harper & Bros., 1931.

BERNSTEIN, IRVING. *The Lean Years: A History of the American Worker, 1920–1933.* Boston: Houghton Mifflin Co., 1960.

GALBRAITH, JOHN KENNETH. *The Great Crash, 1929.* Boston: Houghton Mifflin Co., 1955.

HICKS, JOHN D. *Republican Ascendancy, 1921–1933.* New York: Harper & Bros., 1960.

PROTHRO, JAMES W. *Dollar Decade: Business Ideas in the 1920's.* Baton Rouge: Louisiana State University Press, 1954.

SCHLESINGER, ARTHUR M., JR. *The Crisis of the Old Order, 1919–1933.* Boston: Houghton Mifflin Co., 1957.

SLOSSON, PRESTON W. *The Great Crusade and After: 1914–1928.* New York: Macmillan Co., 1930.

SOULE, GEORGE. *Prosperity Decade: From War to Depression, 1917–1929.* New York: Rinehart & Co., Inc., 1947.

WHITE, WILLIAM ALLEN. *A Puritan in Babylon: The Story of Calvin Coolidge.* New York: Macmillan Co., 1938.

Document 27.1

THE STOCK MARKET CRASH—
A CONTEMPORARY VIEW

A good way to recapture something of the mood of shock, fear, panic, and yet lingering optimism during the final days of the New Era is to examine the day-to-day newspaper reports of the stock market collapse.

(From the *New York Times*, October 25, 1929. Copyright by the *New York Times*; reprinted by permission.)

The most disastrous decline in the biggest and broadest stock market of history rocked the financial district yesterday. In the very midst of the collapse five of the country's most influential bankers hurried to the office of J. P. Morgan & Co., and after a brief conference gave out word that they believe the foundations of the market to be sound, that the market smash has been caused by technical rather than fundamental considerations, and that many sound stocks are selling too low. . . .

The total losses cannot be accurately calculated, because of the large number of markets and the thousands of securities not listed on any exchange. However, they were staggering, running into billions of dollars. Fear struck the big speculators and little ones, big investors and little ones. Thousands of them threw their holdings into the whirling Stock Exchange pit for what they would bring. Losses were tremendous and thousands of prosperous brokerage and bank accounts, sound and healthy a week ago, were completely wrecked in the strange debacle, due to a combination of circumstances, but accelerated into a crash by fear. . . .

Wall Street ended the day in an optimistic frame of mind. The opinion of brokers was unanimous that the selling had got out of hand not because of any inherent weakness in the market but because the public had become alarmed over the steady liquidation of the last few weeks. Over their private wires these brokers counseled their customers against further thoughtless selling at sacrifice prices.

(From the *New York Times*, October 26, 1929. Copyright by the *New York Times*; reprinted by permission.)

WASHINGTON, Oct. 25.—A reassuring statement that the fundamental business of the country was on a sound and prosperous basis was made by President Hoover at the White House this afternoon. It was made in reply to questions by newspaper men asking his opinion on the possible effect on the nation's prosperity of yesterday's collapse in the stock market.

(From the *New York Times*, October 29, 1929. Copyright by the *New York Times*; reprinted by permission.)

The second hurricane of liquidation within four days hit the stock market yesterday. It came suddenly, and violently, after holders of stocks had been lulled into a sense of security by the rallies of Friday and Saturday. It was a country-wide collapse of open-market security values in which the declines established and the actual losses taken in dollars and cents were probably the most disastrous and far-reaching in the history of the Stock Exchange.

That the storm has now blown itself out, that there will be organized support to put an end to a reaction which has ripped billions of dollars from market values, appeared certain last night from statements by leading bankers.

Stock prices virtually collapsed yesterday, swept downward with gigantic losses in the most disastrous trading day in the stock market's history. Billions of dollars in open market values were wiped out as prices crumbled under the pressure of liquidation of securities which had to be sold at any price. . . .

Trading on the New York Stock Exchange aggregated 16,410,030 shares; on the Curb, 7,096,300 shares were dealt in. Both totals far exceeded any previous day's dealings.

From every point of view, in the extent of losses sustained, in total turnover, in the number of speculators wiped out, the day was the most disastrous in Wall Street's history. Hysteria swept the country and stocks went overboard for just what they would bring at forced sale. . . .

There was no quibbling at all between customer and broker yesterday. In any case where margin became thin a peremptory call went out. If there was no immediate answer the stock was sold out "at the market" for just what it would bring. Thousands, sold out on the decline and amid confusion, found themselves in debt to their brokers last night. . . .

Despite the drastic decline, sentiment in Wall Street last night was more cheerful than it has been on any day since the torrent of selling got under way.

PROVIDENCE, R.I., Oct. 29 (AP).—David Korn, 57, proprietor of a coal firm and prominent in charitable activities here, dropped dead in a broker's office in Providence this afternoon as he was watching the ticker. Witnesses said Mr. Korn had appeared worried as news of the stock market crash came into the office. . . .

KANSAS CITY, Oct. 29 (AP).—John G. Schwitzgebel, insurance man, fired two shots into his chest at the Kansas City Club today in an attempt to commit suicide.

"Tell the boys I can't pay them what I owe them," he told friends who rushed to his room.

A brother said he believed Schwitzgebel "had been caught in the market."

Document 27.2

A SPECULATOR'S LAMENT

During the early 1930's the Senate Committee on Banking and Currency conducted a searching investigation into the causes of the stock market crash. The Committee's able general counsel, Ferdinand Pecora, subsequently wrote a book summarizing the results of the probe. Pecora used the following example to denounce certain banking practices of the twenties, but to the historian the illustration has broader meaning for an understanding of the speculative boom and bust.

(From Ferdinand Pecora, *Wall Street under Oath* [New York: Simon and Schuster, Inc., 1939], pp. 84–88)

Mr. Edgar D. Brown was a resident of Pottsville, Pennsylvania. In 1927, he had $100,000 and was looking forward to a trip to California for his health. In 1933, he had nothing, and was clerking for the poor board of Pottsville. Here is his story, typical of those of a great many others, as graphically told to the Senate Committee:

In a national magazine, he saw a persuasive advertisement, reading:

Are you thinking of a lengthy trip? If you are, it will pay you to get in touch with our institution, because you will be leaving the advice of your local banker and we will be able to keep you closely guided as regards your investments.

The advertisement was signed by the National City Bank. It struck Mr. Brown that this just suited his needs, and he made haste to answer it. Soon a representative of the National City Company called upon him. Mr. Brown put himself unreservedly in the latter's hands. He was not suspicious or overcautious, for he had confidence and trust. After all, he was not dealing with some fly-by-night bucket shop or itinerant gold-mining stock peddler, but with the greatest and soundest bank in the world—or so he thought. His one insistence was, that he did not want to buy stocks, but only bonds—fixed interest securities. He was naturally not indifferent to the possibility of profit; but chiefly he wanted safety.

Well, Mr. Brown had asked for bonds, and bonds he got. But not United States Government bonds, such as he had originally owned ($75,000 of his $100,000 was in fact in cash)—these the National City advised him were "all wrong." So they put him, instead, into a bewildering array of Viennese, German, Greek, Peruvian, Chilean, Rhenish,

Hungarian, and Irish governmental obligations, as well as bonds of various private American corporations. These were represented as affording so profitable an opportunity that Mr. Brown was induced not only to risk all of his own $100,000, but to borrow scores of thousands more in order to make additional purchases, until finally his "investments" totaled about $250,000. When these bonds, purchased mostly with borrowed money, declined—instead of enhancing in value, as Mr. Brown had been confidently assured they would do—he complained:

MR. PECORA: You complained to whom?

MR. BROWN: Mr. Rummell [the National City Company representative].

MR. PECORA: Yes?

MR. BROWN: And he said, "Well, that is your fault for insisting upon bonds. *Why don't you let me sell you some stocks?"*

Well, the stock market had been continually moving up. So then I took hook, line, and sinker and said, "Very well, buy stock."

MR. PECORA: Did you tell him what stocks to buy?

MR. BROWN: Never.

MR. PECORA: Did he buy stocks then for your account?

MR. BROWN: Might I answer that facetiously? *Did he buy stock!* (*Great and prolonged laughter.*)

Yes, great and prolonged laughter, but it had proved no laughing matter for Mr. Brown. His faith in the National City was complete: "I bought thousands of shares of stock on their suggestion which I did not know whether the companies they represented made cake, candy, or automobiles." And the National City bought for him so many stocks, and traded in them so violently, that even the unsuspecting Mr. Brown finally complained to the main office of the National City Company in New York. So far as he could tell, he seemed, in spite of all this activity, to be still losing money. He was listened to sympathetically, and once again his portfolio was changed, this time mostly to National City Bank stock and to Anaconda Copper. Still, his stocks kept declining. About October 4, 1929, he took his courage in both hands, went into the National City bank branch in Los Angeles, and "asked them to sell out everything."

MR. BROWN: I was placed in the category of the man who seeks to put his own mother out of his house. I was surrounded at once by all of the salesmen in the place, and made to know that that was a very, very foolish thing to do.

MR. PECORA: That is, to sell your stocks?

MR. BROWN: Especially to sell the National City Bank stocks. . . . I then received an unsolicited wire from their agent in the East . . . (*reading*) "National City Bank now 525. Sit tight."

Once again, Mr. Brown allowed himself to be overpersuaded. The rest of the story is soon told. A few weeks later came the crash. Mr. Brown was naturally sold out, most of his capital irretrievably gone. His efforts to borrow money from the bank in which he had placed such confidence were met with the suave reply that a loan was impossible "unless the borrower has assured earning power and could pay off the loan within six months." But Mr. Brown then had no such earning power, he was "forty years of age—tubercular—almost totally deaf—my wife and family are depending on me solely and alone and because of my abiding faith in the advice of your company I am today a pauper."

Just another little man wiped out, a victim of high-pressure salesmanship!

Document 27.3

CAVEAT EMPTOR—LET THE BUYER BEWARE

The previous document points out one notable characteristic of the stock market boom, namely, that many investors did not know very much about the securities they were so freely purchasing. The Senate investigation revealed one reason why this was so.

(From U.S. Congress, Senate Committee on Banking and Currency, *Report: Stock Exchange Practices*, 73d Congress, 2d Session, Report No. 1455 [Washington, D.C.: U.S. Government Printing Office, 1934], pp. 85, 128–29)

So far as the investor was concerned, the banker frequently did not "have a decent regard for his interests." A glaring instance was the flotation of $90,000,000 bonds of the Republic of Peru sold to the American public in 1927–28 and now in default. The American bankers completely subrogated the interests of the investor to their own interests and to those of their client, Peru. It was admitted by officials of the National City Co., one of the sponsors of the issues, that investors were invited to lend $90,000,000 upon the most precarious of risks, in order to assist Peru in extricating herself from a state of economic and political chaos. . . .

In March 1927 when the tobacco loan was publicly offered the National City Co. issued a prospectus describing the loan in which no information was vouchsafed regarding the bad-debt record of Peru.

MR. PECORA. Do you find any mention in it (the prospectus) whatsoever of the bad credit record of Peru which is embodied in the information I have read into the record from your files?

MR. BAKER [Hugh B. Baker, President of the National City Company]. I should have to read this over, Mr. Pecora. [After perusing document.] No; I do not see anything. It is a secured loan. I do not see any statements in there.

MR. PECORA. No statement or information was given to the American investing public in your circular corresponding to the information that your company possessed in writing among its files concerning the bad debt record of Peru and its being a bad moral and political risk?

MR. BAKER. No, sir.

The $15,000,000 loan was quickly absorbed by the public. Almost immediately negotiations went forward for the flotation of additional loans to Peru on a vast scale.

On December 21, 1927, an issue of $50,000,000 Peruvian Government 6-percent bonds was offered to the public at 91½ by a syndicate composed of National City Co., J. & W. Seligman & Co., Blyth, Witter & Co., the Guaranty Co. of New York, F. J. Lisman & Co., and Central Union Trust Co. The gross spread to the bankers was 5 points.

Between the sale of the $15,000,000 issue and the offering of the $50,000,000 issue, conditions in Peru failed to improve, as indicated in a letter from J. H. Durrell, a vice president and overseas manager of the National City Bank, to Charles E. Mitchell, dated July 27, 1927.

As I see it, there are two factors that will long retard the economic importance of Peru. First, its population of 5,500,000 is largely Indian, two-thirds of whom reside east of the Andes, and a majority consume almost no manufactured products. Second, its principal sources of wealth, the mines and oil wells, are nearly all foreign-owned, and excepting for wages and taxes, no part of the value of their production remains in the country. Added to this, the sugar plantations are in the hands of a few families, a majority of whom reside and invest their profits abroad. Also, for political reasons, the present Government has deported some 400 prominent wealthy conservative families, but allows them to continue to receive and to make use of abroad the income from their Peruvian properties. As a whole, I have no great faith in any material betterment of Peru's economic condition in the near future.

The country's political situation is equally uncertain. President

Leguia, while not having the absolute power possessed by General Gomez in Venezuela, is the last word in all things political, and usually the first word as well. * * * Unfortunately, his health is bad, and it is reported that he must undergo a serious operation soon.

The prospectus on this $50,000,000 loan contained the following statement:

> The Republic of Peru is the third largest country in South America, with an area of approximately 550,000 square miles. It has a population estimated at 6,000,000.

The President of the National City Co. was examined with reference to the omission from the prospectus of the unfavorable factors set forth in Durrell's letter to Mitchell.

MR. PECORA. * * * Why wasn't that detailed information given in this circular along with the statement that the population of Peru was 6,000,000?

MR. BAKER. I cannot answer that.

MR. PECORA. Did you think it would have had a bad effect on the flotation of these bonds if the advices contained in Mr. Durrell's letter of July 27, 1927, had been given to the investing public through the medium of a circular?

MR. BAKER. It might have; yes.

28

DEAN ALBERTSON
Brooklyn College

The New Deal

FRANKLIN DELANO ROOSEVELT stood before thousands of applauding, perspiring delegates to the Democratic National Convention in Chicago on July 2, 1932, to accept the presidential nomination which he and his "brain trust" associates had with consummate political skill managed to wrest from the other contenders. When the cheers and the last booming organ notes of "Happy Days Are Here Again" had stilled, the candidate destined to be the thirty-second President of the United States served notice of a break with the past. "Throughout the nation," he told them, "men and women, forgotten in the political philosophy of the government of the last years look to us here for guidance and for more equitable opportunity to share in the distribution of national wealth. . . ."

And then: "I pledge you, I pledge myself, to a new deal for the American people. Let us all here assembled constitute ourselves prophets of a new order of competence and of courage. This is more than a political campaign; it is a call to arms. . . ."

Two months later, in a campaign address before the plushly conservative Commonwealth Club of San Francisco, Roosevelt pointedly stated one of the primary problems of the new order. He came, he said, to speak not of politics, but of government; not of parties, but of universal principles. "The issue of government has always been whether individual men and women will have to serve some system of government or economics, or whether a system of government and economics exists to serve individual men and women."

The candidate then made an analysis of past American history which was to be the hallmark of New Dealers for a generation. The partnership of laissez-faire government and buccaneering capitalism may have been contributive to American industrial growth at a time when the nation was filling in its frontiers and creating the mightiest productive machinery on earth. But times had changed. The free land of the frontier was gone. The United States had entered World War I as a debtor nation and emerged as the largest international creditor. Infant industries had matured into complex, engulfing giants, unrestrained either by government or by moral self-regulation. Democracy and individualism were thought to be the cornerstones of American greatness. But the old democracy and the old individualism were based on the competitive economics envisioned in Adam Smith's metaphysical "invisible hand" system which saw society automatically propelling itself toward abundance by simply competing in accordance with the laws of the market place—laws which were far beyond the manipulation of mortal men. As the early New Dealers saw it: "The jig is up. The cat is out of the bag. There is no invisible hand. There never was."

Although an industrial revolution and a managerial revolution had occurred since Adam Smith revealed his immutable laws, most Americans continued to glorify the virtue and necessity of competition. Ownership of land, businesses, and factories (and the concomitant fruits of ownership—economic security, success, prestige, and the like) once were available for the many amidst the abundance of America. But by the 1930's, ownership was possible on a modest scale for only a relatively few lucky winners. National and international cartels had replaced the family-owned factory. A managerial elite, hired by corporations on annual salaries to manage their affairs, had superseded the plant owner who had known his foremen and most of his workers by their first names. Within such changes as these, could "democracy" and "individualism" endure by nineteenth-century definitions? Could competition continue to be the guiding principle of business and industry when one tenth of one per cent of American corporations earned nearly half of the net income, and owned over half of the assets, of all corporations in the United States? "Frontier free-booter democracy of the purely individualistic type is definitely gone," said Henry A. Wallace, Secretary of Agriculture, "unless civilization lapses back into the Dark Ages and starts over again. To maintain the good points of the old individualism and the old democracy, and yet to enable modern methods to operate over an entire continent, without injury to the rest of the world, is a challenge to our utmost sympathetic ingenuity."

"The task of government in its relation to business," said Franklin Roosevelt, "is to assist the development of an economic declaration of rights, an economic constitutional order."

This was to be the New Deal. Its obvious problems were inherited from the Old Deal. A depression of pervasive and terrifying dimensions blighted the land. Well over ten million citizens, nearly a quarter of the whole working force, had lost their jobs. Three desperate years of decline had wiped out savings; state funds for the relief of hunger and destitution were exhausted. Foreclosure and bankruptcy stalked the homes, farms, factories, and businesses of the nation. Iowa corn was being burned for fuel while poverty-stricken urbanites shivered in bread lines. Clearly, business must be reinvigorated. The jobless must be sustained, then re-employed. The farmer must be raised from the threat of peasantry. Along with the measures for *recovery*, however, the institutions of the economy must be *reformed* so that the tragedy of depression might not again shake the foundations of democracy.

How was recovery to be achieved? For what purposes was reform to be instigated? Former President Herbert Hoover, too, had sought recovery from depression, but generally within a framework of time-tested dogma which intoned that the national government was not to be trusted. Hated despotism lurked behind each enlargement of federal function; tyranny bestrode every positive executive act (except, of course, such positive acts as appeared in the form of subsidy, tariff, or land grant to business or industry). American democracy was said to follow the paths of "free enterprise" and "individual initiative." How, then, could a free, democratic government "wage war" on national adversity without wrenching the entire political and economic machinery into such a high degree of centralization as to destroy both freedom and individualism? And what reforms could be carried out which hopefully would prevent depression from recurring which would not so alter the American system as to make it unpalatable to the majority vote which democracy (and, incidentally, the Democratic party) required? Three years of failing Republican effort to end depression—during which huge industrial corporations laid off a third of their workers, yet continued to pay dividends—cast some doubt on the amount of individualism remaining for the average man in any case.

During the early years of the New Deal the question emphatically was not whether political democracy still prevailed in the nation. As recently as November, 1932, American democracy was sufficiently viable to throw the Republicans out of office, and presumably might be used at a later date to visit similar retribution on the Democrats. The issue concerned the relevance of political democracy to economic democracy. *If*, as New Dealers suggested, a worker was free no longer to choose his job and be reasonably sure of steady employment, *if* a farmer could be told on market day that his crop would bring less than the cost of growing it, *if* the small businessman had as his only alternatives ruinous competition or the sale of his plant to a chain operation, *if* the ordinary citizen had so little control over his destiny that one third of a nation would be "ill-housed, ill-clad, ill-nourished," then of what practical value was the ballot on election day? It was not, said the New Dealers, government which had taken economic liberty. It was the concentrated wealth and power of business and finance, and a fossilized belief in the inexorability of economic law.

Had the individual become a mere ratchet in the machinery, an exchangeable part, a commodity to be bought and sold on the open market? New Dealers did not think so. At the very heart of the Roosevelt regime lay an optimistic faith in man as an enlightened, rational individual whose abilities of free, democratic choice gave him the collective capacity to master his own social, political, and economic environment. Government and the economy existed to serve individual men and women.

To contemporary observers the New Deal was incredibly confusing because of its many pragmatic inconsistencies and the complexity of its proposals. The personality of its chief architect, President Roosevelt, did little to alleviate the confusion. "There never was a prominent leader," said Rexford G. Tugwell of F.D.R., "who was more determined about his objectives, and never one who was more flexible about his means." This very flexibility, this willingness on the part of Roosevelt and the rest of the New Dealers to "tinker with the works," contributed heavily to the unpatterned quality of the 1933–40 era. And yet, in retrospect, the goals of the "Roosevelt revolution" emerge with singular clarity—to preserve the dignity of the individual and his right to private property within the context of a capitalistic democratic society. Or, as Henry A. Wallace put it, "the New Deal places human rights above property rights and aims to modify special privilege for the few to the extent that such modification will aid in providing economic security for the many."

The immediate response of the New Deal to the problems which it faced was a masterful discernment of the traditional American "middle" way. The new government happily set about following the only mandate given it in solemn referendum by the citizenry—to do *something!* The closed banks were examined, found to be solvent, of course, and reopened. The gold content of the dollar was reduced and the nation moved to a semimanaged currency. City boys were packed

off to the mountains in the dull green uniforms of the Civilian Conservation Corps to hew undergrowth and plant trees. Mild beer and
light wines were provided for a thirsty nation while the Twenty-first
Amendment to the Constitution made its way among the states. Salaries of government workers were cut 15 per cent across the board.
Permissible stock margins were reduced. It was indeed a kaleidoscopic
program. The principal themes of New Deal policy lay buried deep
within the legislation.

The first major tenet of early New Dealism was embodied in a word
which evoked anguished cries from the conservative right—*planning*.
For the prudent householder or the shrewd businessman *not* to plan
ahead was considered the height of folly. But according to the philosophy of rugged individualism, planning by a government was the first
step toward absolute regimentation. "If city planning has been worth
while," asked Secretary of the Interior Harold L. Ickes, "why not plan
nationally? Why not, for instance, plan so that the ample resources
which we have, may be made to go around?" Gloomily replied the
deposed Hoover: "This direction must ultimately be reposed in government bureaus and they are comprised of human beings with dictatorial powers over us all." Rooseveltian planning, however, meant the
formulation of interrelated national programs for rural and urban land
use, for human and resource conservation, and for the overcoming of
the depression. When it came to implementation of national plans,
contrary to Hoover's dire predictions, local individuals concerned
were consulted. In nearly all instances, they passed favorably on the
government's plans by secret ballot, and were asked to staff and to
administer the resultant bureaucracy. The world-renowned Tennessee Valley Authority (TVA) still exists as a monument to govern-
mentally planned resource development.

A second precept of Roosevelt's administrations, "deficit financing,"
caused even greater consternation among the opposition. The President had promised to wage war on the depression. Congress gave him
authority to increase the national debt—to use the people's tax money
for their benefit at a time when they desperately needed it. Thus
armed, the New Deal called forth what William James termed the
"moral equivalents of war" and spent sums which were then thought
to be enormous on work relief and public works. To relief administrator Harry Hopkins, cynics attributed the apocryphal quotation:
"We will tax and tax, spend and spend, elect and elect." But from
John Maynard Keynes, a brilliant British economist, who believed
with Roosevelt that governments existed to serve people, came more

cheering words. "You, Mr. President, having cast off such fetters [as regarding war to be the sole legitimate excuse for deficit financing], are free to engage in the interests of peace and prosperity the technique which has hitherto only been allowed to serve the purposes of war and destruction." New Deal budgets for relief of human suffering between 1933 and 1940 totaled a little over $20 billion. In contrast, by 1958, American short-term consumer credit, mainly for automobiles and household appliances, amounted to $45 billion. Between 1946 and 1958 the federal government spent approximately $440 billion for foreign aid and its own armed forces procurement.

The third aspect of the early New Deal to provoke scorn was its idealistic faith in co-operation. If rational, comprehensive planning, use of deficit financing, and invocation of the moral equivalents could enlist a people to co-operate with its government to fight hunger and poverty, government might utilize the same instruments to achieve an "economic constitutional order." Initially, the Roosevelt administration determined not to attempt ineffectual "trust busting" against the concentrated power of finance and industry. Neither would it attack the "economic royalists" head on by socializing major units of industry. The New Deal would *co-operate* with big business to bring about recovery from depression. The National Recovery Administration (NRA) defined the terms of that co-operation. "Codes of fair competition" set aside the antitrust laws to the extent that each such code became, in direct contravention of the hallowed Sherman Act phrase, an authorization for combination in restraint of trade. Competition of the Adam Smith sort was not obliterated. "It means only," said NRA Administrator Hugh S. Johnson, "that competition must keep its blows above the belt, and that there can be no competition at the expense of decent living."

Having determined government to be the servant of its constituents, the New Deal next was faced with the promised redistribution of opportunity and wealth. Roosevelt approached this problem with a conception of society diametrically opposed to the olive branch of co-operation which had been extended to business and industry. The President saw his constituency in much the same way that TVA Administrator David E. Lilienthal saw his—"people as human beings—not 'the people' in their institutional roles as wage earners or investors or voters or consumers." And yet, how could a President or a government help John Smith to help himself? In certain instances the benevolent planners could reach John Smith as an individual. In many ways, however, John Smith could only be made real in his relation to government and society as an institutionalized being—as a farmer (through the AAA), as a worker (through the AFL or the CIO), or as a small businessman (through the NRA). Co-operation among the individuals *within* each of these groups was the order of the day. Contrary, however, to the best intentions of neo-Freudians and New Dealers alike, competition *between* these large groups might produce the best chance for economic democracy among their memberships. Wittingly or not, the New Deal program was one which created, in the words of Reinhold Niebuhr, "the equilibrium of power which is the basis of justice in any society." Competition between large groups in the old democracy had been, quite simply, uneven conflict between the unorganized financially impotent and the organized financially powerful, with the influence of government thrown usually toward the latter. Henceforth the farmers or the unions, as claimants for shares of the national wealth, might address either government or business on more or less equal terms.

If an equilibrium of power could endow society with a climate of economic justice, there still remained the citizen's desire for material acquisition, i.e., economic security. Under the terms of the old democracy, such security could be had by climbing the ladder of advancement from hired hand to farm tenant to landholder, or from worker to foreman to partner. The goal in either case was ownership. By the 1930's, it was apparent that the ladder to ownership had lost some of its rungs. Tenancy was increasing. Mobility upward from wages to salary was decreasing. Ownership of the nation's land, productive plants, and service enterprises had become concentrated in fewer and fewer hands. Recognizing that an infinitesimal number of tenants or workers would ever achieve ownership, New Deal policies had the effect of bestowing upon the average American at least the *fruits of ownership*—security. Slum-clearance projects, low-interest home purchase loans, bank deposit insurance, and, above all, unemployment and old-age insurance provided an enlarged opportunity for the majority to enjoy some of the material well-being of the opulent and to be freed from a measure of dependence upon the turn of economic fate. President Roosevelt, regarding the Social Security Act as the domestic capstone of his administration, took greater satisfaction from it than anything else he did. For this was the beginning of what since has come to be described as the "cradle-to-grave" security of the welfare state.

By the middle of Roosevelt's second term, times had changed, and so had the New Deal. From Europe came the threatening portents of

World War II. America's unemployed had been largely absorbed by government work relief agencies. The NRA, poorly conceived, badly managed, and business-dominated, had been swept from the scene in one of many laissez-faire decisions by the Supreme Court. Co-operation had failed. As conservatives in both parties gained strength, their demands for the end of a nationally planned economy grew more insistent. Early New Dealers of the planning–co-operation persuasion were dispatched on foreign missions—far from Washington. As their replacements entered the halls of government, the broad view of an interrelated economy, managed with high moral purpose in presumed accordance with the terms of human existence, gave way before "realistic" legalism and attempts to recover and regulate the classical competitive market. In 1933 the Secretary of Agriculture had seen in the first Agricultural Adjustment Act the co-operative, democratically planned use of land, blazing new trails toward a controlled economy, common sense, and social decency. In 1938 the Solicitor of the Department of Agriculture saw in the second Agricultural Adjustment Act an opportunity to move the basic farm legislation from its precarious footing under the Welfare Clause of the Constitution to a more solid foundation under the Commerce Clause. Paraphrasing Reinhold Niebuhr again, the early New Dealers had believed in man's capacity for justice, which made democracy possible; their successors in 1938 believed in man's inclination to injustice, which made democracy necessary.

Never was the New Deal alone able to defeat depression for those who endured its horror from 1929 to 1940. Never did Roosevelt gain suzerainty over the captains of finance and industry. The President, ever keen to achieve a balanced budget, put an end to deficit financing until a severe business recession in 1938 brought the government hastily back to "prime the pump." Defense appropriations, dwarfing the small sums allocated for the war on human misery, soon restored economic good fortune to the nation, obviating the need, many Americans believed, for the co-operative, constructive, reforming impulse which had given so much to the democratic faith—the faith of Franklin Roosevelt. When this man died, the people wept.

Should the New Deal have carried America further toward democratic socialism? Could it have done so? Early New Dealers, such as Rexford G. Tugwell, professed to see the nation at that critical point in its development when it must recognize fundamental changes in the relationship of citizen to government, of government to economy. America, he said, must update its policies to bring them into the twen-

tieth century, or, as he presciently phrased it, the American government would be either "ignored or contemptously brushed aside by
those in the community who have important affairs afoot which they
desire shall not be interferred with." But the Supreme Court, partly in
fear of the overturn of ancient and accepted rites of commerce, and
partly in distaste of the possibility that collective business would dominate collective government, vigorously resisted the "modernization"
of public policy. Congress, in 1937, by refusing to pass legislation for
the creation of additional justices, concurred. And the American citizen, so well instructed in the arts of consumer acquisition, savoring his
little prosperity beefsteak after a half decade of "ground round" depression, remained ignorant of the aspirations of two thirds of the
world's people. The New Deal was not a radical revision of old values.
It set out to save capitalism. It ended by strengthening capitalism and
revitalizing democracy. It could have gone no further.

SUGGESTED READINGS

ARNOLD, THURMAN W. *The Folklore of Capitalism.* New Haven: Yale University Press, 1937.

BURNS, JAMES MACGREGOR. *Roosevelt: The Lion and the Fox.* New York: Harcourt, Brace & Co., 1956.

FARLEY, JAMES A. *Behind the Ballots.* New York: Harcourt, Brace & Co., 1938.

FREIDEL, FRANK. *Franklin D. Roosevelt.* 3 vols. Boston: Little, Brown & Co.,
1952–56.

ICKES, HAROLD L. *The Secret Diary of Harold L. Ickes.* 3 vols. New York: Simon
and Schuster, Inc., 1954.

JOHNSON, HUGH S. *The Blue Eagle from Egg to Earth.* New York: Doubleday
Doran, 1935.

LILIENTHAL, DAVID E. *TVA: Democracy on the March.* New York: Harper &
Bros., 1944.

MOLEY, RAYMOND. *After Seven Years.* New York: Harper & Bros., 1939.

PERKINS, FRANCES. *The Roosevelt I Knew.* New York: Viking Press, Inc., 1946.

ROSENMAN, SAMUEL I. *Working with Roosevelt.* New York: Harper & Bros.,
1952.

ROSENMAN, SAMUEL I. (ed.). *The Public Papers and Addresses of Franklin D.
Roosevelt.* New York: Macmillan Co., 1937. New York: Random House, 1938.
New York: Harper & Bros., 1950.

SCHLESINGER, ARTHUR M., JR. *The Coming of the New Deal.* Boston: Houghton
Mifflin Co., 1959.

SCHLESINGER, ARTHUR M., JR. *The Politics of Upheaval.* Boston: Houghton
Mifflin Co., 1960.

SHERWOOD, ROBERT E. *Roosevelt and Hopkins.* New York: Harper & Bros.,
1948.

TUGWELL, REXFORD G. *The Battle for Democracy.* New York: Columbia University Press, 1935.

TUGWELL, REXFORD G. *The Democratic Roosevelt.* Garden City: Doubleday &
Co., Inc., 1957.

WALLACE, HENRY A. *Democracy Reborn.* RUSSELL LORD (ed.). New York:
Reynal and Hitchcock, 1944.

WALLACE, HENRY A. *New Frontiers.* New York: Reynal and Hitchcock, 1934.

Document 28.1

WE SHALL NOT REST UNTIL THAT MINIMUM IS ACHIEVED

Columbia University Professor of Economics Rexford G. Tugwell was 41 years old when he became a member of Roosevelt's pre-election "brain trust." Soon after the inauguration of the New Deal, he rose from Assistant Secretary of Agriculture to Undersecretary, to become one of the President's principal advisers. An outspoken protagonist of government planning and disciplined industry, he became a favored target of conservative opposition. Leaving Washington in 1937, Tugwell became successively Governor of Puerto Rico and distinguished professor at the University of Chicago. The selections from speeches which he made during 1933 and 1934, given below, illustrate the directions which his followers hoped the President would take during the early New Deal period.

DESIGN FOR GOVERNMENT

(From Rexford G. Tugwell, *The Battle for Democracy* [New York: Columbia University Press, 1935], pp. 1–16)

There is no prearranged field of government which is set apart from the circumstances of those who are governed. Relations here are always interdependent. As the circumstances of the people change, functions of government change. . . . It is a truism, too, to say that what is done by each of its divisions is affected by the whole orientation of the state. Like most truisms, this one contains a kernel of vital truth; it means, as re-spects ourselves, that executive, legislative, and judicial functions are not unalterably fixed, but are subject to revision. Government, or any part of it, is not in itself something; it is for something. It must do what we expect of it or it must be changed so that it will. . . .

Past circumstances produced needs (or supposed needs) which yielded theories in support of them. Toughest of those theories—so tough that, in the thinking of most men, it became an unalterable fact—was that which made competition a vital necessity, an end in itself, to be preserved at all costs. Competition was assumed to be an inherent part of democracy. Indeed competition and democracy came to be thought of as two aspects of one and the same value: a noncompetitive world was an undemocratic world.

Some two decades ago, it began to be apparent—or should have been —that competition and democracy were not Siamese twins, that they were separable, that in fact the separation had to be carried out if democracy were not to be stifled by competition. . . .

Competition, to depart from which was made unlawful, became a matter of legal compulsion. It meant compelled business confusion. Cooperative impulses, demanded by the current economic trend, were thwarted and repulsed. They expressed themselves only indirectly and unhealthily. What was sound and economically necessary was branded as wrong legally. . . .

. . . In this era of our economic existence, I believe it is manifest that a public interest well within the functions of government and well within the authority of government under our Constitution, commands the protection, the maintenance, the conservation, of our industrial faculties against the destructive forces of the unrestrained competition. And certainly the Constitution was never designed to impose upon one era the obsolete economic dogma which may have been glorified under it in an earlier one. For today and for tomorrow our problem is that of our national economic maintenance for the public welfare by governmental intervention—any theory of government, law or economics to the contrary notwithstanding. Hence the National Recovery Act and the Agricultural Adjustment Act of this administration. . . .

. . . Has the theory of a republican form of government explicit in the Constitution been violated by the new Democratic President and Congress? Has the philosophy of "checks and balances" within the Federal Government been infringed? These questions naturally arise; they command respect, for they concern our faith in the organization and functioning of our national Government. But must faiths, political more than economic, be preserved at any cost—that is, in disregard of the obviously necessary requirements of the public welfare? May our faiths in "checks and balances" yield to necessity, or even to expediency? If these faiths, and this necessity for more expeditious government action, are to clash, must we sacrifice efficiency or shall we establish a new faith? . . .

. . . To check and balance government to a point just short of inaction was the desideratum. The prevailing constitutional theory, and therefore the constitutional law, of course corresponded to this prevailing economic outlook.

At the center of this constitutional law was the conception of government as policeman. Government was to stop flagrant abuses, but not, in any circumstances, to do more. It was to be negative and arresting, not positive and stimulating. Its role was minor and peripheral. It was important in this one sense : It was to prevent interferences with the competitive system. Behind that system (so it was said and thoroughly believed) was an invisible hand which beneficently guided warring business men to the promotion of the general welfare.

The jig is up. The cat is out of the bag. There is no invisible hand. There never was. If the depression has not taught us that, we are incapable of education. Time was when the anarchy of the competitive struggle was not too costly. Today it is tragically wasteful. It leads to disaster. We must now supply a real and visible guiding hand to do the task which that mythical, nonexistent, invisible agency was supposed to perform, but never did.

Men are, by impulse, predominantly cooperative. They have their competitive impulses, to be sure ; but these are normally subordinate. Laissez faire exalted the competitive and maimed the cooperative impulses. It deluded men with the false notion that the sum of many petty struggles was aggregate cooperation. Men were taught to believe that they were, paradoxically, advancing cooperation when they were defying it. That was a viciously false paradox. Of that, today, most of us are convinced and, as a consequence, the cooperative impulse is asserting itself openly and forcibly, no longer content to achieve its ends obliquely and by stealth. We are openly and notoriously on the way to mutual endeavors.

And here is the importance of the rediscovery of the Constitution. We are turning our back on the policeman doctrine of government and recapturing the vision of a government equipped to fight and overcome the forces of economic disintegration. A strong government with an executive amply empowered by legislative delegation is the one way out of our dilemma, and on to the realization of our vast social and economic possibilities. . . .

THE ECONOMICS OF THE RECOVERY PROGRAM

(From Rexford G. Tugwell, *The Battle for Democracy* [New York: Columbia University Press, 1935], pp. 78–96)

The general objective is clear and easily stated—to restore a workable exchangeability among the separate parts of our economic machine and to set it to functioning again ; and beyond this to perfect arrangements which may prevent its future disorganization. This means that we must insure adequate income to the farmers, adequate wages to the workers, an adequate return to useful capital, and an adequate remuneration to management. What we want, really, is to provide the opportunity for every individual and every group to work and to be able to consume the product of others' work. This involves a creation of buying power which is coordinate with the creation of goods. We shall not rest nor be diverted to lesser things until that minimum is achieved. . . .

It is quite impossible to predict the shape our newly invented economic institutions may take in the future. That seems to me, in any case, unimportant. What is important is that we have undertaken a venture which is theoretically new in the sense that it calls for control rather than drift. In the years to come much ingenuity will be needed in the effort to isolate and strengthen the nerve centers of industrial civilization. We have yet to discover in determinate fashion what efforts are naturally those of common service, and so require a high degree of socialization, and what ones can safely be left to relatively free individual or group contrivance. We are turning away from the entrusting of crucial decisions, and the operation of institutions whose social consequences are their most characteristic feature, to individuals who are motivated by private interests. . . .

AMERICA TAKES HOLD OF ITS DESTINY

(From Rexford G. Tugwell, *The Battle for Democracy* [New York: Columbia University Press, 1935], pp. 256-67)

The twentieth century found the American people psychologically and financially unprepared to utilize the wealth which the technological revolution of the last thirty years has made possible. . . .

As it became apparent that a more abundant life was within the reach of all our people, if we could only display the social inventiveness necessary to deal with this new abundance in such form as to convert anxious unemployment into secure leisure, we were shaken by a profound moral crisis. On the one side stood the sincere group of wishful beneficiaries of the Old Order, who . . . sat "waiting for the twentieth century to blow over." On the other side stood the mass of our people, who were increasingly bewildered by the failure of the old principles of our society to assure the distribution of those goods which were there for all to see and which were rotting away for want of buyers. The result of this crisis and conflict was the New Deal.

A new deal was absolutely inevitable. People will submit to grave privations and will even starve peaceably, if they realize that actual dearth exists, but no man and no race will starve in the presence of abundance. . . .

The objective of this administration is accordingly a simple one : it is to give our citizens the opportunity for a richer life. But simple and easily stated as this objective is, the methods it imposes are difficult and complex. . . .

In order to understand, it seems to me necessary to keep far up in the foreground always the idea that the possibilities of the future are always greater than were those of any time in the past. . . . That is why, in my opinion, it is a fundamental error to assume that we have now reached the end of the "swing to the left" and that we ought to forego any further important policy changes. The real economic revolution is just beginning and social policy will have to move rapidly to keep pace with it.

I have very little patience, therefore, with those who say we have come to the end of a period of progress, that we must now retrench and economize, hoarding our gains against a poverty-stricken future. . . . We do not seem to realize that it is our own abundance which compels us to make radical changes, first in our ideas and then in the institutions based on our ideas. . . . All the prejudices and shibboleths which survive in people's heads seem to crystallize in government—perhaps because, very rightly, we think of it as somehow sacred. But it will not stay sacred long if it is set apart from change in a changing world. It will simply become atrophied and obsolete and will either be ignored or contemptuously brushed aside by those in the community who have important affairs afoot which they desire shall not be interfered with.

Something like this has been happening to our Government. I think it is fair to say that until last March it was fast becoming ineffectual in its relationships with industry. It insisted on an interpretation of industrial life which belonged to an era which had disappeared. It broke up trusts as a sufficient answer to the pressing problem of control ; and when it discovered that the more they were broken up, the more they remained as they had been, it fell into a kind of trance. It was unwilling to give up competitive theory ; it could therefore think of nothing to do except to restore competition ; and when competition refused to be restored, industry continued to exist in a kind of purgatory—half the heaven of freedom and half the hell of ineffectual public disapproval.

The various recovery acts proceeded from a theory which . . . recognized the changes which had occurred in industrial society and it sought to secure the benefits of industry as it actually existed for the public good. It said, "Industry has developed out of the face-to-face stage ; huge factories exist ; central-office organizations control many even of these organizations, great as they are in themselves ; financial controls are superimposed on this; scientific management has come to stay—therefore, the Government must legalize all these heretofore horrid developments so that it may shape them into social instruments. . . .

. . . Up to now much of the energy of business men has been dissipated in the overpraised conflicts of competition. Each was trying to beat the other fellow—to reach success by standing on the exhausted bodies of fallen competitors. And the success for which all this striving took place was usually defined as the right to exploit consumers by selling them goods of doubtful quality at prices which lowered the general standard of living. . . .

. . . We are fast approaching the time, therefore, when each industry will be able to devote its best energy to the fundamental purpose of industry—which is to produce goods rather than competition. . . .

This reconciliation of differences, however quickly it may come, or whatever contractual relationships it may establish among industries, is not, however, sufficient. For there always remains the essentially defenseless ultimate consumer. The Government may turn out to be his only refuge; and if this is so, the Government will have to assume more and more responsibility for pushing his case.

There are two broad ways in which industrial policy may be shaped from this point on to secure this objective. Industry may be required to define the quality of the goods it offers and to sell them at prices which are suitably low, so that when the transactions of a year, for instance, are totaled up it will be found that our energies and our producing plant have been used to the utmost and that the goods and services they yield have gone to consumers without increase of debt; or industry may be allowed to proceed with the policy of establishing high prices and maintaining them by limitation, and of selling goods whose qualities are mysterious to most consumers; and much of the resulting profits may be taken in taxes and returned to consumers as free goods by the Government—in the form of facilities for health and recreation, insurance against old age, sickness and unemployment, or in other ways. We shall have to accept one or the other of these policies because unless we do we shall sacrifice most of those objectives which we associate with what has been called the New Deal. The choice which lies before us is, therefore, a choice between a socially wise economic policy and the application of socialistic taxation. I prefer the former method.

One, certainly, of the distinguishing characteristics of the present is the power of our industrial machine to produce goods. This power has astonished and frightened us. We have not known what to do about it.

It required that we should either chain it up and prevent its free functioning or that we should reorganize our machinery of distribution so that consumers could take possession of the vast flow of goods. . . .

It is my belief that we shall prove unwilling to accept limitation in this sense as a permanent policy. This does not mean that we may not plan; it does not mean that we may not choose to use our resources in one way rather than another, limiting in some instances and expanding in others, so that all may run smoothly together as a considered and co-ordinated whole. . . .

I think it is perfectly obvious that we can have nothing new in the Government which does not correspond to a new need on the part of our people and of their economic institutions. The New Deal is a very definite attempt to evolve a new governmental-economic relationship in response to the needs and opportunities created by the past methods of operating our economy. To inhibit further growth of these new methods is, therefore, impossible and to attempt to deny their application is the ultimate folly of fossilized ways of thought. Using the traditional methods of a free people, we are going forward toward a realm of cooperative plenty the like of which the world has never seen. It will be no antiseptic utopia and no socialistic paradise, but a changing system in which free American human beings can live their changing lives. . . .

I have also stressed their experimental nature. That seems to me their most important characteristic, and that is something which is American if anything is. . . . There is no reason to think that year by year we shall not learn to better ourselves with the full use of energies and instruments which we have at our disposal. If this be Socialism, make the most of it!

Document 28.2

COMPETITION MUST KEEP ITS BLOWS ABOVE THE BELT

According to the Bloomingdale's Department Store advertisement reproduced here, two seemingly identical men's shirts were offered to the buying public at a 36-cent price differential. The unknown author of the copy makes it clear that the purchaser of the 89-cent shirt is betraying his fellow workers, the NRA, and the nation. Pressure to *co-operate*, to "do his part," extended in the early New Deal period clear down to the unfortunate man with the frayed cuffs.

DAILY NEWS, SATURDAY, OCTOBER 14, 1933   5

WHICH ONE WOULD YOU PREFER TO WEAR?

COLLAR-ATTACHED SHIRT
Pre-shrunk fast color broadcloth of long
staple cotton yarn. Six-button front. **89c.**

COLLAR ATTACHED SHIRT
Pre-shrunk fast color broadcloth of long
staple cotton yarn. Six-button front. **1.25**

This shirt, and tens of thousands like it, were made and sold just a few months ago when the country was not as sound as it is today.

The man that grew the cotton for it lost money. His cotton pickers were not paid with cash...they received canned goods and groceries so that they could eat and have strength to work. The workers in the mill where the cotton was spun into yarn and in the mill where the yarn was woven into fabric received starvation wages...$4 and $5 a week. The girls that fashioned it into a shirt tried to keep the wolf from the door with $5 a week, and in many instances, even less. Their employer lost money. Cut-throat competition, together with curtailed buying power, forced the retailer to sell it at a price which would attract you to buy it, but which netted him a loss.

At 89 cents it was a bargain. A bargain built on misery ...distress...losses...and suffering, all along the line. A bargain that threatened the very structure of this country.

Here is another shirt...manufactured under the Code of the NRA. Looks just like the other one, but it's different.

True, the cotton is the same, the machine-made material is the same, BUT . . . . . the workers now receive at least $13 a week. The workmanship, however, *is different*. Girls that are now receiving a living wage do better work than they did with hungry stomachs and with fear in their hearts.

Yes, it's a different shirt. They will all tell you that ..., from the cotton picker to the one who sells it to you. Thanks to NRA it is *different* . . . . and not a single child labored in its making.

At $1.25, it is a *real* bargain, a *sound* bargain, *sound* for your welfare and *sound* for the welfare of our country. Which one do you prefer to wear?

* * *

Similar Encouraging Facts Could Be Published
Regarding Scores of Other Industries

Written and published in the interest of NRA and all it stands for by

NEW YORK

Document 28.3

AGRICULTURE CANNOT SURVIVE IN A CAPITALISTIC SOCIETY AS A PHILANTHROPIC ENTERPRISE

Henry A. Wallace was Roosevelt's first Secretary of Agriculture, second Vice President, and fourth Secretary of Commerce. In the selections presented here from his books, *New Frontiers* and *Democracy Reborn*, he speaks out sharply on behalf of economic democracy for the farmer. In line with early New Deal thinking, Wallace calls for planning, cooperation, and obedience to the higher moral goals of democracy; contrary to the President's early policy of economic nationalism, Wallace already held definite views on the interrelatedness of the world's peoples and institutions. Seemingly beguiled here by a vision of the neighborly sharing of untrammeled production, the tough-minded Secretary pursued farm parity by administering the Agricultural Adjustment acts as instruments of scarcity capitalism.

AN AGRARIAN DRIVE TO CHANGE THE RULES

(From Henry A. Wallace, *New Frontiers* [New York: Reynal and Hitchcock, 1934], pp. 138–39)

The experimental method of democracy may be slow, but it has the advantage of being sure. When you change people's minds you change the course of a nation.

Though abundance is at hand, we still live by old standards of denial. The situation is confusing. There are those who say that there cannot be a surplus so long as there is a single hungry Chinaman. Fundamentally and eventually this may be true; but these standpat sentimentalists who weep that farmers should practice controlled production do not suggest that clothing factories go on producing *ad infinitum*, regardless of effective demand for their merchandise, until every naked Chinaman is clad. Nor do they feel that plow factories should abandon production control until every hungry Chinaman has a plow. We must play with the cards that are dealt. Agriculture cannot survive in a capitalistic society as a philanthropic enterprise. If the cry of those who bid our farmers think of all those hungry Chinamen, and plant more land, were heeded, it would mean that long before the last hungry Chinamen were taken care of, hundreds of thousands of American farm families would be destroyed.

The feeling that man should live by providing goods for his neighbors, not by withholding goods, goes very deep; and I believe that it is spreading. But the condition of greater balance and justice we now seek, in a capitalistic structure hastily mended, can certainly not be obtained by arranging that everybody work under the profit system except the farmer. The farmer's instinct has always been to be decent and unbusinesslike, to provide to the uttermost, never to deny. This instinct, obeyed by millions of scattered individuals in a society seeking profits and setting prices on a scarcity basis, took our farmers up the long hill to the poorhouse; and killed them as customers. Their death as consumers closed thousands of factories and helped to throw millions out of work. Now we are trying to give our farmers their rightful place in a more decent and balanced system, a system that will work democratically and make for neighborliness and a shared abundance. The people who raise the cry about the last hungry Chinamen are not really criticizing the farmers or the AAA, but the profit system, as we have inherited it from our past.

THE PURPOSES OF THE AAA

(From Henry A. Wallace, *Democracy Reborn* [Russell Lord (ed.)] [New York: Reynal and Hitchcock, 1944], pp. 45–46)

To organize agriculture, co-operatively, democratically, so that the surplus lands on which men and women now are toiling, wasting their time, wearing out their lives to no good end, shall be taken out of production—that is a tremendous task. The adjustment we seek calls first of all for a mental adjustment, a willing reversal, of driving, pioneer opportunism and ungoverned *laissez-faire*. The ungoverned push of rugged individualism perhaps had an economic justification in the days when we had all the West to surge upon and conquer; but this country has filled up now, and grown up. There are no more Indians to fight. No more land worth taking may be had for the grabbing. We must experience a change of mind and heart.

The frontiers that challenge us now are of the mind and spirit. We must blaze new trails in scientific accomplishment, in the peaceful arts and industries. Above all, we must blaze new trails in the direction of a controlled economy, common sense, and social decency. . . .

. . . This Act offers you promise of a balanced abundance, a shared prosperity, and a richer life. It will work, if you will make it yours, and make it work. I hope that you will come to see in this Act, as I do now, a Declaration of Interdependence, a recognition of our essential unity and of our absolute reliance upon one another.

Document 28.4

A GREAT PLAN IS DEMOCRACY'S ANSWER

Born in 1899, David E. Lilienthal became Director of the Tennessee Valley Authority in 1933, Chairman of its Board of Directors in 1941. The following selections from his book, *TVA: Democracy on the March*, make a strong case for public power, which has been part of the Democratic party creed since the age of Roosevelt. In describing government planning in the field of resource development, Lilienthal reveals his fundamental faith in democracy and his deeply felt sense of morality. The implication is clear: A democracy can plan without becoming dictatorial, and it can carry out its plans without enslaving its citizens.

(From David E. Lilienthal, *TVA: Democracy on the March* [New York: Harper & Bros., 1944], pp. 46, 75–76, 105–6, 125, 127, 192–93, 195, 218)

A new chapter in American public policy was written when Congress in May of 1933 passed the law creating the TVA. For the first time since the trees fell before the settlers' ax, America set out to command nature not by defying her, as in that wasteful past, but by understanding and acting upon her first law—the oneness of men and natural resources, the unity that binds together land, streams, forests, minerals, farming, industry, mankind. . . .

People are the most important fact in resource development. Not only is the welfare and happiness of individuals its true purpose, but they are the means by which that development is accomplished; their genius, their energies and spirit are the instruments; it is not only "for the people" but "by the people." . . .

This hankering to be an *individual* is probably greater today than ever before. Huge factories, assembly lines, mysterious mechanisms, standardization—these underline the smallness of the individual, because they are so fatally impersonal. If the intensive development of resources, the central fact in the immediate future of the world, could be made personal to the life of most men; if they could see themselves, because it was true, as actual participants in that development in their own communities, on their own land, at their own jobs and businesses—there would be an opportunity for this kind of individual satisfaction, and there would be something to tie to. . . .

It is the unique strength of democratic methods that they provide a way of stimulating and releasing the individual resourcefulness and inventiveness, the pride of workmanship, the creative genius of human beings whatever their station or function. A world of science and great machines is still a world of men; our modern task is more difficult, but the opportunity for democratic methods is greater even than in the days of the ax and the hand loom. . . .

With the eyes of industry now upon this valley (as they are indeed upon many valleys the world over) planning a considerable industrial expansion here after the war, there is an opportunity to plan and to build so that our resources will endure, our natural beauty be spared despoliation. Here there is a chance to see to it that human well-being in city and town will not, through lack of ingenuity and foresight, be needlessly sacrificed. Shall we succeed? Is the only choice one between pastoral poverty and industrial slums? Can private industry utilize these resources, at a profit, and yet sustain their vigor and longevity? Can business and the common weal both be served? To be able to make an affirmative reply is a matter of the greatest moment.

In the Tennessee Valley the answers will turn to some extent upon how successful the TVA is in its efforts to weld a union of the public interest and the private interests of businessmen. We appear to be uncovering and developing in this valley principles and practices for effecting a jointure of public interests with private, by methods that are voluntary and noncoercive. Our actual experience is unpretentious as measured by the scope of the problem, but it is definitely encouraging and of not a little significance for industry and the people of the country generally. . . .

What the TVA, in specific ways, has sought to do can be simply stated: to accept an obligation to harmonize the private interest in earning a return from resources, with the dominant public interest in their unified and efficient development. The method—and this is the distinctive part of the experiment—is to bring to bear at the grass roots the skills of public experts and administrators not for negative regulation but *to make affirmative action in the public interest both feasible and appealing to private industry*. By public interest I mean the interest of people—people as human beings—not "the people" in their institutional roles as wage earners or investors or voters or consumers. "Underneath all, individuals," men and women and children. . . .

The unified development of resources requires the broadest coalition of effort. This is a job not only for all the people, but for all of the people's institutions. The purpose is national, but the task is one that calls for a partnership of *every* agency of government, state and local as well as federal, that can further the common purpose. Therefore the

grass-roots policy of drawing in private organizations and individuals—
such as those of farmers, workers, and businessmen . . . —has in like
manner been applied by TVA, a *federal* organization, so that the governmental agencies of *local* communities and of the *states* of the Tennessee Valley have become TVA's active and responsible partners.

Decentralizing the administration of government functions that are
clearly national has been carried so far in this valley . . . that, whenever
there is a state or local institution which can perform part of the task
that has been assigned by law to the TVA, we have sought to have that
non-federal agency do it. This way of getting results is an exacting test
of managerial skill in defining functions clearly and in securing a union
of effort. Legalistic arguments about "states' rights" or "federal supremacy" have faded into irrelevance. . . .

In calling upon a state or local agency to share responsibility instead
of setting up a TVA organization to do a specific job alone, and in negotiating the contracts upon which such joint efforts rest, we have deliberately tried to "start something" that local forces might later carry
on, on their own. We have tried to place each new activity into the stream
of the region's life, in the hands of local agencies to be continued when
the initial federal support is withdrawn. . . .

The TVA *is* a planning agency, the first of its kind in the United
States. The great change going on in this valley is an authentic example
of modern democratic planning; this was the expressed intent of Congress, by whose authority we act. . . .

. . . "Unified development" as I have described the idea in action is, in
substance, the valley's synonym for "planning. . . ."

Planning by businessmen, often under some other name, is recognized as necessary to the conduct of private enterprise. It has the virtue
of a single and direct objective, one that can be currently measured, that
is, the making of a profit. . . .

This is admittedly a grave defect of planning by the businessman. For
his legitimate object, namely a profitable business, is not necessarily consistent with the object of society, that is, a prosperous and happy
people. . . .

The idea of unified resource development is based upon the premise
that by democratic planning the individual's interest, the interest of private undertakings, can increasingly be made one with the interest of all
of us, i.e., the community interest. . . .

A great Plan, a moral and indeed a religious purpose, deep and fundamental, is democracy's answer both to our own home-grown would-be
dictators and foreign antidemocracy alike. In the unified development

of resources there is such a Great Plan: the Unity of Nature and Mankind. Under such a Plan in our valley we move forward. True, it is but a step at a time. But we assume responsibility not simply for the little advance we make each day, but for that vast and all-pervasive end and purpose of all our labors, the material well-being of all men and the opportunity for them to build for themselves spiritual strength.

Here is the life principle of democratic planning—an awakening in the whole people of a sense of this common moral purpose. Not one goal, but a direction. Not one plan, once and for all, but *the conscious selection by the people of successive plans.* . . .

We have a choice. There is the important fact. Men are not powerless; they have it in their hands to use the machine to augment the dignity of human existence. True, they may have so long denied themselves the use of that power to decide, which is theirs, may so long have meekly accepted the dictation of bosses of one stripe or another or the ministrations of benevolent nursemaids, that the muscles of democratic choice have atrophied. But that strength is always latent; history has shown how quickly it revives. How we shall *use* physical betterment—that decision is ours to make. We are not carried irresistibly by forces beyond our control, whether they are given some mystic term or described as the "laws of economics." We are not inert objects on a wave of the future. . . .

Document 28.5

COLLECTIVISM IN INDUSTRY COMPELS COLLECTIVISM IN GOVERNMENT

In his hard-hitting acceptance speech before the Democratic National Convention of 1936, Franklin D. Roosevelt began his attack on the "economic royalists"—the "privileged princes of these new economic dynasties, thirsting for power, [reaching] out for control over Government itself." By 1938, the President had gleaned some startling statistics from the income tax rolls: In 1929, for instance, three tenths of one per cent of the American people received 78 per cent of the stock dividends reported by individuals. In 1935–36, 47 per cent of American families were living on less than $1,000 per year, while 1½ per cent of American families were living on incomes totaling the combined income of the 47 per cent. On April 29, 1938, Roosevelt sent his message to Congress on the concentration of economic power, proposing a program to "preserve private enterprise for profit." It is apparent from this message, selections from which are given below, that the earlier New Deal policy of co-operation with business had ended and that competition was to be restored to a government-regulated market. At the same time, it must also be realized that there had been no change whatever in the President's goals of individualism, private property, and democracy. The result of his message was the creation of the Temporary National Economic Committee, with Senator Joseph C. O'Mahoney as Chairman. After three years of hearings, Senator O'Mahoney presented the Committee's recommendations: that national corporations be chartered, that competition be maintained through effective enforcement of the anti-trust laws, and that new business and small enterprise be given tax advantages. By the time the Committee reported its findings, the United States was at war, and the whole matter was left to the searching scrutiny of future economists.

(From Samuel I. Rosenman [ed.], *The Public Papers and Addresses of Franklin D. Roosevelt: War—and Aid to Democracies* [New York: Macmillan Co., 1941], pp. 305-20)

Unhappy events abroad have retaught us two simple truths about the liberty of a democratic people.

The first truth is that the liberty of a democracy is not safe if the people tolerate the growth of private power to a point where it becomes stronger than their democratic state itself. That, in its essence, is Fascism—ownership of Government by an individual, by a group, or by any other controlling private power.

The second truth is that the liberty of a democracy is not safe if its business system does not provide employment and produce and distribute goods in such a way as to sustain an acceptable standard of living.

Both lessons hit home.

Among us today a concentration of private power without equal in history is growing.

This concentration is seriously impairing the economic effectiveness of private enterprise as a way of providing employment for labor and capital and as a way of assuring a more equitable distribution of income and earnings among the people of the nation as a whole. . . .

We believe in a way of living in which political democracy and free private enterprise for profit should serve and protect each other—to ensure a maximum of human liberty not for a few but for all. . . .

That heavy hand of integrated financial and management control lies upon large and strategic areas of American industry. The small business man is unfortunately being driven into a less and less independent position in American life. You and I must admit that.

Private enterprise is ceasing to be free enterprise and is becoming a cluster of private collectivisms: masking itself as a system of free enterprise after the American model, it is in fact becoming a concealed cartel system after the European model. . . .

If you believe with me in private initiative, you must acknowledge the right of well-managed small business to expect to make reasonable profits. You must admit that the destruction of this opportunity follows concentration of control of any given industry into a small number of dominating corporations.

One of the primary causes of our present difficulties lies in the disappearance of price competition in many industrial fields, particularly in basic manufacture where concentrated economic power is most evident—and where rigid prices and fluctuating payrolls are general.

Managed industrial prices mean fewer jobs. It is no accident that in industries, like cement and steel, where prices have remained firm in the face of a falling demand, payrolls have shrunk as much as 40 and 50 per cent in recent months. Nor is it mere chance that in most competitive industries where prices adjust themselves quickly to falling demand, payrolls and employment have been far better maintained. . . .

If private enterprise left to its own devices becomes half-regimented and half-competitive, half-slave and half-free, as it is today, it obviously cannot adjust itself to meet the needs and the demands of the country.

Most complaints for violations of the antitrust laws are made by business men against other business men. Even the most monopolistic business man disapproves of all monopolies but his own. We may smile at this as being just an example of human nature, but we cannot laugh away the fact that the combined effect of the monopolistic controls which each business group imposes for its own benefit, inevitably destroys the buying power of a nation as a whole.

Competition, of course, like all other good things, can be carried to excess. Competition should not extend to fields where it has demonstrably bad social and economic consequences. The exploitation of child labor, the chiseling of workers' wages, the stretching of workers' hours, are not necessary, fair or proper methods of competition. I have consistently urged a federal wages and hours bill to take the minimum decencies of life for the working man and woman out of the field of competition. . . .

But generally over the field of industry and finance we must revive and strengthen competition if we wish to preserve and make workable our traditional system of free private enterprise.

The justification of private profit is private risk. We cannot safely make America safe for the business man who does not want to take the burdens and risks of being a business man. . . .

A discerning magazine of business has editorially pointed out that big business collectivism in industry compels an ultimate collectivism in government.

The power of a few to manage the economic life of the nation must be diffused among the many or be transferred to the public and its democratically responsible government. If prices are to be managed and administered, if the nation's business is to be allotted by plan and not by competition, that power should not be vested in any private group or cartel, however benevolent its professions profess to be.

Those people, in and out of the halls of government, who encourage the growing restriction of competition either by active efforts or by passive resistance to sincere attempts to change the trend, are shouldering a terrific responsibility. Consciously, or unconsciously, they are working for centralized business and financial control. Consciously or unconsciously, they are therefore either working for control of the government itself by business and finance or the other alternative—a growing concentration of public power in the government to cope with such concentration of private power.

The enforcement of free competition is the least regulation business can expect.

The traditional approach to the problems I have discussed has been through the anti-trust laws. That approach we do not propose to abandon. On the contrary, although we must recognize the inadequacies of the existing laws, we seek to enforce them so that the public shall not be deprived of such protection as they afford. To enforce them properly requires thorough investigation not only to discover such violations as may exist but to avoid hit-and-miss prosecutions harmful to business and government alike. . . .

But the existing anti-trust laws are inadequate—most importantly because of new financial economic conditions with which they are powerless to cope. . . .

We have witnessed the merging-out of effective competition in many fields of enterprise. We have learned that the so-called competitive system works differently in an industry where there are many independent units, from the way it works in an industry where a few large producers dominate the market.

We have also learned that a realistic system of business regulation has to reach more than consciously immoral acts. The community is interested in economic results. It must be protected from economic as well as moral wrongs. We must find practical controls over blind economic forces as over blindly selfish men.

Government can deal and should deal with blindly selfish men. But that is a comparatively small part—the easier part—of our problem. The larger, more important and more difficult part of our problem is to deal with men who are not selfish and who are good citizens, but who cannot see the social and economic consequences of their actions in a modern economically interdependent community. They fail to grasp the significance of some of our most vital social and economic problems because they see them only in the light of their own personal experience and not in perspective with the experience of other men and other industries. They, therefore, fail to see these problems for the nation as a whole.

To meet the situation I have described, there should be a thorough study of the concentration of economic power in American industry and the effect of that concentration upon the decline of competition. . . .

It is not intended as the beginning of any ill-considered "trust-busting" activity which lacks proper consideration for economic results. . . .

It is a program whose basic purpose is to stop the progress of collectivism in business and turn business back to the democratic competitive order.

It is a program whose basic thesis is not that the system of free private enterprise for profit has failed in this generation, but that it has not yet been tried. . . .

29

ROBERT H. FERRELL
Indiana University

President Roosevelt and the Coming of the War

FOR MANY who admire the late President Franklin D. Roosevelt, it is disturbing to say that in 1939–41 he felt obliged to pursue a sometimes devious course in leading his country into involvement in the second World War. In his days of power the President was a most attractive individual, one of the master political leaders of all time— he of the wide grin, the uplifted cigarette holder, the Harvard-accented voice of the radio fireside chats, the ready quip to newspapermen. Almost all Americans today take pride in Roosevelt's leadership of the nation in the difficult years of the Great Depression and the war against Germany and Japan. Moreover, American entrance into the conflict in December, 1941, was a long-overdue event; few people would argue any more that the country's involvement in the second World War was a mistake. Still, the people of the United States were profoundly pacific, if not pacifist, when, on September 1, 1939, the war began in Europe. And when the Japanese attacked Pearl Harbor a little over two years later, the nation was bewildered, angry, and stunned. In spite of agonized soul searching as to whether the country should enter the conflict, the general feeling probably was against such action as late as December, 1941. The President personally favored strong measures to help the Allies. He believed he had to move carefully. He chose methods that were—or at least now appear—sideways and oblique.

Perhaps his choice of means reflected his own personality, which was a mixture of forthrightness and guile. He was both a lion and a fox, as James M. Burns's biography has described him. When in command of a cause, he was magnificent, moving it forward by sheer personal magnetism, charging the people of the country—in his radio chats—to carry out the nation's purpose. Whenever he came to the front of an issue and asked for support, there was tremendous force behind whatever he was championing. Few, if any, presidents have expressed the aspirations of the American people—and, in his own terms, the hopes of the free world—as did Roosevelt. He must be numbered among the handful of truly great American presidents.

There was also the other side of his personality—the foxy side, if you will. In a democracy no really successful politician—and Roosevelt was one—can proceed by meeting every issue head on. The President, like most men of good will, tended to be at his worst when he could not confront an issue. He was inclined to verbal formulas to disguise his movements. He hated unpleasantness and, to avoid it, occasionally would take refuge in remarks that smacked of insincerity. There were, for example, the Senate elections of 1938, when he was seeking to purge errant conservative senators, most of them southern, who had opposed his effort to pack the Supreme Court. While campaigning against them in their home states, the President met Senator Walter George (D.) of Georgia, one of the men on his purge list. "God bless you, Walter," said he.

No effort will be made here to set down the events that took the country to war by December 7, 1941; but it is easily possible, in examining the record of the years 1939–41, to see some of Roosevelt's foxiness when confronting the nearly overwhelming sentiment for peace on the part of his countrymen. The President's side-stepping of issues, or his glossing of pro-Allied measures, produced a quite remarkable record in the months before Pearl Harbor.

When war opened in Europe with the German attack on Poland, the President could do little other than declare American neutrality. Admittedly, the Continent's political balance seemed fairly even, the chances of eventual Nazi victory not large. Poland would fall, and did after less than a month of Blitzkrieg; but France and Britain would remain at war, and with time and supplies from the factories of America, they could redress their armament deficiencies and triumph.

After some months of so-called "Sitzkrieg" came the denouement of April-June, 1940: the German invasion of the Netherlands and of Belgium, and the fall of France after collapse of the supposedly invincible French army. Soon the British were alone, and Winston Churchill was making the most magnificent speech of his generation. That greatest statesman in British history defiantly announced in Parliament that "we shall not flag or fail. We shall go on to the end ... we shall fight in the seas and oceans, we shall fight with growing confidence and growing strength in the air, we shall defend our island, whatever the cost may be, we shall fight on the beaches, we shall fight on the landing-grounds, we shall fight in the fields and in the streets, we shall fight in the hills; we shall never surrender, and even if, which I do not for a moment believe, this island or a large part of it were subjugated and starving, then our Empire beyond the seas, armed and guarded by the British Fleet, would carry on the struggle, until, in God's good time, the New World, with all its power and might, steps forth to the rescue and the liberation of the Old."

At once Roosevelt undertook measures admittedly energetic, if not altogether in line with orthodox constitutional practices in the United States. In the summer of 1940 the President instructed the War Department to sell back some of its new weapons to the manufacturers, so the latter could sell them to the British. The government also released stocks of first World War weapons. Last but not least, there was the destroyers-bases deal of September 2, 1940. This arrangement was in the form of an executive agreement and not a treaty (the President probably could not have obtained either the two-thirds Senate majority necessary for a treaty or the simple majority of Senate and House necessary for a joint resolution). Roosevelt wished to give the British fifty over-age destroyers, four-stackers of 1917–18 vintage which had been laid up for years. Could he do so constitutionally? He consulted his Attorney General, Robert H. Jackson, who gave an affirmative opinion. Under the President's constitutional powers as Commander-in-Chief and director of foreign relations, Jackson said, F.D.R. could obtain the British bases by executive agreement rather than treaty. Two acts of Congress—of 1883 and June, 1940—together with a Supreme Court decision gave the President authority to dispose of the over-age destroyers. An act of 1917 permitted sending the ships to Britain, even though England was at war and the United States was nominally neutral, because the destroyers, when constructed during the first World War, had not been intended for sale to a belligerent power. Fortified with this legal blank check, the President instructed Secretary of State Cordell Hull to trade the over-age destroyers for ninety-nine-year leases of specified naval bases: Newfoundland, Bermuda, the Bahamas, Jamaica, Santa Lucia, Trinidad, Antigua, and British Guiana. To a surprised nation, F.D.R. announced this swap as "the most important action in the reinforcement of our national defense . . . since the Louisiana Purchase."

A few months later, in November, 1940, came the presidential elections, in which the country's desire to stay neutral was perhaps the prime political fact, or so the two opposing candidates—Roosevelt and

Wendell L. Willkie—appear to have believed. To their credit, both men advocated aid to the Allies. The tight place in the campaign, however, turned out not to be aid to the Allies but whether American troops eventually might have to go again to Europe. Willkie announced foolishly that "if you elect me president I will never send an American boy to fight in any European war." Not to be outdone, the President, at Boston on October 30, 1940, made the following rebuttal: "And while I am talking to you, fathers and mothers, I give you one more assurance. I have said this before, but I shall say it again, and again and again. Your boys are not going to be sent into any foreign wars." Three days afterward, in Buffalo, he declared: "Your President says this country is not going to war."

Neither Roosevelt (who should have known better) nor Willkie (who might have) displayed major statesmanship in such remarks. The electoral promises of 1940 were vaguely reminiscent of one of Benjamin Franklin's aphorisms: "When you come to a low place, stoop." Not long after the campaign, American troops were en route to Greenland and Iceland; a little more than a year later the President had to renege on his promise completely.

Once re-elected, Roosevelt addressed himself to a major program designed to give Britain aid of a sort that would enable Churchill's government not merely to hold on but to fight aggressively. By early 1941 the British were fast approaching the end of their funds. When this had happened during the first World War, the United States had lent large sums to the Allies, and there had followed the arid war-debt arguments of the 1920's and 1930's when the Allies proved unable or unwilling to repay the debts. Roosevelt wanted no repetition of that experience. In 1941 the British could not possibly repay loans. Furthermore, the Johnson Debt Default Act of 1934 forbade them. The President therefore decided to remove "the nasty old dollar sign" from American aid to Britain, and proposed to Congress a measure that subsequently became known as "lend-lease." The President would have charge of a huge initial open appropriation of $7 billion to "lend, lease, or otherwise dispose of" to any country whose defense was vital to the United States. The original lend-lease appropriation would make fiscal history: It was the largest single appropriation ever presented to Congress. It was more than ninety times the amount of the national debt which Secretary of the Treasury Alexander Hamilton had refunded in 1790. (Eventually, over $50 billion was disbursed under the successive lend-lease enactments.)

Debate over the original lend-lease measure was extremely bitter, particularly because isolationists in Congress realized they were being outwitted. To the President's opponents, lend-lease looked suspicious. No one seemed to know who had written the proposed legislation when it turned up in Congress, although rumor had it that the bill was composed in the White House. The President refused to say that lend-lease was a *war* measure—which, in fact, it was. He thought of it as a *defense* measure. Its title was "An Act to Promote the Defense of the United States." Representative Dewey Short (R.) of Missouri smelled a conspiracy. He told his fellow legislators that "you can dress this measure up all you please, you can sprinkle it with perfume and pour powder on it, masquerade it in any form you please . . . , but it is still foul and it stinks to high heaven. It does not need a doctor, it needs an undertaker."

The isolationist Senator Burton K. Wheeler (D.) of Montana described lend-lease with an allusion to the Agricultural Adjustment Act of 1933: "The lend-lease-give program is the New Deal's triple A foreign policy; it will plow under every fourth American boy." Roosevelt, incensed, told a press conference that the Senator's remark was the "most untruthful, . . . the most dastardly, unpatriotic thing that has ever been said. Quote me on that. That really is the rottenest thing that has been said in public life in my generation."

After one of the most impassioned Congressional debates in the country's history, lend-lease became law on March 11, 1941.

It immediately gave rise to a new problem, namely, that of transporting material, once produced, across three thousand miles of ocean to the British government. German wolf-pack submarines were getting the best of the British navy in the early spring and summer of 1941. Many of the Atlantic convoys were sailing without sufficient protection, and losses were approaching a critical level. To any clear-thinking individual in possession of the facts, it should have been evident that the enormous increase in transatlantic cargoes after passage of the Lend-Lease Act would require the United States navy to convoy merchantmen—both American and British—to Britain or at least some part of the ocean nearby.

Again the fox took over. The President steadily denied any intention of instituting convoys. He said he preferred something known as "patroling." In reply to a newspaper correspondent's question, Roosevelt, on April 25, 1941, made his famous distinction between a convoy and a patrol. There was the same difference between the two operations, he said, as between a cow and a horse ("if one looks at a cow and calls it a horse that is all right with the president, but that does not make a cow a horse"). It became known that ships of the American navy were operating far out in the Atlantic "on neutrality patrol," flashing news of alien ships in uncoded messages to which anyone could listen—and British warships and planes invariably did. On April 9 the President included Greenland in "our sphere of co-operative hemispheric defense." In reality, it was a base for convoys. On July 7, he extended hemispheric defense to Iceland.

There followed the inevitable incidents. On September 4, 1941, a German submarine attacked the United States destroyer U.S.S. *Greer*, after the latter had trailed the Nazi vessel and broadcast its position for three hours and twenty-eight minutes, during which a British plane had dropped four depth charges. The President took a strong view of this engagement. He made a radio talk on September 11, in which he said the vessel "was carrying American mail to Iceland. . . . She was then and there attacked by a submarine. . . . I tell you the blunt fact that the German submarine fired first upon this American destroyer without warning, and with deliberate design to sink her. . . . We have sought no shooting war with Hitler. We do not seek it now. But neither do we want peace so much that we are willing to pay for it by permitting him to attack our naval . . . ships while they are on legitimate business . . . when you see a rattlesnake poised to strike, you do not wait until he has struck before you crush him. These Nazi submarines and raiders are the rattlesnakes of the Atlantic." He announced that he had given "sink on sight" orders to the navy, a decision which he said was the "result of months and months of constant thought and anxiety and prayer."

Then, on October 17, came the torpedoing, with severe damage, of the destroyer U.S.S. *Kearny* by a German submarine west of Iceland, with loss of eleven American lives. F.D.R., on October 27, delivered a long and vehement address, in the course of which he said: "America has been attacked. The U.S.S. *Kearny* is not just a Navy ship. She belongs to every man, woman, and child in this Nation." What he did not say was that the *Kearny* had been depth-bombing German submarines when she was torpedoed.

In everything but name, there was open war in the Atlantic. The destroyer U.S.S. *Reuben James* was torpedoed on the night of October 30, 1941, with loss of 115 lives.

Meanwhile, the President had confronted the Japanese in the Pacific; but toward the people and government of Japan, it was less necessary to be careful. Americans had been tiring of Japanese aggression in Asia; and most of them, including the isolationists, were willing to have a showdown—although, admittedly, not in the form of an attack on the great naval base at Pearl Harbor. In the Roosevelt administration's Pacific policy of 1940–41, there was much more of the lion than of the fox. American policy toward Japan had a straightforwardness which was lacking in policy toward Germany.

In the years 1940–41, events in the Pacific moved rapidly to their climax. At first the Japanese had wavered in purpose, unsure of whether to proceed north against the Soviet Union or south toward possessions of the Dutch, British, French, and Americans. The fall of France in June, 1940, helped make up the Japanese mind. The southward move—which offered the major Pacific archipelagoes, including Australia—also was far more attractive than Siberia. In July, 1941, President Roosevelt froze Japanese assets in the United States, cutting off any possibility of trade, including oil, which Japan greatly needed. In Tokyo the military soon afterward completely took over the government, and the result was the Pearl Harbor disaster. The attack occurred without warning; it was in the tradition of all of Japan's modern wars—against China in 1894, Russia ten years later, German possessions in China in 1914.

One allegation ought to be set at rest for now and all time, namely, the extraordinary contention, occasionally heard, that President Roosevelt arranged the attack at Pearl Harbor. After the end of the second World War the historian-sociologist Harry Elmer Barnes and a considerable group of like-minded scholars (who took the name of "revisionists") sought to prove that the President had exposed the American fleet at Hawaii in 1941. F.D.R. knew, they said, that the Germans were too occupied in Russia to take up the challenge he had given in the Atlantic; the Nazis had attacked the Soviet Union in June, 1941, and by early December were in the grand climactic moment of their campaign, having reached the very gates of Moscow. The American President, the revisionists believed, considered that it would be far easier to provoke the Japanese to war—they were not so involved elsewhere, were less astute, and would fall for a stratagem. The President did not anticipate so large an attack as took place at Pearl Harbor, it was argued, but he was not unnerved by loss of the Pacific battleship fleet and over 2,300 American lives;. Such a loss would take the United States into the second World War with a unity that the country otherwise could never have had. The Barnes thesis, suffice it to say, has never been proved. On the basis of all available evidence, there is utterly no truth in it. And there never possibly could have been: Apart from Franklin D. Roosevelt's essential nobility of mind, any student of American politics knows that the government of the United States is too large a contraption to enable anyone, even a president, to set on foot such a malignant conspiracy. It would of necessity have involved too many people; somewhere, some place, there would have to be written records.

There remains the record of presidential foxiness prior to Pearl Harbor, a record which raises the ancient issue of ends and means. Moralistic Americans will be troubled by the President's methods of propelling his reluctant country toward the conflict in Europe. They may wish that somehow their fathers and grandfathers, voters in the years 1939–41, could have been presented clearly with the issues, could have read the signs of those times and seen the need for their nation's involvement in the crusade against the most amoral government since the statistically clouded time of Genghis Khan. Could the President somehow, in some way, have enlightened them to their interests? Could he have done so short of losing all of his political influence and leadership? Admittedly, education is a slow, halting way to get people to do anything, even when a crisis is clearly at hand. Perhaps the pessimists and cynics are essentially right in believing that the citizens of a democracy cannot always grasp quickly the major issues of the complicated twentieth century.

SUGGESTED READINGS

BARNES, HARRY ELMER (ed.). *Perpetual War for Perpetual Peace.* Caldwell, Idaho: Caxton Printers, Ltd., 1953.

BEARD, CHARLES A. *President Roosevelt and the Coming of the War: A Study in Appearances and Realities.* New Haven: Yale University Press, 1948.

BURNS, JAMES M. *Roosevelt: The Lion and the Fox.* New York: Harcourt, Brace & Co., 1956.

KIMMEL, HUSBAND E. *Admiral Kimmel's Story.* Chicago: Henry Regnery Co., 1955.

LANGER, WILLIAM L. and GLEASON, S. EVERETT. *The Challenge to Isolation: 1937–40.* New York: Harper & Bros., 1952. *The Undeclared War: September 1940–December 1941.* New York: Harper & Bros., 1953.

THEOBALD, ROBERT A. *The Final Secret of Pearl Harbor: The Washington Contribution to the Japanese Attack.* New York: Devin-Adair Co., 1954.

Document 29.1

"WE MUST BE THE GREAT ARSENAL OF DEMOCRACY"

Roosevelt's most effective means of rallying the American people behind his policies and programs was the radio fireside chat. The President, a masterful speaker, clearly enjoyed addressing the nation over the air waves; he accompanied his words with gestures which in the days before television unfortunately could not be seen by the audience. The principal ideas expressed in this fireside chat on national security, December 29, 1940, were to be repeated in a presidential address to Congress delivered eight days later.

(From Samuel I. Rosenman [ed.], *The Public Papers and Addresses of Franklin D. Roosevelt: War—and Aid to Democracies* [New York: Macmillan Co., 1941], pp. 633–44)

My friends:

This is not a fireside chat on war. It is a talk on national security; because the nub of the whole purpose of your President is to keep you now, and your children later, and your grandchildren much later, out of a last-ditch war for the preservation of American independence and all the things that American independence means to you and to me and to ours.

Tonight, in the presence of a world crisis, my mind goes back eight years to a night in the midst of a domestic crisis. It was a time when the wheels of American industry were grinding to a full stop, when the whole banking system of our country had ceased to function.

I well remember that while I sat in my study in the White House, preparing to talk with the people of the United States, I had before my eyes the picture of all those Americans with whom I was talking. I saw the workmen in the mills, the mines, the factories; the girl behind the counter; the small shopkeeper; the farmer doing his spring plowing; the widows and the old men wondering about their life's savings.

I tried to convey to the great mass of American people what the banking crisis meant to them in their daily lives.

Tonight, I want to do the same thing, with the same people, in this new crisis which faces America.

We met the issue of 1933 with courage and realism.

We face this new crisis—this new threat to the security of our nation —with the same courage and realism.

Never before since Jamestown and Plymouth Rock has our American civilization been in such danger as now.

For, on September 27, 1940, by an agreement signed in Berlin, three powerful nations, two in Europe and one in Asia, joined themselves together in the threat that if the United States of America interfered with or blocked the expansion program of these three nations—a program aimed at world control—they would unite in ultimate action against the United States.

The Nazi masters of Germany have made it clear that they intend not only to dominate all life and thought in their own country, but also to enslave the whole of Europe, and then to use the resources of Europe to dominate the rest of the world.

It was only three weeks ago their leader stated this: "There are two worlds that stand opposed to each other." And then in defiant reply to his opponents, he said this: "Others are correct when they say: With this world we cannot ever reconcile ourselves. . . . I can beat any other power in the world." So said the leader of the Nazis.

In other words, the Axis not merely admits but *proclaims* that there can be no ultimate peace between their philosophy of government and our philosophy of government.

In view of the nature of this undeniable threat, it can be asserted, properly and categorically, that the United States has no right or reason to encourage talk of peace, until the day shall come when there is a clear intention on the part of the aggressor nations to abandon all thought of dominating or conquering the world.

At this moment, the forces of the states that are leagued against all peoples who live in freedom, are being held away from our shores. The Germans and the Italians are being blocked on the other side of the Atlantic by the British, and by the Greeks, and by thousands of soldiers and sailors who were able to escape from subjugated countries. In Asia, the Japanese are being engaged by the Chinese nation in another great defense.

In the Pacific Ocean is our fleet.

Some of our people like to believe that wars in Europe and Asia are of no concern to us. But it is a matter of most vital concern to us that European and Asiatic war-makers should not gain control of the oceans which lead to this hemisphere.

One hundred and seventeen years ago the Monroe Doctrine was conceived by our Government as a measure of defense in the face of a threat against this hemisphere by an alliance in Continental Europe. Thereafter, we stood on guard in the Atlantic, with the British as neighbors. There was no treaty. There was no "unwritten agreement."

And yet, there was the feeling, proven correct by history, that we as neighbors could settle any disputes in peaceful fashion. The fact is that during the whole of this time the Western Hemisphere has remained free from aggression from Europe or from Asia.

Does anyone seriously believe that we need to fear attack anywhere in the Americas while a free Britain remains our most powerful naval neighbor in the Atlantic? Does anyone seriously believe, on the other hand, that we could rest easy if the Axis powers were our neighbors there?

If Great Britain goes down, the Axis powers will control the continents of Europe, Asia, Africa, Australasia, and the high seas—and they will be in a position to bring enormous military and naval resources against this hemisphere. It is no exaggeration to say that all of us, in all the Americas, would be living at the point of a gun—a gun loaded with explosive bullets, economic as well as military.

We should enter upon a new and terrible era in which the whole world, our hemisphere included, would be run by threats of brute force. To survive in such a world, we would have to convert ourselves permanently into a militaristic power on the basis of war economy.

Some of us like to believe that even if Great Britain falls, we are still safe, because of the broad expanse of the Atlantic and of the Pacific.

But the width of those oceans is not what it was in the days of clipper ships. At one point between Africa and Brazil the distance is less than from Washington to Denver, Colorado—five hours for the latest type of bomber. And at the North end of the Pacific Ocean America and Asia almost touch each other.

Even today we have planes that could fly from the British Isles to New England and back again without refueling. And remember that the range of the modern bomber is ever being increased.

During the past week many people in all parts of the nation have told me what they wanted me to say tonight. Almost all of them expressed a courageous desire to hear the plain truth about the gravity of the situation. One telegram, however, expressed the attitude of the small minority who want to see no evil and hear no evil, even though they know in their hearts that evil exists. That telegram begged me not to tell again of the ease with which our American cities could be bombed by any hostile power which had gained bases in this Western Hemisphere. The gist of that telegram was: "Please, Mr. President, don't frighten us by telling us the facts."

Frankly and definitely there is danger ahead—danger against which we must prepare. But we well know that we cannot escape danger, or the fear of danger, by crawling into bed and pulling the covers over our heads.

Some nations of Europe were bound by solemn non-intervention pacts with Germany. Other nations were assured by Germany that they need *never* fear invasion. Non-intervention pact or not, the fact remains that they *were* attacked, overrun and thrown into the modern form of slavery at an hour's notice, or even without any notice at all. As an exiled leader of one of these nations said to me the other day—"The notice was a minus quantity. It was given to my Government two hours after German troops had poured into my country in a hundred places."

The fate of these nations tells us what it means to live at the point of a Nazi gun.

The Nazis have justified such actions by various pious frauds. One of these frauds is the claim that they are occupying a nation for the purpose of "restoring order." Another is that they are occupying or controlling a nation on the excuse that they are "protecting it" against the aggression of somebody else.

For example, Germany has said that she was occupying Belgium to save the Belgians from the British. Would she then hesitate to say to any South American country, "We are occupying you to protect you from aggression by the United States"?

Belgium today is being used as an invasion base against Britain, now fighting for its life. Any South American country, in Nazi hands, would always constitute a jumping-off place for German attack on any one of the other Republics of this hemisphere.

Analyze for yourselves the future of two other places even nearer to Germany if the Nazis won. Could Ireland hold out? Would Irish freedom be permitted as an amazing pet exception in an unfree world? Or the Islands of the Azores which still fly the flag of Portugal after five centuries? You and I think of Hawaii as an outpost of defense in the Pacific. And yet, the Azores are closer to our shores in the Atlantic than Hawaii is on the other side.

There are those who say that the Axis powers would never have any desire to attack the Western Hemisphere. That is the same dangerous form of wishful thinking which has destroyed the powers of resistance of so many conquered peoples. The plain facts are that the Nazis have proclaimed, time and again, that all other races are their inferiors and therefore subject to their orders. And most important of all, the vast resources and wealth of this American Hemisphere constitute the most tempting loot in all the round world.

Let us no longer blind ourselves to the undeniable fact that the evil forces which have crushed and undermined and corrupted so many others are already within our own gates. Your Government knows much about them and every day is ferreting them out.

Their secret emissaries are active in our own and in neighboring countries. They seek to stir up suspicion and dissension to cause internal strife. They try to turn capital against labor, and vice versa. They try to reawaken long slumbering racial and religious enmities which should have no place in this country. They are active in every group that promotes intolerance. They exploit for their own ends our natural abhorrence of war. These trouble-breeders have but one purpose. It is to divide our people into hostile groups and to destroy our unity and shatter our will to defend ourselves.

There are also American citizens, many of them in high places, who, unwittingly in most cases, are aiding and abetting the work of these agents. I do not charge these American citizens with being foreign agents. But I do charge them with doing exactly the kind of work that the dictators want done in the United States.

These people not only believe that we can save our own skins by shutting our eyes to the fate of other nations. Some of them go much further than that. They say that we can and should become the friends and even the partners of the Axis powers. Some of them even suggest that we should imitate the methods of the dictatorships. Americans never can and never will do that.

The experience of the past two years has proven beyond doubt that no nation can appease the Nazis. No man can tame a tiger into a kitten by stroking it. There can be no appeasement with ruthlessness. There can be no reasoning with an incendiary bomb. We know now that a nation can have peace with the Nazis only at the price of total surrender.

Even the people of Italy have been forced to become accomplices of the Nazis; but at this moment they do not know how soon they will be embraced to death by their allies.

The American appeasers ignore the warning to be found in the fate of Austria, Czechoslovakia, Poland, Norway, Belgium, the Netherlands, Denmark, and France. They tell you that the Axis powers are going to win anyway; that all this bloodshed in the world could be saved; that the United States might just as well throw its influence into the scale of a dictated peace, and get the best out of it that we can.

They call it a "negotiated peace." Nonsense! Is it a negotiated peace if a gang of outlaws surrounds your community and on threat of extermination makes you pay tribute to save your own skins?

Such a dictated peace would be no peace at all. It would be only another armistice, leading to the most gigantic armament race and the most devastating trade wars in all history. And in these contests the Americas would offer the only real resistance to the Axis powers.

With all their vaunted efficiency, with all their parade of pious purpose in this war, there are still in their background the concentration camp and the servants of God in chains.

The history of recent years proves that shootings and chains and concentration camps are not simply the transient tools but the very altars of modern dictatorships. They may talk of a "new order" in the world, but what they have in mind is only a revival of the oldest and the worst tyranny. In that there is no liberty, no religion, no hope.

The proposed "new order" is the very opposite of a United States of Europe or a United States of Asia. It is not a Government based upon the consent of the governed. It is not a union of ordinary, self-respecting men and women to protect themselves and their freedom and their dignity from oppression. It is an unholy alliance of power and pelf to dominate and enslave the human race.

The British people and their allies today are conducting an active war against this unholy alliance. Our own future security is greatly dependent on the outcome of that fight. Our ability to "keep out of war" is going to be affected by that outcome.

Thinking in terms of today and tomorrow, I make the direct statement to the American people that there is far less chance of the United States getting into war, if we do all we can now to support the nations defending themselves against attack by the Axis than if we acquiesce in their defeat, submit tamely to an Axis victory, and wait our turn to be the object of attack in another war later on.

If we are to be completely honest with ourselves, we must admit that there is risk in any course we may take. But I deeply believe that the great majority of our people agree that the course that I advocate involves the least risk now and the greatest hope for world peace in the future.

The people of Europe who are defending themselves do not ask us to do their fighting. They ask us for the implements of war, the planes, the tanks, the guns, the freighters which will enable them to fight for their liberty and for our security. Emphatically we must get these weapons to them in sufficient volume and quickly enough, so that we and our children will be saved the agony and suffering of war which others have had to endure.

Let not the defeatists tell us that it is too late. It will never be earlier. Tomorrow will be later than today.

Certain facts are self-evident.

In a military sense Great Britain and the British Empire are today the spearhead of resistance to world conquest. They are putting up a fight which will live forever in the story of human gallantry.

There is no demand for sending an American Expeditionary Force outside our own borders. There is no intention by any member of your Government to send such a force. You can, therefore, nail any talk about sending armies to Europe as deliberate untruth.

Our national policy is not directed toward war. Its sole purpose is to keep war away from our country and our people.

Democracy's fight against world conquest is being greatly aided, and must be more greatly aided, by the rearmament of the United States and by sending every ounce and every ton of munitions and supplies that we can possibly spare to help the defenders who are in the front lines. It is no more unneutral for us to do that than it is for Sweden, Russia and other nations near Germany, to send steel and ore and oil and other war materials into Germany every day in the week.

We are planning our own defense with the utmost urgency; and in its vast scale we must integrate the war needs of Britain and the other free nations which are resisting aggression.

This is not a matter of sentiment or of controversial personal opinion. It is a matter of realistic, practical military policy, based on the advice of our military experts who are in close touch with existing warfare. These military and naval experts and the members of the Congress and the Administration have a single-minded purpose—the defense of the United States.

This nation is making a great effort to produce everything that is necessary in this emergency—and with all possible speed. .This great effort requires great sacrifice.

I would ask no one to defend a democracy which in turn would not defend everyone in the nation against want and privation. The strength of this nation shall not be diluted by the failure of the Government to protect the economic well-being of its citizens.

If our capacity to produce is limited by machines, it must ever be remembered that these machines are operated by the skill and the stamina of the workers. As the Government is determined to protect the rights of the workers, so the nation has a right to expect that the men who man the machines will discharge their full responsibilities to the urgent needs of defense.

The worker possesses the same human dignity and is entitled to the same security of position as the engineer or the manager or the owner. For the workers provide the human power that turns out the destroyers, the airplanes and the tanks.

The nation expects our defense industries to continue operation without interruption by strikes or lock-outs. It expects and insists that management and workers will reconcile their differences by voluntary or legal means, to continue to produce the supplies that are so sorely needed.

And on the economic side of our great defense program, we are, as you know, bending every effort to maintain stability of prices and with that the stability of the cost of living.

Nine days ago I announced the setting up of a more effective organization to direct our gigantic efforts to increase the production of munitions. The appropriation of vast sums of money and a well coordinated executive direction of our defense efforts are not in themselves enough. Guns, planes, ships and many other things have to be built in the factories and arsenals of America. They have to be produced by workers and managers and engineers with the aid of machines which in turn have to be built by hundreds of thousands of workers throughout the land.

In this great work there has been splendid cooperation between the Government and industry and labor; and I am very thankful.

American industrial genius, unmatched throughout the world in the solution of production problems, has been called upon to bring its resources and its talents into action. Manufacturers of watches, farm implements, linotypes, cash registers, automobiles, sewing machines, lawn mowers and locomotives are now making fuses, bomb packing crates, telescope mounts, shells, pistols and tanks.

But all our present efforts are not enough. We must have more ships, more guns, more planes—more of everything. This can only be accomplished if we discard the notion of "business as usual." This job cannot be done merely by superimposing on the existing productive facilities the added requirements of the nation for defense.

Our defense efforts must not be blocked by those who fear the future consequences of surplus plant capacity. The possible consequences of failure of our defense efforts now are much more to be feared.

After the present needs of our defenses are past, a proper handling of the country's peace-time needs will require all the new productive capacity—if not more.

No pessimistic policy about the future of America shall delay the immediate expansion of those industries essential to defense. We need them.

I want to make it clear that it is the purpose of the nation to build now with all possible speed every machine, every arsenal, every factory that we need to manufacture our defense material. We have the men—the skill—the wealth—and above all, the will.

I am confident that if and when production of consumer or luxury goods in certain industries requires the use of machines and raw materials that are essential for defense purposes, then such production must yield, and will gladly yield, to our primary and compelling purpose.

I appeal to the owners of plants—to the managers—to the workers—to our own Government employees—to put every ounce of effort into producing these munitions swiftly and without stint. With this appeal I give you the pledge that all of us who are officers of your Government will devote ourselves to the same whole-hearted extent to the great task that lies ahead.

As planes and ships and guns and shells are produced, your Government, with its defense experts, can then determine how best to use them to defend this hemisphere. The decision as to how much shall be sent abroad and how much shall remain at home must be made on the basis of our over-all military necessities.

We must be the great arsenal of democracy. For us this is an emergency as serious as war itself. We must apply ourselves to our task with the same resolution, the same sense of urgency, the same spirit of patriotism and sacrifice as we would show were we at war.

We have furnished the British great material support and we will furnish far more in the future.

There will be no "bottlenecks" in our determination to aid Great Britain. No dictator, no combination of dictators, will weaken that determination by threats of how they will construe that determination.

The British have received invaluable military support from the heroic Greek army, and from the forces of all the governments in exile. Their strength is growing. It is the strength of men and women who value their freedom more highly than they value their lives.

I believe that the Axis powers are not going to win this war. I base that belief on the latest and best information.

We have no excuse for defeatism. We have every good reason for hope—hope for peace, hope for the defense of our civilization and for the building of a better civilization in the future.

I have the profound conviction that the American people are now determined to put forth a mightier effort than they have ever yet made to increase our production of all the implements of defense, to meet the threat to our democratic faith.

As President of the United States I call for that national effort. I call for it in the name of this nation which we love and honor and which we are privileged and proud to serve. I call upon our people with absolute confidence that our common cause will greatly succeed.

Document 29.2

THE ATTORNEY GENERAL GIVES AN OPINION

American presidents often have depended upon experts from the various executive departments of the federal government to produce legal justification for acts of dubious constitutionality. For example, in 1917—prior to the nation's entry into World War I—Woodrow Wilson circumvented a Senate filibuster designed to prevent the arming of merchant vessels by obtaining an opinion from Secretary of State Robert Lansing which held that such action could be taken under terms of an unrepealed statute of 1797. Attorney General Robert H. Jackson's opinion of August 27, 1940, justifying lend-lease, displays more than a little ingenuity.

(From *Department of State Bulletin*, Vol. III, No. 63 [September 7, 1940], pp. 201–7)

My Dear Mr. President:

In accordance with your request I have considered your constitutional and statutory authority to proceed by Executive Agreement with the British Government immediately to acquire for the United States certain off-shore naval and air bases in the Atlantic Ocean without awaiting the inevitable delays which would accompany the conclusion of a formal treaty. . . .

The questions of constitutional and statutory authority, with which alone I am concerned, seem to be these.

First. May such an acquisition be concluded by the President under an Executive Agreement or must it be negotiated as a Treaty subject to ratification by the Senate?

Second. Does authority exist in the President to alienate the title to such ships . . . , and if so, on what conditions?

Third. Do the statutes of the United States limit the right to deliver . . . the over-age destroyers by reason of the belligerent status of Great Britain? . . .

Happily, there has been little occasion in our history for the interpretation of the powers of the President as Commander-in-Chief of the Army and Navy. I do not find it necessary to rest upon that power alone to sustain the present proposal. But it will hardly be open to controversy that the vesting of such a function in the President also places upon him a responsibility to use all constitutional authority which he may possess to provide adequate bases and stations for the utilization of the naval and air weapons of the United States at their highest efficiency in our defense. It seems equally beyond doubt that present world conditions forbid him to risk any delay that is constitutionally avoidable.

The second power to be considered is that control of foreign relations which the Constitution vests in the President as a part of the Executive function. . . . The President's power over foreign relations . . . is not unlimited. Some negotiations involve commitments as to the future which would carry an obligation to exercise powers vested in the Congress. Such Presidential arrangements are customarily submitted for ratification by a two-thirds vote of the Senate before the future legislative power of the country is committed. However, the acquisitions which you are proposing to accept are without express or implied promises on the part of the United States to be performed in the future. The consideration . . . is completed upon transfer of the specified items. The Executive Agreement obtains an opportunity to establish naval and air bases for the protection of our coastline but it imposes no obligation upon the Congress to appropriate money to improve the opportunity. It is not necessary for the Senate to ratify an opportunity that entails no obligation.

There are precedents which might be cited, but not all strictly pertinent. The proposition falls far short in magnitude of the acquisition by President Jefferson of the Louisiana Territory from a belligerent during a European war, the Congress later appropriating the consideration and the Senate later ratifying a treaty embodying the agreement.

I am also reminded that in 1850, Secretary of State Daniel Webster acquired Horse Shoe Reef, at the entrance of Buffalo Harbor, upon condition that the United States would engage to erect a lighthouse and maintain a light but would erect no fortification thereon. This was done without awaiting legislative authority. Subsequently the Congress made appropriations for the lighthouse, which was erected in 1856. . . .

It is not believed, however, that it is necessary here to rely exclusively upon your constitutional power. . . . I think there is also ample statutory authority to support the acquisition of these bases, and the precedents perhaps most nearly in point are the numerous acquisitions of rights in foreign countries for sites of diplomatic and consular establishments—perhaps also the trade agreements recently negotiated under statutory authority and the acquisition in 1903 of coaling and naval stations and rights in Cuba. . . .

The transaction now proposed represents only an exchange with no statutory requirement for the embodiment thereof in any treaty and involving no promises or undertakings by the United States that might raise the question of the propriety of incorporation in a treaty. I therefore advise that acquisition by Executive Agreement of the rights proposed to be conveyed to the United States by Great Britain will not require ratification by the Senate.

The right of the President to dispose of vessels of the Navy . . . finds clear recognition in at least two enactments of the Congress and a decision of the Supreme Court—and any who assert that the authority does not exist must assume the burden of establishing that both the Congress and the Supreme Court meant something less than the clear import of seemingly plain language [acts of March 3, 1883 and June 28, 1940; *Levinson* v. *United States*, 258 U.S. 198, 201]. . . .

Whether the statutes of the United States prevent the dispatch to Great Britain, a belligerent power, of the . . . over-age destroyers depends upon the interpretation to be placed on section 3 of title V of the act of June 15, 1917. . . . This section reads:

"During a war in which the United States is a neutral nation, it shall be unlawful to send out of the jurisdiction of the United States any vessel, built, armed, or equipped as a vessel of war, or converted from a private vessel into a vessel of war, with any intent or under any agreement or contract, written or oral, that such vessel shall be delivered to a belligerent nation, or to an agent, officer, or citizen of such nation, or with reasonable cause to believe that the said vessel shall or will be employed in the service of any such belligerent nation after its departure from the jurisdiction of the United States."

This section . . . is inapplicable to vessels, like the over-age destroyers, which were not built, armed, equipped as, or converted into, vessels of war with the intent that they should enter the service of a belligerent. . . .

In this connection it has been noted that during the war between Russia and Japan in 1904 and 1905, the German Government permitted the sale to Russia of torpedo boats and also of ocean liners belonging to its auxiliary navy. . . .

Accordingly, you are respectfully advised:

a) That the proposed arrangement may be concluded as an Executive Agreement, effective without awaiting ratification.

b) That there is presidential power to transfer title and possession of the proposed considerations. . . .

c) That . . . there is no legal obstacle to . . . delivery.

Respectfully submitted,

ROBERT H. JACKSON
Attorney General

Document 29.3

ROOSEVELT SPEAKS IN BOSTON

President Roosevelt's speech of October 30 came shortly after Wendell L. Willkie, his Republican opponent in the 1940 election campaign, told a GOP rally in Baltimore: "If you elect him [Roosevelt] you may expect war in April, 1941." Roosevelt and his jittery advisers believed they had to reassure the mothers and fathers of America that their sons were not ticketed for slaughter on the battlefield. They were particularly anxious because of the location. Boston was marked by the Anglophobia of its citizens of Irish descent, and Massachusetts Democratic Senator David I. Walsh was a pronounced isolationist. Consequently, in his address the President catered to national fears and to local prejudices; he had sufficient political courage, however, to emphasize the necessity of extending further American aid to the British.

(From the *New York Times*, October 31, 1940. Copyright by the *New York Times*; reprinted by permission.)

Mr. Mayor, my friends of New England:

I've had a glorious day here in New England. And I don't need to tell you that I've been glad to come back to my old stamping ground in Boston. There's only one thing about this trip that I regret. I have to return to Washington tonight, without getting a chance to go into my two favorite States, Maine and Vermont.

This is the third inning. In New York City, two nights ago, I showed . . . how Republican leaders, with their votes and in their speeches, have been playing and still are playing politics with national defense.

Even during the past three years, when the dangers to all forms of democracy throughout the world have been obvious, the Republican team in the Congress has been acting only as a party team.

Time after time, Republican leadership refused to see that what this country needs is an all-American team. . . .

Our objective is to keep any potential attacker as far from our continental shores as we possibly can.

And you, here in New England, know well and visualize it, that within the past two months your government has acquired new naval and air bases in British territory in the Atlantic Ocean, extending all the way from Newfoundland on the north to that part of South America where the Atlantic Ocean begins to narrow, with Africa not far away. . . .

And while I am talking to you, fathers and mothers, I give you one more assurance.

I have said this before, but I shall say it again, and again and again. Your boys are not going to be sent into any foreign wars.

They are going into training to form a force so strong that, by its very existence, it will keep the threat of war far away from our shores. Yes, the purpose of our defense is defense. . . .

I have discussed the falsifications which Republican campaign orators have been making about the economic condition of the nation, the condition of labor and the condition of business.

They are even more ridiculous when they shed those old crocodile tears over the plight of the American farmer.

Now, if there is any one that a Republican candidate loves more than the laboring man in October and up to election day, it's the farmer.

And the very first one that he forgets after election day is the farmer. . . .

No, the American farmers will not be deceived by pictures of Old Guard candidates, patting cows and pitching hay in front of moving-picture cameras. . . .

Now, among the Republican leaders, among the Republican leaders who have voted against . . . practically every . . . farm bill for the United States is the present chairman of the Republican National Committee, that "peerless leader," that "farmers' friend"—Congressman Joe Martin of Massachusetts. . . .

I will have to let you in on a secret. It will come as a great surprise to you, and it's this:

I'm enjoying this campaign and I am really having a fine time. . . .

Document 29.4

"THIS WAS PIRACY"

President Roosevelt's fireside chat of September 11, 1941, was an explanation and defense of his administration's policy of naval and air patrols in the Atlantic. The occasion for it was the sinking of an American destroyer by a German submarine a week earlier.

(From the *New York Times*, September 12, 1941. Copyright by the *New York Times*; reprinted by permission.)

My Fellow-Americans:

The Navy Department of the United States has reported to me that on the morning of Sept. 4 the United States destroyer Greer, proceeding in full daylight toward Iceland, had reached a point southeast of Greenland. She was carrying American mail to Iceland. She was flying the American flag. Her identity as an American ship was unmistakable.

She was then and there attacked by a submarine. Germany admits that it was a German submarine. The submarine deliberately fired a torpedo at the Greer, followed later by another torpedo attack. In spite of what Hitler's propaganda bureau has invented, and in spite of what any American obstructionist organization may prefer to believe, I tell you the blunt fact that the German submarine fired first upon this American destroyer without warning, and with deliberate design to sink her.

Our destroyer, at the time, was in waters which the Government of the United States had declared to be waters of self-defense, surrounding outposts of American protection in the Atlantic. . . .

This was piracy, piracy legally and morally. It was not the first nor the last act of piracy which the Nazi government has committed against the American flag in this war, for attack has followed attack. . . .

In the face of all this we Americans are keeping our feet on the ground. Our type of democratic civilization has outgrown the thought of feeling compelled to fight some other nation by reason of any single piratical attack on one of our ships. We are not becoming hysterical or losing our sense of proportion. Therefore, what I am thinking and saying tonight does not relate to any isolated episode. . . .

To be ultimately successful in world mastery, Hitler knows that he must get control of the seas. He must first destroy the bridge of ships which we are building across the Atlantic and over which we shall continue to roll the implements of war to help destroy him, to destroy all his works in the end. He must wipe out our patrol on sea and in the air if he is to do it. He must silence the British Navy. . . .

This attack on the Greer was no localized military operation in the North Atlantic. This was no mere episode in a struggle between two nations. This was one determined step toward creating a permanent world system based on force, on terror and on murder. . . .

Normal practices of diplomacy—note writing—are of no possible use in dealing with international outlaws who sink our ships and kill our citizens. . . .

We have sought no shooting war with Hitler. We do not seek it now. But neither do we want peace so much that we are willing to pay for it by permitting him to attack our naval and merchant ships while they are on legitimate business.

I assume that the German leaders are not deeply concerned tonight, or any other time, by what the real Americans or the American Government says or publishes about them. We cannot bring about the downfall of nazism by the use of long-range invective.

But when you see a rattlesnake poised to strike, you do not wait until he has struck before you crush him.

These Nazi submarines and raiders are the rattlesnakes of the Atlantic. They are a menace to the free pathways of the high seas. They are a challenge to our own sovereignty. They hammer at our most precious rights when they attack ships of the American flag—symbols of our independence, our freedom, our very life. . . .

Do not let us be hair-splitters. Let us not ask ourselves whether the Americans should begin to defend themselves after the first attack, or the fifth attack, or the tenth attack, or the twentieth attack.

The time for active defense is now.

Do not let us split hairs. Let us not say, "We will only defend ourselves if the torpedo succeeds in getting home, or if the crew and the passengers are drowned." . . .

Upon our naval and air patrol—now operating in large number over a vast expanse of the Atlantic Ocean—falls the duty of maintaining the American policy of freedom of the seas—now. That means, very simply, very clearly, that our patrolling vessels and planes will protect all merchant ships—not only American ships but ships of any flag—engaged in commerce in our defensive waters. They will protect them from submarines; they will protect them from surface raiders.

This situation is not new. The second President of the United States, John Adams, ordered the United States Navy to clean out European privateers and European ships of war which were infesting the Caribbean and South American waters, destroying American commerce.

The third President of the United States, Thomas Jefferson, ordered the United States Navy to end the attacks being made upon American and other ships by the corsairs of the nations of North Africa.

My obligation as President is historic; it is clear; yes, it is inescapable.

It is no act of war on our part when we decide to protect the seas that are vital to American defense. The aggression is not ours. Ours is solely defense.

But let this warning be clear. From now on, if German or Italian vessels of war enter the waters the protection of which is necessary for American defense, they do so at their own peril. . . .

I have no illusions about the gravity of this step. I have not taken it hurriedly or lightly. It is the result of months and months of constant thought and anxiety and prayer. . . .

The American people have faced other grave crises in their history. . . .

And with that inner strength that comes to a free people conscious of their duty, conscious of the righteousness of what they do, they will—with divine help and guidance—stand their ground against this latest assault upon their democracy, their sovereignty and their freedom.

30

JOHN E. WILTZ
Indiana University

The United States and National Security

AT 9:07 A.M., Sunday, September 2, 1945, the pride of the United States fleet, the superdreadnought *Missouri*, scrubbed and polished, rode at anchor in Tokyo Bay. Low-hanging clouds obscured the sun, but the air was warm, and a refreshing breeze moved across the bay, causing the water to splash gently against the thick armor of the ship's hull. From the veranda deck fluttered the flags of the United States, Great Britain, China, and the Soviet Union. On the gallery deck below, in the shadow of the ship's fearsome sixteen-inch guns, General Douglas A. MacArthur, Supreme Commander of Allied forces in the Pacific, leaned over a long table and with trembling hand affixed his signature to the document proclaiming the surrender of the empire of Japan. The second World War was ending—six years plus one day after it began.

As the ceremony aboard the *Missouri* closed, the sun burst through the clouds; for the typical American of September 2, 1945, this circumstance seemed symbolic. For him, the ceremony marked the end of an unfortunate interruption in the normal tempo of American life. It was an interruption which had not proved specially agonizing. No bombs had fallen on American cities. American battle casualties, relative to those of other nations, were light. The war, moreover, had brought unprecedented economic prosperity; and the principal concern of the average American on September 2, 1945, was enjoyment of his new affluence. He had accepted patriotically the inconveniences of war—rationing, the housing shortage, inability to purchase a new automobile. But the war was over, and he wanted to dismantle the huge American military establishment and return to peacetime pursuits as quickly as possible.

The world of September, 1945, of course, was not that of September, 1939—or December, 1941. Global war had brought many changes.

There were changes in weapons. During the war, scientists and technicians had waged a battle of drawing boards, and out of this competition had come developments which even in the second World War made a shambles of traditional military and diplomatic equations. The long-range bombing plane appeared in the war's latter stages. Where the Wellingtons and Heinkels and B–17's of the early war years could strike targets several hundred miles from base, the long-range bomber spanned oceans and continents. Then, there was the rocket-powered missile, developed by Germany and used late in the war. The German rockets had limited range and accuracy. But scientists had visions of missiles capable of delivering deadly warheads with pinpoint accuracy upon targets 1,500 miles away and more.

One scientific and technical achievement, of course, made all others seem rudimentary and inconsequential: During the war, man unlocked the secret of nuclear energy. Only a handful of people had understood the possibilities of splitting the atom, and Americans were amazed to learn in August, 1945, that a single B–29 bomber with one bomb had leveled the Japanese city of Hiroshima. Nuclear energy held undreamed-of promise for promoting the happiness and comfort of man; it also placed in man's hands the capacity for his own extermination.

The war brought significant social and political changes. Western and central Europe had suffered vast destruction. For two thousand years the western two thirds of Europe had served as the bastion of Western civilization and all it implied in Hebraic-Christian, Greek, and Roman ideas. Not only had Europe preserved Western civilization through the centuries, but it had spread that civilization's influence to the ends of the world. Yet, in the short space of thirty years in the twentieth century, Europe squandered its human and material resources during two devastating wars. On September 2, 1945, much of the Continent lay in ruins. It lacked the means, if not the will, to ward off enemies.

The war had brought changes in other parts of the world. It had set in motion a revolution for countless millions in that great area of the globe from West Africa to the South China Sea. People in much of that area never had known political independence or social equality. Times were changing. Many of these people had fallen under Axis domination during the war. They had lost respect for the European imperial governments—Great Britain, France, the Netherlands—which could not defend their overseas interests. Moreover, they had contributed to expulsion of the Axis powers, and believed they had earned a right to a new social and political order. They also were not unaware of the exalted phrases of the Atlantic Charter that everyone had a right to a choice of government, dignity, and equal opportunity. All of these developments combined to prevent restoration of the old imperial order, and the result over the next fifteen years was the appearance of a host of new nations.

Most of these new nations rested on shaky foundations. Individually, most of these countries lacked the physical bases for prosperity and security. Their populations had slight knowledge of modern technology. Their people often lacked unity and traditions of stability. Leaders usually lacked political experience. Taken as a whole, these former colonial areas had enormous human resources and a substantial part of those mineral resources which hitherto had helped insure the prosperity and power of the great nations of the world. Yet the new nations, like Europe weak and almost defenseless, constituted a vast power vacuum.

In addition to Europe and the newly emerging nations, a third group of countries had felt profoundly the effects of war. These nations—in Latin America, the Far East, the Middle East—had come out of the war years in varying conditions, but all continued to suffer the twin evils of feudalism and poverty. Their corrupt, oppressive, and inefficient governments were mainly interested in preserving a wealthy elite. The mass of people lived in poverty and state-condoned illiteracy. Yet, through the curtains of ignorance and censorship had filtered the new gospel of human rights. This gospel, sanctioned in the Charter of the United Nations, stirred people in these countries to new determination to achieve the promise of the good life of the twentieth century.

The war brought the rise of a new Eurasian "superpower," the Soviet Union. When Adolf Hitler launched the invasion of June, 1941, Soviet Russia hardly ranked as a first-rate power. The past ninety years had seen a succession of Russian humiliations on the battlefield—in the Crimean War of 1854–56, the Russo-Japanese War of 1904–5, the first World War, the Russo-Polish War of 1920–21, the Russo-Finnish War of 1939–40. But the Red Army, supported by the fierce determination of the Soviet people and the productive capacity of Russian and American factories, ultimately repelled the German invader. When fighting ended in May, 1945, Soviet soldiers occupied half of Europe.

The triumph of Russian armies in the second World War meant more than increase in the power of the Soviet state, for its armies carried the hope of the world communist movement. Russian communism, born of the rubble of the first World War, emerged in 1945 with enormous strength and confidence. Inspired by a mixture of historic Russian nationalism and more recent Marxism-Leninism, Soviet leaders determined to expand their power. The most alluring object was western Europe, the heart of Western civilization. But there were the newly emerging nations and those countries ill with feudalism and poverty.

Did the people of the United States in September, 1945, comprehend the changes of the previous six years?

Americans surely knew of the technical changes, in part because they had produced many of them. But they less clearly assessed the war's social and political changes. They understood machines better than men. They failed to grasp the implications of the destruction of Europe. They did not appreciate the new ambitions of Soviet Russia. They were virtually unaware that the war had aroused half the world to a sense of its poverty and ignorance and a desire to share in twentieth-century progress. They hoped to turn their tanks and battleships into automobiles and washing machines, and to return to the tranquil pursuits of the past.

Here was a tragic miscalculation by Americans of the war generation. Nationalism would be less shrill in the early 1960's than it had been in the early 1930's. The United Nations would prove only slightly more effective as a guarantor of peace than had the League of Nations. In place of the old balance of power, the post-1945 world produced a new balance of nuclear terror. Liberty and democracy stood in as great, if not greater, jeopardy than in the time of Hitler and Mussolini. Americans found it impossible to relax behind the world organization, to restore conditions under which they could concentrate on domestic affairs almost to the exclusion of world affairs.

Why did Americans miscalculate?

Americans were essentially a parochial people in 1945. From the time the first white men settled in the New World, their largest challenges had appeared from within the western hemisphere. So overwhelming were the problems—so tempting were the rewards—presented by the vast territory in North America that Americans seldom paused to consider the affairs of Europe and Asia. When the habit of looking inward reasserted itself in 1945, the result was failure to note the far-reaching and ominous developments which had come from the second World War.

Not historically minded, Americans in 1945, moreover, failed to ponder the lessons of the past. To the average American, history was an Indian arrowhead, a Fourth-of-July parade, a Civil War battlefield. He seldom saw history as a stream of causes and effects, a contest among ideas, a struggle by people to control and improve their environment.

If Americans had so understood history in 1945, they might have seen matters differently. They would have taken a more realistic view of the United Nations. They would have noted that the UN suffered the very same structural weaknesses that had hindered the American government of 1775–89, the German Confederation of the nineteenth century, and the League of Nations. Of particular importance was the UN's lack of financial independence and its inability to enforce decisions. And a better understanding of the past would have revealed that the failure of the League of Nations had not resulted from absence of American membership. In the years after 1939 the notion was widespread that the United States could have averted the second world conflict had the American people listened to President Woodrow Wilson in 1919–20. This alluringly simple explanation hardly squared with the complicated facts of history. Given the American nation's own frustrations, disillusions, and prejudices of the interwar period, it seems fair to say that United States membership in the League would have altered slightly the tragic course of events of those years.

Americans in 1945 did not understand Soviet Russia. They looked upon the individual Russian as an East European. If one applied geographical criteria, he could legitimately define the Russian as such. But in truth, the Russian long had been well removed from the Latin culture of most of Europe. In the past five hundred years, four events, more than any others, had influenced Europeans: the Renaissance, the Reformation, the discovery of the New World, and the French Revolution. These events had made slight impact upon the Russians. As a consequence, the average Russian had small attachment to—or understanding of—Western ideals of liberty, equality, fraternity.

Americans were at best imperfectly aware of the history of Russian expansionism. Few could recall the era before the World War of 1914–18 when Russia had been in the European race for empire. Or perhaps they gave excessive credence to the Soviet Union's commitment to the Marxist dogma of anti-imperialism. Still, Russians, whether tsarist or communist, were Russians, and for a thousand years had looked to the West. They had breached the gates of Europe on several occasions. In pursuit of Napoleon in 1814, they had taken over territories in eastern Europe, withdrawing only under pressure by the Congress of Vienna. During the Russo-Turkish War of 1877, they had made another thrust toward the West, but the Congress of Berlin of 1878 determined that the Russian conquest could not prevail. In the period between 1878 and 1914 the Russians had sought to spread their influence in eastern Europe, especially in the Balkans, and their ambitions helped bring on the first World War. The Bolsheviks, after 1917, demonstrated dedication to anti-imperialism by withdrawing from territories occupied under the tsar, but in 1939 the Soviets took advantage of Hitler's problems to strike a bargain with the Nazi dictator and occupy part of eastern Europe. Hitler expelled them from this conquest in 1941; but in 1944 and 1945, they returned and took even more.

Finally, by September 2, 1945, Americans had forgotten—or at least put in the recesses of their minds—the history of Russian communism to 1941. Many of them had looked with mixed emotions upon Hitler's invasion of the Soviet Union, but Germany's stunning early victories forced the conclusion that any country under attack by the Nazis merited Western support. During the war, it became fashionable to portray the Soviets as courageous fighters (which they were) and honorable friends (which they were not). Ignored was the Marxist-Leninist dogma about world communist revolution. Americans chose to overlook Stalin's purges of the 1930's, the pact with Hitler in 1939, the invasions of Poland and Finland in 1939. When the war ended in 1945, they continued under the happy illusion that the Soviets, after all, were not such bad fellows; that they had forgotten the Marxist-Leninist world revolution; that the wartime alliance could endure in peace.

If the people of the United States were living in a dream world in September, 1945, within the next two years they had to face reality. They saw the weakness of the United Nations, learned that the war had not altered the ambitions of Russian nationalism or the Soviet commitment to Marx and Lenin. They awakened to an understanding of the state of Europe and began to comprehend what was happening in the newly emerging nations and the feudalistic regimes of Latin America, the Middle East, and China. They came to realize that only they stood between these areas and Soviet imperialism.

When the Soviet menace became apparent in the years 1946–47—when disillusion set in over failure of the second great war to make the world safe for democracy—the temptation was considerable to withdraw to a "Fortress America." Such a response would have been consistent with American tradition. Yet, most Americans concluded in the late 1940's that the United States must try to contain the Soviets within their existing territory. Occasionally, there was some wild talk about a preventive war, an attempt to roll back the Iron Curtain and destroy the communist threat with a massive atomic attack on the Soviet Union. But no responsible leader was prepared to assume responsibility for manifold Hiroshimas and Nagasakis. The very idea was unthinkable.

The American alternative in the years 1947–50 was a series of bold departures from past policies. The Truman Doctrine bolstered the anticommunist regimes in Turkey and Greece, and prevented those countries from falling behind the Iron Curtain. Next, and most important of all, came the Marshall Plan, which poured massive economic assistance into central and western Europe. Acting on the theory that chaos and economic collapse would make inevitable a communist coup, the United States determined to restore the physical resources and morale of Europeans still outside the Soviet empire. The Marshall Plan was a spectacular success. Then, in 1948 the Soviets challenged the new American "containment" policy by blockading American-British-French land routes to Berlin—a jointly controlled city one hundred miles behind the Iron Curtain. A massive airlift of food and supplies prevented Western sectors of Berlin from falling to the Russians. In this same period the United States entered into its first formal military alliance since the year 1800, the North Atlantic Treaty Organization (NATO) of 1949. Its aim was to create a powerful establishment which would deter a Soviet military conquest of Europe. Almost concurrently came the Point Four program, aimed at bolstering underdeveloped countries of the world. Because of poverty and shaky politics, American leaders reasoned, these countries otherwise might fall to communism.

Such programs were expensive and strained American resources. Yet, despite caution by prewar isolationists such as Republican Senator Robert A. Taft of Ohio and occasional assertions that the Marshall Plan and the Point Four program were a "global WPA," opposition in Congress was small. This remarkable bipartisanship on foreign policy was due in large measure to the patient work of another Republican, Senator Arthur H. Vandenberg, a former isolationist from Michigan.

But in 1949–50 a new wave of disillusion swept the United States and almost threatened to turn the country once again to isolation. Several developments contributed to this mood. There came the shattering news of early 1949 that the communists had taken over China. Many Americans, especially isolationists, always had felt a strange affection for General Chiang Kai-shek and the Chinese Nationalists. For the isolationist, there was an ocean between America and Europe, but Asia seemed part of the American land mass. During the war years, isolationists had urged more aid to Chiang; and in the postwar era, when the United States was pouring money into Europe, they demanded still more assistance to Nationalist China. While the isolationist appeal seemed consistent with the containment policy, planners in the State Department had little faith in Chiang Kai-shek and suspected that aid to him would go for nought. The only way to save Chiang, they reasoned, was a massive land assault in China by American troops or a preventive war on the entire communist world—neither of which courses Americans wanted. Supporters of Chiang in the United States did not see matters in this light. After his fall, they argued that large-scale military and economic assistance could have saved him, and concluded that containment was a farce and that traitors or dupes in the State Department had "sold Chiang down the river."

While Americans were pondering the communist conquest of China, they were appalled by the case of Alger Hiss, a young Harvard-trained lawyer who had held important posts in the administrations of Franklin D. Roosevelt. Evidence indicated that Hiss, in the 1930's, had passed classified information to Soviet spies. To Main Street America the sophisticated Hiss typified the intellectual leadership in Washington—presumably in the State Department or in the White House inner circle—which had championed policies allegedly leading to the loss of China.

Before the Hiss case had reached a conclusion, Americans in the autumn of 1949 received the distressing news that the Soviets had set off an atomic explosion. The nuclear monopoly of the United States was no more. Hardly had Americans digested this information when they learned in February, 1950, that the Soviets had gained access to American atomic secrets via Dr. Klaus Fuchs, a high-level scientist in the service of the British government.

The communist invasion of South Korea followed in June, 1950. President Harry S. Truman's decision to dispatch American forces to check the communist advance in the name of the United Nations met general approval, although some congressmen, including Senator Taft, criticized the President for acting without Congressional consent. After several months, United Nations forces—mainly American and South Korean—halted the communists and in a series of splendid maneuvers pushed the enemy to the Manchurian border. But with victory in sight, UN troops met disaster when communist China hurled large forces across the Yalu River to bolster the North Koreans. Before the end of the year 1950, a second heartbreaking retreat began down the Korean peninsula. In frustration, many Americans criticized UN members for making token contributions to the Korean fighting. Simultaneously, they assailed Secretary of State Dean G. Acheson for a speech "inviting" the communist attack in the first place (in a speech of January, 1950, Acheson had omitted South Korea and Formosa from the American area of defense in the Far East).

In this setting of frustration and disillusion, public discussion of America's Far Eastern and world policy reached a climax. The debate resembled that of ten years before, when Americans had pondered entering the fight against Hitler. As in 1940, argument revolved around isolationism. Yet, there were differences. In 1940, isolationists had denied that the United States had an enemy and had contended that if the nation would isolate itself from foreign embroilments, it could remain without one. In 1950, isolationists (they preferred to be called nationalists) acknowledged that the United States had an enemy, but argued that the nation could best cope with this enemy by sharply reducing—or even eliminating—its commitments overseas and concentrating its strength in the western hemisphere—in a "Fortress America."

Debate opened a few days after the Congressional elections of November, 1950. Election results had encouraged critics of "Truman-Acheson" foreign policies, causing Senator Taft—"Mr. Republican" of the United States—to press for revision of American policy along lines more to his liking. In an interview at Cincinnati on November 10, 1950, he announced that only an idiot would be an isolationist but then significantly asked: "Is Europe our first line of defense? Is it defensible at all?" He called for a thorough re-examination of American policy.

Taft's remarks brought a counterblast from Secretary of State Acheson. "We are told," he said, ". . . that all isolationists are extinct, as dead as the dodo or the saber-toothed tiger. But there is a new species that has come on the horizon, and this new species I call the 're-examinist.'" Acheson compared re-examinists with the farmers who pulled up his crops in the morning to see how they had done during the night. While Acheson's reply to Taft was clever, it came at the wrong psychic moment. Most Americans were in no mood for witticisms.

The debate enlarged. A new champion of the neoisolationism entered the lists—Joseph P. Kennedy, a Democrat, prewar isolationist and former American Ambassador to Great Britain. Speaking before the University of Virginia Law School Forum, Kennedy urged withdrawal from all overseas areas: "Where are we now? What have we in return for this effort? Friends? We have far fewer friends than we had in 1945. In Europe they are still asking for our dollars but what kind of friendship have we bought there?" A first step, Kennedy declared, was "to get out of Korea—indeed, to get out of every point in Asia which we do not plan realistically to hold in our own defense. . . . The next step in pursuit of this policy is to apply the same principle to Europe." He saw little good from the American effort to contain communism in Europe and shrugged off the Marshall Plan and the Berlin airlift. "What have we gained," he asked, "by staying in Berlin?" Conceding that Europe might fall to the communists, Kennedy said that such an event would be unfortunate, but ought not to deter the United States from building Fortress America.

Kennedy's remarks were raucously applauded, and approving letters poured into newspaper offices. The *Wall Street Journal* printed three columns of letters endorsing the Kennedy view. The editors explained the absence of critical letters by observing that none had been received.

The next prominent speaker in the debate was Governor Thomas E. Dewey of New York, unsuccessful Republican candidate for president in 1948. Representing the internationalist wing of the Republican party, Dewey urged a dramatic increase in American military power. He declared, moreover, that "we will still need strong, powerful friends elsewhere in the world. . . . Nothing will make them rearm and nothing will give them the will to fight if they do rearm, without a new degree of strength and leadership from this country in world affairs. So . . . our Government should state its aims and objectives specifically for all the world to see and know. . . . Unless we are going to shrink within our own borders and wait to be conquered by a Communist world, we must boldly make decisions that will keep friends of our cause both in Europe and in Asia."

Next evening, December 15, 1950, President Truman, in a radio address declaring a national emergency and ordering stepped-up mobilization, made recommendations similar to those of the man he had defeated in the election two years before. He said that "the defense of Europe is of the utmost importance to the security of the United States. . . . The Communist rulers are trying their best to split the free nations apart. If they should succeed, they would do staggering damage to the cause of freedom. Unity with our allies is now, and must continue to be, the foundation of our effort. Working together, the free nations can present the common front, backed by strength, which is necessary if we are to negotiate with the Kremlin for peaceful settlements."

But a few days later the forces of the new isolationism brought out their best spokesman, former President Herbert Hoover. Having lived down his unfortunate reputation as a depression President, Hoover had become a highly respected elder statesman. Speaking before a national radio audience, he said: "The foundation of our national policies must be to preserve for the world this Western Hemisphere Gibraltar of Western Civilization." Hoover saw no need for a large land army. With powerful air and naval forces, he believed, the United States could hold the Atlantic and Pacific oceans. America's lines of defense would recede to include Great Britain, Japan, Formosa, and the Philippines. As for Korea, he said, the communists had won there. As for Europe, "before we land another man or another dollar on their shores," the Europeans "should show they have spiritual strength and unity to avail themselves of their own resources."

No speech of the 1950 debate equaled Hoover's in impact. It stirred the deepest emotions. For many Americans, it offered the prospect of return to happy days of splendid aloofness from world embroilments. It promised relief from taxes. The seventy-six-year-old former President also sounded the economy note when he said: "We could, after initial outlays for more air and naval equipment, greatly reduce our expenditures, balance our budget and free ourselves from the dangers of inflation and economic degeneration." Following the address, New York's Senators Irving Ives and Herbert Lehman reported their mail running better than ninety to one in favor of the Hoover program. Hoover's secretary reported receipt of more than 5,000 letters, less than 100 of which were critical. The Hoover program delighted the Soviets. *Pravda* immediately printed the entire speech.

Not all Americans, however, were isolationists, and many considered Hoover's program a cowardly and dangerous retreat. Historian Arthur M. Schlesinger, Jr., recalling Hoover's opposition to sending American troops to France in 1917 and his isolationism of 1940, wrote that Hoover showed inability to learn by experience: "He was clearly wrong in 1917 and 1940, and he is equally wrong now." Ralph McGill, in the *Atlanta Constitution*, wrote that what Hoover "proposes is national suicide." In Washington a "leading Republican" said of the Hoover speech: "It was just an open invitation for Stalin to take over all of Western Europe, without a struggle." Former Secretary of War

Robert Patterson, also a Republican, called Hoover's words "the counsel of discouragement, despair, and defeat." Secretary Acheson told a press conference on December 22 that the National Security Council many times had considered withdrawal into the western hemisphere and had always rejected such action because "it spells defeat and frustration, it has no possibility of success, and therefore it is not an attitude which this Government can usefully take."

To issue a formal reply to Hoover, the State Department commissioned John Foster Dulles, a Republican foreign policy adviser, and the man who would become Secretary of State in 1953. Speaking before the American Association for the United Nations on December 29, Dulles pointed out that one of the principal American assets in the cold war was industrial superiority—a superiority of three or four to one over the communist nations in terms of steel, aluminum, electric power, oil. If the United States yielded the Ruhr and the Middle East to the Soviets in pursuit of Fortress America, it would relinquish that superiority. Said Dulles: "It is possible to plan, on paper, and describe in words, what it seems should be an impregnable defense, a China Wall, a Maginot Line, a Rock of Gibraltar, an Atlantic and Pacific Moat. But . . . such a defense carries within itself the seeds of its own collapse. A defense that accepts encirclement quickly decomposes. That has been proved a thousand times." He concluded: "A United States which could be an inactive spectator while the barbarians overran and desecrated the cradle of our Christian civilization would not be the kind of United States which could defend itself."

It became clear that for the moment, at least, there would be no retreat to Fortress America. And later, in the presidential election of 1952, it became evident that the Kennedy-Hoover type of isolation was dead. The Republicans, then led by General Dwight D. Eisenhower, believed in reducing waste and inefficiency in overseas programs. Yet, interestingly, the GOP—since 1920 the party of isolationism—indicated a willingness to move more boldly in world affairs than the Democrats. They argued that containment was a negative approach to the communist conspiracy, that the United States should think in terms of rolling back the Iron Curtain and of "liberating" the Soviet-dominated countries of eastern Europe. Once in power in 1953, the Eisenhower administration found it inexpedient to expel the Russians from eastern Europe but remained loyal to American commitments to bolster anticommunist countries and contain the Soviets. The only change of consequence was that more foreign aid went into guns, tanks, and planes and less into economic assistance.

Arguments for a grand withdrawal continued throughout the 1950's, but since total American retreat from Europe and the Far East was unlikely, opponents began to emphasize that the United States ought to reduce its commitments. Economic assistance was the special target. Critics of the 1950's dubbed this program, with its large annual appropriations, a massive "giveaway," and contended that the United States had few friends, despite it. Late in the 1950's, when the country's balance-of-payments problem attracted attention, increased pressure developed to restrict foreign aid, military and economic, on the ground that it was draining the American gold reserve.

The Democrats returned to national power in 1961, and the new administration of John F. Kennedy, the son of Joseph P. Kennedy, was as committed to massive overseas military and economic programs as were the preceding administrations of Truman and Eisenhower. Yet, before long, critics of such programs stepped up demands for revision —a substantial cutback. Large opposition to the Kennedy foreign assistance program was heard in Congress, and observers noted that neither Presidents Truman nor Eisenhower had succeeded in selling to the man in the street and on the farm the virtues of foreign aid. The American of Buncombe County or of Peoria had no personal contact with the farmer or shopkeeper in Bangkok or Baghdad. Usually, he had only a faint idea where such places were and cared little about their condition or destiny. Foreign aid meant higher taxes. Let the denizens of Bangkok and Baghdad help themselves! Millions of Americans continued to see foreign assistance, especially economic aid, as nothing less than charity. They concurred with Republican Congressman H. R. Gross of Iowa that "the waste, the extravagance, the outright corruption in this vast foreign give-away program almost defies the imagination. What have we bought with this incredible outpouring of our treasure . . . ? The record is clear that the billions of dollars we have lavished on foreign governments has bought neither friends nor respect. Neither has it fashioned a world that is peaceful, prosperous, or free."

As the 1960's moved on, Americans continued to re-evaluate their position in the world. The continuing deficit in the balance of payments worried them, though few had any idea what it was all about. Premier Charles de Gaulle of France began to assert his independence of the Western alliance more vigorously than in the past; he thwarted American attempts to prepare for British entry into the booming European economic community; he rebuffed American efforts to persuade him against creation of an expensive and superfluous French nuclear force; and he went so far as to recognize the government of communist China. These slaps (at least, that is what Americans considered them) by a country which the United States had saved in critical days during and after the war caused no little bitterness. The temptation was to say "to hell with" the French—and the rest of the world, too.

In March, 1963, came the Clay report, which seemed to question the American commitment overseas. This report resulted from a study of the American foreign assistance program by a committee of private citizens, most of them industrialists and bankers of conservative background, appointed by President Kennedy. Chairman of the committee was General Lucius D. Clay, who had been in charge of American forces in Germany during the Berlin blockade of 1948–49. The Clay report did not advocate retreat to Fortress America. Yet, if accepted, it would bring substantial reduction of the American commitment overseas. While praising the goals of America's foreign-aid program, the report insisted that Italy, Canada, the United Kingdom, France, and Japan—nations recovered from the war and enjoying substantial prosperity—should contribute more to foreign aid because "the present burden is falling unfairly on the United States." It recommended that economic assistance to Africa, for example, should come from countries in western Europe that formerly had colonies there. The report opposed American aid to countries such as Yugoslavia and Poland, which did not share American political and economic ideals. It opposed aid to any government which fostered "socialism"—government-owned industrial and commercial enterprises which competed with private endeavors. Apparently impressed by the Clay report, President Kennedy promptly reduced his fiscal 1964 budget recommendations for foreign aid from $4.9 billion to $4.5 billion.

The debate over American security in a chaotic world doubtless will continue for years to come. Powerful sentiment in the United States has continued to call for reduction of American commitments overseas. Suggestions range from the modest withdrawal advocated in the Clay report to the total retreat demanded by members of the John Birch Society and the Daughters of the American Revolution, who would eliminate foreign aid, withdraw American membership from the United Nations, and expel the UN organization from the United States. Congress has shown marked sympathy for curtailment of foreign aid. Restrictive amendments to the recent Foreign Aid Act have required suspension of aid to any country expropriating privately owned United States property without "adequate" compensation, and have banned aid to communist countries "except in extraordinary circumstances." Objects of this latter amendment were Poland and Yugoslavia, two countries which have managed a certain freedom of thought and a quasi-independent relationship with the West which many Americans consider healthy and hopeful. Congress has shown determination to slash foreign aid, despite the remarkable appeal of Secretary of Defense Robert S. McNamara, who preferred reducing American military power. In hearings before the House Foreign Affairs Committee on April 8, 1963, McNamara warned that a return to isolationism "would lead not to self-preservation, but to slow suicide."

How will the debate progress? No one can say, but as long as the present world stalemate continues, there will be arguments in the United States over the nation's overseas commitments. And as long as western Europe and Japan enjoy rapid economic growth and booming prosperity—coupled with America's sluggish economy and outflow of gold—there will be determination to pass a larger share of the United States's burden of containing communism to its allies.

SUGGESTED READINGS

ACHESON, DEAN G.   *Power and Diplomacy.* Cambridge: Harvard University Press, 1958.

AGAR, HERBERT.   *The Price of Power: America since 1945.* Chicago: University of Chicago Press, 1957.

BEAL, JOHN R.   *John Foster Dulles: A Biography.* New York: Harper & Bros., 1957.

BOYD, ANDREW.   *United Nations: Piety, Myth and Truth.* Baltimore: Penguin Books, 1962.

BUCHAN, ALASTAIR.   *NATO in the 1960's: The Implications of Interdependence.* New York: Frederick A. Praeger, Inc., 1963.

CARLETON, WILLIAM G.   *The Revolution in American Foreign Policy: Its Global Range.* New York: Random House, 1963.

CASTLE, EUGENE W.   *The Great Giveaway: The Realities of Foreign Aid.* Chicago: Henry Regnery Co., 1957.

DEUTSCHER, ISAAC.   *The Great Contest: Russia and the West.* New York: Oxford University Press, 1960.

FARIS, DONALD K.   *To Plow with Hope.* New York: Harper & Bros., 1958.

GOLDMAN, ERIC F.   *The Crucial Decade—and After: America, 1945–1960.* New York: Alfred A. Knopf, Inc., 1960.

GRAEBNER, NORMAN A.   *Cold War Diplomacy, 1945–1960.* Princeton: Princeton University Press, 1962.

GRAEBNER, NORMAN A.   *The New Isolationism.* New York: Ronald Press Co., 1956.

JORDAN, AMOS A., JR. *Foreign Aid and the Defense of Southeast Asia.* New York: Frederick A. Praeger, Inc., 1962.

KENNAN, GEORGE F. *American Diplomacy, 1900–1950.* Chicago: University of Chicago Press, 1951.

KENNAN, GEORGE F. *Russia, the Atom, and the West.* New York: Harper & Bros., 1957.

KNORR, KLAUS (ed.). *NATO and American Security.* Princeton: Princeton University Press, 1959.

LISKA, GEORGE. *The New Statecraft: Foreign Aid in American Foreign Policy.* Chicago: University of Chicago Press, 1960.

LOEBER, THOMAS S. *Foreign Aid: Our Tragic Experiment.* New York: W. W. Norton & Co., Inc., 1961.

MCNEILL, WILLIAM H. *Greece: American Aid in Action, 1947–1956.* New York: Twentieth Century Fund, 1957.

MONTGOMERY, JOHN D. *The Politics of Foreign Aid: American Experience in Southeast Asia.* New York: Frederick A. Praeger, Inc., 1962.

MORGENTHAU, HANS J. *In Defense of the National Interest.* New York: Alfred A. Knopf, Inc., 1951.

OSGOOD, ROBERT E. *NATO: The Entangling Alliance.* Chicago: University of Chicago Press, 1962.

PRICE, HARRY B. *The Marshall Plan and Its Meaning.* Ithaca: Cornell University Press, 1955.

SALVADORI, MASSIMO. *NATO: A Twentieth-Century Community of Nations.* Princeton: Princeton University Press, 1957.

SETON-WATSON, HUGH. *Neither War Nor Peace: The Struggle for Power in the Postwar World.* New York: Frederick A. Praeger, Inc., 1962.

SPANIER, JOHN. *American Foreign Policy Since World War II.* New York: Frederick A. Praeger, Inc., 1962.

THOMPSON, KENNETH W. *Political Realism and the Crisis of World Politics.* Princeton: Princeton University Press, 1960.

Document 30.1

THE CASE FOR AND AGAINST THE MARSHALL PLAN

Secretary of State George C. Marshall outlined his plan for European recovery from the devastation of the second World War in an address at Harvard University on June 5, 1947. Over the next several months, there was much discussion of the so-called "Marshall Plan." A strong supporter, the veteran Kentucky Senator, Alben W. Barkley, explained Marshall's position in a speech over the National Broadcasting Company radio network on July 18, 1947.

(From *Congressional Record*, Vol. 93, Pt. 12, *Appendix*, July 24, 1947, pp. A3777–A3778)

I am glad of this opportunity to discuss with my listeners among the American people the proposal advanced by Secretary of State Marshall for coordinating all efforts in behalf of European recovery.

I take it for granted that no serious-minded American now doubts the necessity of American aid in the stabilization of Europe particularly, and it may be of other countries, especially parts of Asia.

While our Nation was not in any way responsible for World War II, which devastated vast areas of the earth's surface, and destroyed billions of dollars worth of property and of homes, and disorganized world economy more completely and universally than ever before, human destiny has placed upon our doorsteps the responsibility of aiding in the economic, moral, and political stabilization of the nations of the world in the interests of peace.

These efforts on our part are not dictated merely by the emotions of charity, worthy as they are. They are not based solely upon a Christian duty, which we acknowledge in our pews, but sometimes deny in our politics, to serve mankind in any way that may lift his standard of life, and his enjoyment of freedom and self-government.

These efforts on our part are justified on the sole ground of national self-interest, because we know that we cannot long prosper if the rest of the world lies prostrate, and we know that democracy in America and the Western Hemisphere cannot be safe and secure so long as it is in danger, or has been destroyed in the rest of the world.

Already we have granted aid in the way of loans to Great Britain, to France, to Poland, to China, and to Italy, and to some of the other nations of Europe. Almost overnight a situation developed in Greece and Turkey that made it necessary for us to come to their aid to the extent of $400,-000,000 in order that they might maintain their independence and the integrity of their nationality. It was my good fortune to be in Turkey and Greece during the discussion of these two loans in the Congress of the United States, and it was actually pathetic to observe the renewed faith and confidence that the Greek and Turkish people had in themselves and their own economic and political independence by even the prospect of help from the United States. . . .

In addition to these direct loans, we have afforded a large amount of aid in the form of food and materials, in order to help rebuild the economy of the devastated nations of Europe, and along with our allies, we have been compelled to assume a large and continuing obligation in the occupied sections of Germany.

General Marshall has recognized that this aid cannot continue indefinitely on a piecemeal basis. The industrial situation in Europe must be improved in order that the dwellers in the city may be able to purchase the food produced by the farmers. The exchange of food for industrial products between city and country, based upon the medium of a sound currency, constitutes the basis of economic prosperity. So long as the industrial workers of Europe, by reason of unemployment or pitifully low wages, or for any other economic reason, are unable to purchase the products of European farmers, outside efforts will have to be brought to bear to feed and clothe them until they can restore their own economy.

Hunger and despair breed anarchy and chaos. Destructive ideologies feed upon hunger and despair and hopelessness, and we know already, I regret to say, that there are certain nations in Europe who are, apparently, seeking to compound the suffering of the European people, in order that they may find a fertile field for the propagation of their totalitarian ideas among people of normal democratic habits and instincts. Realizing this situation, as it has become crystal clear in recent months, General Marshall, in his address at Harvard University, suggested that the nations of Europe come together and take account of their own situation, tabulate their needs, and make a survey of their own ability to help themselves, in order that they and we might know the situation from the standpoint of need and ability. In the meantime, the President of the United States has appointed three separate commissions to make a survey of our own resources and ability to aid the distressed nations of the world to get on their feet, and thereby restore their own political independence, and increase their ability to resist outside pressure.

These commissions will, undoubtedly, report as soon as it is humanly possible to gather all the facts.

In the meantime, the Foreign Ministers of Great Britain, France, and Russia, met in Paris recently for the purpose of discussing the possibility of a European conference to carry out the suggestions of our Secretary of State to take stock of European needs, not for the purpose of presenting us a one-sided bill for collection, but in order, by their mutual conference and mutual efforts, to determine what they can do for themselves, so that we may determine for ourselves how much of the balance we are able to do, as well as what other nations are able to contribute to the general results.

As so often happens, the Russian Foreign Minister made the conference of the three ministers impossible of success. He packed up his bags and returned to Moscow. Whereupon, Mr. Ernest Bevin, Foreign Minister of Great Britain, and Mr. Georges Bidault, Foreign Minister of

France, issued invitations for 22 European nations, including Russia and her satellites, to meet in conference in Paris to do what General Marshall suggested in his speech at Harvard University a few weeks before. So far Russia has declined, and 4 of her satellites have declined. One of them, Czechoslovakia, first accepted, but, under pressure from Moscow, withdrew the acceptance. But, if that nation had been free to accept upon their own responsibility, without outside pressure, they would be sitting in the Paris Conference today with the other European nations. I believe the same may be said of the other nations which declined, including Poland, Hungary, Rumania, and Bulgaria. But, be that as it may, there are 16 European nations now in session at Paris, seeking to take stock of their conditions, of their own abilities, in order that they and we may present a picture to the world and to our own people, which may be the basis of cooperative action designed to restore human happiness, human prosperity, and preserve the peace of the world by preserving it in every nation.

We do not know what will come out of this conference in Paris. It has begun its deliberations with commendable zeal and speed. It seems to have sensed the responsibility which rests upon the statesmen of Europe to tighten their belts and reduce their necessities to a figure which can be easily understood by those upon whom they call for assistance. It is impossible to speculate as to how much money it will be found these nations need from the outside world. But, we know that in order for the American people to put their hand to the plow with a determination which the situation may require, we must give them the facts. We must tell them the truth. General Marshall has emphasized this necessity in every utterance he has made, and I think the Congress of the United States recognizes the necessity of taking the American people into their confidence, insofar as it can be done. There are, of course, certain facts surrounding the conditions abroad, and certain delicate, diplomatic difficulties, which cannot be publicized, at least until all the facts are known. But, what we are trying to do, and our Secretary of State and President, and all of us, without regard to partisan politics, are trying to do, is organize our efforts upon a sound and stable basis, and organize the recuperative ability of all the nations who need help, so that they may not be led to believe that they may rely solely upon our own largess, in order that they may reap the benefits of a long and prosperous peace in the years to come.

We feel that the recovery of Europe is not a one-way street. We are willing to go the full length of the requirements, so long as we feel that the nations we are trying to help are, in good faith, trying to help themselves. We know that the peace of the world cannot be long maintained, if there is chaos in Europe and Asia. We know that democracy in America cannot be maintained if it is to be surrounded by the antithesis of democracy in every other continent of the world. Realizing this, the American people and American Government are willing to team up with every other nation that is, in good faith, seeking to help itself. We are willing to pull even the major part of the load, if necessary, in order that the vehicle may go forward—the vehicle of peace, of contentment, of happiness and confidence in the future—the vehicle of self-government, and of political and economic integrity in every nation whose independence is essential to the advancement of democratic ideals in all portions of the world and their preservation wherever they exist today.

It is, therefore, my view that this suggestion, or plan, or proposal, of General Marshall's, whatever it may be called, is one of the most constructive approaches to world rehabilitation that has been made, and it is my sincere hope and belief that, if the nations who are the victims of the ravages of war, and victims of internal and external pressures designed to eat into the foundation of their national integrity, rise to the opportunity which now faces them, by cooperating fully with our Government and among themselves, we shall find a solution of the problems that beset Europe and the rest of the world and constitute such a pall upon the horizon of liberty and democracy. We are willing to cooperate with all nations that are willing to cooperate with us. We would prefer to cooperate with every nation, regardless of the form of its government, but, if we cannot enlist all of them in this international effort to restore normal conditions, to restore employment, and production, and the stability of currencies, and all the other things so essential in the production of the essentials of happiness and contentment, we shall do the best we can to cooperate with those nations that are willing to meet us halfway on this highway to peace and progress.

There was less opposition to the Marshall Plan than one might have anticipated, considering America's isolationist traditions. Still there were critics, such as West Virginia's Republican Representatve, Hubert S. Ellis, who, on December 19, 1947, entered into the *Congressional Record* a statement by former Congressman Samuel B. Pettengill, Democrat of Indiana.

THE RAT HOLE OF ZLIN

(From the *Congressional Record*, Vol. 93, Pt. 13, *Appendix*, December 19, 1947, p. A4926)

Let's measure the Marshall plan with a yardstick we can understand. Let's apply it to what was once the largest shoe factory in the world—the Bata plant in Czechoslovakia. This plant was founded by a poor shoemaker's son in the tiny village of Zlin. He started with a capital of 800 florins. But he had something else. He had elbow grease and freedom. His plant grew until its 12,000 employees, making 75,000 shoes a day, had a world-wide market.

Last year, the Socialist government of Czechoslovakia took over the Bata plant. In 10 months, cash reserves of 1,000,000 crowns were wasted. Its debt was increased 300,000,000 crowns. Its directors, superintendents and foremen—2,000 men with the "know-how"—were kicked out. Shoe prices were raised out of reach. The morale of the workingmen was destroyed. It now takes four men to produce what one man had done.

Is General Marshall to pour his money and ours down that rat hole? Are American shoemakers to be taxed to make good the ruin caused not by the war, but by Socialist politicians? . . .

No one can understand $18,000,000,000. No one can understand Europe with its 25 nations, its 400,000,000 people who have hated and killed each other for centuries. But everyone can understand the rat hole at Zlin. It is only one of thousands. How do you help these 12,000 Bata families? How do you keep them fed as long as they have to live under the same government that ruined them?

Yet our State Department says we must not ask these Socialist governments to get off their people's backs as a condition for our aid. We might offend them, they say.

So, while these governments continue to redistribute the jobs to their armies of political retainers, are we to stuff the rat holes as fast as they dig them? (The increase in the number of bureaucrats under Attlee in England is one-third the number of her coal miners.) Are we to rebuild the trains blown up by their strikers? Fill their coal bins as they reduce their working hours?

WHAT IS PROSPERITY?

What does our prosperity consist of? Is it our automobiles, bathtubs, gadgets and dollars? No. These are only yardsticks. But these things are not the cause of our prosperity. They are the effect. The source of our prosperity is something far different. It is the American spirit, our initiative, our risk-taking, private property, and our Constitution which protected from confiscation those who have sweated and saved during 150 years. If all the gadgets were burned, the American spirit, if we retain it, could rebuild them in a few brief years.

Europe could rebuild, too, if it had the American spirit. Without it—fill in the answer yourself.

Are we to fill rat holes in Europe, and go socialist at home? . . .

Document 30.2

THE GREAT CHINA DEBATE

News arriving early in 1949 of communist victories in China—a country for which they always had special affection—came as a shock to Americans. A widely accepted view was that a fumbling United States policy of the years 1945–49 now was delivering the Far East to communism. One individual who spoke out in criticism of the China policy of recent Democratic administrations was a thirty-one-year-old Democratic Congressman from Boston, John F. Kennedy.

(From the *Congressional Record*, Vol. 95, Pt. 12, *Appendix*, February 21, 1949, p. A993)

Over these past few days we have learned the extent of the disasters befalling China and the United States. . . .

At the Yalta Conference in 1945 a sick Roosevelt, with the advice of General Marshall and other Chiefs of Staff, gave the Kurile Islands as well as the control of various strategic Chinese ports, such as Port Arthur and Darien, to the Soviet Union. . . .

Our policy in China has reaped the whirlwind. The continued insistence that aid would not be forthcoming unless a coalition government with the Communists was formed, was a crippling blow to the national government. So concerned were our diplomats and their advisers, the Lattimores and the Fairbanks, with the imperfections of the diplomatic system in China after 20 years of war, and the tales of corruption in high places, that they lost sight of our tremendous stake in a non-Communist China.

There were those who claimed, and still claim, that Chinese communism was not really communism at all but merely an advanced agrarian movement which did not take directions from Moscow.

Listen to the words of the Bolton report: "Its doctrines follow those of Lenin and Stalin. Its leaders are Moscow-trained (of 35 leading Chinese Communist political leaders listed in the report, over a half either spent some time or studied in Moscow). Its policies and actions, its strategy and tactics are Communist. The Chinese Communists have followed faithfully every zigzag of the Kremlin's line for a generation."

This is the tragic story of China whose freedom we once fought to preserve. What our young men had saved, our diplomats and our President have frittered away. . . .

The standard defense of America's China policy was that Chiang Kai-shek and the Chinese Nationalists fell before the communists not for want of American support, but in spite of it. Such was the position of Secretary of State Dean G. Acheson, who, on January 12, 1950, spoke before the National Press Club.

(From the *Congressional Record*, Vol. 96, Pt. 1, Senate, January 20, 1950, pp. 672–73)

. . . Let's come now to the matters which Asia has in common. There is in this vast area what we might call a developing Asian consciousness, and a developing pattern, and this, I think, is based upon two factors which are pretty nearly common to the entire experience of all these Asian people.

One of these factors is a revulsion against the acceptance of misery and poverty as the normal condition of life. Throughout all of this vast area, you have that fundamental revolutionary aspect in mind and belief. The other common aspect that they have is the revulsion against foreign domination. Whether that foreign domination takes the form of colonialism or whether it takes the form of imperialism, they are through with it. They have had enough of it and they want no more. . . .

Since the end of the war in Asia, we have seen over 500,000,000 people gain their independence and over seven new nations come into existence in this area.

We have the Philippines with 20,000,000 citizens. We have Pakistan, India, Ceylon, and Burma with 400,000,000 citizens, southern Korea with 20,000,000, and within the last few weeks, the United States of Indonesia with 75,000,000. . . .

Nobody, I think, says that the Nationalist Government fell because it was confronted by overwhelming military force which it could not resist. Certainly no one in his right mind suggests that. Now, what I ask you to do is to stop looking for a moment under the bed and under the chair and under the rug to find out these reasons, but rather to look at the broad picture and see whether something doesn't suggest itself.

The broad picture is that after the war, Chiang Kai-shek emerged as the undisputed leader of the Chinese people. Only one faction, the Communists, up in the hills, ill-equipped, ragged, a very small military force, was determinedly opposed to his position. He had overwhelming military power, greater military power than any ruler had ever had in the entire history of China. He had tremendous economic and military support and backing from the United States. He had the acceptance of all other foreign countries, whether sincerely or insincerely in the case of the Soviet Union is not really material to this matter. Here he was in this position and 4 years later what do we find? We find that his armies have melted away. His support in the country has melted away. His support largely outside the country has melted away and he is a refugee on a small island off the coast of China with the remnants of his forces.

As I said, no one says that vast armies moved out of the hills and defeated him. To attribute this to the inadequacy of American aid is only to point out the depth and power of the forces which were miscalculated or ignored. What has happened, in my judgment, is that the almost inexhaustible patience of the Chinese people in their misery ended. They did not bother to overthrow this government. There was really nothing to overthrow. They simply ignored it throughout the country. They took the solution of their immediate village problems into their own hands. If there was any trouble or interference with the representatives of the government, they simply brushed them aside. They completely withdrew their support from this government and when that support was withdrawn, the whole military establishment disintegrated. Added to the grossest incompetence ever experienced by any military command was this total lack of support both in the armies and in the country, and so the whole matter just simply disintegrated.

The Communists did not create this. The Communists did not create this condition. They did not create this revolutionary spirit. They did not create a great force which moved out from under Chiang Kai-shek. But they were shrewd and cunning to mount it, to ride this thing into victory and into power. . . .

Document 30.3

THE HISS CASE

The Alger Hiss perjury trial and revelation that a Soviet spy ring had secured American atomic secrets brought a wave of suspicion that communists had infiltrated the United States government and were "boring from within" to destroy the American system. Remarks by administration leaders—such as Secretary Acheson's statement that he would not turn his back on Alger Hiss and President Truman's reference to spy hunts as "red herrings"—provided potent ammunition to critics of recent American policies. Senator Edward Martin, Republican of Pennsylvania, speaking to his constituents on February 13, 1950, is typical of these critics.

(From the *Congressional Record,* Vol. 96, Pt. 13, *Appendix,* February 17, 1950, pp. A1175–A1176)

There is no doubt that the disclosures of the Alger Hiss trial have been tremendously important. Now no one can fail to be convinced—despite official denials—that Communists had worked their way into high places in our Government and were coloring our foreign and domestic policies.

I don't know whether these men have all been rooted out yet. I do know that much of their influence remains.

I do know that some of the policies which the Administration has been following at home and abroad are policies which Communists, or fellow travelers, or their innocent dupes, would set in motion and support.

Think that over. I'll come back to it later. . . .

I want to talk briefly about Dean Acheson, the Secretary of State. In the press and in my mail there have been many demands for his impeachment.

First of all, I am sure he is not a Communist. But I do believe he made a bad and indecent blunder when, after the conviction of Alger Hiss, Mr. Acheson said in effect that this traitor was his friend, and that even if the Supreme Court should uphold the conviction, he, Acheson, would not desert his friend.

Had Dean Acheson first resigned as Secretary of State, and then made that statement, it might have been a courageous and noble thing. He, as a private individual, would be standing by a friend. But Dean Acheson did not resign. He is not merely a private citizen.

Dean Acheson stands at the head of the department which makes, directs, and carries out the foreign policy for this Nation of 150,000,000 men, women, and children. Dean Acheson speaks not only for that department, but to the rest of the world he is the official spokesman for the United States.

Alger Hiss was formerly a high official of the State Department. Alger Hiss betrayed his country by stealing secrets of the State Department and transmitting them to a foreign dictatorship whose sole aim is to enslave the world by climbing over a prostrate America.

Thus we have the head of our State Department endorsing and supporting a man in his own department who resorted to perjury and hide his part in a disloyal conspiracy.

And, as I said earlier, Dean Acheson's policies regarding China and other places strongly indicate that he is the victim of policies laid down by Communists and Communist sympathizers, like Alger Hiss. . . .

Then Mr. Truman went on to make another charge. He declared that these investigations into a spy system working right here in Washington, in Government agencies, was—and I quote—"a red herring."

Surely you all remember that. It was the considered judgment of an administration which asks you to trust it to make foreign and domestic policy in your best interests.

There was still another Presidential statement in June 1948, when Mr.

Truman was pooh-poohing what he called a red herring. He said—and I quote:

"I went to Potsdam in 1945 * * * with the kindliest feelings toward Russia and we made certain agreements, specific agreements. I got very well acquainted with Joe Stalin and I like old Joe. He's a decent fellow." End of quote.

Do you folks all remember that?

My fellow Pennsylvanians, I have a confession to make.

I like old Harry. I believe that deep down he's a decent fellow.

But let me add this. I'd like old Harry a lot better if he would just confess error once in a while.

I'd like him a lot better if he'd admit to the country that he was wrong about the red herring and wrong about Joe Stalin.

I'd like him a lot better if he'd clamp down on his high officials so they would not go around extending the hand of friendship to traitors to our country.

I'd like him a lot better if he'd admit that a terrible blunder was made at Yalta—that a sick Franklin Roosevelt, influenced by Communist Alger Hiss, sold out anti-Communist China to Joe Stalin and the Soviet Union.

I'd like him a lot better if he would admit that he, Harry Truman, blundered terribly when, fooled by his pro-Communist advisers, he made a deal which gave us a zone of Berlin but without a highway leading to it, so that we had to use the airlift, and are having more trouble even now.

I'd like old Harry better if he'd admit error in the Chinese policy which caused us to sell out the Nationalists to the Communists.

But I guess he won't.

The disclosures of the Hiss case and the more recent revelation that atomic secrets have been betrayed to Soviet Russia make it imperative for every American to be on his guard. . . .

Document 30.4

THE POLICIES OF DEAN G. ACHESON

In his speech before the National Press Club on January 12, 1950, Secretary Acheson considered the question of American military security in the Pacific. He spoke of the American defensive perimeter—which did not include Korea. For five and one-half months, North Korean communists attacked South Korea, and soon critics were assailing Acheson for inviting the Red attack by omitting South Korea from the defensive perimeter. Acheson also spoke of United Nations guarantees, and his defenders have argued that these passages implied possible American intervention in case of armed aggression. Decide for yourself, from the following excerpt, whether the Secretary, in effect, invited Red aggression.

(From the *Congressional Record*, Vol. 96, Pt. 1, Senate, January 20, 1950, pp. 674–75)

In the first place, the defeat and the disarmament of Japan has placed upon the United States the necessity of assuming the military defense of Japan so long as that is required, both in the interest of our security and in the interests of the security of the entire Pacific area and in all honor in the interest of Japanese security. We have American and there are Australian troops in Japan. I am not in a position to speak for the Australians, but I can assure you that there is no intention of any sort of abandoning or weakening the defenses of Japan and that whatever arrangements are to be made, either through permanent settlement or otherwise, that defense must, and shall be, maintained.

This defensive perimeter runs along the Aleutians to Japan and then goes to the Ryukyus. We hold important defense positions in the Ryukyu Islands and those we will continue to hold. In the interest of the population of the Ryukyu Islands, we will at an appropriate time offer to hold these islands under trusteeship of the United Nations. But they are essential parts of the defensive perimeter of the Pacific and they must, and will be, held.

The defensive perimeter runs from the Ryukyus to the Philippine Islands. Our relations, our defensive relations with the Philippines, are contained in agreements between us. Those agreements are being loyally carried out and will be loyally carried out. Both peoples have learned by bitter experience the vital connections between our mutual defense requirements. We are in no doubt about that and it is hardly necessary for me to say an attack on the Philippines could not and would not be tolerated by the United States. But I hasten to add that no one perceives the imminence of any such attack.

So far as the military security of other areas in the Pacific is concerned, it must be clear that no person can guarantee these areas against military attack. But it must also be clear that such a guarantee is hardly sensible or necessary within the realm of practical relationship. Should such an attack occur—one hesitates to say where such an armed attack could come from—the initial reliance must be on the people attacked to resist it and then upon the commitments of the entire civilized world under the Charter of the United Nations which so far has not proved a weak reed to lean on by any people who are determined to protect their independence against outside aggression. But it is a mistake, I think, in considering Pacific and far-eastern problems to become obsessed with military considerations. Important as they are, there are other problems that press and these other problems are not capable of solution through military means. These other problems arise out of the susceptibility of many areas and many countries in the Pacific area to subversion and penetration. That cannot be stopped by military means. . . .

The fall of Nationalist China, the Hiss case, the Soviet spy ring, and Korea brought forth torrents of criticism of Secretary of State Dean G. Acheson. Many Americans demanded his resignation; and in the elections of 1950 and 1952, he became an object of virulent political attack. Yet, he was not without defenders. One interesting retort to the Acheson critics came from an important Republican newspaper.

(From the *San Francisco Chronicle*, December 2, 1950)

We're getting a little tired of that refrain. When an able man is doing an earnest and competent job in a difficult situation, and the fate of all of us depends upon how well he does the job, we favor letting him see it through. We have seen too often in history this situation: A calm and competent man of vision puts his case before a people. But the people are befuddled by hysteria and hysteria-mongers, and throw him out.

Secretary Acheson is doing such a job in such a situation. We don't happen to agree with his boss politically, but there can be only one President and one Secretary of State at a time, and while he's there he's representing all of us, Democrats, Republicans, Prohibitionists, and everyone else. If he loses it will be just as expensive for us as though we had put him there personally. So we want to give Acheson the leeway he needs. We don't want him loaded down with needless handicaps that are going to prevent him from serving us to the best of his ability.

He is currently being overburdened with that kind of handicap. We would estimate that the trouble he gets at the hands of Vishinsky and Stalin and Mao Tse-tung doesn't slow him down half so much as the trouble he gets from the Americans who keep bleating, "Throw him out, throw him out."

What has he done or failed to do to merit this kind of vicious carping? What's the bill of particulars against him?

The old China policy grudge is still the only thing the critics really hold against him. The Communists won in China, Chiang Kai-shek was whipped, and Acheson got the blame. All the weaknesses of Chiang's regime, the corruption that surrounded him, the eagerness with which his own forces deserted by the milions to the enemy camp—all that is forgotten or ignored. Acheson single-handedly defeated Chiang and turned China over to the Communists. That's the gist of the critics' argument, and Acheson has been built up as the great symbol of the failure of American foreign policy.

We don't go along with that.

We don't think, in the first place, that American foreign policy has failed—yet. Certainly, we could have done better in China, if we could have availed ourselves of second sight. But Acheson didn't have it, and neither did his critics. And we don't go along with the smug Monday-morning quarter-backing when, as now, there's far more pressing work ahead. . . .

Acheson has done a distinguished over-all job as Secretary of State. He has plugged patiently and ably for European strength and unity and won a fair degree of success there. He rose splendidly in the Korean crisis. He has championed the United Nations while turning back the Russian effort to convert it to an instrument of Soviet will. It was Acheson who came up with the answer to the Russian veto in the Security Council, and cleared the way for authority to be transferred to the veto-free Assembly, where it now resides. That was a stroke of master statesmanship, managing as it did to save the United Nations and enhance its authority. And now he has outlined a policy of long-range strategy that aims at rearing the maximum strength and unity by free nations while holding to the minimum the likelihood of world war III.

We doubt that Acheson could satisfy his tormentors by any move short of resigning, but if he undertook to follow their counsel on foreign policy we should have real cause for alarm. What they want, judging from the tenor of their criticism, is for the United States to sever all bonds with the United Nations, defy the friendly world, and set out along our solitary way to whip the communist empire.

We think Acheson's program, though admittedly more complicated, makes far more sense, and we support him in his effort to work it out under circumstances that grow more trying by the hour. . . .

Document 30.5

BIPARTISANSHIP IN FOREIGN AFFAIRS: EISENHOWER SUPPORTS "PROGRAMS OF MUTUAL SECURITY"

America's program of containing communism in all corners of the world, begun under the Democratic President Harry S. Truman, had the unqualified support of President Dwight D. Eisenhower, a Republican.

This was interesting, inasmuch as the Republican party, since 1920, had been the party of isolation. Eisenhower expressed his position in an address on May 21, 1957.

(From the *Congressional Record*, Vol. 107, Pt. 12, Senate, August 15, 1961, pp. 15915–17)

Just 1 week ago I talked with you about our Federal budget as a whole. Tonight I want to talk with you about one part of it : our mutual-security programs. These programs are the source of military and economic strength for our alliance throughout the free world. They form, in fact, a saving shield for freedom.

Although the cost of these programs amounts to only 5 percent of the budget, I am talking exclusively about them tonight for two simple reasons.

First.   In my judgment these programs do more than any other— dollar for dollar—in assuring the safety of our country and the peaceful lives of all of us.

Second.   They are the most misunderstood of any of the Federal Government's activities. Their nature, their purposes, their results are vitally important to all of us—but little known to many of us.

Their common label of "foreign aid" is gravely misleading—for it inspires a picture of bounty for foreign countries at the expense of our own. No misconception could be further from reality. These programs serve our own basic national and personal interests. . . .

. . . We must recognize that, whenever any country fails under the domination of communism, the strength of the free world—and of America—is by that amount weakened and communism strengthened. If this process, through our neglect or indifference, should proceed unchecked, our continent would be gradually encircled. Our safety depends upon recognition of the fact that the Communist design for such encirclement must be stopped before it gains momentum—before it is again too late to save the peace.

This recognition dictates two tasks. We must maintain a common worldwide defense against the menace of international communism. And we must demonstrate and spread the blessings of liberty—to be cherished by those who enjoy these blessings, to be learned and sought by those now denied them.

This is not a new policy nor a partisan policy.

Defense Cannot Be with Guns Alone

This is a policy for America that began 10 years ago when a Democratic President and a Republican Congress joined in a historic declaration. They then declared that the independence and survival of two countries, Greece and Turkey—then menaced by Communist aggression—were so important to the security of America that we would give them military and economic aid.

That policy saved those nations. And it did so without the cost of American lives.

That policy has since been extended to all critical areas of the world. It is expressed concretely in mutual-security treaties embracing 42 other nations. And these treaties reflect a solemn finding by the President and by the Senate that our own peace would be endangered if any of these countries were conquered by international communism.

The lesson of Greece and Turkey 10 years ago has been repeated in the saving of other lands and peoples. A recent example is the southeast Asian country of Vietnam, whose President has just visited us as our honored guest.

CRISIS IN SOUTHEAST ASIA

Two years ago it appeared that all southeast Asia might be overrun by the forces of international communism. The freedom and security of nations for which we had fought throughout World War II and the Korean war again stood in danger. The people of Vietnam responded bravely—under steadfast leadership.

But bravery alone could not have prevailed.

We gave military and economic assistance to the Republic of Vietnam. And we entered into a treaty—the Southeast Asia Security Treaty—which plainly warned that an armed attack against this area would endanger our own peace and safety, and that we would act accordingly. Thus Vietnam has been saved for freedom.

This is one of the nations where we have been spending large amounts of so-called "foreign aid." What could be plainer than the fact that this aid has served not only the safety of another nation—but also the security and interests of our own? . . .

When the Congress last year approved the mutual-security programs, I believed—as did many others—that it was time to review their whole concept. Since then careful studies have been completed by committees of the Congress, by competent private groups, and by two public groups of leading citizens from all walks of life.

All these studies unanimously agreed that these programs are vital to our national interest and must be continued.

Some important revisions in the structure of our programs were recommended by these various studies. And my message to the Congress today has proposed certain changes therein.

The whole design of this defense against Communist conspiracy and encirclement cannot be with guns alone. For the freedom of nations can be menaced not only by guns—but by the poverty that communism can exploit.

You cannot fight poverty with guns.

You cannot satisfy hunger with deadly ammunition.

Economic stability and progress—essential to any nation's peace and well being—cannot be assured merely by the firepower of artillery or the speed of jets.

And so our mutual security programs today—at a total cost of some $4 billion—are designed to meet dangers in whatever form they may appear. Thus, they have three key purposes:

First. To help friendly nations equip and support armed forces for their own and our defense.

Second. To help, in a sustained effort, less-advanced countries grow in the strength that can support freedom as their way of life.

Third. To meet emergencies and special needs affecting our own national security and interest.

Examining each of these purposes briefly, I speak first of the military aspect of these programs.

This accounts for about three-fourths of their total cost—just under $3 billion. This sum serves—indeed it belongs to—our own national defense. And to recognize that fact, I have today requested the Congress henceforth to appropriate funds for military assistance as part of the regular budget of the Department of Defense.

Our system of collective defense unites us with all those 42 countries with which we have defense treaties. It embraces the Organization of American States in this Western Hemisphere, and defense arrangements with many Far Eastern countries like Korea and the Republic of China. It includes our readiness to cooperate in the Middle East with any free country threatened by Communist aggression and seeking our aid.

In Europe this collective effort is symbolized by NATO—the 15 countries in the North Atlantic Treaty alliance. And NATO's strength involves much more than symbols. In addition to our forces, NATO has more than 80 trained divisions, Active and Reserve, some 5,000 modern aircraft, 600 major naval vessels. Here—as elsewhere throughout the world—our allies provide manpower, resources, and bases, while we help with weapons and military training.

COST OF STANDING ALONE

Here again we see in the most concrete and practical way how collective effort and collective security serve our own national good. For our Nation to try, completely alone, to counter the Communist military threat would be not only more hazardous strategy; it would also be far more costly.

It would demand many billions of dollars more in defense expenditures.

It would mean raising the draft calls throughout our land. It would mean more of our sons in uniform. It would mean longer service for them. . . .

Now let us look at mutual security on the economic front.

The peril here can be just as great to us as in the military arena.

Today in many countries 1 billion free people—across three continents—live in lands where the average yearly income of each man is $100 or less. These lands include the 19 nations that have won their independence since World War II. Most of them are on the frontier of the Communist world, close to the pressure of Communist power. For centuries the peoples of these countries have borne a burden of poverty. Now they are resolved to hold on to political independence, they are resolved to achieve the economic strength to sustain that independence and to support rising standards of living.

In these lands no government can justify rule, or even survive, which does not reflect this resolve, which does not offer its people hope of progress. And wherever moderate government disappears, Communist extremists will extend their brand of despotic imperialism.

Our own strength would suffer severely from the loss to the Communists of these lands and of their people and resources. But, as these lands improve their standards of living, they will be stronger allies in defense of freedom. And there will be widening opportunity for trade with them.

We seek to help these people to help themselves.

We cannot export progress and security to them.

Essentially, they must achieve these for themselves. But there are practical ways by which we can help—especially in the early struggles of these young nations to survive.

For one thing, they need the knowledge of skilled people—farm experts, doctors, engineers—to teach new techniques to their people. Our program of technical cooperation aims to do this. It will cost $150 million next year. . . .

In this whole program, we do not seek to buy friends.

We do not seek to make satellites.

We do seek to help other peoples to become strong and to stay free—and learn, through living in freedom, how to conquer poverty, how to know the blessings of peace and progress.

This purpose—I repeat—serves our own national interest.

It also reflects our own national character. We are stirred not only by calculations of self-interest but also by decent regard for the needs and hopes of all our fellow-men. I am proud of this fact, as you are. None of us would wish it to be otherwise.

This is not mere sentimentality. This is the very nature of America— the spiritual nature of America—realistically understood and applied.

If ever we were to lose our sense of brotherhood, our sense of kinship with all freemen, we would have entered upon our Nation's period of decline. Without vision—without a quick sense of justice and compassion—no people can claim greatness.

Now, there remains—in addition to continuing defense and economic aid—a final aspect to our mutual security programs. This entails assistance to meet various special needs, including sudden crises against which prior planning is impossible. Such crises generally demand the swiftest action.

We have seen several such examples in recent years. . . .

All such situations—as in Iran, Guatemala, Jordan—have been tense moments in the world struggle. Each such moment vitally touches our own national interest.

I have asked the Congress for the sum of $300 million to enable us to act—and to act swiftly—in any such moment as it may strike.

Only such part of that sum will be used as is clearly needed to serve our national interest. But the history of these years surely means one thing: To give saving help at such moments is true economy on a world scale—for it can mean the saving of whole nations and the preservation of peace.

These, then, are the kinds of help and action that make up our mutual security programs, for which I have asked the Congress to appropriate less than $4 billion—one-twentieth of our national budget. This is not a mathematical guess or an arbitrary sum. It reflects economies already achieved in some aspects of military aid.

It is a reasoned figure.

And, considering the issues at stake, it is a minimum figure.

I know of no more sound or necessary investment that our Nation can make. I know of no expenditure that can contribute so much—in the words of the Constitution—to our common defense and to securing the blessings of liberty for ourselves and our posterity.

It is not always easy to see all the day-to-day results of these programs in concrete terms. They operate in distant lands whose histories, even their names, seem remote. Often the results are not swift and dramatic, but gradual and steady. They operate rather like police or fire protection in our own cities. When they are least in the news, they are doing their most effective work.

We live at a time when our plainest task is to put first things first. Of all our current domestic concerns—lower taxes, bigger dams, deeper harbors, higher pensions, better housing—not one of these will matter if our Nation is put in peril. For all that we cherish and justly desire—for ourselves or our children—the securing of peace is the first requisite.

We live in a time when the cost of peace is high.

Yet the price of war is higher and is paid in different coin—with the lives of our youth and the devastation of our cities.

The road to this disaster could easily be paved with the good intentions of those blindly striving to save the money that must be spent as the price of peace.

It is no accident that those who have most intimately lived with the horrors of war are generally the most earnest supporters of these programs to secure peace.

To cripple our programs for mutual security in the false name of "economy" can mean nothing less than a weakening of our Nation.

To try to save money at the risk of such damage is neither conservative nor is it constructive.

It is reckless.

It could mean the loss of peace. It could mean the loss of freedom. It could mean the loss of both.

I know that you would not wish your Government to take such a reckless gamble.

I do not intend that your Government take that gamble.

I am convinced of the necessity of these programs of mutual security—for the very safety of our Nation. For upon them critically depends all that we hold most dear—the heritage of freedom from our fathers, the peace and well-being of the sons and daughters who will come after us. . . .

Document 30.6

MAC ARTHUR VERSUS TRUMAN

Following the military disasters in Korea of November and December, 1950, American enthusiasm for the Korean War declined perceptibly. Then, in the spring of 1951 came the debate between General Douglas A. MacArthur, Supreme Commander in the Far East, and the Truman administration over the desirability of extending the war by bombing communist bases in China. When this debate led to dismissal of MacArthur, a popular hero of both the first and second world wars, there was a sharp public protest. In a radio address on April 12, 1951, President Truman attempted to explain America's determination to resist Red aggression in Korea and at the same time avoid extending the war.

(From the *Congressional Record*, Vol. 97, Pt. 12, *Appendix*, April 12, 1951, pp. A1981–A1983)

I want to talk plainly to you tonight about what we are doing in Korea and about our policy in the Far East.

In the simplest terms what we are doing in Korea is this: We are trying to prevent a third world war.

I think most people in this country recognized that fact last June. And they warmly supported the decision of the Government to help the Republic of Korea against the Communist aggressors. But many persons, even some who applauded the decision to defend Korea, have forgotten the basic reason for our action.

It is right for us to be in Korea. It was right last June. It is right today.

I want to remind you why this is true.

The Communists in the Kremlin are engaged in a monstrous conspiracy to stamp out freedom all over the world. If they were to succeed, the United States would be numbered among their principal victims. It must be clear to everyone that the United States cannot—and will not—sit idly by and await foreign conquest. The only question is: When is the best time to meet the threat and how?

The best time to meet the threat is in the beginning. It is easier to put out a fire in the beginning when it is small than after it has become a roaring blaze.

And the best way to meet the threat of aggression is for the peace-loving nations to act together. If they don't act together, they are likely to be picked off, one by one.

Assaults Inaction of Thirties

If they had followed the right policies in the 1930's—if the free countries had acted together, to crush the aggression of the dictators, and if they had acted in the beginning, when the aggression was small—there probably would have been no World War II.

If history has taught us anything, it is that aggression anywhere in the world is a threat to peace everywhere in the world. When that aggression is supported by the cruel and selfish rulers of a powerful nation who are bent on conquest, it becomes a clear and present danger to the security and independence of every free nation.

This is a lesson that most people in this country have learned thoroughly. This is the basic reason why we joined in creating the United Nations. And, since the end of World War II, we have been putting that lesson into practice—we have been working with other free nations to check the aggressive designs of the Soviet Union before they can result in a third world war.

That is what we did in Greece, when that nation was threatened by the aggression of international communism.

The attack against Greece could have led to general war. But this country came to the aid of Greece. The United Nations supported Greek resistance. With our help, the determination and efforts of the Greek people defeated the attack on the spot.

Another big Communist threat to peace was the Berlin blockade. That, too, could have led to war. But again it was settled because free men would not back down in an emergency.

The aggression against Korea is the boldest and most dangerous move the Communists have yet made.

The attack on Korea was part of a greater plan for conquering all of Asia. . . .

We do not want to see the conflict in Korea extended. We are trying to prevent a world war—not to start one. The best way to do that is to make it plain that we and the other free countries will continue to resist the attack.

But you may ask, why can't we take other steps to punish the aggressor? Why don't we bomb Manchuria and China itself? Why don't we assist Chinese Nationalist troops to land on the mainland of China?

POINTS TO RISK OF WORLD WAR

If we were to do these things we would be running a very grave risk of starting a general war. If that were to happen, we would have brought about the exact situation we are trying to prevent.

If we were to do these things we would become entangled in a vast conflict on the continent of Asia and our task would become immeasurably more difficult all over the world.

What would suit the ambitions of the Kremlin better than for our military forces to be committed to a full-scale war with Red China? . . .

I have thought long and hard about this question of extending the war in Asia. I have discussed it many times with the ablest military advisers in the country. I believe with all my heart that the course we are following is the best course.

I believe that we must try to limit the war to Korea for these vital reasons: To make sure that the precious lives of our fighting men are not wasted; to see that the security of our country and the free world is not needlessly jeopardized; and to prevent a third world war.

A number of events have made it evident that General MacArthur did not agree with that policy. I have, therefore, considered it essential to relieve General MacArthur so that there would be no doubt or confusion as to the real purpose and aim of our policy.

It was with the deepest personal regret that I found myself compelled to take this action. General MacArthur is one of our greatest military commanders. But the cause of world peace is more important than any individual.

The change in commands in the Far East means no change whatever in the policy of the United States. We will carry on the fight in Korea with vigor and determination in an effort to bring the war to a speedy and successful conclusion. . . .

Dismissal of General Douglas A. MacArthur and the military situation in the Far East brought a seven-week investigation by the Joint Armed Services and Foreign Relations committees of the Senate in May and June, 1951. The committees issued no formal report, but Republican members prepared a statement of their findings and conclusions on such topics as Truman's removal of MacArthur, alleged diplomatic bungling which had brought disaster in the Far East, Truman's method of committing American forces to Korea, and the administration's policy of limited objectives in Korea.

(From the *Congressional Record*, Vol. 97, Pt. 15, *Appendix*, October 20, 1951, pp. A6849–A6850)

I. The President's Removal of General MacArthur

1. While the President's authority for the removal of a military officer is readily conceded, his method of removal was ill-advised and the reasons assigned for the removal were utterly inadequate to justify the act.

2. General MacArthur had never violated any military directives.

3. There was no serious disagreement between General MacArthur and the Joint Chiefs of Staff as to military strategy in Korea.

4. The military in no way initiated or recommended the recall of General MacArthur.

5. The sincerity of MacArthur's motives in recommending military policy to end the Korean conflict in victory remains unquestioned. Throughout the hearings, many tributes were paid to his integrity, abil-

ity, and accomplishments. His contribution toward preventing the spread of communism in Japan is universally acknowledged.

II. Diplomatic Bungling and Unpreparedness That Led to War

1. The administration's Far East policy has been a catastrophic failure, and sole responsibility for this failure rests with the State Department. Far-eastern policy was never a part of the so-called bipartisan foreign policy.

2. The foreign policy of the United States since the middle 1940's has been based on expediency rather than the principles of liberty and justice. Our military victory of 1945 in the Pacific has been squandered by our diplomats.

3. Yalta—a great tragedy of American diplomacy—was the turning point of American Far East foreign policy. The myths that Russian participation in the Japanese War was a military necessity, and that the Yalta concessions were necessary to achieve that participation, have been adequately refuted.

4. The advice and information of our ablest and most experienced officials has been ignored. Ambassador Hurley was not informed of the Yalta agreements; Admiral Leahy's advice on the lack of necessity for Russian entry into the Pacific war was not followed. General MacArthur was not consulted on the Far East situation when Marshall went to China, as Special Ambassador in 1945, nor was he consulted in 1950 before the President's decision to fight in Korea; General Wedemeyer's recommendations on China and Korea were ignored and suppressed; Admiral Badger's advice on the need for military assistance to the Republic of China was not accepted.

5. It has not been the consistent policy of the United States to support the Republic of China; some United States officials were so opposed to Chiang Kai-shek that they were automatically on the side of the Red regime. Despite administration claims that it is the "firm and continuing" policy of the United States to support the Nationalist Government, the record is replete with evidence of a lack of both moral and material support.

6. The administration has been unduly preoccupied with the defense of America in Europe to the neglect of the defense of America in Asia. If the Republic of China had received effective military aid from the United States as late as 1948, the Chinese Communists might have been defeated. The myth that the Republic of China fell because the Chinese troops refused to fight is again refuted by sworn testimony.

7. Throughout the hearings, it was not possible to determine who wrote the 1945 mission to China instructions for General Marshall. Under these orders he was to bring about the "unification of China" by encouraging acceptance of Communist officials into the anti-Communist Chiang Kai-shek government on a coalition basis, at a time when Russian domination of Chinese Communists was already known to United State officialdom.

8. The administration believed that Chinese Communists would work in harmony with the Nationalists in a coalition government despite our previous experience that the Communist objective is invariably to take over, "lock, stock, and barrel," any government of which Communists become a part.

9. The propaganda campaign against the Chinese Nationalist Government and the attacks on the leadership of Chiang Kai-shek were vicious. Mismanagement and corruption are not confined to the Orient; it ill behooves the Government of the United States to cast the first stone.

10. The State Department directive of December 23, 1949—announcing to our Foreign Service officers that Formosa was not of strategic importance to the United States and that control of Formosa by the Communists would not imperil our Far East position—was a policy statement calculated to prepare the way for the abandonment of Formosa to the Chinese Reds.

11. The military potential of the United States has not been maintained at a level commensurate with our potential commitments or financial expenditures since VJ-day. From 1945 to the outbreak of the Korean war, $95,000,000,000 was spent on national defense; yet General Vandenberg testified that we still have only a "shoestring" Air Force, and Generals Marshall, Bradley, and Collins acknowledged the inadequacy of our present defenses.

12. The failure of the United States Government to train adequately and to supply equipment to the South Koreans made them tempting targets of aggression. Since the State Department and the United Nations [have] the sole responsibility in Korea, they must answer also for the failure of the intelligence missions to anticipate the June 25, 1950, attack.

13. The publication of the 1947 Wedemeyer report on Korea might have alerted the Government and the people of the United States; but General Marshall, then Secretary of State, suppressed the report.

14. The problem of Communist infiltration in our Government is still unsolved. It is difficult to secure information from an administration which is determined to keep the facts from the Congress and the people.

III. Presidential Action and United States–United Nations Conduct of the War

1. The involvement of the United States Armed Forces in the Korean conflict is without precedent in American history. Congress has not declared war nor has the President proclaimed a state of war. The Korean conflict, with its 200,000 American casualties, is improperly labeled a "police action." The United States should never again become involved in war without the consent of Congress.

2. Political considerations have prevented full exploitation of American air and naval superiority in the Korean war. The Secretary of State has assumed military functions. Despite these facts, our Armed Forces in Korea have acquitted themselves with a gallantry unsurpassed in our history.

3. The command function delegated to the United States by the United Nations has not worked out in practice and has been subjected to veto by a minority of participating nations. There has been a lack of adequate military support from United Nations allies; at the same time, we are unable to comprehend why the administration has persisted in its attitude of refusing the offer of 33,000 fighting men advanced by Chiang Kai-shek. Some of our allies, moreover, have displayed an unfortunate attitude with respect to economic sanctions against Red China.

4. The thirty-eighth parallel in Korea has no military significance, and its political significance has never been satisfactorily explained by anyone in the administration.

IV. Prospects of Achieving a Decisive Victory and Peace

1. The administration has no positive plan for achieving a decisive victory. The successful completion of the Korean conflict is essential since the United States cannot afford the costly destruction of its manpower. The immoral policy of a military strategy which involves merely the killing of more Chinese Communists is unlikely to produce victory or to enhance the stature of the United States in the family of nations.

2. The risk of precipitating world war III through adoption of a positive program for victory in Korea is no greater now than before. It is utterly inconsistent for the administration to take the calculated risk of provoking Russia in Europe through the Atlantic Pact while cowering at taking a similar risk in Asia.

3. The limited war now being fought in Korea by the United States is impossible to define. Cessation of hostilities, based upon restoration of

the status quo at the thirty-eighth parallel, will be a victory for aggression. Any peace short of the liberation and unification of Korea is a delusion. Any settlement at the thirty-eighth parallel is a Chinese Communist victory. The termination of hostilities in Korea will not eliminate responsibility in that area.

4. The United States will not allow Formosa to fall into hostile hands. It will continue to support the Government of the Republic of China. In the MacArthur hearings, no administration official advocated the unseating of the Nationalist Government or the seating of the Communist government of China in the United Nations. Time will tell whether the administration will hold to this admirable determination.

Document 30.7

THE POLICIES OF JOHN FOSTER DULLES

President Dwight D. Eisenhower's secretary of state, John Foster Dulles, in November, 1954, spoke on the goal of American foreign policy. In this address, he spoke of the need for constant military vigilance and of the importance of spiritual resources, a characteristic of his approach to diplomacy.

(From the *Congressional Record*, Vol. 100, Pt. 12, Senate, November 30, 1954, pp. 16182-84)

Let me begin by emphasizing the goal of our foreign policy—it is to enable you and me and our children to enjoy in peace the blessings of liberty. That purpose is back of everything we do.

The task is not an easy one, for international communism threatens both peace and liberty, by many means, at many places.

COEXISTENCE

One ever-present danger is the danger of being fooled into dropping our guard before the peril is really past.

The international Communists are masters at the trick of using words which mean one thing to them and another thing to us.

It took us time to learn that the word "democracy" means, to Communists, a dictatorship—what they call "dictatorship of the proletariat." . . .

Now the tricky word is "coexistence." To us it means tolerance of differences. It remains to be seen what it means to international Communists. It is true that the Russian Communists have recently talked more softly. But it is equally true that the Chinese Communists have talked and acted with increasing violence. They break their armistice agreements and they outrage the elemental decencies of international conduct.

Perhaps international communism is trying by a new way to divide the free nations. They seek to be soothing in Europe. They are provocative in Asia. . . .

DEFENSE OF THE UNITED STATES AGAINST ARMED ATTACK

There are some people in the United States, and there are more in other lands, who contend that it is wrong to be ready and able to fight. They say that the true peace-lovers should be unarmed and neutral.

We have tried that and it did not work.

We were unarmed and neutral in 1914 when the First World War came. The aggressors felt that they could count us out.

We were unarmed and neutral in 1939 when the Second World War came. Again the aggressors thought they could count us out.

The Korean war came after we had largely disarmed, and withdrawn our troops from Korea, and the aggressors thought that they would be unopposed.

Today we take a different view. We believe that the greatest contribution we can make to peace is to be ready to fight, if need be, and to have the resources and the allies to assure that an aggressor would surely be defeated. That does not mean being truculent or provocative or militaristic. It does mean seeking peace not only with the heart, but also with the mind.

In that mood, we make military preparations which, we believe, will deter war. That requires, basically, that a potential aggressor shall not think that aggression is a paying proposition. He must know that he cannot destroy the United States by sudden attack and that we have the capacity to counterattack.

So, we are developing continental defense in a major way. It will consist of an elaborate series of early warning systems and interceptors which apply the latest scientific knowledge. These should enable us to knock down a very high percentage of any Red bombers engaged in hostile missions against the United States.

Then, we have our Strategic Air Command which is capable of delivering retaliatory blows against vital parts of the Soviet Union. These blows, we calculate, would do damage far in excess of that which Red planes could inflict upon the United States.

You may ask what foreign policy has to do with this. My answer is: everything. Our continental defense system depends on Canada. And the free nations cannot have effective retaliatory power to deter aggression without airfields in widely scattered places.

Therefore, a vital part of our foreign policy is to have friendly relations with many other countries so that we can work together for our common defense.

I can report that we do have such friendly relations, and that, as a result, we can make it unprofitable for any nation to attack the United States. . . .

THE CAPTIVE PEOPLES

There is one final aspect of our policies to which I would allude. We believe, as Abraham Lincoln said, that our Declaration of Independence, promises "liberty, not alone to the people of this country, but hope for the world for all future time."

Today, a third of the human race is in fearful bondage to Communist dictatorships. But we do not regard that as immutable.

There is, we know, vast human discontent among the 800 million people whom international communism rules. That comes from the enslavement of labor, the suppression of religion and of individual initiative, and the national humiliation of the satellite countries.

Liberation normally comes from within. But it is more apt to come from within if hope is constantly sustained from without. That we are doing in many ways. . . .

CONCLUSION

There is often a tendency on the part of free peoples to see their own faults and weaknesses and to exaggerate the strength and successes of others. Of course, we should subject ourselves to constant self-criticism. That is the way to betterment.

We need not, however, feel that we are now failing in the great struggle which has been forced upon us. We are entitled to be confident because we are strong in ourselves and strong in the good partnership we have with our allies.

The reality of the matter is that the United States, by every standard of measurement, is the world's greatest power not only materially but spiritually. We have national policies which are clear and sound. They fit a civilization based on religious faith. They are strongly implemented and at a cost we can afford to live with. They have evolved on a non-partisan basis and, in broad outline, they are overwhelmingly backed by our people. Such policies, I am supremely confident, will peacefully prevail.

Secretary John Foster Dulles, in 1954, reiterated the policy of "massive retaliation." This meant that if the communists challenged the noncommunist world at any point, they—presumably the Russians and the Chinese—faced the threat of a full-scale nuclear retaliatory blow by the United States. Dulles sought to assuage fears which the policy inspired in the Western world by stating that the capacity to retaliate instantly did not impose the necessity of unleashing atomic weapons in each case of attack. Still, many Americans and western Europeans feared that massive retaliation narrowed the range of choice to total inaction or the atomic mushroom cloud. A chief advantage of massive retaliation, of course, was that it seemed to provide more security for less cost—"a bigger bang for a buck," in the parlance of 1954. It seemed less expensive to rely on a few menacing atomic weapons than upon a range of guns, tanks, warships, and airplanes with masses of soldiers, sailors, and airmen.

(From John Foster Dulles, "Policy for Security and Peace," *Foreign Affairs*, April, 1954, pp. 353–64)

. . . Most areas within the reach of an aggressor offer less value to him than the loss he would suffer from well-conceived retaliatory measures. Even in such areas, however, local defense will always be important. In every endangered area there should be a sufficient military establishment to maintain order against subversion and to resist other forms of indirect aggression and minor satellite aggressions. This serves the indispensable need to demonstrate a purpose to resist, and to compel any aggressor to expose his real intent by such serious fighting as will brand him before all the world and promptly bring collective measures into operation. Potential aggressors have little respect for peoples who have no will to fight for their own protection or to make the sacrifices needed to make that fighting significant. Also, they know that such peoples do not attract allies to fight for their cause. For all of these reasons, local defense is important. But in such areas the main reliance must be on the power of the free community to retaliate with great force by mobile means at places of its own choice.

A would-be aggressor will hesitate to commit aggression if he knows in advance that he thereby not only exposes those particular forces which he chooses to use for his aggression, but also deprives his other assets of "sanctuary" status. That does not mean turning every local war into a world war. It does not mean that if there is a Communist attack somewhere in Asia, atom or hydrogen bombs will necessarily be dropped on the great industrial centers of China or Russia. It does mean that the free world must maintain the collective means and be willing to use them in the way which most effectively makes aggression too risky and expensive to be tempting. . . .

Initially this reshaping of the military program was misconstrued in various respects. Some suggested that the United States intended to rely wholly on large-scale strategic bombing as the sole means to deter and counter aggression. What has already been said should dispose of this erroneous idea. The potential of massive attack will always be kept in a state of instant readiness, but our program will retain a wide variety in the means and scope for responding to aggression. Others interpreted the program as a move away from collective security. The exact opposite is the case, as has been shown. Our policies are based squarely on a collective security system and depend for their success on its continuing vitality. Still others feared that we intended to withdraw our forces from abroad in the interest of mobility. Now that the fighting is ended in Korea, our forces in the Far East will be reduced in numbers, as has previously been announced, but the kind of force that remains will have great striking power. Moreover, the program does not mean that we intend to pull our forces out of Europe. It is, of course, essential that the continental nations themselves provide a harmonious nucleus of integrated defense. If they do so, the United States would expect to maintain substantial forces of its own in Europe, both in support of the forward strategy of defense and for political reasons. . . .

Document 30.8

THE COMMUNIST CHALLENGE: TWO VIEWPOINTS

Early in the 1960's, Americans—smarting under defeat in Cuba and feeling the effect of Soviet pressure in West Berlin, Laos, and South Vietnam—debated the question of how the United States should respond to such developments. Should the United States risk nuclear war to eliminate Fidel Castro from Cuba or save West Berlin from Nikita Krushchev? Counsel for moderation and caution came from Senator Wayne Morse, Democrat of Oregon.

(From the *Congressional Record*, Vol. 107, Pt. 10, Senate, July 20, 1961, pp. 13987–88)

. . . There must not be a time when Soviet Russia, or Communist China, can be permitted to believe that a military aggression on the part of either one will go unchallenged or unresisted. It must be evident at all times that the Communist powers have nothing whatever to gain, but do have everything to lose, from an aggressive action.

As President Kennedy has put it: "The NATO shield was long ago extended to cover West Berlin, and we have given our word that an attack upon that city would be regarded as an attack upon us all." I have not the slightest doubt that the United States would live up to its pledges, nor have I the slightest doubt that the American people would support whatever effort is necessary to make those pledges good.

But in my opinion, there is much more to this matter than has yet been discussed as much as it deserves. It relates to the frequency with which we hear that our only two alternatives are either to surrender to the Russians which is unthinkable, or to destroy both ourselves and Russia with a nuclear war.

No one ever described a nuclear war between two nations more accurately than did General MacArthur in his recent visit to the Philippines, when he called it double suicide. General MacArthur moved the American occupation forces into Japan after years of assault upon it with bombing planes, and after the dropping of just two atomic bombs by the United States. Many of you here today saw that result. All of you know what modern war does to civilian populations. Casualties today are not suffered just by the soldiers on a distant battlefield.

In World War II, London was as much a battlefield as El Alamein, and the Netherlands was destroyed not on any battlefield at all, but at Rotterdam. The casualties are not soldiers in modern war, but women, children, and the elderly, too.

With the exception of the American Civil War, we have fought our enemies on territory outside the United States.

We are now confronted with the unpleasant fact that the next war will see Charleston, W. Va., and Portland, Oreg., objects of devastation and mass death.

The scientists who discuss this subject with the Senate Foreign Relations Committee, of which I am a member—and they are the same scientists who devised the nuclear weapons with which the American forces are now armed—freely predict that a nuclear war with Russia would produce between 30 and 50 million casualties in the United States. They indicate that as few as 50 intercontinental missiles armed with nuclear warheads landing on the North American Continent would render the United States and Canada almost uninhabitable for many decades.

This is one aspect of a nuclear war that is seldom mentioned in the United States. But before we allow our emotions over Berlin to run away with us, we must remember that the United States has as much to lose as Russia has in a nuclear war.

A second part of the nuclear war talk that seldom comes up is what the political situation would be when it was over. Again, I express only a personal opinion, but I believe a nuclear war between ourselves and Russia would obliterate Berlin, along with our own two countries, and that Communist China would probably be left as the most powerful nation in the world.

It is one of the sad facts of war that the issue on which it began is not usually around at the end, but instead a whole new series of problems has been created by the war itself.

Suppose that some specific action of the Communists to interfere with our access into Berlin occurs, and we respond as so many of our military planners have recommended—with a nuclear strike against Russia? There is virtually no chance that we could avoid the retaliation of Soviet missiles.

I think that the result would be not the protection of Berlin, or of our rights there, but its destruction. Neither would the Soviet Union or the United States have protected itself, but only destroyed iself in exchange for destroying its enemy.

Moreover, we all know that modern war is not the breeding ground of prosperity and liberty, but of misery and revolution. In this century, it has been wars which have given communism its greatest opportunity to seize power, and it has only been where the United States has stepped in afterward, as we did in Europe with the Marshall plan, that we have saved these areas from Communist domination. The cost is one we are still paying in foreign aid, and this year it is going to cost us some $4 billion.

What I am saying is that destruction of the Soviet Union will not destroy communism, especially when there is no longer a rich and powerful United States left in the picture, either.

The loss of a significant portion of America's wealth and our capacity to help finance freedom in other countries would pull down the great dike against communism in the underdeveloped continents of Asia, Africa, and South America.

It is well to keep these things in mind as we talk about Berlin, because a nuclear war resulting from this contest will have far-reaching consequences. We ought to consider those consequences carefully before we make such an irrevocable decision.

I am not saying it will not come to such a decision, or that anything is better than a nuclear war.

But what I am saying is that the United States must make every effort, try every path, and use every means of finding a way to preserve our rights and the freedom of Berlin without nuclear war.

A different view came from Senator Barry Goldwater, Republican of Arizona, who believed the United States had not reacted vigorously and courageously to communist challenges in the era since 1945. He deplored peaceful coexistence with communism as a farce and a disgrace, and urged the United States to place less emphasis upon the opinions of so-called "neutral" nations when establishing policy. He declined to advocate nuclear retaliation to each communist challenge, although insisting that there was no substitute for victory. Goldwater believed that if the United States displayed willingness to unleash its atomic power, the communists would retreat in Cuba, South America, Berlin, and southeast Asia. But Goldwater's critics charged that his policies, carried to their logical conclusion, could end only in an atomic holocaust. The Senator outlined his views in a speech before the Virginia State Bar Association in August, 1961.

(From the *Congressional Record*, Vol. 107, Pt. 12, Senate, August 16, 1961, pp. 15952–54)

. . . If there is any doubt as to what victory in the cold war means, let me say that it means the opposite of defeat; it means freedom instead of slavery; it means the right of every man to worship God; of nations to determine [their] own destiny free of force and coercion. Victory in the cold war means the sum total of all the hopes of freemen throughout the world. It means human dignity, freedom of choice, the right to work, and achieve with the skills and capabilities with which man was endowed by his Creator. And it means peace with honor for men who prize liberty above death.

Now, can victory be achieved without a nuclear war? Senator Fulbright would like us to believe that there can be no cold war victory without the destruction of civilization. This is precisely what the Communists and the Russians also would like us to believe. Their whole line of attack, through propaganda and adroit economic, political and military moves, is directed toward making us think in terms of fear. They want to make sure that we believe the risk is too great to employ any of our strength. Their purpose is intimidation and it's working too well.

Indeed, a cold war victory over the Communists is entirely possible. It won't be easy because we have lost too much valuable time and too many golden opportunities. But it can be done with the proper integrated strategy—a strategy that aims at victory, that retains our economic strength; that incorporates the principles of political, military, economic, and psychological strength in meeting Soviet challenges and in presenting some challenges of our own. Those who argue against any use of strength, against any military risk, against any unilateral action fail to understand that political victory in the cold war is the only way to avoid a strictly military solution of the East-West crisis. It involves some risk, but our experience shows us that this risk is greatly overexaggerated. Every time we have stood up to the Russians they have backed down. Our trouble is we haven't stood up to them enough. Despite the arguments of Communists and leftwing propagandists who want us to believe that the present ideological struggle will inevitably lead to a shooting war, just the reverse is true. A shooting war can only be avoided by winning the cold war. And unless we win the cold war, we will be an easy pushover for the Khrushchevs, the Castros, and the Mao Tse-tungs when they decide the time is ripe to push their strategy into a shooting phase. . . .

Of course, if victory is not our official aim, then there would appear to be no point in bringing all our arguments—be they military, economic, political, or psychological—to bear on the side of freedom. But can we be sure that if we completely eliminate the possible use of nuclear weapons that the Russians will follow suit? Can we risk our future and the future of mankind on exclusive emphasis on conventional rather than ultimate weapons? Can we make any assumptions that would diminish our strength—in any field—when dealing with the Russians? Merely to ask the questions is to answer them. We can assume nothing where the Russians are concerned. We can trust nothing that the Russians say. We can accept nothing that the Russians sign as a conclusive guarantee.

Theirs is a policy of deliberate, calculated attrition which eats away steadily at the landmass represented by the freeworld and at the individual and collective liberties of its people. Unless we develop the will to win and the strategy to achieve victory—and do it soon—that attrition will engulf us. It has already been moving in 7 league boots over the surface of the globe and advances to within 90 miles of our own country. It hasn't slowed down because there is a risk of military action involved. It moves right on, inexorably increasing Communist power in strategic areas. And it steps up the tempo every time fear of possible consequences paralyzes the West in a posture of caution and indecision. Is there any wonder that the Communists welcome policy declarations which question whether the United States could win the cold war without a holocaust? Is there any wonder why they promote the mirage of peaceful coexistence which merely means that we stand immobilized while they advance their overall design? Is it any wonder that the Communists feel free to push their plan to build Cuba into an anti-American bastion in the Western Hemisphere?

The whole Communist operation makes the element of time a vital factor. Time is running out on the West while it is working in favor of international communism—at least under our present policy. For, I would remind you the policy we are following today is the same one which we have followed—with a few exceptions—since the end of World War II. It is the policy of spending in the hope of gaining allies. It is the policy which has permitted the Communists to gain in almost every area of the world while the cause of freedom has been losing. . . .

Let me assure you that a world without arms, a world living peacefully and adjusting its grievances in a global regime of law and order is more than an objective. It is a dream and its name is "Utopia." Even if it were practical, such an objective has no direct application against the urgent problems which beset the world today. We haven't the time for implementing dreams right now. We must deal with reality, the ever-present threat of Communist tyranny which is not going to submit the kind of civilizing Senator Fulbright envisions.

Suppose there is a big fire in your neighborhood. What do you think about first? You think of saving your home from destruction and your family from death. And if the flames have already enveloped your garden fence, do you lose time planning to build a dream house next year or next decade in a nonexistent city and in a theoretical country? Of course, you don't. You go right to work fighting the flames to save the house you've already got in the city and country where you live now.

This is the way it is today with our country and with the world. There is a fire in the world and its Communist flames are threatening to destroy the American way of life. Not next year, or in the next decade, or in a future century, but right now—today. These ugly red flames are already brushing our shores and they continue to rage unchecked.

And I suggest that this is no time for an American foreign policy objective designed to erect an impractical international dream city of the future. It is long past the time when our objective should be the practical means of dousing the fire and smothering the flames of international communism.

So what can we do? Our job, first and foremost, is to persuade the enemy that we would rather follow the world to kingdom come than consign it to hell under communism. Having made that clear, we must seize opportunities as they arise to protect freedom and demonstrate our strength. Many such opportunities have arisen in the past, some of which we have used to good advantage. For example, we were told by the weak of heart and the peddlers of despair that unless we yielded Quemoy and Matsu to the Communists, a terrible war would result. The Eisenhower administration said, in effect, very well, if the Communist world chooses to go to war to occupy these islands, then that's the way it will have to be. But the Communist world did not so choose, and Quemoy and Matsu are free today. And they will be free tomorrow and just as long as our resolution lasts. The story was repeated in Lebanon. We sent in marines there against the advice and quaking of those who fear a display of determination and strength. And Lebanon is free today. We acted from strength, too, when Berlin was threatened in 1948, and Berlin remains free. In Korea, our trouble was that Stalin didn't know that we meant business, and the result was a costly, unnecessary war which we would not have had to fight if the Russians had been assured in advance of our determination.

On the other hand, our resolve was not strong enough in Cuba to back our intent with the strength required and which we possessed. The result is that Cuba languishes in chains while a bearded Communist dictator thumbs his nose at the United States and plays the enemy's game to the hilt. And when Senator Fulbright worries lest we alienate the rest of Latin America by taking affirmative action in Cuba, I'm sure Castro guffaws. Much of Latin America has already been alienated by the timidity and ineffectiveness of our American policy. The Latins cannot understand why a world power, such as the United States, allows a two-bit Kremlin stooge to spit in our eye. And they wonder what source of support we could possibly be to them when communism pushes its expansion program throughout the Western Hemisphere. They see us weak and baffled in an area of vital concern, not only to them but to our own existence. . . .

And, in laying that groundwork, there are a number of immediate steps we should take to reorient our policy for maximum U.S. effectiveness in the cold war. They include the following:

1. We must stop believing that our primary objective must be to humor the public opinion of neutral or uncommitted nations rather than to defend our strategic interests, cooperate closely with our allies, and to advance our positions of strength. This we must do the more readily because much of this so-called opinion which entrances our coexistence proponents is fabricated by the Communists to our detriment; and since we have no proper method by which we can judge what public opinion really believes throughout the world.

2. We must stop lying to ourselves and our friends about disarma-

ment. We must stop advancing the cause of the Soviet Union by playing along with this great Communist-inspired deception. We must abandon the illusion that the Soviets, in their disarmament policies, are interested in furthering peace rather than baiting a trap for us. Their objective is to contrive our unilateral disarmament while they continue to arm themselves secretly as fast as they can.

It is not dialectics but schizophrenia when we increase our military budget by 15 percent and the Soviets theirs by 33 percent while, at the same time, we proclaim that disarmament is our highest goal and a practical method of composing the present conflict. The American people can stand the truth, but they cannot prosper under an official policy of self-deception.

3. We must get rid of the ban on nuclear testing. This is the worst and most transparent trap into which the United States has fallen during the course of the cold war. The ban does nothing but serve the Soviet Union to improve its nuclear weapons by clandestine testing, to stop our own advances in offensive and defensive nuclear technology and, ultimately, lead to a situation where we wake up confronted with superior Soviet weapons.

4. We must stop negotiating about things that are nonnegotiable, such as the rights of our allies, compromises of our security, treaties like the test ban which can be neither controlled nor enforced. We must not deceive ourselves and our friends into believing that nuclear weapons and modern technology can be negotiated out of existence.

5. We must stop helping communism, whether by trade, political concessions, technical disclosures, soft talk in the United Nations, recognition of Outer Mongolia, pilgrimages to Moscow or support for revolutionaries of the Castro type.

6. We must avoid economic collapse by scaling down extravagant and useless domestic programs and halt the squandering of our money on unrealistic worldwide aid programs.

Now, in conclusion I would remind you that in a mortal struggle there is no substitute for victory. The way I propose, the way of strength, is not an easy way. It is a hard course requiring determination and hard decisions involving risk. But it is the way of peace, not war; of freedom, not slavery. It is the way of all Americans, Republicans and Democrats alike; the way of all free people with the will to remain free. Thank you.

31

LOUIS RUCHAMES
Smith College

Segregation and Discrimination in the Twentieth Century

As HAS BEEN SUGGESTED in Professor Grady McWhiney's preceding essay (Chapter XVII, "The Negro in the 'New South,'" pp. 21–35), the yawning gulf between profession and practice in America's treatment of its minority groups, especially the Negro, is one of the great paradoxes of American history. On the one hand, we have the Declaration of Independence with its affirmation of human equality and the Judaeo-Christian heritage with its emphasis upon the dignity and worth of the individual; on the other, slavery, segregation, discrimination, and persecution.

The problem had its origin in 1619 with the landing of a cargo of Negro slaves in Jamestown, Virginia; it was intensified when slaves were introduced into Massachusetts and other colonies; and its implications became evident when Maryland, Virginia, and Massachusetts, the first two in 1664 and the latter in 1705, enacted laws prohibiting intermarriage between Negroes and whites. Segregation in America, then, was first born within societies committed to slavery; its primary purpose was to help maintain slavery; and it was dedicated to the proposition that the slave, identified by his black skin, was too inferior and degraded to enter into the relationship of marriage with a white person. Beginning as a "badge of servitude," segregation has continued to serve that purpose, even in our own day, though slavery has long since ended.

While segregation grew out of slavery, its greatest development came after abolishment of the "peculiar institution." The reason is quite clear. Even under slavery, segregation laws were of greatest use in regulating the status of the free Negro. While the laws of slavery were adequate to prevent slaves as a class from rising out of bondage, the existence of the free Negro represented both an anomaly and a threat to the entire system. Segregation served to remind the free Negro that though his status resulted from an accident of fate, nevertheless, by reason of his race, he partook of the inferiority of all Negroes. He was neither to consider himself nor to be considered by others as equal to a white man. And he was not to enter white society except as an inferior. The status of the free Negro was directly related to that of the slave; the inferiority of the former was both reinforced and confirmed by the servitude of the latter.

When slavery disappeared in the North after the colonial period, racial attitudes toward the Negro which had prevailed under it did not disappear but, in fact, were strengthened by the continued existence of slavery in the South. The result in some states was an increase in segregation. In Massachusetts, for instance, "Jim Crow" railroads and an antimiscegenation law existed as late as the 1840's, and Negro children were segregated in Boston's public schools until 1855.

Similarly, segregation in the South received its greatest development years after the end of slavery and some time after the close of the Reconstruction period in 1877. Not only did it grow out of attitudes concerning Negro inferiority prevailing under slavery; but, indeed, it served as a substitute for slavery. Segregation helped to keep the Negro "in his place" and guaranteed that he would remain a docile "hewer of wood and drawer of water," subservient and obedient to the white man's will. Consequently, beginning with the end of Reconstruction and continuing until the early thirties of this century, there gradually evolved, at first slowly and hesitantly but then more quickly, a dense network of racial segregation covering almost every area of society in the South.

A popular misconception is that the history of racial discrimination in America has been one of gradual improvement and progress. Nothing could be further from the truth. In 1900, Negro discrimination and segregation were far worse than they had been 25 years earlier; 25 years later, in many respects, the situation had further deteriorated. Charles W. Chesnutt, a Negro novelist, remarked at the turn of the century that "the rights of the Negro are at a lower ebb than at any time during the thirty-five years of their freedom, and the race-prejudice more intense and uncompromising." Professor C. Vann Woodward, in a recent study of segregation, has written: "Wide agreement prevailed in the early years of the century that there was less sympathy, tolerance, and understanding between the races than there had been during the Reconstruction period, and some put the case even more strongly."

For the Negro the years of the twentieth century before the first World War were marked by mob violence and lynchings, disfranchisement, relegation to menial and low-paid jobs, and increasing segration in all walks of life by state and municipal laws as well as informal custom. These trends continued well after the war. As late as 1944, Gunnar Myrdal, the Swedish economist and sociologist, could say that "segregation is now becoming so complete that the white Southerner practically never sees a Negro except as his servant and in other standardized and formalized caste situations."

Reasons for the increasing segregation were many, but two are of particular importance. First, in the 1890's, southern conservative political leaders raised the banner of segregation to help destroy the regional Populist movement, which had threatened to unite Negroes and lower class whites against the dominant political and economic groups. And second, the Supreme Court showed overt hostility toward legislative efforts to protect Negro rights while at the same time approving state Jim Crow legislation. Indeed, in two notable decisions, the Court paved the way for much of the segregation that followed. In the civil rights cases of 1883, it invalidated the Congressional Civil Rights Act of 1875, which had prohibited denial to Negroes of equal access to accommodations in inns and hotels, theaters, and railroads. In effect, the Court negated the right of Congress under the Thirteenth and Fourteenth amendments to legislate against segregation and discrimination in these areas of society. In 1896, in *Plessy* v. *Ferguson*, the Supreme Court upheld the right of a state to segregate Negroes on public conveyances and, by implication, in education and elsewhere. This decision opened the way to a flood of state segregationist legislation during the ensuing decades. One member of the Court, Justice John M. Harlan, refused to conform to the temper of the times and vigorously dissented in both cases. "Our Constitution is color-blind, and neither knows nor tolerates classes among citizens," said Harlan, a former Kentucky slaveholder. He characterized segregation as a "badge of servitude." When the Supreme Court, on May 17, 1954, declared segregation in public education illegal, Justice Harlan's dissent was finally vindicated.

Despite Myrdal's doleful observation regarding segregation in 1944, conditions were already maturing which were to lead to an improvement in the Negro's status throughout the nation and to a weakening of the entire structure of racial discrimination. These conditions included (1) the movement of Negroes from South to North and a subsequent increase in their political influence in several northern states; (2) growing Negro group-consciousness and militancy, marked by the decline of Booker T. Washington's philosophy of accommodation and the growth of the National Association for the Advancement of Colored People, with its aggressive, mass-action strategy for securing Negro rights; (3) the liberal tide which flowed across the country during the 1930's, symbolized in Franklin D. Roosevelt's New Deal, with its greater concern for the oppressed and poverty-stricken; (4) the assistance given by New Deal agencies to the Negroes, thereby stimulating among them a new sense of their own worth and dignity; (5) the increased interest of major religious organizations in the expansion of opportunities for all minority groups, including Negroes; (6) the insistence by the newly formed CIO upon equality of treatment for white and Negro workers, and the admission of numerous Negroes into the organization; and (7) the emergence of new and influential organizations, such as the American Civil Liberties Union and the Southern Conference for Human Welfare, which were deeply concerned for the rights of minority groups.

In June, 1941, several months before the United States entered the war and in the midst of a mounting defense effort, these conditions converged to bring about one of the major advances in the history of Negro and other minority groups. It was an advance which in turn helped pave the way, thirteen years later, for the epochal Supreme Court decision barring segregation in public education. This was the issuance by President Franklin D. Roosevelt of Executive Order 8802, which prohibited discrimination in government employment and defense industries because of race, creed, color, or national origin. A Fair Employment Practice Committee was created to enforce the order. The President's action came in response to a prolonged campaign by Negro and other organizations; it had culminated in a threatened march on Washington by more than 100,000 Negroes.

Executive Order 8802 had a twofold significance. It challenged the widely held belief shared by historians, social scientists, and political leaders that racial discrimination and segregation could not be eliminated through legal action. Such had been the position taken by the Supreme Court in *Plessy* v. *Ferguson*, when it ruled that "legislation is powerless to eradicate social instincts or to abolish distinctions based upon physical differences, and the attempt to do so can only result in accentuating the difficulties of the present situation." And it opened the way to almost unlimited economic opportunities for Negroes and other minority groups in many of the most important sectors of the economy. Negro leaders hailed the order as "the most significant move on the part of the Government since the Emancipation Proclamation."

The Fair Employment Practice Committee existed for about five years. It practically ceased functioning in 1943, but was revived by a new executive order on May 27, 1943, and continued in effect until June 28, 1946. During its lifetime the FEPC was subjected to unremitting attack by southern members of Congress and was obliged to endure a hostile Congressional investigation. It suffered from insufficient funds; indifference, if not hostility, from other government agencies; and sharply curtailed powers. Despite these handicaps, the FEPC achieved notable results.

The Committee held public hearings, investigated complaints, brought the glare of publicity and the power of the presidential office to bear upon recalcitrant employers and labor unions, issued educational materials, and succeeded in opening many opportunities in industry and government to Negroes and others where previously none had existed. Whereas, in March, 1942, Negroes were only 2.5 per cent of all workers employed in war production, by November, 1944, they made up approximately 8 per cent of the war workers for whom statistics were available. A very significant increase also took place in the employment of Negroes in government. While these developments in both industry and government were due partly to the wartime labor shortage, much of it undoubtedly came from FEPC efforts. Available statistics indicate that plants involved in public hearings or otherwise investigated by Committee members showed a greater increase in Negro employment than did defense industries in general. Numerous employers who at one time had discriminated against Negroes or other minority groups hired a few Negroes as a result of FEPC persuasion; subsequently, they employed other workers without any discrimination. These included, among others, aircraft firms on the West Coast, the New York Telephone Company, the Philadelphia Transportation Company, and the A.O. Smith Company of Milwaukee, Wisconsin. Diminishing, too, were those forms of segregation which had resulted from the hiring of Negroes for only certain types of work. In many instances where Negroes and whites began to work side by side and to learn more about one another, prejudice seemed to lessen. And finally, political leaders and the well-informed public generally began to realize that law, even in the form of an executive order which did not confer all the powers of a Congressional statute, could be effective in eliminating discrimination.

These lessons, learned on a national level, stimulated passage of FEPC laws in states and cities throughout the North. On March 12,

1945, New York enacted the first state Fair Employment Practice law. By July, 1960, seventeen states and over forty municipalities had passed similar laws. These frequently were expanded to include prohibitions against educational, housing, and other forms of discrimination. The antidiscrimination laws had a significant impact upon segregation and racial bias in the North.

As the climate of opinion in America during the late 1930's and 1940's veered toward a more sympathetic view of Negro needs and rights, so too did the Supreme Court, which both symbolized the change and contributed toward it. In far-reaching decisions, it pronounced against the South's white primaries, judicial enforcement of racial restrictive covenants, segregation in interstate travel, and unequal provisions for Negro and white students in segregated schools. But its greatest contribution to equal rights was made on May 17, 1954, and again on May 31, 1955, when, in what are now popularly known as the "school segregation cases," it ruled that "in the field of public education the doctrine of 'separate but equal' has no place." "Separate educational facilities are inherently unequal," the Court affirmed; and Negro pupils, by being segregated, are "deprived of the equal protection of the laws guaranteed by the Fourteenth Amendment." Not only did the Court rule against school segregation in these decisions; it also implicitly challenged the entire system of legalized segregation as it existed in twenty-one states and the District of Columbia.

How effective have the decisions been? Substantial integration on the elementary and high school levels has been achieved in the District of Columbia and West Virginia, and to a lesser extent in Missouri, Kentucky, Delaware, Oklahoma, and Maryland. But only token integration exists in Arkansas, Florida, North Carolina, and Virginia; and none in Georgia, except for Atlanta, which has had limited integration in its high schools; while in Louisiana, it has been confined to New Orleans, where one school district·is partially desegregated. No public school integration on the elementary or high school level has taken place in Alabama, Mississippi, or South Carolina. In September, 1962, eight years after the Supreme Court's decision, one observer estimated that fewer than 10,000 of the 2.8 million Negro children in the South were attending mixed classes. (For a comprehensive summary of the status of segregation-integration in the South as of November, 1962, see the publication of the Southern Education Reporting Service, *Statistical Summary of School Segregation-Desegregation in the Southern and Border States* [Nashville, Tenn., November, 1962].)

These results are disappointing. They are in part due to the fierce resistance with which southern political leaders and large sections of the southern population have met the decision. Furthermore, they are partially inherent in the nature of the judicial process, in which each ruling pertains to the case at hand, while its application to other school systems requires additional lawsuits which also may be carried to the Supreme Court. Moreover, each evasion, if it is to be overcome, likewise can be corrected only through court action, which may also be litigated up to the Supreme Court. Thus the possibilities for delaying action are almost infinite. Finally, President Eisenhower, by giving less than positive and wholehearted support to effectuating the decision, hardly accelerated the snail-like pace of school desegregation.

Perhaps the most cogent argument advanced by white southerners is that the Court's decision, while helping the black man, plays havoc with the civil liberties of white men, since it deprives them of the right to choose those with whom they associate—in school or elsewhere. The logical reply is that, especially under segregation, individual white southerners do not have this right. More than ever before, perhaps even for the first time, they now will have it. Moreover, in a public school system, under compulsory education, the pupil does not have an opportunity to select other members of his class. To grant one child such freedom at the expense of another is destructive of the equal right to an education which is at the basis of democracy.

What of the future? Admittedly, the progress made in integration in education thus far has been relatively minor, and southern opposition to it shows little sign of decreasing. Nevertheless, the outlook remains hopeful. Seen nationally, segregation is today a constantly narrowing and decreasing way of life. At one time, it was supported by the national government and the Supreme Court, and its area extended throughout the United States; today, it is being challenged everywhere, and its area of dominance is gradually being compressed further and further into the deep South. It should be remembered, too, that as a result of President Harry S. Truman's Executive Order 9981, issued in July 1948, the army, the navy, and the air force are now completely integrated. The hundreds of thousands of young men who pour into the services each year are given an experience in integrated living which is bound to have an impact on their attitudes when they return home. Even the South itself has been the scene of changes which sooner or later are bound to be felt. Despite terror and intimidation, many more Negroes are voting today than ever before. They have been elected to some school boards, they are sitting on juries in increasing numbers, they participate in professional athletics, and they are beginning to enter southern colleges and universities, even in the deep South. Some southern cities have desegregated their parks, museums, and public libraries. Though segregation remains the dominant pattern, the cracks within it already are noticeable.

Perhaps the most significant development in this area is the attitude of the Negro people themselves. It takes two races to make segregation work. The increasing resistance of Negroes to every manifestation of segregation, and their refusal to accept anything less than equal treatment and equal rights, are guarantees that the problem will never be solved except on the basis of complete integration. The constructive results of department store "sit-ins" in various southern cities, the sustained efforts of "freedom riders," the continuous testing of segregation ordinances, the voter registration drives in the South—despite the use of police dogs and prisons by state and local officials—are an indication of the new Negro spirit.

So fundamental has been the change in Negro attitudes and actions that it may be justly regarded as a revolution, as Louis E. Lomax has called it in his very perceptive book, *The Negro Revolt*. The onset of this change may be traced to December, 1955, when Mrs. Rosa Parks, a Negro woman of Montgomery, Alabama, refused to surrender her seat in a municipal bus to a white passenger and was subsequently arrested. Her arrest evoked the bus boycott by Montgomery Negroes which lasted for months, showed masterful organization and determination, and ended in a complete victory with the issuance of a United States Supreme Court decision, in October, 1956, which declared segregated seating on municipal buses illegal.

The Montgomery boycott catapulted into national prominence the Reverend Martin Luther King, Jr., who perhaps better than any other Negro leader articulated the feelings and hopes of his people. It also inspired Negroes throughout the country to emulate the Montgomery protest. Typifying the new Negro spirit were two forms of action which ensued: the sit-ins and the freedom rides.

The sit-ins began in February, 1960, when four freshmen from an all-Negro college in Greensboro, North Carolina, entered a Woolworth store, sat down at a white lunch counter, and refused to move until served. The tactic spread to numerous other cities and states across the nation. Associated with it was the technique of nonviolent, direct mass action perfected by the Congress of Racial Equality, or CORE, and taught by CORE representatives to sit-in participants throughout the country. Over eight hundred sit-ins occurred; and as

Louis E. Lomax notes, these "involved more people than any other civil rights movement in history": about seventy thousand Negroes and whites in over a hundred cities with more than four thousand arrested, "most of them Negro students." In many cities, such as Nashville, sit-ins were accompanied by economic boycotts by the entire Negro community; and the combined pressure, frequently proving decisive, brought success to the advocates of integration.

Freedom rides were initiated by James Farmer, a former Methodist clergyman and program director for the NAACP, who had resigned from the latter organization to become national director of CORE in February, 1961. In March, 1961, CORE announced its intention to test segregation in interstate travel terminals, by undertaking freedom rides, and on May 4 the first freedom riders headed south from the national capital. Soon other groups—the Nashville Student Movement, the Student Non-Violent Coordinating Committee, and Martin Luther King's Southern Christian Leadership Conference—sent riders southward. About a thousand persons, both Negro and white, were involved. Facilities were tested in several cities, among which were Nashville; New Orleans; Montgomery; Birmingham; Augusta and Athens, Georgia; and Jackson, Mississippi. The riders met with violence and bloodshed in several municipalities, but they subsequently achieved their objective when, at the request of President Kennedy, the Interstate Commerce Commission (on September 22, 1961) banned segregation in interstate terminals. Its order became effective on November 1, 1961.

Sit-ins and freedom rides confirmed the importance of nonviolent mass action, accompanied where feasible by an economic boycott, as the vital catalytic agents for achieving results in the drive against discrimination and segregation. Such became evident in the Birmingham racial crisis of April and May, 1963, in which thousands of Negroes— men, women, and children—demonstrated for more than a month. They were beaten, shot at, attacked by dogs, sprayed by hoses, and imprisoned. Yet, they refused to submit. Finally, through mass action and economic boycott, they forced the Birmingham white community —or at least some of its more important business and civic leaders— to accede to several of their demands and to begin the process of desegregation.

In any evaluation of the success achieved by the Negro revolt, one point bears stressing: Had similar demonstrations occurred at the turn of the century in cities and towns of the deep South, they would have been ruthlessly crushed; indeed, they would probably have been confronted with violence and bloodshed on a scale unimaginable today. In 1963 the beatings and bombings were relatively infrequent, and even the dogs were used with some restraint. The difference lies not only in a changed climate of opinion but in the even more important fact that today the judicial and executive branches of the federal government are pledged to support the basic Negro objectives—elimination of segregation and discrimination, and achievement of full equality of opportunity. Freedom rides and attempts at school desegregation, for instance, were first made feasible by Supreme Court rulings on interstate travel and education. The successful entrance of James Meredith, a Negro veteran, into the University of Mississippi in September, 1962, and of two Negroes into the University of Alabama in June, 1963, despite opposition from the governors of both states, was due ultimately to the support given to Court decisions by the late President Kennedy, however vacillating his efforts may have seemed during the early stages of the Meredith case.

In recent years, tactical questions have come increasingly to the fore among Negro organizations. CORE and the Southern Christian Leadership Conference, the latter headed by Dr. Martin Luther King, Jr., have advocated and practiced nonviolent mass action. The same strategy has been followed by the Student Non-Violent Coordinating Committee, which has participated in sit-ins, voter registration programs, and freedom rides. The National Association for the Advancement of Colored People, the largest and most influential Negro organization on the American scene, is theoretically in favor of mass action. In recent years, however, it has concentrated primarily on legal action through test cases in the courts. Confronted by the sit-ins, freedom rides, and other forms of mass action, the NAACP has increased its support and sponsorship of such efforts.

A few leaders of the Negro community do not accept the principle of nonviolence. Robert F. Williams, a former President of the local NAACP branch in Monroe, North Carolina (and presently in Cuba after fleeing to avoid prosecution), has advocated meeting violence with violence where necessary. Birmingham Negroes, after suffering police brutality without retaliation for more than a month, finally turned upon the police in an outburst of violence. Similar instances have occurred elsewhere. The Black Muslims, who represent a small but growing minority voice in the Negro community, neither advocate nor abjure violence as a matter of policy. Yet, they frequently express hatred of the white man, advocate the complete separation of Negroes and whites, demand the establishment of a separate Negro state, and emphasize the innate supremacy of the black man. The ability of Negroes to gain their objectives through the tactics advocated by the established organizations has undoubtedly limited Black Muslim growth. Further gains toward integration and the acceptance of the Negro as a full-fledged, equal member of American society would make its program of separation, based upon hatred of the white man, even less tenable.

As one looks upon the racial scene today, the situation is hopeful. Noteworthy gains already have been made, and others are unquestionably in the offing. Of great importance is the Civil Rights Act of 1964—signed by President Lyndon B. Johnson into law on July 2, 1964—which provides for the elimination of discrimination in public accommodations, education, voter registration, and employment. Yet, progress in the future, as the past suggests, will not come automatically. It will result from continued struggle on the part of the Negro people, supported by whites who are willing to join with them. Much too will depend upon the efforts of President Johnson and other officers of the federal government to enforce the Civil Rights Act and the decisions of the Supreme Court. As the world becomes smaller and human interdependence grows greater, as people everywhere begin to demand recognition of their worth and dignity, segregation and discrimination become ever more outworn, to be discarded as the relics of a barbarous age.

SUGGESTED READINGS

ASHMORE, HARRY. *An Epitaph for Dixie.* New York: W. W. Norton & Co., Inc., 1958.

BERGER, MORROE. *Equality by Statute: Legal Controls over Group.Discrimination.* New York: Columbia University Press, 1952.

GOLDEN, HARRY. *Mr. Kennedy and the Negroes.* Cleveland: World Publishing Co., 1964.

GREENBERG, JACK. *Race Relations and American Law.* New York: Columbia University Press, 1959.

KONVITZ, MILTON R. *A Century of Civil Rights,* with a study, *State Law against Discrimination,* by THEODORE LESKES. New York: Columbia University Press, 1961.

LOMAX, LOUIS E. *The Negro Revolt.* New York: Harper & Bros., 1962.

QUINT, HOWARD H. *Profile in Black and White: A Frank Portrait of South Carolina.* Washington, D.C.: Public Affairs Press, 1958.

RUCHAMES, LOUIS. *Race, Jobs and Politics: The Story of FEPC.* New York: Columbia University Press, 1953.

WARREN, ROBERT PENN. *Segregation: The Inner Conflict of the South*. New York: Random House, 1956.

WOODWARD, C. VANN. *The Strange Career of Jim Crow*. New and rev. ed. New York: Oxford University Press, 1957.

WORKMAN, WILLIAM D., JR. *The Case for the South*. New York: Devin-Adair Co., 1960.

Document 31.1

"THE DOCTRINE OF 'SEPARATE BUT EQUAL' HAS NO PLACE"

Reversing the "separate but equal" doctrine enunciated in *Plessy* v. *Ferguson* (1896), the Supreme Court, in 1954, established the principle that segregation in public education is unconstitutional. Defenders of white supremacy criticized the decision on the grounds that (1) it constituted an unwarranted interference with states' rights and (2) the court depended upon sociological data rather than upon legal precedent.

(From *Brown* v. *Board of Education of Topeka*, 347 U.S. 483 [1954])

WARREN, C.J.: These cases come to us from the States of Kansas, South Carolina, Virginia, and Delaware. They are premised on different facts and different local conditions, but a common legal question justifies their consideration together in this consolidated opinion.

In each of the cases, minors of the Negro race, through their legal representatives, seek the aid of the courts in obtaining admission to the public schools of their commuunitly on a nonsegregated basis. In each instance, they had been denied admission to schools attended by white children under laws requiring or permitting segregation according to race. This segregation was alleged to deprive the plaintiffs of the equal protection of the laws under the Fourteenth Amendment. In each of the cases other than the Delaware case, a three-judge federal district court denied relief to the plaintiffs on the so-called "separate but equal" doctrine announced by this Court in *Plessy* v. *Ferguson*. . . . Under that doctrine, equality of treatment is accorded when the races are provided substantially equal facilities, even though these facilities be separate. In the Delaware case, the Supreme Court of Delaware adhered to that doctrine, but ordered that the plaintiffs be admitted to the white schools because of their superiority to the Negro schools.

The plaintiffs contend that segregated public schools are not "equal" and cannot be made "equal," and that hence they are deprived of the equal protection of the laws. Because of the obvious importance of the question presented, the Court took jurisdiction. Argument was heard in the 1952 Term, and reargument was heard this Term on certain questions propounded by the Court.

Reargument was largely devoted to the circumstances surrounding the adoption of the Fourteenth Amendment in 1868. It covered exhaustively consideration of the Amendment in Congress, ratification by the states, then existing practices in racial segregation, and the views of proponents and opponents of the Amendment. This discussion and our own investigation convince us that, although these sources cast some light, it is not enough to resolve the problem with which we are faced. At best, they are inconclusive. The most avid proponents of the post-War Amendments undoubtedly intended them to remove all legal distinctions among "all persons born or naturalized in the United States." Their opponents, just as certainly, were antagonistic to both the letter and the spirit of the Amendments and wished them to have the most limited effect. What others in Congress and the state legislature had in mind cannot be determined with any degree of certainty.

An additional reason for the inconclusive nature of the Amendment's history, with respect to segregated schools, is the status of public education at that time. In the South, the movement toward free common schools, suppored by general taxation, had not yet taken hold. Education of white children was largely in the hands of private groups. Education of Negroes was almost nonexistent, and practically all of the race were illiterate. In fact, any education of Negroes was forbidden by law in some states. Today, in contrast, many Negroes have achieved outstanding success in the arts and sciences as well as in the business and professional world. It is true that public education had already advanced further in the North, but the effect of the Amendment on Northern States was generally ignored in the congressional debates. Even in the North, the conditions of public education did not approximate those existing today. The curriculum was usually rudimentary; ungraded schools were common in rural areas; the school term was but three months a year in many states; and compulsory school attendance was virtually unknown. As a consequence, it is not surprising that there should be so little in the history of the Fourteenth Amendment relating to its intended effect on public education.

In the first cases in this Court construing the Fourteenth Amendment, decided shortly after its adoption, the Court interpreted it as proscribing all state-imposed discriminations against the Negro race. The doctrine of "separate but equal" did not make its appearance in this Court until 1896 in the case of *Plessy* v. *Ferguson* . . . involving not education but transportation. American courts have since labored with the doctrine for over half a century. In this Court, there have been six cases involving the "separate but equal" doctrine in the field of public education. In *Cumming* v. *County Board of Education* . . . [1899], and *Gong Lum* v. *Rice* . . . [1927], the validity of the doctrine itself was not challenged. In more recent cases, all on the graduate school level, inequality was found in that specific benefits enjoyed by white students were denied to Negro students of the same educational qualifications. . . . [Gaines, Sipuel, Sweatt, McLaurin.] In none of these cases was it necessary to reexamine the doctrine to grant relief to the Negro plaintiff. And in *Sweatt* v. *Painter* . . . , the Court expressly reserved decision on the questions whether *Plessy* v. *Ferguson* should be held inapplicable to public education.

In the instant cases, that question is directly presented. Here, unlike *Sweatt* v. *Painter*, there are findings below that the Negro and white schools involved have been equalized, or are being equalized, with respect to buildings, curricula, qualifications and salaries of teachers, and other "tangible" factors. Our decision, therefore, cannot turn on merely a comparison of these tangible factors in the Negro and white schools involved in each of the cases. We must look instead to the effect of segregation itself on public education.

In approaching this problem, we cannot turn the clock back to 1868 when the Amendment was adopted, or even to 1896 when *Plessy* v. *Ferguson* was written. We must consider public education in the light of its full development and its present place in American life throughout the Nation. Only in this way can it be determined if segregation in public schools deprives these plaintiffs of the equal protection of the laws.

Today, education is perhaps the most important function of state and local governments. Compulsory school attendance laws and the great expenditures for education both demonstrate our recognition of the importance of education to our democratic society. It is required in the performance of our most basic public responsibilities, even service in the armed forces. It is the very foundation of good citizenship. Today it is a principal instrument in awakening the child to cultural values, in preparing him for later professional training, and in helping him to adjust normally to his environment. In these days, it is doubtful that any child may reasonably be expected to succeed in life if he is denied the opportunity of an education. Such an opportunity, where the state has undertaken to provide it, is a right which must be made available to all on equal terms.

We come then to the question presented. Does segregation of children in public schools solely on the basis of race, even though the physical facilities and other "tangible" factors may be equal, deprive the children of the minority group of equal educational opportunities? We believe that it does.

In *Sweatt* v. *Painter*, . . . in finding that a segregated law school for Negroes could not provide them equal educational opportunities, this Court relied in large part on "those qualities which are incapable of objective measurement but which make for greatness in a law school." In *Mc-Laurin* v. *Oklahoma State Regents*, . . . the Court, in requiring that a Negro admitted to a white graduate school be treated like all other students, again resorted to intangible considerations: ". . . his ability to study, to engage in discussions and exchange views with other students, and, in general, to learn his profession." Such considerations apply with added force to children in grade and high schools. To separate them from others of similar age and qualifications solely because of their race generates a feeling of inferiority as to their status in the community that may affect their hearts and minds in a way unlikely ever to be undone. The effect of this separation on their educational opportunities was well stated by a finding in the Kansas case by a court which nevertheless felt compelled to rule against the Negro plaintiffs:

> Segregation of white and colored children in public schools has a detrimental effect upon the colored children. The impact is greater when it has the sanction of the law; for the policy of separating the races is usually interpreted as denoting the inferiority of the Negro group. A sense of inferiority affects the motivation of a child to learn. Segregation with the sanction of law, therefore, has a tendency to retard the educational and mental development of Negro children and to deprive them of some of the benefits they would receive in a racially integrated school system.

Whatever may have been the extent of psychological knowledge at the time of *Plessy* v. *Ferguson*, this finding is amply supported by modern authority. Any language in *Plessy* v. *Ferguson* contrary to this finding is rejected.

We conclude that in the field of public education the doctrine of "separate but equal" has no place. Separate educational facilities are inherently unequal. Therefore, we hold that the plaintiffs and others similarly situated for whom the actions have been brought are, by reason of the segregation complained of, deprived of the equal protection of the laws guaranteed by the Fourteenth Amendment. This disposition makes unnecessary any discussion whether such segregation also violates the Due Process Clause of the Fourteenth Amendment.

Because these are class actions, because of the wide applicability of this decision, and because of the great variety of local conditions, the formulation of decrees in these cases presents problems of considerable complexity. On reargument, the consideration of appropriate relief was necessarily subordinated to the primary question—the constitutionality of segregation in public education. We have now announced that such segregation is a denial of the equal protection of the laws. In order that we may have the full assistance of the parties in formulating decrees, the cases will be restored to the docket, and the parties are requested to present further argument on Questions 4 and 5 previously propounded by the Court for the reargument this Term. The Attorney General of the United States is again invited to participate. The Attorneys General of the states requiring or permitting segregation in public education will also be permitted to appear as *amici curiae* upon request to do so by September 15, 1954, and submission of briefs by October 1, 1954.

It is so ordered.

(From *Brown* v. *Board of Education of Topeka*, 349 U.S. 294 [1955])

Mr. Chief Justice Warren delivered the opinion of the Court.

These cases were decided on May 17, 1954. The opinions of that date, declaring the fundamental principle that racial discrimination in public education is unconstitutional, are incorporated herein by reference. All provisions of federal, state, or local law requiring or permitting such discrimination must yield to this principle. There remains for consideration the manner in which relief is to be accorded.

Because these cases arose under dfferent local conditions and their disposition will involve a variety of local problems, we requested further argument on the question of relief. In view of the nationwide importance of the decision, we invited the Attorney General of the United States and the Attorneys General of all states requiring or permitting racial discrimination in public education to present their views on that question. The parties, the United States, and the States of Florida, North Carolina, Arkansas, Oklahoma, Maryland, and Texas filed briefs and participated in the oral argument.

These presentations were informative and helpful to the Court in its consideration of the complexities arising from the transition to a system of public education freed of racial discrimination. The presentations also demonstrated that substantial steps to eliminate racial discrimination in public schools have already been taken, not only in some of the communities in which these cases arose, but in some of the states appearing as *amici curiae*, and in other states as well. Substantial progress has been made in the District of Columbia and in the communities in Kansas and Delaware involved in this litigation. The defendants in the cases coming to us from South Carolina and Virginia are awaiting the decision of this Court concerning relief.

Full implementation of these constitutional principles may require solution of varied local school problems. School authorities have the primary responsibility for elucidating, assessing, and solving these problems; courts will have to consider whether the action of school authorities constitutes good faith implementation of the governing constitutional principles. Because of their proximity to local conditions and the possible need for further hearings, the courts which originally heard these cases can best perform this judicial appraisal. Accordingly, we believe it appropriate to remand the cases to those courts.

In fashioning and effectuating the decrees, the courts will be guided by equitable principles. Traditionally, equity has been characterized by a practical flexibility in shaping its remedies and by a facility for adjusting and reconciling public and private needs. These cases call for the exercise of these traditional attributes of equity power. At stake is the personal interest of the plaintiffs in admission to public schools as soon as practicable on a nondiscriminatory basis. To effectuate this interest may call for elimination of a variety of obstacles in making the transition to school systems operated in accordance with the constitutional principles set forth in our May 17, 1954, decision. Courts of equity may properly take into account the public interest in the elimination of such obstacles in a systematic and effective manner. But it should go without saying that the vitality of these constitutional principles cannot be allowed to yield simply because of disagreement with them.

While giving weight to these public and private considerations, the courts will require that the defendants make a prompt and reasonable start toward full compliance with our May 17, 1954, ruling. Once such a start has been made, the courts may find that additional time is necessary to carry out the ruling in an effective manner. The burden rests upon the defendants to establish that such time is necessary in the public interest and is consistent with good faith compliance at the earliest practicable date. To that end, the courts may consider problems related to administration, arising from the physical condition of the school plant, the school transportation system, personnel, revision of school districts and attendance areas into compact units to achieve a system of determining admission to the public schools on a nonracial basis, and revision of local laws and regulations which may be necessary in solving the foregoing problems. They will also consider the adequacy of any plans the defendants may propose to meet those problems and to effectuate a transition to a racially nondiscriminatory school system. During this period of transition, the courts will retain jurisdiction of these cases.

The judgments below, except that in the Delaware case, are accordingly reversed and remanded to the District Courts to take such proceedings and enter such orders and decrees consistent with this opinion as are necessary and proper to admit to public schools on a racially nondiscriminatory basis with all deliberate speed the parties to these cases. The judgment in the Delaware case—ordering the immediate admission of the plaintiffs to schools previously attended only by white children—is affirmed on the basis of the principles stated in our May 17, 1954, opinion, but the case is remanded to the Supreme Court of Delaware for such further proceedings as that court may need necessary in light of this opinion.

It is so ordered.

Document 31.2

"SEPARATE AND BE SAVED!"

The Black Muslim movement, although in existence for several years, has only recently gained national attention. Its program and objectives, as enunciated by its leader and theoretician, Elijah Muhammad, born Elijah Poole, a former Baptist clergyman, stand in open opposition to those of other Negro organizations.

(From *Muhammad Speaks*, August 2, 1963, pp. 1, 9)

The unwillingness of the slaves to leave their masters is due to their great love for the slave masters. If America is unwilling to grant her 20,000,000 ex-slaves freedom to go for self today, it is the same unwillingness of white America's forefathers in dealing with our parents less than 100 years ago.

During the time of the Emancipation Proclamation, we were scattered to the winds without any knowledge or ability to undertake the responsibilities of a half freedom. Our fathers, lacking the skills and the training of how to provide for themselves, were forced to remain with the masters in order to receive even the barest necessities of life.

Our former slave masters knowing of our dependence upon them, maliciously and hatefully adopted attitudes and social and educational systems that have deprived us of the opportunity to become free and independent right up to the present day.

But we, the black slaves, of this soil of bondage were not deprived of the freedom to fight in America's wars, but are deprived of the right to fight for our own freedom.

The opposition met by our forefathers who fought for their freedom is a chilled memory that history will not forget. The black people are given the freedom to give their lives for the American Cause of tyranny, but are not free to fight for their own freedom and independence.

As long as my people are the blind lovers of their enemies, they will seek to forever return to the bosom of their masters in no better status or position than that of a slave.

Our foreparents' desire was to see us free indeed and not only are some of our people willing to betray those of our blood and kindred who died before us, but are now willing to betray the fruition of freedom to our generations to come. Allah will help us to get this freedom, justice, and equality and some of this earth that we can call our own.

I say to the American white citizens who are in a position; to oppose or hasten the separation of the two or suffer the consequences as did the Egyptians' opposition to Jehovah and His Servant Moses.

We must have some of this earth that we can call our own! We and our fathers have been robbed of all that we originally possessed. And now we are left without anything to go for self like wealth and modern instruments to start a civilization as you have; though we helped you to get what you have. We, now, must have justice and some of this earth and its wealth that we can call our own.

HURRY AND JOIN UNTO YOUR OWN KIND! THE TIME OF THIS WORLD IS NOW AT HAND.

Document 31.3

"CAN NEGROES AFFORD TO BE PACIFISTS?"

Robert F. Williams, a militant ex-marine from Monroe, North Carolina, was removed from his post as local NAACP leader by the national organization because of his alleged advocacy of violent Negro retaliation to white violence.

(From Robert F. Williams, "Can Negroes Afford to Be Pacifists?" *Liberation*, September, 1959, pp. 4–7)

In 1954 I was an enlisted man in the United States Marine Corps. As a Negro in an integrated unit that was overwhelmingly white, I shall never forget the evening we were lounging in the recreation room watching television as a news bulletin flashed on the screen. This was the historic Supreme Court decision that segregation in the public schools is unconstitutional. Because of the interracial atmosphere, there was no vocal comment. There was for a while complete silence. I never knew how the Southern white boys felt about this bulletin. Perhaps I never will, but as for myself, my inner emotions must have been approximate to the Negro slaves' when they first heard about the Emancipation Proclamation. Elation took hold of me so strongly that I found it very difficult to refrain from yielding to an urge of jubilation. I learned later that night that other Negroes in my outfit had felt the same surge of elation.

On this momentous night of May 17, 1954, I felt that at last the government was willing to assert itself on behalf of first-class citizenship, even for Negroes. I experienced a sense of loyalty that I had never felt before. I was sure that this was the beginning of a new era of American democracy. At last I felt that I was a part of America and that I belonged. That was what I had always wanted, even as a child.

I returned to civilian life in 1955 and the hope I had for Negro liberation faltered. I had returned to a South that was determined to stay the hand of progress at all cost. Acts of violence and words and deeds of hate and spite rose from every quarter. An attitude prevailed that Negroes had a court decree from the "Communist inspired court," but the local racist had the means to initiate the old law of the social jungle called Dixie. Since the first Negro slaves arrived in America, the white supremacists have relied upon violence as a potent weapon of intimidation to deprive Negroes of their rights. The Southerner is not prone to easy change; therefore the same tactics that proved so successful against Negroes through the years are still being employed today. There is open defiance to law and order throughout the South today. Governor Faubus and the Little Rock campaign was a shining example of the Southern racists' respect for the law of the land and constituted authority.

The State of Virginia is in open defiance of federal authority. States like my native state of North Carolina are submitting to token integration and openly boasting that this is the solution to circumvention of the Supreme Court decisions. The officials of this state brazenly slap themselves on the back for being successful in depriving great numbers of their colored citizens of the rights of first-class citizenship. Yes, after having such great short-lived hope, I have become disillusioned about the prospect of a just, democratic-minded government motivated by politicians with high moral standards enforcing the Fourteenth Amendment without the pressure of expediency.

News Blackout

Since my release from the Marine Corps I could cite many cases of unprovoked violence that have been visited upon my people. Some, like the Emmett Till case, the Asbury Howard case and the Mack Parker incident, have been widely publicized. There are more, many many more, occurring daily in the South that never come to light of the press because of a news blackout sponsored by local racist officials.

Laws serve to deter crime and to protect the weak from the strong in civilized society. When there is a breakdown of law and the right of equal protection by constituted authority, where is the force of deterrent? It is the nature of people to respect law when it is just and strong. Only highly civilized and moral individuals respect the rights of others. The low-mentality bigots of the South have shown a wanton disregard for the wellbeing and rights of their fellowmen of color, but there is one thing that even the most savage beast respects, and that is force. Soft, polished words whispered into the ears of a brute make him all the more confused and rebellious against a society that is more than he can understand or feel secure in. The Southern brute respects only force. Nonviolence is a very potent weapon when the opponent is civilized, but nonviolence is no match or repellent for a sadist. I have great respect for the pacifist, that is, for the pure pacifist. I think a pure pacifist is one who resents violence against nations as well as individuals and is courageous enough to speak out against jingoistic governments (including his own) without an air of self-righteousness and pious moral individuality. I am not a pacfist and I am sure that I may safely say that most of my people are not. Passive resistance is a powerful weapon in gaining concessions from oppressors, but I venture to say that if Mack Parker had had an automatic shotgun at his disposal, he could have served as a great deterrent against lynching.

"Turn-the-Other-Cheekism"

Rev. Martin Luther King is a great and successful leader of our race. The Montgomery bus boycott was a great victory for American democracy. However, most people have confused the issues facing the race. In Montogmery the issue was a matter of struggle for human dignity. Nonviolence is made to order for that type of conflict. While praising the actions of those courageous Negroes who participated in the Montgomery affair, we must not allow the complete aspects of the Negro struggle throughout the South to be taken out of their proper perspective. In a great many localities in the South Negroes are faced with the necessity of combating savage violence. The struggle is for mere existence. The Negro is in a position or begging for life. There is no lawful deterrent against those who would do him violence. An open declaration of non-violence, or turn-the-other-cheekism is an invitation that the white racist brutes will certainly honor by brutal attack on cringing, submissive Negroes. It is time for the Negro in the South to reappraise his method of dealing with his ruthless oppressor.

In 1957 the Klan moved into Monroe and Union County. In the beginning we did not notice them much. Their numbers steadily increased to the point wherein the local press reported as many as seventy-five hundred racists massed at one rally. They became so brazen that mile-long motorcades started invading the Negro community. These hooded thugs fired pistols from car windows, screamed, and incessantly blew their automobile horns. On one occasion they caught a Negro woman on the street and tried to force her to dance for them at gun point. She escaped into the night, screaming and hysterical. They forced a Negro merchant to close down his business on direct orders from the Klan. Drivers of cars tried to run Negroes down when seen walking on the streets at night. Negro women were struck with missiles thrown from passing vehicles. Lawlessness was rampant. A Negro doctor was framed to jail on a charge of performing an abortion on a white woman. This doctor, who was vice-president of the N.A.A.C.P., was placed in a lonely cell in the basement of a jail, although men prisoners are usually confined upstairs. A crowd of white men started congregating around the jail. It is common knowledge that a lynching was averted. We have had the usual threats of the Klan here, but instead of cowing, we organized an armed guard and set up a defense force around the doctor's house. On one occasion, we had to exchange gunfire with the Klan. Each time the Klan came on a raid they were led by police cars. We appealed to the President of the United States to have the Justice Department investigate the police. We appealed to Governor Luther Hodges. All our appeals to constituted law were in vain. Governor Hodges, in an underhanded way, defended the Klan. He publicly made a statement, to the press, that I had exaggerated Klan activity in Union County—despite the fact that they were operating openly and had gone so far as to build a Klan clubhouse and advertise meetings in the local press and on the radio.

CRINGING NEGRO MINISTERS

A group of nonviolent ministers met the city Board of Aldermen and pleaded with them to restrict the Klan from the colored community. The city fathers advised these cringing, begging Negro ministers that the Klan had constitutional rights to meet and organize in the same way as the N.A.A.C.P. Not having been infected by turn-the-other-cheekism, a group of Negroes who showed a willingness to fight caused the city officials to deprive the Klan of its constitutional rights after local papers told of dangerous incidents between Klansmen and armed Negroes. Klan motorcades have been legally banned from the City of Monroe.

The possibility of tragedy's striking both sides of the tracks has caused a mutual desire to have a peaceful coexistence. The fact that any racial brutality may cause white blood to flow as well as Negro is lessening racial tension. The white bigots are sparing Negroes from brutal attack, not because of a new sense of morality, but because Negroes have adopted a policy of meeting violence with violence.

THE SCREAMS OF THE INNOCENT

I think there is enough latitude in the struggle for Negro liberation for the acceptance of diverse tactics and philosophies. There is need for pacifists and nonpacifists. I think each freedom fighter must unselfishly contribute what he has to offer. I have been a soldier and a Marine. I have been trained in the way of violence. I have been trained to defend myself. Self-defense to a Marine is a reflex action. People like Rev. Martin Luther King have been trained for the pulpit. I think they would be as out of place in a conflict that demanded real violent action as I would be in a pulpit praying for an indifferent God to come down from Heaven and rescue a screaming Mack Parker or Emmett Till from an ungodly howling mob. I believe if we are going to pray, we ought to pass the ammunition while we pray. If we are too pious to kill in our own self-defense, how can we have the heart to ask a Holy God to come down to this violent fray and smite down our enemies?

As a race, we have been praying for three hundred years. The N.A.A.C.P. boasts that it has fought against lynching for fifty years. A fifty-year fight without victory is not impressive to me. An unwritten anti-lynch law was initiated overnight in Monroe. It is strange that so-called Negro leaders have never stopped to think why a simple thing like an anti-lynch law in a supposedly democratic nation is next to impossible to get passed. Surely every citizen in a republic is entitled not to be lynched. To seek an anti-lynch law in the present situation is to seek charity. Individuals and governments are more inclined to do things that promote the general welfare and well-being of the populace. A prejudiced government and a prejudiced people are not going to throw a shield of protection around the very people in the South on whom they vent pent-up hatreds as scapegoats. When white people in the South start needing such a law, we will not even have to wait fifty days to get it.

STOP LYNCHING WITH VIOLENCE

On May 5, 1959, while president of the Union County branch of the National Association for the Advancement of Colored People, I made a statement to the United Press International after a trial wherein a white man was supposed to have been tried for kicking a Negro maid down a flight of stairs in a local white hotel. In spite of the fact that there was an eyewitness, the defendant failed to show up for his trial, and was completely exonerated. Another case in the same court involved a white man who had come to a pregnant Negro mother's home and attempted to rape her. In recorder's court the only defense offered for the defendant was that "he's not guilty. He was just drunk and having a little fun." Despite the fact that this pregnant Negro mother was brutally beaten and driven from her home because she refused to submit, and a white woman neighbor testified that the woman had come to her house excited, her clothes torn, her feet bare, and begging her for assistance, the court was unmoved. The defendant's wife was allowed to sit with him throughout the trial, and his attorney asked the jury if they thought this white man would leave "this beautiful white woman, the flower of life for this Negro woman." Some of the jurymen laughed and the defendant went free. This great miscarriage of justice left me sick inside, and I said then what I say now. I believe that Negroes must be willing to defend themselves, their women, their children and their homes. They must be willing to die and to kill in repelling their assailants. There is no Fourteenth Amendment, no equal protection under the law. Negroes *must* protect themselves, it is obvious that the federal government will not put an end to lynching; therefore it becomes necessary for us to stop lynching with violence. We must defend ourselves. Even though I made it known that I spoke as an individual American citizen, I was suspended by the N.A.A.C.P. for advocating violence. The N.A.A.C.P. was so fearful of the consequence of this statement that I heard about my suspension over the radio before I got an official notice. The radio announcer tried to give local Negroes the impression that the N.A.A.C.P. advocated turn-the-other-cheekism. The thing that struck me most was not the suspension, but the number of letters and telegrams I received from Negroes all over America who showed a readiness to fight. The Negro on the street who suffers most is beginning to break out of the harness of the nonviolent race preachers. The fact that the N.A.A.C.P. had to issue a statement saying, "The N.A.A.C.P. has never condoned mob violence but it firmly supports the right of Negroes individually and collectively to defend their person, their homes and their property from attack" is a strong indication of the sentiment among the masses of Negroes. How can an individual defend his person and property from attack without meeting violence with violence? What the N.A.A.C.P. is advocating now is no more than I had advocated in the first place. I could never advocate that Negroes attack white people indiscriminately. Our branch of the N.A.A.C.P. in Union County is an interracial branch.

KING CASHES IN ON WAR

It is obvious that the Negro leadership is caught in a terrible dilemma. It is trying to appease both white liberals who want to see Negro liberation given to us in eye-dropper doses and the Negro masses, who are growing impatient and restive under brutal oppression. There is a new Negro coming into manhood on the American scene and an indifferent government must take cognizance of this fact. The Negro is becoming more militant, and pacifism will never be accepted wholeheartedly by the masses of Negroes so long as violence is rampant in Dixie. Even Negroes like King who profess to be pacifists are not pure pacifists and at times speak proudly of the Negro's role of violence in this violent nation's wars. In a speech at the N.A.A.C.P. convention, he said, "In spite of all of our oppression, we have never turned to a foreign ideology to solve our problems. Communism has never invaded our ranks. And now we are simply saying we want our freedom, we have stood with you in every crisis. For you, America, our sons died in the trenches of France, in the foxholes of Germany, on the beachheads of Italy and on the islands of Japan. And now, America, we are simply asking you to guarantee our freedom." King may not be willing to partake in expeditions of violence, but he has no compunction about cashing in on the spoils of war. There are too many Negro leaders who are afraid to talk violence against the violent racist and are too weak-kneed to protest the warmongering of the atom-crazed politicians of Washington.

Some Negro leaders have cautioned me that if Negroes fight back, the racist will have cause to exterminate the race. How asinine can one get? This government is in no position to allow mass violence to erupt, let alone allow twenty million Negroes to be exterminated. I am not half so worried about being exterminated as I am about my children's growing up under oppression and being mentally twisted out of human proportions.

We live in perilous times in America, and especially in the South. Segregation is an expensive commodity, but liberty and democracy too, have their price. So often the purchase check of democracy must be signed in blood. Someone must be willing to pay the price, despite the scoffs from the Uncle Toms. I am told that patience is commendable and that we must never tire of waiting, yet it is instilled at an early age that men who violently and swiftly rise to oppose tyranny are virtuous examples to emulate. I have been taught by my government to fight, and if I find it necessary I shall do just that. All Negroes must learn to fight back, for nowhere in the annals of history does the record show a people delivered from bondage by patience alone.

Document 31.4

A PLEA FOR NONVIOLENT RESISTANCE

One of those who replied to Williams' article was the Reverend Martin Luther King, Jr., who is generally accepted as the leading national spokesman for Negro nonviolent mass action.

(From Martin Luther King, Jr., "The Social Organization of Nonviolence," *Liberation*, October, 1959, pp. 5–6)

Paradoxically, the struggle for civil rights has reached a stage of profound crisis, although its outward aspect is distinctly less turbulent and victories of token integration have been won in the hard-resistance areas of Virginia and Arkansas.

The crisis has its origin in a decision rendered by the Supreme Court more than a year ago which upheld the pupil placement law. Though little noticed then, this decision fundamentally weakened the historic 1954 ruling of the Court. It is imperceptibly becoming the basis of a *de facto* compromise between the powerful contending forces.

The 1954 decision required for effective implementation resolute Federal action supported by mass action to undergird all necessary changes. It is obvious that Federal action by the legislative and executive branches was half-hearted and inadequate. The activity of Negro forces, while heroic in some instances, and impressive in other sporadic situations, lacked consistency and militancy sufficient to fill the void left by government default. The segregationists were swift to seize these advantages, and unrestrained by moral or social conscience, defied the law boldly and brazenly.

The net effect of this social equation has led to the present situation, which is without clearcut victory for either side. Token integration is a developing pattern. This type of integration is merely an affirmation of a principle without the substance of change.

It is, like the Supreme Court decision, a pronouncement of justice, but by itself does not insure that the millions of Negro children will be educated in conditions of equality. This is not to say that it is without value. It has substantial importance. However, it fundamentally changes the outlook of the whole movement, for it raises the prospect of long, slow change without a predictable end. As we have seen in Northern cities, token integration has become a pattern in many communities and remained frozen, even though environmental attitudes are substantially less hostile to full integration than in the South.

THREE VIEWS OF VIOLENCE

This then is the danger. Full integration can easily become a distant or mythical goal—major integration may be long postponed, and in the quest for social calm a compromise firmly implanted in which the real goals are merely token integration for a long period to come.

The Negro was the tragic victim of another compromise in 1878, when his full equality was bargained away by the Federal Government and a condition somewhat above slave status but short of genuine citizenship become his social and political existence for nearly a century.

There is reason to believe that the Negro of 1959 will not accept supinely any such compromises in the contemporary struggle for integration. His struggle will continue, but the obstacles will determine its specific nature. It is axiomatic in social life that the imposition of frustration leads to two kinds of reactions. One is the development of a wholesome social organization to resist with effective, firm measures any efforts to impede progress. The other is a confused, anger-motivated drive to strike back violently, to inflict damage. Primarily, it seeks to cause injury to retaliate for wrongful suffering. Secondarily, it seeks real progress. It is punitive—not radical or constructive.

The current calls for violence have their roots in this latter tendency. Here one must be clear that there are three different views on the subject of violence. One is the approach of pure nonviolence, which cannot readily or easily attract large masses, for it requires extraordinary discipline and courage. The second is violence exercised in self-defense, which all societies, from the most primitive to the most cultured and civilized, accept as moral and legal. The principle of self-defense, even involving weapons and bloodshed, has never been condemned, even by Gandhi, who sanctioned it for those unable to master pure nonviolence. The third is

the advocacy of violence as a tool of advancement, organized as in warfare, deliberately and consciously. To this tendency many Negroes are
being tempted today. There are incalculable perils in this approach. It is
not the danger or sacrifice of physical being which is primary, though it
cannot be contemplated without a sense of deep concern for human life.
The greatest danger is that it will fail to attract Negroes to a real collective struggle, and will confuse the large uncommitted middle group,
which as yet has not supported either side. Further, it will mislead Negroes into the belief that this is the only path and place them as a minority
in a position where they confront a far larger adversary than it is possible
to defeat in this form of combat. When the Negro uses force in self-
defense he does not forfeit support—he may even win it, by the courage
and self-respect it reflects. When he seeks to initiate violence he provokes
questions about the necessity for it, and inevitably is blamed for its consequences. It is unfortunately true that however the Negro acts, his
struggle will not be free of violence initiated by his enemies, and he will
need ample courage and willingness to sacrifice to defeat this manifestation of violence. But if he seeks it and organizes it, he cannot win. Does
this leave the Negro without a positive method to advance? Mr. Robert
Williams would have us believe that there is no effective and practical
alternative. He argues that we must be cringing and submissive or take
up arms. To so place the issue distorts the whole problem. There are other
meaningful alternatives.

The Negro people can organize socially to initiate many forms of
struggle which can drive their enemies back without resort to futile and
harmful violence. In the history of the movement for racial advancement,
many creative forms have been developed—the mass boycott, sitdown
protests and strikes, sit-ins,—refusal to pay fines and bail for unjust
arrests—mass marches—mass meetings—prayer pilgrimages, etc. Indeed, in Mr. Williams' own community of Monroe, North Carolina, a
striking example of collective community action won a significant victory
without use of arms or threats of violence. When the police incarcerated
a Negro doctor unjustly, the aroused people of Monroe marched to the
police station, crowded into its halls and corridors, and refused to leave
until their colleague was released. Unable to arrest everyone, the authorities released the doctor and neither side attempted to unleash violence. This experience was related by the doctor who was the intended
victim.

There is more power in socially organized masses on the march than
there is in guns in the hands of a few desperate men. Our enemies would

prefer to deal with a small armed group rather than with a huge, unarmed but resolute mass of people. However, it is necessary that the mass-action method be persistent and unyielding. Gandhi said the Indian people must "never let them rest," referring to the British. He urged them to keep protesting daily and weekly, in a variety of ways. This method inspired and organized the Indian masses and disorganized and demobilized the British. It educates its myriad participants, socially and morally. All history teaches us that like a turbulent ocean beating great cliffs into fragments of rock, the determined movement of people incessantly demanding their rights always disintegrates the old order.

It is this form of struggle—non-cooperation with evil through mass actions—"never letting them rest"—which offers the more effective road for those who have been tempted and goaded to violence. It needs the bold and the brave because it is not free of danger. It faces the vicious and evil enemies squarely. It requires dedicated people, because it is a backbreaking task to arouse, to organize, and to educate tens of thousands for disciplined, sustained action. From this form of struggle more emerges that is permanent and damaging to the enemy than from a few acts of organized violence.

Our present urgent necessity is to cease our internal fighting and turn outward to the enemy, using every form of mass action yet known—create new forms—and resolve never to let them rest. This is the social lever which will force upon the door to freedom. Our powerful weapons are the voices, the feet, and the bodies of dedicated, united people, moving without rest toward a just goal. Greater tyrants than Southern segregationists have been subdued and defeated by this form of struggle. We have not yet used it, and it would be tragic if we spurn it because we have failed to perceive its dynamic strength and power.

CASHING IN ON WAR?

I am reluctant to inject a personal defense against charges by Mr. Williams that I am inconsistent in my struggle against war and too weak-kneed to protest nuclear war. Merely to set the record straight, may I state that repeatedly, in public addresses and in my writings, I have unequivocally declared my hatred for this most colossal of all evils and I have condemned any organizer of war, regardless of his rank or nationality. I have signed numerous statements with other Americans condemning nuclear testing and have authorized publication of my name in advertisements appearing in the largest circulation newspapers in the country, without concern that it was then "unpopular" to so speak out.

Document 31.5

"STRONG LOCAL GOVERNMENT IS THE FOUNDATION OF OUR SYSTEM"

Alabama Governor George C. Wallace, in an official statement, protested "federal coercion" of the state to force the admission of two Negroes into the University of Alabama. He argues here that such coercion is illegal.

(From the *New York Times*, June 12, 1963. Copyright by the *New York Times*; reprinted by permission.)

As Governor and Chief Magistrate of the State of Alabama, I deem it to be my solemn obligation and duty to stand before you representing the rights and sovereignty of this state and its peoples.

The unwelcomed, unwanted, unwarranted and force-induced intrusion upon the campus of the University of Alabama today of the might of the Central Government offers frightful example of oppression of the rights, privileges and sovereignty of this state by officers of the Federal Government. This intrusion results solely from force, or threat of force, undignified by any reasonable application of the principle of law, reason and justice. It is important that the people of this state and nation understand that this action is in violation of rights reserved to the state by the Constitution of the United States and the Constitution of the State of Alabama. While some few may applaud these acts, millions of Americans will gaze in sorrow upon the situation existing at this great institution of learning.

Only the Congress makes the law of the United States. To this date no statutory authority can be cited to the people of this country which authorizes the Central Government to ignore the sovereignty of this state and attempt to subordinate the rights of Alabama and millions of Americans. There has been no legislative action by Congress justifying this intrusion.

When the Constitution of the United States was enacted, a Government was formed upon the premise that people, as individuals, are endowed with the rights of life, liberty and property, and with the right of local self-government. The people and their local self-governments formed a Central Government and conferred upon it certain stated and limited powers. All other powers were reserved to the states and to the people.

Strong local government is the foundation of our system and must be continually guarded and maintained. The 10th Amendment to the Constitution of the United States reads as follows:

"The powers not relegated to the United States by the Constitution, nor prohibited by it to the states, are reserved to the states respectively, or to the people." This amendment sustains the right of self-determination, and grants the state of Alabama the right to enforce its laws and regulate its internal affairs.

This nation was never meant to be a unit of one but a united of the many—that is the exact reason our freedom-loving forefathers established the states, so as to divide the rights and powers among the many states, insuring that no central power could gain massive government control.

There can be no submission to the theory that the Central Government is anything but a servant of the people. We are God-fearing people —not Government-fearing people. We practice today the free heritage bequeathed to us by the founding fathers.

I stand here today, as Governor of this sovereign state, and refuse to willingly submit to illegal usurpation of power by the Central Government. I claim today for all the people of the state of Alabama those rights reserved to them under the Constitution of the United States. Among those powers so reserved and claimed is the right of state authority in the operation of the public schools, colleges and universities. My action does not constitute disobedience to legislative and constitutional provisions. It is not defiance for defiance sake, but for the purpose of raising basic and fundamental constitutional questions. My action is a call for strict adherence to the Constitution of the United States as it was written—for a cessation of usurpation and abuses. My action seeks to avoid having state sovereignty sacrificed on the altar of political expediency.

Further, as the Governor of the State of Alabama, I hold the supreme executive power of this state, and it is my duty to see that the laws are faithfully executed. The illegal and unwarranted actions of the Central Government on this day, contrary to the laws, customs and traditions of this state, is calculated to disturb the peace.

I stand before you today in place of thousands of other Alabamians whose presence would have confronted you had I been derelict and neglected to fulfill the responsibilities of my office. It is the right of every citizen, however humble he may be, through his chosen officials of representative government to stand courageously against whatever he believes to be the exercise of power beyond the constitutional rights conferred upon our Federal Government. It is this right which I assert for the people of Alabama by my presence here today.

Again I state—this is the exercise of the heritage of freedom and liberty under the law—coupled with responsible government.

Now, therefore, in consideration of the promises, and in my official capacity as Governor of the State of Alabama, I do hereby make the following solemn proclamation:

Whereas, the Constitution of Alabama vests the supreme executive powers of the state in the Governor as the chief magistrate, and said Constitution requires of the Governor that he take care that the laws be faithfully executed; and,

Whereas, the Constitution of the United States, Amendment 10, reserves to the states respectively or to the people, those powers not delegated to the United States, nor prohibited to the states; and,

Whereas, the operation of the public school system is a power reserved to the State of Alabama under the Constitution of the United States and Amendment 10 thereof; and,

Whereas, it is the duty of the Governor of the State of Alabama to preserve the peace under the circumstances now existing, which power is one reserved to the State of Alabama and the people thereof under the Constitution of the United States and Amendment 10 thereof:

Now, therefore, I, George C. Wallace, as Governor of the State of Alabama, have by my action raised issues between the Central Government and the sovereign State of Alabama, which said issues should be adjudicated in the manner prescribed by the Constitution of the United States; and now being mindful of my duties and responsibilities under the Constitution of the United States, the Constitution of the State of Alabama, and seeking to preserve and maintain the peace and dignity of this state, and the individual freedoms of the citizens thereof, do hereby denounce and forbid this illegal and unwarranted action by the Central Government.

Document 31.6

A SOUTHERN MODERATE TAKES HIS STAND

A view contrary to that of Governor George C. Wallace by a southern white moderate was presented by Mayor Ivan Allen, Jr., of Atlanta, before the Commerce Committee of the United States Senate. Atlanta has been a pioneer southern city in seeking to bring about a just and peaceful solution to the race problem.

As the Mayor of the Southeast's largest city, I can say to you out of first-hand experience and first-hand knowledge that nowhere does the problem of eliminating discrimination between the races strike so closely home as it does to the local elected public official.

He is the man who cannot pass the buck.

From this viewpoint, I speak of the problem as having been brought into sharp focus by decisions of the Supreme Court of the United States and then generally ignored by the Presidents and Congresses of the United States. Like a foundling baby, this awesome problem has been left on the doorsteps of local governments throughout the nation.

It is true that Atlanta has achieved success in eliminating discrimination in areas where some other cities have failed, but we do not boast of our success. Instead of boasting, we say with the humility of those who believe in reality that we have achieved our measure of success only because we looked facts in the face and accepted the Supreme Court's decisions as inevitable and as the law of our land. Having embraced realism in general, we then set out to solve specific problems by local cooperation between people of goodwill and good sense representing both races.

In attacking the specific problems, we accepted the basic truth that the solutions which we sought to achieve in every instance granted to our Negro citizens rights which white American citizens and businesses previously had reserved to themselves as special privileges.

These special privileges long had been propped up by a multitude of local ordinances and statewide laws which had upheld racial segregation in almost every conceivable form.

In Atlanta we find plenty of these props of prejudice to contend with when we set out to solve our specific problems of discrimination. In attacking these problems, I want to emphasize that in not one single instance have we retained or enhanced the privileges of segregation.

'A Long Process'

It has been a long, exhausting and often discouraging process and the end is far from being in sight.

Atlanta has achieved only a measure of success. I think it would assist you in understanding this if I explained how limited so far has been this transition from the old segregated society of generations past, and also how limited so far has been the participation of the Negro citizens.

Significant as is the voluntary elimination of discrimination in our leading restaurants, it affects so far only a small percentage of the hundreds of eating places in our city.

And participation by Negroes so far has been very slight. For example, one of Atlanta's topmost restaurants served only 16 out of Atlanta's 200,000 Negro citizens during the first week of freedom from discrimination.

The plan for eliminating discrimination in hotels as yet takes care only of convention delegates. Although prominent Negroes have been accepted as guests in several Atlanta hotels, the Negro citizens as a whole seldom appear at Atlanta hotels.

Underlying all the emotions of the situation is the matter of economics. It should be remembered that the right to use a facility does not mean that it will be used or misused by any group, especially the groups in the lower economic status.

Now I would like to submit my personal reasons why I think Atlanta has resolved some of these problems, while in other cities solutions have seemed impossible and strife and conflict have resulted.

As an illustration, I would like to describe a recent visit of an official delegation from a great Eastern city which has a Negro population of over 600,000 consisting of in excess of 20 per cent of its whole population.

The members of this delegation at first simply did not understand and would hardly believe that the business, civic and political interests of Atlanta had intently concerned themselves with the Negro population. I still do not believe that they are convinced that all of our civic bodies backed by the public interest and supported by the city government have daily concerned themselves with an effort to solve our gravest problem—which is relations between our races.

Gentlemen, Atlanta has not swept this question under the rug at any point. Step by step—sometimes under court order—sometimes voluntarily moving ahead of pressures—sometimes adroitly—and many, many times clumsily—we have tried to find a solution to each specific problem through an agreement between the affected white ownership and the Negro leadership.

To do this, we have not appointed a huge general bi-racial committee, which too often merely becomes a burial place for unsolved problems. Each time a specific problem has come into focus, we have appointed the people involved to work out the solution—theater owners to work with top Negro leaders—or hotel owners to work with the top leadership—or certain restaurant owners have of their own volition dealt with the top

Negro leadership. By developing the lines of communication and respectability, we have been able to reach amicable solutions.

COURT RULINGS CITED

I do not believe that any sincere American citizen desires to see the rights of private business restricted by the Federal Government unless such restriction is absolutely necessary for the welfare of the people of this country.

On the other hand, following the line of thought of the decisions of the Federal courts in the past 15 years, I am not convinced that current rulings of the courts would grant to American business the privilege of discrimination by race in the selection of its customers.

Here again we get into the area of what is right and what is best for the people of this country. If the privilege of selection based on race and color should be granted, then would we be giving to business the right to set up a segregated economy? And if so, how fast would this right be utilized by the nation's people? And how soon would we again be going through the old turmoil of riots, strife, demonstrations, boycotts, picketing?

Are we going to say that it is all right for the Negro citizen to go into the bank on Main Street and to deposit his earnings or borrow money, then to go to department stores to buy what he needs, to go to the supermarket to purchase food for his family, and so on along Main Street until he comes to a restaurant or a hotel—in all these other business places he is treated just like any other customer—but when he comes to the restaurant or the hotel, are we going to say that it is right and legal for the operators of these businesses, merely as a matter of convenience, to insist that the Negro's citizenship be changed and that, as a second-class citizen, he is to be refused service?

I submit that it is not right to allow an American's citizenship to be changed merely as a matter of convenience.

If the Congress should fail to clarify the issue at the present time, then by inference it would be saying that you could begin discrimination under the guise of private business. I do not believe that this is what the Supreme Court has intended with its decisions. I do not believe that this is the intent of Congress or of the people of this country.

I am not a lawyer, Senators. I am not sure I clearly understand all of the testimony involving various amendments to the Constitution and the Commerce Clause which has been given to this committee. I have a fundamental respect for the Constitution of the United States. Under this

Constitution we have always been able to do what is best for all of the people of this country. I beg of you not to let this issue of discrimination drown in legalistic waters. I am firmly convinced that the Supreme Court insists that the same fundamental rights must be held by every American citizen.

Atlanta is a case that proves that the problem of discrimination can be solved to some extent. And I use this "some extent" cautiously, as we certainly have not solved all of the problems; but we have met them in a number of areas. This can be done locally, voluntarily, and by private business itself.

DEFIANCE IS DISCERNED

On the other hand, there are hundreds of communities and cities, certainly, throughout the nation that have not ever addressed themselves to the issue, whereas others have flagrantly ignored the demand, and today stand in all defiance to any change.

The Congress of the United States is now confronted with a grave decision. Shall you pass a public accommodation bill that forces this issue? or, shall you create another round of disputes over segregation by refusing to pass such legislation?

Surely, the Congress realizes that after having failed to take any definite action on this subject in the last 10 years, to fail to pass this bill would amount to an endorsement of private business setting up an entirely new status of discrimination throughout the nation. Cities like Atlanta might slip backward. Hotels and restaurants that have already taken this issue upon themselves and opened their doors might find it convenient to go back to the old status.

Failure by Congress to take definite action at this time is by inference an endorsement of the right of private business to practice racial discrimination and, in my opinion, would start the same old round of squabbles and demonstrations that we have had in the past.

Gentlemen, if I had your problem, armed with the local experience I have had, I would pass a public accommodation bill. Such a bill, however, should provide an opportunity for each local government first to meet this problem and attempt to solve it on a local, voluntary basis, with each business making its own decision.

REASONABLE TIME ASKED

I think a public accommodation law now should stand only as the last resort to assure that discrimination is eliminated, but that such a law would grant a reasonable time for cities and businesses to carry out this function before Federal intervention.

It might even be necessary that the time factor be made more lenient in favor of smaller cities and communities, for we all know that large metropolian areas have the capability of adjusting to changes more rapidly than smaller communities.

Perhaps this, too, should be given consideration in your legislation. But the point I want to emphasize again is that now is the time for legislative action. We cannot dodge the issue. We cannot look back over our shoulders or turn the clock back to the eighteen-sixties. We must take action now to assure a greater future for our citizens and our country.

A hundred years ago the abolishment of slavery won the United States the acclaim of the whole world when it made every American free in theory.

Now the elimination of segregation, which is slavery's stepchild, is a challenge to all of us to make every American free in fact as well as in theory—and again to establish our nation as the true champion of the free world.

Document 31.7

"RACE HAS NO PLACE IN AMERICAN LIFE OR LAW"

President John F. Kennedy's forthright statement on the crisis at the University of Alabama represented a vigorous affirmation of his determination to further the cause of integration and Negro rights.

(From Office of the White House Press Secretary, "Remarks of the President on Nationwide Radio and Television," June 11, 1963. Courtesy Pierre Salinger, Press Secretary to the President.)

Good evening, my fellow citizens.

This afternoon, following a series of threats and defiant statements, the presence of Alabama National Guardsmen was required on the University of Alabama to carry out the final and unequivocal order of the United States District Court of the Northern District of Alabama. That order called for the admission of two clearly qualified young Alabama residents who happened to have been born Negro.

That they were admitted peacefully on the campus is due in good measure to the conduct of the students of the University of Alabama, who met their responsibilities in a constructive way.

I hope that every American, regardless of where he lives, will stop and examine his conscience about this and other related incidents. This Nation was founded by men of many nations and backgrounds. It was founded on the principle that all men are created equal, and that the rights of every man are diminished when the rights of one man are threatened.

Today we are committed to a worldwide struggle to promote and protect the rights of all who wish to be free, and when Americans are sent to Viet-Nam or West Berlin, we do not ask for whites only. It ought to be possible, therefore, for American students of any color to attend any public institution they select without having to be backed up by troops.

It ought to be possible for American consumers of any color to receive equal service in places of public accommodation, such as hotels and restaurants and theaters and retail stores, without being forced to resort to demonstrations in the street, and it ought to be possible for American citizens of any color to register and to vote in a free election without interference or fear of reprisal.

It ought to be possible, in short, for every American to enjoy the privileges of being American without regard to his race or his color. In short, every American ought to have the right to be treated as he would wish to be treated, as one would wish his children to be treated. But this is not the case.

The Negro baby born in America today, regardless of the section of the Nation in which he is born, has about one-half as much chance of completing a high school as a white baby born in the same place on the same day, one-third as much chance of completing college, one-third as much chance of becoming a professional man, twice as much chance of becoming unemployed, about one-seventh as much chance of earning $10,000 a year, a life expectancy which is seven years shorter, and the prospects of earning only half as much.

This is not a sectional issue. Difficulties over segregation and discrimination exist in every city, in every State of the Union, producing in many cities a rising tide of discontent that threatens the public safety. Nor is this a partisan issue in a time of domestic crisis. Men of good will and generosity should be able to unite regardless of party or politics. This is not even a legal or legislative issue alone. It is better to settle these matters in the courts than on the streets, and new laws are needed at every level, but law alone cannot make men see right.

We are confronted primarily with a moral issue. It is as old as the scriptures and is as clear as the American Constitution.

The heart of the question is whether all Americans are to be afforded equal rights and equal opportunities, whether we are going to treat our fellow Americans as we want to be treated. If an American, because his skin is dark, cannot eat lunch in a restaurant open to the public, if he cannot send his children to the best public school available, if he cannot vote for the public officials who represent him, if, in short, he cannot enjoy the full and free life which all of us want, then who among us would be content to have the color of his skin changed and stand in his place? Who among us would then be content with the counsels of patience and delay?

100 years of delay have passed since President Lincoln freed the slaves, yet their heirs, their grandsons, are not fully free. They are not yet freed from the bonds of injustice. They are not yet freed from social and economic oppression, and this Nation, for all its hopes and all its boasts, will not be fully free until all its citizens are free.

We preach freedom around the world, and we mean it, and we cherish our freedom here at home, but are we to say to the world, and much more importantly, to each other that this is a land of the free except for the Negroes; that we have no second-class citizens except Negroes; that we have no class or cast [*sic*] system, no ghettoes, no master race except with respect to Negroes?

Now the time has come for this Nation to fulfill its promise. The events in Birmingham and elsewhere have so increased the cries for equality that no city or State or legislative body can prudently choose to ignore them.

The fires of frustration and discord are burning in every city, North and South, where legal remedies are not at hand. Redress is sought in the streets, in demonstrations, parades and protests which create tensions and threaten violence and threaten lives.

We face, therefore, a moral crisis as a country and as a people. It cannot be met by repressive police action. It cannot be left to increased demonstrations in the streets. It cannot be quieted by token moves or talk. It is a time to act in the Congress, in your State and local legislative body and, above all, in all of our daily lives.

It is not enough to pin the blame on others, to say this is a problem of one section of the country or another, or deplore the fact that we face. A great change is at hand, and our task, our obligation, is to make that revolution, that change, peaceful and constructive for all.

Those who do nothing are inviting shame as well as violence. Those who act boldly are recognizing right as well as reality.

Next week I shall ask the Congress of the United States to act, to make a commitment it has not fully made in this century to the proposition that race has no place in American life or law. The Federal Judiciary has upheld that proposition in a series of forthright cases. The Executive Branch has adopted that proposition in the conduct of its affairs, including the employment of Federal personnel, the use of Federal facilities, and the sale of Federally financed housing.

But there are other necessary measures which only the Congress can provide, and they must be provided at this session. The old code of equity law under which we live commands for every wrong a remedy, but in too many communities, in too many parts of the country, wrongs are inflicted on Negro citizens as there are no remedies at law. Unless the Congress acts, their only remedy is in the street.

I am, therefore, asking the Congress to enact legislation giving all Americans the right to be served in facilities which are open to the public—hotels, restaurants, theaters, retail stores and similar establishments.

This seems to me to be an elementary right. Its denial is an arbitrary indignity that no American in 1963 should have to endure, but many do.

I have recently met with scores of business leaders urging them to take voluntary action to end this discrimination and I have been encouraged by their response, and in the last two weeks over 75 cities have seen progress made in desegregating these kinds of facilities. But many are unwilling to act alone, and for this reason, nationwide legislation is needed if we are to move this problem from the streets to the courts.

I am also asking Congress to authorize the Federal Government to participate more fully in lawsuits designed to end segregation in public education. We have succeeded in persuading many districts to desegregate voluntarily. Dozens have admitted Negroes without violence. Today a Negro is attending a State-supported institution in every one of our 50 States, but the pace is very slow.

Too many Negro children entering segregated grade schools at the time of the Supreme Court's decision nine years ago will enter segregated high schools this fall, having suffered a loss which can never be restored. The lack of an adequate education denies the Negro a chance to get a decent job.

The orderly implementation of the Supreme Court decision, therefore, cannot be left solely to those who may not have the economic resources to carry the legal action or who may be subject to harassment.

Other features will be also requested, including greater protection for the right to vote. But legislation, I repeat, cannot solve this problem alone. It must be solved in the homes of every American in every community across our country.

In this respect, I want to pay tribute to those citizens North and South who have been working in their communities to make life better for all. They are acting not out of a sense of legal duty, but out of a sense of human decency.

Like our soldiers and sailors in all parts of the world, they are meeting freedom's challenge on the firing line, and I salute them for their honor and their courage.

My fellow Americans, this is a problem which faces us all—in every city of the North as well as the South. Today there are Negroes unemployed two or three times as many compared to whites, inadequate in education, moving into the large cities, unable to find work, young people particularly out of work without hope, denied equal rights, denied the opportunity to eat at a restaurant or lunch counter or go to a movie theater, denied the right to a decent education, denied almost today the right to attend a State university even though qualified. It seems to me that these are matters which concern us all, not merely Presidents or Congressmen or Governors, but every citizen of the United States.

This is one country. It has become one country because all of us and all the people who came here had an equal chance to develop their talents.

We cannot say to ten percent of the population that you can't have that right; that your children can't have the chance to develop whatever talents they have; that the only way that they are going to get their rights is to go into the streets and demonstrate. I think we owe them and we owe ourselves a better country than that.

Therefore, I am asking for your help in making it easier for us to move ahead and to provide the kind of equality of treatment which we would want ourselves; to give a chance for every child to be educated to the limit of his talents.

As I have said before, not every child has an equal talent or an equal ability or an equal motivation, but they should have the equal right to develop their talent and their ability and their motivation to make something of themselves.

We have a right to expect that the Negro community will be responsible, will uphold the law, but they have a right to expect that the law will be fair; that the Constitution will be color blind, as Justice Harlan said at the turn of the century.

This is what we are talking about and this is a matter which concerns this country and what it stands for, and in meeting it I ask the support of all of our citizens.

Thank you very much.

Document 31.8

"I HAVE A DREAM"

Perhaps nowhere have the aspirations of the American Negro been expressed so eloquently as by the Reverend Martin Luther King, Jr., at the great civil rights rally sponsored by the National Association for the Advancement of Colored People held in Washington, D.C., on August 28, 1963.

DR. MARTIN LUTHER KING, JR., SOUTHERN CHRISTIAN LEADERSHIP CONFERENCE

(From the *New York Times*, August 28, 1963. Copyright by the *New York Times*; reprinted by permission.)

Now is the time to make real the promises of democracy. Now is the time to rise from the dark and desolate valley of segregation to the sunlit path of racial justice. Now is the time to lift our nation from the quicksands of racial injustice to the solid rock of brotherhood. Now is the time to make justice a reality for all of God's children.

There will be neither rest nor tranquility in America until the Negro is granted his citizenship rights. The whirlwinds of revolt will continue to shake the foundations of our nation until the bright day of justice emerges.

And that is something that I must say to my people who stand on the threshold which leads to the palace of justice. In the process of gaining our rightful place we must not be guilty of wrongful deeds.

Again and again, we must rise to the majestic heights of meeting physical force with soul force. The marvelous new militancy which has engulfed the Negro community must not lead us to a distrust of all white people, for many of our white brothers as evidence by their presence here today have come to realize that their destiny is tied up with our destiny!

'Never Be Satisfied'

There are those who are asking the devotees of civil rights, "When will you be satisfied?" We can never be satisfied as long as the Negro is the victim of the unspeakable horrors of police brutality. We can never be satisfied as long as our bodies, heavy with the fatigue of travel, cannot gain lodging in the motels of the highways and the hotels of the cities.

We can never be satisfied as long as our children are stripped of their selfhood and robbed of their dignity by signs stating "for whites only." We cannot be satisfied as long as the Negro in Mississippi cannot vote and the Negro in New York believes he has nothing for which to vote.

No, we are not satisfied and we will not be satisfied until justice rolls down like water and righteousness like a mighty stream.

Now, I am not unmindful that some of you have come here out of great trials and tribulations. Some of you have come fresh from narrow jail cells.

Continue to work with the faith that honor in suffering is redemptive. Go back to Mississippi, go back to Alabama, go back to South Carolina, go back to Georgia, go back to Louisiana, go back to the slums and ghettos of our Northern cities, knowing that somehow this situation can and will be changed. Let us not wallow in the valley of despair.

Now, I say to you today, my friends, so even though we face the difficulties of today and tomorrow, I still have a dream. It is a dream deeply rooted in the American dream. I have a dream that one day this nation will rise up and live out the true meaning of its creed: "We hold these truths to be self-evident, that all men are created equal."

I have a dream that one day on the red hills of Georgia the sons of former slaveowners will be able to sit down together at the table of brotherhood.

I have a dream that one day even the state of Mississippi, a state sweltering with the people's injustice, sweltering with the heat of oppression, will be transformed into an oasis of freedom and justice.

I have a dream that my four little children will one day live in a nation where they will not be judged by the color of their skin, but by the content of their character.

This is our home. This is the faith that I go back to the South with— with this faith we will be able to hew out of the mountain of despair a stone of hope.